COLLECTIBLE
TOYS

Toys on cover courtesy of Bill Bertoia

Cover photo by George Kerrigan

This is a registered trademark of Random House, Inc.

© 1990 by Random House, Inc.

Published by: The House of Collectibles
201 East 50th Street
New York, New York 10022

Distributed by Ballantine Books, a division of Random House, Inc., New York, and simultaneously in Canada by Random House of Canada Limited, Toronto.

Manufactured in the United States of America

ISBN: 0-876-37803-3

Fifth Edition: June 1990

10 9 8 7 6 5 4 3 2 1

This book is dedicated to Bernard Barenholtz, who so generously shared his vast knowledge of toys and folk art over the years. Barney's own personal collection was legendary, yet he placed a far greater value on the wonderful people he met with a special interest in toys.

Table of Contents

✳ ✳ ✳

Acknowledgments

For their invaluable assistance, I would like to extend appreciation to the following: Carl Burnet, San Diego, CA; Noel Barrett Auctions, Carversville, PA; Bernard Barenholtz, Marlboro, NH; Nan and Bill Bopp, Walpole, NH; Blair Whitton, Keene, NH; Lee and Rally Dennis, Peterborough, NH; Linda Mullen, Los Angeles, CA; Dana Hawkes, Collectibles Department, Sotheby's, NYC; Eric Alberta and Henry Kurtz, Phillips Auctioneering & Appraising, NYC; Joanne C. Grant, Mid-Hudson Galleries, Cornwall-on-Hudson, NY; Mildred Ewing (toys and dolls specialist) and Alicia Barry Gordon, publicity, both of Skinner Auctions, Bolton, MA; Brian Riba of Riba Auctions, Glastonbury, CT; Alex Acevedo of Alexander Gallery, NYC; Richard Opfer of Opfer Auctioneering, Timonium, MD; and Dale Kelley, Antique Toy World, Chicago, IL.

The beauty of a good toy is that
it picks out the really important things.
Oarsmen who actually row, for instance,
or the steamer's great walking beam,
or a good loud bell on a train.
Imagination does the rest. Any boy knows that.
A toy is very like a primitive painting,
a crude imitation of life;
yet for all that a very shrewd glimpse at it too,
for the collection we exhibit here
is kind of a push-pull
pageant of American history.

—Dec. 1959, American Heritage

INTRODUCTION

How to Use This Guide

The toys in this book are grouped alphabetically by category, and within each grouping we have again broken them down into ABC order. The exceptions are in the Military Miniatures section, where we have classified the Britains toys sequentially by the manufacturer's set numbers. We have added over 100 more toy maker listings with identifying marks and other data to assist you in documenting your toys. Unlike the old Bob and Ray radio skit where ace sports reporter Wally Ballou would rattle off Saturday's football results without giving the names of the teams, we hope this guide gives you the score and a lot more to help you determine what to buy and how much to pay.

The Prices in This Book

No doubt you've heard all about the pitfalls of consulting a price guide. That it is outdated by the time it hits the bookstands. That it fails to compensate for geographical and market variables. That it doesn't stress *strongly* enough that these prices reflect toys in like-new condition, with each flaw exacting its toll from the final asking price. Further, that dealers and auction houses will take *their* pound of flesh, thereby further shrinking profits by a third to half the guided price. Then too, there is the old bromide frequently cited as a caveat in many price guides, that the only true barometer of price is that established between a willing buyer and willing seller.

However, that age-old question still prevails—"How much *is* it worth?" In trying to come up with an answer in this volatile hobby, we have elected to borrow a page from the world of antiquarian books. In this field, as a barometer, many dealers and collectors alike rely almost exclusively on *actual* prices realized at a given time at various book auctions and shows. There has been so much exciting auction and sale activity in the toy world over the past several years that we are including special sections (by toy category) that provide auction prices from such blockbusters as the Perelman Sale, the Game Preserve Museum Sale, the Barenholtz Sales at Skinner, the Atlanta Toy Museum Sale, Opfer Christmas Auctions, and the Phillips Christmas Auction, from 1988. Here again, prices may have been dictated by such variables as condition, rarity, the prestige of having come from a major private collection or museum, or even the ego of the participants. Coupled with price estimates, however, we feel this guide will help give you a much clearer picture as to the value of a given toy.

Toy Market Overview

In the past two years alone, more significant toy and game collections have come to market than we've witnessed in 25 years in the hobby.

First and foremost, there was the dispersal of the Perelman Toy Museum collection at a series of rather exclusive tag sales last autumn in Philadelphia, known as the Great Grab of '88. Not since the heralded Jerry Smith collection of 6,000 toys purveyed by Hallmark Cards in the mid–1970s or the Toy Museum of Atlanta series of auctions in 1986, has there been anything to compare in terms of sheer anticipation, scope, and ultimate rarities.

On the very weekend of the first of the Perelman extravaganzas, the Game Preserve Museum collection of vintage board games was gaveled down at Skinner in Bolton, Massachusetts.

Less than a month later at private sale, collector Al Davidson purchased the bank collection of Gertrude and the late Covert Hagerty of Coaltown, Pennsylvania, to the tune of $3.2 million. Davidson, who had sold off part of his own vast mechanical bank horde at Sotheby's in 1988, upgraded via the Hagerty sale as well as gained a number of choice and unique mechanicals and lead and brass patterns. Most of the balance of the Hagerty collection, comprising some 95% of the total, has since been recirculated throughout the hobby. Davidson hinted that a number of banks he'd resold have exceeded the record price of $250,000, exacted for the Freedman's bank at the Perelman sale.

In December 1988, at Richard Opfer's auction in Timonium, Maryland, the Arnie Hed bank collection came on the block with an impressive selection of over 600 mechanicals and stills, ringing up $275,000.

Thus, within a span of 90 days, over 10 million dollars worth of premier banks came to market—an unprecedented windfall.

Another private sale, which had less of an impact on the toy world, was that of Manhattanite Robert Lesser. This sale involved a million dollar transaction, revolving around his collection of comic/character toys. The entrepreneur in the Lesser sale, as well as in the Perelman, Hagerty, and Barenholtz megadeals, was the flamboyant Alex Acevedo of Manhattan, a man hailed as the Donald Trump of the antique toy world, but whose takeovers have been anything but hostile.

Certainly the most spectacular of the two sales was the Perelman Big Grab of '88. When thieves broke into Philadelphian Leon Perelman's private toy museum last fall, tied up his caretaker, and made off with a stash of antique marbles, no less, Perelman promptly closed the museum. A few days later, he sold off the entire collection of over 5,000 toys, plus the museum itself. Alex Acevedo, the buyer, quickly lined up an on-the-premises, by-invitation-only tag sale, including 36 of the hobby's elitists. Those privileged to attend, however, were required to spend a minimum of $50,000. Two well-known toy/bank specialists assisted in pricing each item: Don Markey of Lititz, Pennsylvania, who had orchestrated the celebrated Mosler bank sale in 1983, and Bill Bertoia of Vineland, New Jersey, who, along with Noel Barrett, masterminded the Atlanta Toy Museum auctions in 1986.

Prospective buyers at the Perelman sale were allowed three hours to examine, but not touch, the merchandise. Then, as cable TV cameras ground away, Acevedo, attired in tuxedo, fired a cap pistol from the museum's collection, signaling that the mad rush was on.

Within ten minutes there wasn't a bank left in the place in the $30,000-and-up range. By day's end, all but 5–10% of hundreds of mechanical and still banks had been sold. A prized collection of lead and brass bank patterns was sold intact for $125,000, as was the 19th-century cap pistol collection, for $115,000.

The first day conclave, and several subsequent public sales held in early October, yielded more than $5,000,000. All remaining toys, including a number from the museum attic (some 1,000 toys in all), were purchased by noted toy restorer/dealer Russ Harrington of Baltimore.

It is far too early to assess the impact of all this activity and its filter-down effect on the entire toy market. One thing is certain—a month later, at the Allentown Toy Show, ex-Perelman toys were in evidence at table after table, all at substantially enhanced prices and with no ground-swell rush to buy. None of the ultimate rarities from the Perelman sale, however, were in evidence. The truly great pieces, the ones that may surface once in a lifetime, are ensconced in the hands of collectors and are likely to remain so for some time to come.

The following toy categories reflect intensive activity and sustained interest among dealers and collectors at recent auctions, shows, and exhibitions. They represent trendsetters to keep an eye on now and into the 1990s.

NINETEENTH-CENTURY BOARD GAMES

The Game Preserve collection sale at Skinner, in September 1988, might well have heralded a new beginning. It had all the fanfare to propel previously undervalued vintage board games to new highs going into the 1990s.

Over a span of 35 years, Lee and Rally Dennis had accumulated a vibrant, colorful array of board games, puzzles, and bagatelles from primarily the late 19th century. Their museum in Peterborough, New Hampshire, was a mecca for lovers of these genteel diversions. Over 1,100 parlor games were apportioned into 315 lots at Skinner. A mini collection of vintage playing cards had been sold some time ago, but the balance of the Dennis treasures were offered intact, fresh on the market, and unsullied by any skim-off of choice examples.

The Game Preserve collection has received extensive exposure over the years, having been the subject of a PBS telecast, numerous magazine and newspaper write-ups, and intense scrutiny in Lee Dennis' book, *Antique American Games/1840–1940* (see Bibliography).

The sale averaged over $450 per lot, clearly abetted by such stunners as the McLoughlin "Man in the Moon Game," at $5,060; 22 other large-sized parlor games, primarily by McLoughlin, Milton Bradley, and Parker Brothers, sold for $1,000 and more. From the 1930s, a limited edition of Charles Darrow's "Monopoly" soared to $2,640, while related "Monopoly" ephemera and Darrow's less heralded "Bulls & Bears" board game was a steep $3,740. What may be overlooked, as the dust clears from this landmark auction, is that a number of very choice smaller games that were lotted together were hammered down at very reasonable prices.

A few weeks following the Game Preserve outing, we noted that dealers on the field at the Howlands Flea Market in Amherst, New Hampshire, and at several subsequent toy shows, including Allentown, had been busily marking up their prices on board games.

On the other hand, at a Riba auction a month later in Wethersfield, Connecticut, a popular "Game of Baseball" (McLoughlin Bros., circa 1886) entry rallied to $550. This game in similar condition at the Game Preserve sale took off to $2,530.

Bruce Whitehill, known as The Big Game Collector and one of the founders of the American Game Collectors Association, offered this postscript on the Game Preserve auction in the February 1989 issue of *Antique Toy World*:

> There are some extraordinary games that select collectors will pay a premium for. But 98% of the games out there do not warrant such high prices. Dealers who have doubled the prices of their more common games—I hope—are going to be unable to unload their merchandise. Because a turn-of-the-century, large McLoughlin board game sells for four figures doesn't mean that an "Authors" game should sell for $50 because it's also a McLoughlin and from the 1880s.

Ironically, the price of a board game is still governed principally by the stunning lithographic illustration on the box, with little regard to the collection housed inside it. ("The Man in the Moon," for example, has a very mundane checkerboard inside with illustrations of the phases of the moon.) Good advice for the 1990s, therefore, is to look for gameboards and puzzles with powerful graphics and with tie-ins to famous personages and events. Examples might include: "Teddy Roosevelt at San Juan," "The North Pole Game," "Pikes Peak or Bust," "Dewey's Victory," and "Round the World with Nellie Bly." Also, any similar diversions relating to sports and blacks should be pursued.

CAST-IRON TRANSPORTATION TOYS

Cast-iron toys are indigenous to these shores and are by-products of the Industrial Revolution of the late 19th century.

Examples of English and German cast-iron toys exist, of course, but it is the homegrown artisans who dominate—Messrs. Ives, Harris, Carpenter, Hubley, Arcade, J. & E. Stevens, Dent, Kenton, Wilkins, and Pratt & Letchworth. These masters combined to make cast-iron creations (most notably horse-drawn rigs and, later, motor toys) truly an American art form. Up through the 1960s, cast-iron toys dominated the hobby and prices quickly escalated.

Then something happened. There seemed to be a sudden awakening on the part of advanced collectors to the classic 19th-century, painted, tin clockwork toys, as well as the exquisite early 20th-century, European clockwork tin boats, roadsters, and trains of Märklin, Bing, and Carette. At the same time, as is often the case when the supply of premier pieces cannot possibly meet the demand, cast-iron reproductions flooded the market. No longer spurned, cast-iron transportation toys, particularly the ultimate rarities, rebounded with a vengeance. American collectors had apparently become more sophisticated and lost their fear of reproductions, having had the cooling-off period to study authentic toys and detect the differences. A few years ago when the dollar dropped, many Europeans, particularly the Germans, entered the bidding fray for our early cast-iron examples.

Pennsylvania dealer Bob Schneider, in a recent interview with Lil Gottshalk in *Maine Antique Digest*, offered this caveat, however: "Great things are in demand and bring great prices. Boat anchors are just that and will always be the same, regardless of the sale they are in." (Schneider refers to cumbersome, common cast-iron toys as lacking the detail, great design, craftsmanship, and/or condition to energize upscale collectors.)

The following prices for ultimate rarity cast-iron toys in superb condition were achieved at the Perelman sale and at several recent auctions, and they are indeed something to ponder over:

Horse-drawn Barouche, Pratt & Letchworth, *$6,000*.
Animated Circus Wagon, Kyser & Rex, *$6,500*.
Double Bicyclists, Wilkins, *$22,500*.
Four Bicycle Riders on Tandem, Ives, *$28,000*.
Four-seater Brake, Wilkins, *$32,000*.
Reindeer Sleigh, oversized, Hubley, *$37,500*.
Revolving Monkey Cage, Hubley, *$30,000*.
Two-seater Brake, Hubley, *$6,000*.

At Opfer's Christmas Auction, 1988:

Three-seater Brake, Hubley, *$8,250.*
Horse-drawn Fire Pumper, with original box, Carpenter, *$7,150.*
Horse-drawn Ladder Truck, Pratt & Letchworth, *$3,300.*

Small cast-iron auto toys, ranging from four to six inches long and primarily from the 1920s and early 1930s, proved far more affordable at Opfer. A Chrysler Airflow, 6 inches long, brought $302.50; the others sold at $22 to $176.

At Lloyd Ralston Toy Auction, Darien, Connecticut, November 1988:

Royal Circus Farmer Van Wagon, Hubley, *$4,500* (vs. *$4,000* at Perelman).
Hubley Trap, 13 inches long, *$2,300.*
Fire Water Tower Wagon, Wilkins, cast iron and steel, *$2,000.*

A Tally-Ho's Ups and Downs

Not all exotic cast-iron toys are immune to the vagaries of auction goers. A coveted Carpenter Tally-Ho coach-and-four was snapped up at $15,000 at Perelman. An example at the Raymond Holland collection auction at Sotheby's in 1985, estimated at $6,500–$8,500, failed to reach reserves. A few months later, it brought $1,650 at Opfer's sale. Holland had purchased the Tally-Ho at Opfer's '84 Christmas Auction at $2,750! "If the thing is painted *right*, it should bring $3,500," observed Baltimore dealer Frank Whitson, who should know; he once owned the toy many years prior to this transaction.

COMIC/CHARACTER TOYS

The "top bananas" in this toy category got a good ride over the past year. At Bill Spicer's toy auction in North Kingston, Rhode Island, in April 1989, a Marx Buck Roger's Rocket Ship, with original box, went out of orbit at $2,500, a new high for that rather common toy. Celluloid Mickey Mouse riding Pluto on wheels brought $6,600 at auction, certainly a record for a plastic toy. Alexander Acevedo, in his Christmas 1988 auction, offered a similar example at $4,500, as well as Mickey on Rocking Horse at $5,500 and Donald Duck Whirligig at $4,500. These fragile Japanese toys from the 1930s have found new respectability among Walt Disney collectors.

There were more surprises. A Mickey Mouse Waddle Book, made in 1934 and featuring four paper Disney characters that could be assembled with brass fittings to waddle down a runway, was priced in Acevedo's Christmas catalog at $10,000.

Perhaps the record for *any* comic toy was posted at the Perelman Great Grab of '88. A Kenton, circa 1910 double eagle chariot with Happy Hooligan and Foxy Grandpa nodders, and with Gloomy Gus as driver, sold at $40,000; Captain & The Kids bell toy: $15,000; a Hubley Happy Hooligan Phaeton: $13,500! After a lull, cast-iron comic toys are back with a vengeance.

The Holy Grail among Disney celluloid toys is the Mickey Mouse pulled by Horace toy. Introduced at the City of Paris department store in San Francisco during the height of the Depression, there is only one known in mint condition and it recently sold as part of the Robert Lesser collection. Alex Acevedo asserted that if another ever came to market he'd willingly "pay $15,000 for it and I wouldn't sell it for less than $20,000."

Also in 1989, Mel Birnkrant, a well-known collector of Disneyana, purchased Oswald the Rabbit, the first Disney-designed stuffed doll, from dealer Richard Wright for $5,000.

There was a time, back in the 1960s, when cast-iron horse-drawn toys and motor toys were all the rage, and comic/character toys in tin, celluloid, and steel enjoyed less than exalted status, hovering in the $25, $50, and perhaps $100 range. There was a recession in 1969, so there was a period until the mid–1970s when prices were still low. According to Bob Lesser, "If you bought the right things, before there were any books to guide you, you could have a fortune in the 1980s."* The first real breakthrough occurred in the 1970s when Nebraska collector/author Ken Harman (*Comic Strip Toys*; see Bibliography) sold Popeye in the Rowboat for $5,000 to a pair of New York collectors.

In buying comic/character toy "futures," it's worth consid-

*From *Of Men and Mice; Witty Toys on View*, by Rita Reif, *New York Times*, January 17, 1988.

ering that the average collector under thirty probably wouldn't
know Happy Hooligan from a new rock group and thinks Tom
Mix plays for the Oakland Raiders. At least, with toys the likes
of Charlie Chaplin, Mickey and Minnie Mouse, Popeye, and Little
Orphan Annie, the memory lingers on as long as there are Saturday morning kiddie cartoon shows and national shrines such
as Disneyland.

Not all comic toys have kept pace with the rarer, more desirable examples, however. We remember selling a rather extensive comic collection some 20 years ago, and although we'd love
to have some of them back today (i.e., Powerful Katrinka, Smitty
on Scooter, Barney Google, and Sparkplug), surprisingly a number of other comic toys have been marking time. B.O. Plenty and
Joe "Wanna Buy a Duck" Penner, for example, are still available at 1970s selling prices, or even less, if you factor in infla-
tion. This may be attributable, in part, to the embarrassment of
riches a few years back when Louis Marx held a bankruptcy sale
of their entire warehouse stock. Another factor may be that a
new breed of young affluent collectors finds no nostalgic bridge
between themselves and these toys, which lie beyond their era
of consciousness.

Several other comic toys seem to have taken a pratfall recently. Hi-Way Henry, once considered the consummate comic
action car, commanded as high as $4,500 in its heyday. Al-
though an example brought $3,000 at Perelman, we've seen it
go as low as $1,100 at an Opfer auction. The latter toy did have
a replaced stove and restored clothes pole (the toy is notoriously
flimsy), and such defects are a sure-fire way to cool off bidders.
Another comic classic, a toy that had always eluded us, was
Jiggs & His Jazzcar. The toy had once peaked at $2,500, but
despite its excellent condition, a similar example surprisingly
fetched but $660 at a recent auction. Also relegated to the "it's
past history" status is the "Skidoodle" German toy, which once
supposedly had comic strip connections. Lacking this pedigree,
the "Skidoodle" now sells in the $250 range, or about a fifth of
its going price two or three years ago. Alex Acevedo predicted
"a price jump soon, but only on the higher-priced toys—say from
$10,000 to $15,000."

There is a shark feed going on, with a number of big-time
buyers trying to buy up all the premier comic strip toys. If it's
any consolation, there will *still* be plenty of the more common,
but every bit as diverting, comic toys available at affordable
prices.

MECHANICAL BANKS

Mechanical banks reign supreme in the antique toy world and are considered the domain of the last of the big spenders. Certainly prices have risen dramatically throughout the 1980s and the recent sale of three major collections* portends that the more exotic specimens in pristine condition will go for a king's ransom into the 1990s.

In no other toy category is condition so closely equated with price. In a Frank Donegan article, titled "Banks That Move," in the April 1989 issue of *Americana*, Bill Bertoia is quoted as saying, "Condition is everything in this field. It's like location in real estate." Steven Weiss of Hillman-Gemini, a New York City toy emporium, applies this formula: "If a bank with 90% of its paint is worth $1,000, then one with 95% will sell for $2,000; one with 99% plus may be worth $5,000."

Higher prices for the *crème de la crème* of mechanicals appear to be elevating prices at even the lowest level. According to Don Markey, banks worth $3,500 are now going for $9,500. A case in point: a rather common Eagle & Eaglets bank, normally no higher than $200 B.P. (Before Perelman), recently sold for $1,000. When we talked with Ernest Long, a venerable California dealer, at Allentown a few weeks following the Perelman sale, he pointed out that banks had gone up between 35% and 40% since the Mosler sale in 1982.

In reality, only a handful of bank patrons are prepared to spend anything like the $250,000 doled out for the Freedman's bank at Perelman, The Darky With Watermelon, at $245,000, or the Old Woman in the Shoe, which commanded nearly $245,000 in an Al Davidson sell-off from the Hagerty horde.

While it is true that you can't buy *any* bank for what you paid two years ago, those who have been in this hobby long enough know that everything goes in a cycle. The worst scenario could happen if too much attention is focused on these overblown prices and a lot of disgruntled collectors are driven right out of the marketplace.

Meanwhile, the best advice to bank collectors, particularly those at entry level, would be to sit back and bide your time. The Annie Hed Bank Collection Sale at Opfer's last October saw

---

*The Perelman Museum collection, the Arnie Hed collection, and the Covert and Gertrude Hagerty collection, all of which sold within 90 days in 1988.

a lot of specimens go for reasonable prices. The price differential between a Charles Bailey "Springing Cat," for example, was startling indeed. The Hed entry brought only $6,600, as compared with $14,000 at a Charles Duff sale and $16,500 at Perelman. Lil Gottschalk, reporting on the Opfer Christmas 1988 Auction, in *Maine Antique Digest*, cited a Bull Dog bank that had sold at the Hed outing for $550. Consigned by the buyer to the Christmas sale, "this time around it sold for $1,155, closer to its true market value."

The alchemy of today's mechanical bank market can gild more than a few faded "lilies." Look for these treasures to seek their own level, hopefully with prices on this galaxy.

MILITARY MINIATURES

In the third and fourth editions of our *Official Price Guide to Collectible Toys*, we commented about the vastly accelerated prices generated at auction by military miniatures by such makers as Britains, Courtenay, Stadden, Heyde, Lucotte, and Mignot.

The war games folks—the vest-pocket Napoleons and Bismarcks who deploy their troops like chess pieces on micro-sized battlefields—are at it again. In recent years, these rather astounding prices were realized at auction: a 15th-century Knights Tournament scene with 25 figures, primarily Stadden and Lassett, $1,430; a Britains U.S. Military Band issued from 1956–1959, $4,180; a Britains Louow Wepener Regiment, "Armies of the World," $2,860; a Tipco Mercedes Fuhrermobile, early 1940s, $1,320; a Hauser Half-Truck Prime Mover and Troop Carrier, $2,530. An unboxed #2184 Britains set of Bahama Police brought $2,530 while a Britains "Walking Elephant," circa 1890, sold for the same. From the heralded Natalie Hammond Hayes collection sold at Phillips in 1987, a set of 18 Richard Courtenay Fighting Knights soared to $13,500, an average of nearly $700 per figure. A mounted replica of Sir John Havering wielding a battle-ax, reached $1,650. Gebruder Heinrich, a contemporary maker and rival to Heyde, was represented by a boxed set of khaki-clad U.S. cavalry troopers, at $1,045 or over twice pre-sale estimates.

In late 1988, Phillips, New York City, held a Collectibles Sale in which a new record was set for a single lead soldier at auction. A Richard Courtenay figure of an English archer falling wounded brought $2,750. Other prices for the fast-rising Courtenays* included $2,090 for Thomas, Lord Braose, astride a "jockey horse" bareheaded, holding battle-ax in right hand, and $1,540 for Sir Stephen Cossington, mounted with battle-ax in movable right arm, shield in left, and kettle helmet. A 67-piece Britains display set, #73, with General Officer, Royal Horse Artillery, 17th Lancers, Life Guards with trumpeter and officer, Royal Norfolk, Scots Greys, and the Black Watch marching at slope with piper and officer sold for $3,850. An extremely uncommon group of Buck Rogers figures by Britain, exclusively for John Dille, including Buck Rogers, Wilma Deering, Dr. Huter, and Ardella, plus two robots, circa 1935, also brought $3,850. Britains set #2093, the Band of the Royal Berkshire Regiment (1954–1959), brought a $2,970 hammer price.

The Burtt Ehrich collection sale at Guernsey's, New York City, in 1989, proved that even non-military miniatures have moved high up on the covetability scale. A Britains #1550 Noah's Ark (see "Military Miniatures" section for details on this sale) far exceeded the guided price at $6,600, the same top bid as realized for a very scarce Britains Victorian Family.

Entry-level collectors should be forewarned that Military Band sets, with their flair for pageantry and sophisticated instrumental detail, are almost preordained to go high in the 1990s. Leading the parade among the numerous quality militariana makers will be Britains, ". . . the best documented, most extensive line . . . with wonderful illustrated boxes."**

PEDAL CARS

In the past several years, we have covered several sizable estate auctions of pedal-powered or battery-powered child-size automobiles. Like many an endangered species, the comparatively large size of these fascinating vehicles may well have hastened their demise. Julie Collier, Director of Collectibles at Christie's East, New York City, was quoted recently in *Antiques & Collecting* as saying "They are the kind of object you leave behind when you move. Most . . . were three feet long, often longer, with an average size of approximately 45 inches." Despite their rel-

---

*Ten of the 32 Courtenays offered topped the $1,000 mark; two exceeded $2,000.
**Phillips specialist Henry Kurtz, as quoted in "Standing Armies" by Duncan Christy, in the June 1988 issue of *Americana Magazine*.

ative scarcity, or perhaps because of it, child-size autos, construction rigs, farm tractors, train engines, and even airplanes are cooking on all cylinders with a growing coterie of collectors, many of whom have an affinity for the adult-size vintage models as well. The most desirable are those in pristine condition, superbly crafted, and authentically detailed to replicate specific adult-size models. A 40-inch pedal car, modeled after a late 1920s Hudson, for example, produced by American National Co., Toledo, Ohio, recently sold at $2,200 at a Christie's East auction. A baby blue, pedal-powered Austin two-seater, with battery-powered headlights and lift-up hood, circa 1920s, sold for $750 at Sotheby's in New York City recently, while what outwardly appeared to be a more desirable toy—a restored Packard two-seater touring car with canvas top—at the same auction failed to meet reserves. The operative word here is "restored."

Summary: Here is a case where a select number of "rabid" private collectors are vying for a dwindling number of motor toys that were produced in limited quantities from their very *inception.*

SOFT TOYS

Echoing through the toy auction halls from Los Angeles to London is the chant, "There's nothing 'soft' about the market for soft toys." Noel Barrett and Bill Bertoia, who managed the Atlanta Toy Museum Sale in Philadelphia in 1986, could point to their offering of early Steiff swivel neck with center seam character dolls, for example. A Steiff French legionnaire doll brought $1,500; a chef, $1,100; a black-shirted cadet, $1,200! (A Sunny Jim doll, meanwhile, which could not be positively identified as Steiff, managed only $325. Ah, the magic of a name.) Even a pair of Steiff rabbits multiplied to $700. A very uncommon Lenci Aviatrix doll at the Atlanta Toy Museum sale soared to $1,200. Meanwhile, some time ago, at Skinner Auctions in Bolton, Massachusetts, a Steiff German foot soldier, circa 1915, in full uniform, more than doubled pre-sale estimates at $2,090; this is not to mention a grouping of Steiff teddy bears that ranged in price (depending on wear and tear) from $550 to $1,000. Even some of the small Steiff animal toys from the 1960s averaged over $30 apiece at the Skinner Sale. Just as we go to press, a Steiff teddy bear set an astonishing new high of $86,350 at Sotheby's. Steiff Mickey and Minnie Mouse toys achieved $3,500 each in Opfer's 1989 pre-Christmas sale.

History of Toys

✳ ✳ ✳

Those delightful artifacts we call toys have existed in many subtle guises in almost every culture and period since the dawn of civilization. Single-movement string-worked toys have survived from over 5,000 years ago in the Indus Valley. Articulated toys, dolls, board games, and rattles have been discovered in Egyptian tombs dating back 2,000 years; limestone pull toys from Persia pre-date the birth of Christ. The British Museum has in its vast holdings a wooden tiger from Thebes circa 1,000 B.C. Toy horses and chariots mounted on wheeled platforms and pulled by strings date from the 4th or 5th century B.C.; Roman youngsters played with baked clay marbles and rag dolls. Toy Roman banks were discovered in the ruins of Pompeii. Unaccountably, toys were simple and few, particularly following the decline of the Roman Empire to the 13th century. It was not until the 16th century that Germany, with Nuremberg and Sonnenberg as major toy centers, developed lever-manipulated wooden and tin toys as an offshoot of local craft guilds. The word ''toy'' itself dates to this era. Daniel Defoe, in *History of the Life and Adventures of Mr. Duncan Campbell*, refers to toys being bought in a toy shop in Edinburgh in 1720.

From the fascinating Hieronymus Bestelmeier illustrated catalogs dating from the 1790s to 1807, we have a rare glimpse of the toys of the period: dolls, games, wooden villages, and zoos, as well as tiny armies of lead soldiers and painted tinplate warships. With the decline of the forests in Germany, mass-production techniques and ''mother necessity'' led to the innovation of the casting of iron and stamping of tinplate toys. Metal toys were produced in substantial quantities, beginning in 1840. By the 1870s Germany was exporting toys to France, Great Britain, and America. From 1890 to 1914, Nuremberg boasted as many as 300 toy factories, over two-thirds of which were engaged in the metal toy trade.

Germany produced the first clockwork train sets from 1865 to 1867, with zinc and lead decorations and painted tinplate engines and stock. In France, two leading firms, Rossignol and Martin, turned to manufacturing automata. Salvaging old tin soon became a minor Paris industry. In France, quality toy production reached its zenith from 1903 to 1914, their La Belle Epoque.

Germany and France were not alone in invading the field of child's play. Some of the most marvelous, highly collectible wood toys were fashioned by itinerant carvers in America, particularly in Pennsylvania Dutch country. The folk art toys of Wilhelm Schimmel (1817–1890), Aaron Mountz during the second half of the 19th century, and George Huguenin in the late 19th century, reflect whimsical barnyard scenes, Noah's arks, crude animals, eagles, and churches.

Although less prolific than the German manufacturers, their U.S. counterparts, the Pattersons of Berlin and New Britain, Connecticut, for example, made toys from scrap as early as the late 18th century. The earliest known clockwork toys patented in America are the Walking Zouve, a Stevens & Brown, Forestville, Connecticut, walking doll and Autoperipatetikos by Enoch Morrison and manufactured by Martin & Runyan, New York City. July 15, 1862, is the patent date. By 1848, the Philadelphia Tin Toy Mfg. Co. was producing brightly colored horses, cows, locomotives, and boats. In 1856, George Brown featured a veritable menagerie on wheels, all handsomely stencil decorated. Hot air toys emerged in the late 1860s by Ives & Blakeslee, Plymouth, Connecticut. Moving figures were fitted with pulleys and with paper wheels and placed over a lamp, register, or gas burner to ingeniously set the toy in motion.

J. & E. Stevens, Cromwell, Connecticut, was probably the first American manufacturer to produce cast-iron toys, introducing their firecracker pistols beginning in 1859. By the late 1860s, Stevens, along with James Fallows, J. Hall, and J. Serrell, began to turn out hundreds of variations of still and mechanical banks in tin and cast iron.

The first American cast-iron toys appeared as miniature trains, horse-drawn drays, brakes, landaus, hansoms, tally-hos,

and wagons. They were rather crude and stiff imitations of earlier tin incarnations. Soon, however, manufacturers began paying closer attention to authenticity and detail. In the golden era
of cast-iron toys, the 1880s and 1890s, the premier makers were
F.W. Carpenter of Harrisville, New York; John Hubley, Lancaster, Pennsylvania; Henry Dent, Fullerton, Pennsylvania; Pratt &
Letchworth, Buffalo, New York; E.R. Ives, Plymouth, Connecticut; and James Wilkins, Keene, New Hampshire.

In 1850, the U.S. Census Bureau listed 47 toy makers; by
1880, the number had quadrupled to 173 toy and game manufacturers, with annual sales figures equivalent to such successful industries as sporting goods, telephone and telegraph,
cleaning and dyeing.

In the 1850s, the dean of wooden toy manufacturers was William Tower of South Hingham, Massachusetts. With Joseph Ja-
cobs, Crocker Wilder, and several other members, Tower created
a cooperative workshop known as the Tower Guild. Other wood
toy innovators included three generations of the Charles Crandall family from Pennsylvania and New York (1867 through the
1890s); Joel Ellis, Springfield, Vermont; Brown & Eggleston and
A. Christian & Son, New York City (1856); R. Bliss, Pawtucket,
Rhode Island (1870s); Morton Converse, Winchendon, Massachusetts (1884); and W.S. Reed, Leominster, Massachusetts
(1875). These firms produced handsomely lithographed paper-
on-wood Noah's arks, churches, transportation toys, doll houses,
and doll furniture, as well as hobby horses.

Fanciful cast-iron bell toys were led by Gong Bell Mfg., East
Hampton, Connecticut. Gong Bell may well have produced the
first example, the Revolving Chimes Bell, in 1873. Another East
Hampton maker, Watrous Mfg. (1880s–1930s), which later
merged with N.N. Hill (circa 1890), produced bell toys.

The major collecting focus today is on toys that have been
mass produced from mid-19th century on—American toys with
obvious European exceptions. Many leading collectors establish
the turn of the century as a cut-off point. Cast-iron toy specialists, however, are more inclined to extend their parameters to
include later examples by Hubley, Kenton, and Arcade, and a
handful of other U.S. firms that continued to produce superb
toys up to World War II. The scarcity and expense of adding
vintage examples to one's collection has prompted a whole new
cult of enthusiasts to seek solace in space and robot toys and
transportation toys of the postwar period.

History of Toy Collecting

✳ ✳ ✳

Toy collecting is a relatively recent phenomenon. Only in the last twenty or so years has the hobby lured significant numbers of collectors, as well as scholars and antiquarians. John Brewer, in his essay *Childhood Revisited: The Genesis of the Modern Toy*, explained that in 17th-century colonial America the play of both adults and children was condemned as a sinful and idle pursuit. In England as well, there was a noticeable lack of toys in the household. Dr. Johnson's *Dictionary* defined "toy" as "a petty commodity; a trifle; a thing of no value; a plaything or bauble."

Somehow, the philosopher John Locke and another free-thinker, Frederick Froebel, were instrumental in helping to break the moralist hold of the Calvinists and Puritans, leading to a more advanced approach of encouraging the development of a child's intelligence through the liberalization of play. "Even so," added Brewer, "it was an affluent audience in America and in England who had the time, the money, and the social predisposition to lavish attention on their children." Patrick Murray, in his book *Toys*, points out that in Victorian England toys were referred to as "rich boy's pretties."

Murray adds that one single event helped to swing the tide of public sentiment: the manufacturer Gebruder Maerklin, of Göppingen, a name synonymous with originality and quality, staged an exhibition at the Leipzig Spring Fair in 1891 that clearly foretold the imaginative potential of the hobby. As early as the 1870s the Bavarian Museum in Nuremberg displayed collections of old and new toys. The designs and mechanisms of these toys were closely scrutinized and widely copied by manufacturers of that period.

Ernest King, an eminent English toy collector at the turn of this century, specialized in the ha'penny tuppeny (now simply known and coveted as "penny toys") in Lilliputian-sized tin toys from the late Victorian and Edwardian era (1890–1914). In 1917, he endowed the British Toy Museum with his fabulous collection of over 1,650 penny toys. In 1957, the King Collection went on display in the Children's Room at Kensington Palace in London. In covering the event, toy author Leslie Daikin wrote in *The Illustrated London News*, "Thanks to the late Ernest King, we may recapture in microcosm something of a social pattern that is forgotten."

On these shores, toys may well have been "discovered" on the coattails of folk art. The Whitney Studio club of New York City mounted the first folk art exhibition in 1924. By the early 1930s, major exhibitions including folk art and toys were staged by the Museum of Modern Art and by the Newark Museum. In the late 1920s, the Ives Co. recalled their glory days of the 1880s in their advertisements and catalogs. They also promoted themselves in their New York showrooms, with a special display of vintage Ives clockwork toys. After the crash of 1929, business failed, but Lionel, which absorbed Ives a few years later, assembled the earlier display with their own vast collection of early train sets. Toys were well on their way—"on track," so to speak—in striving for respectability.

Numerous collecting societies materialized in the United States in the 1960s, including The Antique Toy Collectors of America, Mechanical Bank Collectors of America, and the American Train Collectors Association. In 1985, The American Game Collector's Association was founded. (See additional organizations listed under "Collecting Organizations" in the back of this book.)

John Brewer writes, "Toys are cultural messages—sometimes simple, occasionally complex and ambiguous, but invariably revealing." An endless multitude of enthusiasts are discovering the infinite variety and fascination of toys.

How to Gain
Greater Satisfaction
From Toy Collecting

*   *   *

The following guidelines, distilled from the teachings of some of the most prominent collectors in the hobby, may prove helpful to beginning, as well as seasoned, toy enthusiasts.

1. Most toy people tend to gravitate toward a category that they can pinpoint in time which is from their own realm of experience. In many cases, specialization is an extension of one's profession or trade. While it may sound simplistic, it is essential to collect what *you* like. Resist if you will the follow-the-leader syndrome that occurs in toy collecting and other hobbies. A few years back, the big crunch was for Lehmann toys among one of the toy societies. Suddenly, even the more uncommon Lehmanns were almost impossible to find, except at ridiculous prices. Leading collector/author Bernard Barenholtz counsels: "Make sure that the toys you are interested in are within your financial grasp. Buy the best you can afford. One fine toy is worth five ordinary ones."

2. Familiarization breeds contentment. Visit as many museums and private collections as possible. A few years ago, we were privileged to visit the exhibition, "Built to Last: The Toys of Kingsbury," at the New Hampshire Historical Society in Concord, New Hampshire. We came away with a far deeper appreciation for Kingsbury toys and their predecessor, Wilkins. In addition to a variety of pressed steel examples, it was obvious that Wilkins' Brownie Fire Department, twin cyclists, sidewheelers, and other cast-iron toys compared favorably with the best of Ives and Carpenter.

3. Research, research, and more research. Surround yourself with as many toy books, reference guides, trade catalogs, advertising trade cards, billheads from various toy makers, newspaper clippings, and photographs as possible and don't let this material gather dust in your files and library shelves. Consult your sources frequently.

4. Get to know your fellow collectors. There are any number of clubs and organizations that will open their doors to you. Many groups conduct seminars, museum tours, reprint toy catalogs, and serve as a conduit of information on everything relating to the hobby. Other groups are merely social, but the importance of interfacing with others who have the same infectious enthusiasm for toy collecting cannot be underestimated. Through seminars at conventions, club auctions, and simple conversation with fellow club members, you'll be exposed to more quality toys than you are likely to come across in a lifetime. To quote Barney Barenholtz again (from his book *American Antique Toys*), "The most important reason [to collect] may not be intrinsic to the toys themselves, but to the wonderful people we have met all over the world, whose paths never would have crossed ours but for the sharing of this special interest in antique toys." Many leading collectors we know, for example, are simply not "joiners." They still find ample opportunities to make contact with fellow collectors at major toy auctions. There is also today such a proliferation of toy extravaganzas and exhibitions, enough to fill out one's social calendar for an entire year, that there is every opportunity to make contact with collectors with areas of specialization akin to your own.

5. Noted collector/author Lillian Gottschalk, in an interview in *Antique Toy World* several years ago, had this to say about learning the toy field backwards and forwards: "I feel [the toy] with my hands, with my eyes. Then experience and knowledge take over." Learn to observe fellow collectors, particularly at major shows and toy auctions where it is often crowded and there are many distractions. Note the thoroughness with which they examine any toy they might be intent on purchasing. One collector of our acquaintance always carries the following in her handbag: a loupe or magnifying glass, a black light, a magnet, and [seriously] a dose of smelling salts. The latter pulls her through those rather feverish bidding duels at auctions.

6. Seek out only the more knowledgeable, experienced dealers whose integrity and judgment are respected within the hobby. Toy collecting has grown by leaps and bounds in recent

years, and there are scores of new faces among us. The field is, nevertheless, a tightly knit universe and the word is soon out as to who is reputable and who is not.

A surprising number of prominent collectors rely on their "pet" dealers to locate rarities for them, even going so far as to keep them on retainer. To maintain a low profile (*why*, we have never been able to ascertain), some collectors even have their dealers execute bids in their behalf at auction. (One wonders whatever happened to the thrill of the chase?) Implicit in any transaction with toy dealers or auction houses is that your money be fully refundable if, for any reason, the specific toy fails to match up to its advertised or "as stated" condition.

7. Despite all the articles and books that talk about "collecting for fun and profit," approaching toys from an investment standpoint can be an expensive lesson. Someone once said that mutual funds, government bonds, and real estate would be safer investments. We feel rather strongly that a toy collection was meant to be lived with, not stored in safety deposit boxes or otherwise "squirreled away," under lock and key. There is no denying, however, that collectors should have a thorough understanding of the value of the toy they own.

8. This leads up to an essential point: too many of us fail to sit back and determine which direction our collection is to take and which limits need to be set. To quote Yogi Berra: "If you don't know where you're going, you'll wind up somewhere else." Running off in all directions at once and acquiring toys willy-nilly inevitably results in a squandering of time and money. Avoid also those so-called real "buys"—toys missing a wheel, an arm, a driver—those toys bereft of paint, rusted out, which appear to have been run over by a steamroller. Unless you are a professional restorer, the cost of returning this toy to its original condition will be prohibitive.

9. Resign yourself to the prospect that somewhere along the line you will make errors of judgment. Take heart; mistakes can often pay for themselves if they are factored in as part of the total experience. They will only heighten your perception in future transactions.

10. Dave Bausch, a venerable collector for over 30 years from Allentown, Pennsylvania, offered this conclusion in an interview in *Collectors' Showcase*: "The best piece of advice I can give . . . is to be patient. All too often someone wants to build a collection overnight. It can be a very expensive lesson. Learn as much as you can and have *fun*. That's what it's all about."

How to Document a Toy By Maker and Date of Manufacture

❋ ❋ ❋

There are those compulsive accumulators of toys who could care less about a toy's history—whether it be fashioned in a large city factory, somebody's backyard, or at the North Pole by elves. Others are less concerned with age or pedigree than with its visceral impact—its patina, form, and condition. To these enthusiasts, the *toy* is the thing.

We like to think that historical elements connected with a toy not only add to its value but to the enjoyment of the toy as well.

DATING TOYS

A neat bit of detective work can uncover the actual or approximate date of a toy even when there are few clues to go by. Only a few U.S. toys were patented in the mid-1850s. After 1870, most examples were patented or trademarked, indicating a copyright. Should any stenciled, embossed, or printed patent numbers appear on the toy itself or on its original box, the year of issue can be traced by using the chart found under "Toy Patents." For a nominal fee, a number can be verified by the U.S. Patent Office as to original patent application and names of both inventor and manufacturer. Major libraries and historical societies are additional sources for various patent data. German patents date back to 1878, and two recent books, *German Patent Books Vol. I: 1878–1915* and *Vol. II: 1916–1940*, should prove indispensable for the serious collector. Patent dates, of course, can sometimes be misleading. Ernest Paul Lehmann, for example, bought the patent rights to the original Tom the Climbing Monkey on string (from an American, William Pitt Shattuck) in 1881. Over the past 75 years Lehmann produced five European variations, including a 1953 version of Tom with his little red fez.

MAKERS' MARKS

Represented on the following pages are makers' marks covering over 50 of the giants in the U.S. and European toy industry, many of which have existed since toys were first mass produced.

In compliance with the McKinley Tariff Act of 1891, imported toys made from that time forth were marked with the country of origin. Unfortunately, many of these toys either bore no makers' marks or, if they had paper labels, they may have long since disappeared. Some of the best sources for identifying unmarked toys are manufacturers' and jobbers' wholesale and retail catalogs, flyers, broadsides, and order forms. A number of toy organizations and museums have reprinted much of this valuable material. You'll also find examples advertised in various toy trade journals, such as *Antique Toy World, Collectors' Showcase*, and *The Antique Trader*. For more recent vintage toys, back issues of jobber trade publications, such as *Toys and Novelties*, provide new-product announcements, trade gossip, and a myriad of advertisements which help unscramble the puzzle of which toys were made to whose specifications (as with broker George Borgfeldt, who marketed many toys under a "no name" line). Borgfeldt was also the American representative for Steiff and Nifty toys, and the New York broker for Gibbs Mfg. of Canton, Ohio.

Harris Toy Co. of Cleveland, to further complicate matters, acted as jobbers for their competition, Dent, Hubley, and Wilkins, in addition to producing their own premier cast-iron horse-drawn rigs. In the early years of Hubley Mfg., the firm produced all manner of spare parts for other companies. Now you can begin to see why identifying toys by manufacturer is far from child's play!

An excellent sourcebook for identifying Walt Disney franchised merchandise by manufacturer was produced by Herman "Kay" Kamen from 1934 to 1950 (there were seven 48-page United Artists Corp. catalogs in all). Actually, the catalogs have become collectors' items in themselves. Sears & Roebuck's cat-

Bliss, U.S.

Carette, German

Chein, U.S.

Gunthermann, German

Ideal, U.S.

Lehmann, German

Bing

CHARRETTES PEUGEOT

Peugeot, French

Charles Rosignol,
French

Manoil, U.S.

Lionel, U.S.

PARIS

Cuberly, Blondell, Gerbeau,
French

Oro Werke Neill,
German

Jouet de Paris (JEP),
French

Muller–Kadeder, German

Righter, German

Brimtoy, G.B.

French Toy Seal of Quality

Greppert, Kelch, German

Arcade, U.S.

Strauss, U.S.

Metalgraf, Italian

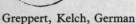

Ives, U.S.

Wilhelm, Kraus, German

D.S

Dessein, German

Hess, German

Marx, U.S.

Maerklin, German

Walter Stock, German

Kenton, U.S.

Gray Iron, U.S.

Meccano, G.B.

J.P.
FRANCE

Edmond Faire, French

Rossignol, French

TOYS

Althof Bergmann, U.S.

Britains, G.B.

TRADE   MARK

MADE IN ENGLAND

Burnett Ltd., G.B.

Fischer, German

alogs from the '30s and '40s also provide excellent reference material for Mickey Mouse and various other comic collectibles enthusiasts.

IDENTIFYING GERMAN TOYS
BY TRADEMARK INITIALS

Figures or combinations of letters often appear as follows:

George Carette	G.C. & Co.
Greppert Kelch	G.&K.
Kellerman	C.K.O.
Karl Bub	K.B.N.
Wilhelm Kraus	J.K. & Co.
Hathius Hess	H.J.L.
Muller & Kadeder	M.K.
Walter Stock	Marke Stocke
Siegfried Gunthermann	
& Adolph Weige	SG.AW
Tipp & Co.	T.C.O.
Johann Distler	J.D.N.
Theodor Frederich	
Wilhelm Marklin	G.M.; G.M. & Co.
Oro Muller	OROBR
Richter & Company	J.S.
Johann Philipp Meier	No letters used but a small image of dog pulling cart. Usually appears on underside of toy. Meier registered the logo in 1894.

TOY PATENTS, 1860–1942

Toys may be dated and identified by maker by listings in the annual *U.S. Patent Gazette*, but in many cases the data is very sketchy. The best solution is to write the U.S. Patent Office in Washington, D.C., with a list of patent numbers required, and for a nominal fee they will send you copies of the patent drawings with copy description in printed form.

The only drawback with patent papers is that there is no way of determining if the toy was ever manufactured. Here is where cross-referencing with manufacturers' catalogs, business record books, and toy trade magazines will assist you in making a positive identification.

Year	Patent Number	Year	Patent Number
1860	26,642	1895	531,619
1861	31,005	1896	552,502
1862	34,045	1897	574,369
1863	37,266	1898	596,467
1864	41,047	1899	616,871
1865	45,685	1900	640,167
1866	51,784	1901	664,827
1867	60,658	1902	690,385
1868	72,959	1903	717,521
1869	85,503	1904	748,567
1870	98,460	1905	778,834
1871	110,617	1906	808,618
1872	122,304	1907	839,799
1873	134,504	1908	875,679
1874	146,120	1909	908,436
1875	158,350	1910	945,010
1876	171,641	1911	980,178
1877	185,813	1912	1,013,095
1878	198,733	1913	1,049,326
1879	211,078	1914	1,083,267
1880	223,211	1915	1,123,212
1881	236,137	1916	1,166,419
1882	251,685	1917	1,210,389
1883	269,820	1918	1,251,458
1884	291,016	1919	1,290,027
1885	310,163	1920	1,326,899
1886	333,494	1921	1,364,063
1887	355,291	1922	1,401,948
1888	375,720	1923	1,440,362
1889	395,305	1924	1,478,996
1890	418,665	1925	1,521,590
1891	443,987	1926	1,568,040
1892	466,315	1927	1,612,790
1893	488,976	1928	1,654,521
1894	511,744	1929	1,696,897

Year	Patent Number	Year	Patent Number
1930	1,742,181	1936	2,026,510
1931	1,787,424	1937	2,066,309
1932	1,839,190	1938	2,101,004
1933	1,892,663	1939	2,142,080
1934	1,944,449	1940	2,185,170
1935	1,985,878	1941	2,227,418
		1942	2,268,540

Manufacturers

✳ ✳ ✳

Acme Toy Works, Chicago, Illinois
1903–1907
Founder: Jacob Lauth
Specialty: Clockwork toy autos.

All Metal Products Co. (see *Wyandotte Toys*)

All-NU Products Inc., New York City, New York
1938–1945
Founder: C. Frank Krupp
Specialty: Military miniatures. Krupp originated and sculpted Barclay's tin helmeted soldier line, then left to form own company. Krupp went into bankruptcy in 1945, but resumed business a year later under the name Faben Products Inc.

Alps Shojo Ltd., Tokyo, Japan
1948 to date
Specialty: Toy vehicles and novelties, many of which are battery operated; mixed tinplate and tin. Space toys are among the most popular. Trademark: ALPS.

Althof, Bergmann, New York City, New York
1867–1880
Founders: Three Bergmann brothers and the jobber, L. Althof.
Specialty: One of first U.S. toy makers to produce carpet-running tinplate trains; renowned for its painted tin clockwork toys, notably the hoop variety; also bell toys, still banks, horse-drawn vehicles.

American Flyer, Chicago, Illinois
1907–1938 (Acquired by A.C. Gilbert)
Specialty: Electric train engines and rolling stock. Also produced a popular line of comic figures on bicycle gravity toys, including Charlie Chaplin, Uncle Sam, and Roosevelt Bears (circa 1912). A.C. Gilbert revitalized the ailing American Flyer line; following World War II, it moved to "S" gauge models, retaining the American Flyer name.

American National Co., Toledo, Ohio
Early 1900s
Founders: Walter, Harry, and William Diemer
Slogan: "Raise the Kids on Wheels"
Trade Name: "Giant"
Specialty: Produced sidewalk toys (scooters, bicycles) and pressed-steel trucks, competing briefly with Keystone and Buddy "L" in the late 1920s.

American Soldier Co., Brooklyn, New York
1898–1930 (Purchased by Selchow & Righter)
Founder: C.W. Beiser
Specialty: "American Hero" cowboy and Indian sets. Trademark "Eureka" was used up through 1903. Beiser innovated a special stand-up figure display tray which he licensed to Britains and several other firms.

Andes Foundry Co., Lancaster, Pennsylvania
1919–1930s
Founder: Eugene Andes
Specialty: First made paper caps and cast-iron components for Kilgore cap guns and cannons. Merged with Kilgore and Federal Mfg. in 1927, and became American Toys until the company dissolved a few years later. Specialized in Arctic ice cream wagons, airplanes, stake and dump trucks.

Arcade Mfg. Co., Freeport, Illinois
1868–1946
(Originally under name Novelty Iron Works)
Slogan: "They Look Real" (adopted in 1920)
Founder: E.H. and Charles Morgan
Specialty: First made toys and coffee mills in 1884.
As late as 1939, Arcade's toy line included over 300 toy items.
Yellow Cab was first successful toy. Andy Gump in 348 and
Chester Gump in His Pony Cart (all three pictured) were other
popular toys with collectors. Arcade also made toy banks, doll
house furniture, and cast-iron penny toys.

Arnold Co., Nuremberg, Germany
1906 to date
Founder: K. Arnold
Specialty: Stationary steam accessories; nautical toys. Introduced "Rapido" gauge "N" model railroads in 1960s.

Auburn, Auburn, Indiana (Double Fabric Tire Corp.)
1913–1968 (Made first toys in 1935)
Specialty: English Palace Guard toy soldiers, as well as military
miniatures for European and American branches of service.
Made number of animal and wheeled vehicle toys. Toy division
moved to Deming, New Mexico, in 1960.

Automatic Toy Works, New York City, New York
1868–1874
Founder: Robert J. Clay
Specialty: Clockwork tin toys, i.e., Girl Skipping Rope, Toy
Gymnast, Creeping Baby; was precursor of all Ives articulated,
dancing platform toys. Bought out by Ives in 1874.

Barclay Mfg. Co., Hoboken, New Jersey
1923–1971
Founders: Leon Donze, a Frenchman, and Michael Levy
Specialty: Introduced line of toy soldiers in 1932; became the
largest U.S. producer of toy soldiers up to World War II.

Barton & Smith, Philadelphia, Pennsylvania
1890s–?
Founder: J. Barton
Specialty: Cast-iron mechanical banks, including "Boy on Trapeze."

Bassett-Lowke, Northampton, England
1899 to date
Founder: Wenman J. Bassett-Lowke
Specialty: The first to recognize the quality workmanship of
German toy train manufacturers (i.e., Maerklin, Bing, Carette,
and Ismayer) and to commission specific British designs.
Bassett-Locke also innovated the mail-order catalog of toys concept, mailing its first edition, with tipped-in photographs, in
1899.

Bing Corp., New York City, New York
1924–1935
Founder: John Bing
Specialty: Spinoff of German firm, Gebruder Bing; served as jobber for parent firm with mechanical boats, zeppelins, steam engines.

Gebruder Bing, Nuremberg, Germany
1866–1933
Founders: Brothers Ignatius and Adolph Bing
Specialty: Wide-range spring-driven cars, buses, boats. Perhaps

its biggest coup was a line of trains initiated in 1882. Bing went under during the crash of 1929; Karl Bub acquired the toy trains division and Fleischmann the toy boats.

R. Bliss Mfg. Co., Pawtucket, Rhode Island
1832–1914 (Sold to Mason & Parker, Winchendon, Massachusetts)
Founder: Rufus Bliss
Specialty: Bliss had over a one-hundred-year history, although the earliest known advertisement for toys appeared in *New England Business Directory* in 1871. Pioneered in development of lithographed paper on wooden toys, including dolls' houses, boats, trains, and building blocks.

Blomer & Schüler, Nuremberg, Germany
1930 to date
Specialty: Tin mechanical motor toys; logo features elephant with howdah.

George Borgfeldt & Co., New York City, New York
1881–1962
Founders: George Borgfeldt, and Marcell and Joseph Kahle
Specialty: Importer and wholesaler of toys, including comic novelty tin wind-ups under name "Nifty." Trademark was "Nifty"

smiling moon face. Also distributed "Oh Boy" pressed steel trucks and cars.

James H. Bowen, Philadelphia, Pennsylvania
1877–1906
Founder: James H. Bowen
Specialty: Pattern maker for J. & E. Stevens mechanical banks, including such classics as "Reclining Chinaman," "Darktown Battery," "Girl Skipping Rope."

Bowman, Norwich, England
1920s–1935
Specialty: Steam-driven locomotives and rolling stock.

Milton Bradley & Co., Springfield, Massachusetts
1861 to date
Founder: Milton Bradley
Slogan: "Maker of the World's Best Games"
Specialty: Variously identified as Milton Bradley Company, Milton Bradley & Co., and Milton Bradley Co. Launched his business with "The Checkered Game of Life," a board game with high moral overtones. Milton Bradley also became well known for educational games, books, kindergarten teaching aids, and school supplies, as well as a small range of toys.

William Britains Ltd., London, England
1893 to date
Founder: William Britain
Specialty: Introduced a three-dimensional hollow toy soldier line, faithfully replicating over 100 British Army regiments in their first decade of doing business. Britains expanded to become the world's largest producer of lead toy soldiers. (Since 1966, alas, the figures have been produced in plastic.)

George W. Brown & Co., Forestville, Connecticut
1856–1880
Founders: George W. Brown and Chauncey Goodrich
Specialty: The first manufacturer to produce toys with clockwork mechanisms, beginning perhaps as early as 1850. Known for classic boats, vehicles, animal platform toys, dancing figures, and hoop bell toys fashioned in painted tin. Merged with J. & E. Stevens in 1868.

Karl Bub, Nuremberg, Germany
1851–1966
Founder: Karl Bub
Specialty: A superbly enameled (and later lithographed) line of clockwork tin transportation toys, including trains. Many Bub toys reached the American market via exclusive distributor F.A.O. Schwarz, New York City, during the 1920s–1930s.

Buddy "L," Salem, Massachusetts
1910 to date
Founder: Fred Lundahl
Specialty: Known under the following corporate names through the years: Moline Press Steel (1910–1913); Buddy "L" Wood Products (1944); Buddy "L" Manufacturing (1930); Buddy "L" Corp. (to date). Buddy "L" toys were named after the founder's son. Lundahl introduced the line in 1921. Starting with a small pressed-steel pickup truck, Buddy "L" had expanded to a veritable fleet of almost 30 cranes, steam rollers, trucks, and other construction toys some five years later.

Buffalo Toy & Tool Works, Buffalo, New York
1924–1968
Specialty: Lightweight pressed-steel aeronautical, automotive, and carousel toys, many of which were activated by a special spiral rod connected to a spring.

Burnett Ltd., London, England
1920s–1930s
Specialty: Painted and lithographed tin clockwork vehicles, including London autobuses.

Butler Brothers, New York City, New York
1876–1950s
Specialty: One of the largest wholesale distributors of toys in the United States during the first quarter of the 20th century, carry-

ing the most elite lines. Sold by catalog exclusively to merchants, with sample houses in most major U.S. cities.

Cardini, Omegna, Italy
1922–1928
Specialty: Five main lines of small toy automobiles; Cardini's innovative packaging included outer box that could be transformed into car's garage. Toys were identified by large Cardini crest; wheels were marked "Pirelli-cord."

Georges Carette, Nuremberg, Germany
1886–1917
Founder: Georges Carette (with Gebruder Bing's backing)
Specialty: Tin mechanical cars, boats, trains, mostly lithographed. Best known for electric streetcars and model trains. Carette, as a French citizen, was deported from Germany in 1917, thus closing the firm.

Carlisle & French Co., Cincinnati, Ohio
1895–1915 (For toy line. Firm continues to date as marine lighting manufacturer)
Founders: Robert Finch and Morton Carlisle
Specialty: Produced first successful electrically run toy train in the United States in 1897. Later expanded line to include steam outline locomotives and rolling stock. Also functioned as distributor, handling the first toy automobile (made by Knapp Electric in 1900).

Francis W. Carpenter, Port Chester, New York
1880–1890 (Sold patent rights and inventory to Pratt & Letchworth, but produced several outstanding toys on his own through the first decade of the 20th century)
Specialty: Cast-iron, horse-drawn vehicles, including what many collectors regard as the *crème de la crème,* the tally-ho.

N.D. Cass, Athol, Massachusetts
1890s to date
Specialty: Wooden toys, some with clockwork mechanisms, including autos, trucks, doll houses, and barns.

Chad Valley, Birmingham, England
1823 (Under name Johnson Brothers Ltd.; assumed Chad Valley name in 1929) to date
Founder: Anthony Bunn-Johnson
Specialty: Lightweight metal cars, construction kit models, Teddy Bears. Palitoy, a subsidiary of General Mills, UK Ltd., purchased Chad Valley Co. in 1978.

Champion Hardware Co., Geneva, Ohio
1883–1954 (Toys from 1930–1936)
Founders: John and Ezra Hasenpflug
Specialty: Cast-iron transportation toys; cast-iron parts for other leading toy makers.

J. Chein & Co., New York City, New York, and Harrison, New Jersey
1903–1979 (Toy producing years)
Founder: Julius Chein
Specialty: Lithographed tin mechanical toys, banks, drums, tea sets. Chein's line of comic and circus tin toys received wide acceptance in the 1930s and leading up to World War II. Became known as Chein Industries, Inc., in 1970s.

Andre Citroen, Paris, France
1919 to date (Toys first produced in 1923)
Founder: Andre Citroen
Specialty: Exact replicas of the automotive manufacturer's real thing, the full-size models (as an advertising gimmick); later, other brands of autos were replicated. A stencil on the underside usually identifies Citroen.

D.P. Clark, Dayton, Ohio
1898–1909 (Renamed Schieble Toy & Novelty in 1909)
Founder: David P. Clark
Specialty: Sheet-steel novelty and automotive toys with friction and flywheel mechanisms.

Clark & Sowdon, New York City, New York
Early 1890s–1910
Specialty: Board games such as "Rough Riders," "Game of Golf," "Yacht Race."

E.O. Clark, New York City, New York
1897–early 1900s
Founder: E.O. Clark (Successor to Clark & Sowdon)
Specialty: Board games, including "The Charge," "The Hippodrome," "The Owl & The Pussycat."

Comet Metal Products, Queens, New York
1919–1950s
Founder: Abraham Slonin
Specialty: Originally a die-casting business; produced line of 55 mm solid military toys in late 1930s. In World War II, produced warship identification models for U.S. Navy. In 1946, introduced military line, "Authenticast," with plants in Richmond Hill, New York, and Galway, Ireland. Designer was Holger Eriksson; South African connection was established following fire which destroyed Galway plant. (See *S.A.E.*)

Morton E. Converse Co., Winchenden, Massachusetts
1878–1934 (Mason & Converse until 1883)
Founder: Morton Converse
Specialty: "Toytown Complex" was once recognized as largest wood toy factory in the world. Known for Noah's arks, ABC blocks, and doll furniture, many of which were lithograph on wood. Made steel toys in the 1890s, comprised mainly of transportation vehicles with clockwork mechanisms.

Corcoran Mfg. Co., Washington, Indiana
1920s–1940s
Specialty: Large, pressed-steel riding toy autos and trains under trademark "Cor-Cor."

Corgi Toys, Mettoy Playcraft Ltd., Swansea, South Wales
Since 1956 (Mettoy Playcraft Ltd. originated in 1934)
Specialty: Miniature toy vehicles in metal and plastic.

Courtenay Miniatures, Doran, England
1938–1963
Founders: Richard and Vida Courtenay; an extension of a Doran
   toy maker which dates back to 1892
Specialty: Very limited production, pewter royalty figures, including Knights of the Round Table. Peter Greenhill purchased
the Courtenay molds in the early 1960s and continues to market
miniatures under the Courtenay and Greenhill names.

Charles M. Crandall, Covington, Pennsylvania
1867–1905 (Relocated to Montrose, Pennsylvania, in 1875; to
   Waverly, New York, 1888)
Founder: Charles Crandall
Specialty: Interlocking tongue-and-groove lithograph paper-on-
wood joints that children used to create multiple figure forms.
Some of the most popular sets: "District School House," "Acrobats," and "Treasure Box." Charles' son Jesse started his own
toy business soon after the Civil War, relocating in Brooklyn.
Jesse Crandall was issued a number of patents for rocking toys,
alphabet blocks, and construction toys.

Jesse Crandall, Brooklyn, New York
1840s–1880s
Specialty: Hobby horses, rocking horses, velocipedes, and board
games.

Crescent Toy Co., Ltd., Great Britain
1921–late 1970s
Specialty: Hollowcast lead soldiers and plastic figures, including
"Dan Dare, Pilot of the Future"; also made die-cast motor miniatures.

A.A. Davis, Nashua, New Hampshire
1860s–?
Specialty: Novelty toys featuring small lithographed figures of
celebrities, animals, butterflies with movable parts set in wooden
cups, covered by glass (i.e., "Magic Major General Grant"; see
"Political" listing).

Dayton Friction Toy Works, Dayton, Ohio
1909–1935
Founder: D.P. Clark (see *D.P. Clark*)
Specialty: Pressed-steel friction toys with patented horizontal

flywheel (1926) under trade name "Gyro"; maker of child-size, up to 24 inches long, SON-NY line of motor toys.

Dayton Toy & Specialty Co., Dayton, Ohio
1920s–early 1930s
Specialty: Large, heavy-gauge, pressed-steel transportation toys.

Dent Hardware Co., Fullerton, Pennsylvania
1895–1937 (Continued to manufacture cold storage hardware until 1973)
Founders: Henry H. Dent, with four additional partners
Specialty: Cast-iron and aluminum transportation toys and banks. "Pioneer" fire truck, Ford Tri-Motor, and large hook-and-ladder toys were popular items.

Johann Distler, Nuremberg, Germany
1900–1968
Founder: Johann Distler. In 1917, Distler took on Messrs. Brown & Mayer as partners. In 1923, partners took over after Distler's death. Brown & Mayer sold out to Ernst Volk in 1935. From 1962–1968, a Belgian firm assumed toy business.
Specialty: Lithographed tin penny toys; comic and erratic action transportation toys.

Charles William Doepke Manufacturing Co., Rossmoyne, Ohio
1920s and 1930s
Specialty: Faithful replicas of transportation, fire fighting, farm, and construction vehicles under name "Model Toys." Known for rugged, heavy-gauge steel construction and ease of operation.

Doll Et Cie (& Co.), Nuremberg, Germany
1868–Post–World War II
Founders: Peter Doll and J. Sondheim. Firm was taken over

by Fleischmann in 1938 but the name was retained until 1948. Specialty: Steam engines and accessories; novelty trains and cars, some of which were steam propelled. Trademark based on initials "D.C."

Dowst (Tootsietoy), Chicago, Illinois
Late 1890s
Founders: Charles O. and Samuel Dowst
Specialties: Miniature cast-metal cars, trains, and planes. Tootsietoy name introduced in 1922 when Dowst introduced a line of doll furniture (named after a Dowst granddaughter, Toots). Merged with Cosmo Mfg. in 1926; acquired Strombeck-Becker toy line in 1961 and made name change as Strombecker Corp.

Hans Eberl, Nuremberg, Germany
Circa 1900 to late 1920s
Founder: Hans Eberl
Specialty: Automotive toys bearing initials H.E.N.; Borgfeldt was a factory agent for Eberl.

Edmund's Traditional Toy Soldiers
1950s–?
Founder: Edmund Fangonilo
Specialty: Confederate Regiment replicas in limited editions of 100 sets, created by the artist, Fangonilo.

EFFanBEE, New York City, New York
1910 to date
Founders: Fleischaker and Baum (from which the trade name derives)
Specialty: Early on, EFFanBEE specialized in bisque, cloth, and composition baby and toddler dolls, with slogan: "They Walk, They Talk, They Sleep." Later the firm made a number of celebrity puppets and ventriloquists' dolls, including Charlie McCarthy, W.C. Fields, and Howdy Doody.

Gebruder Einfalt, Nuremberg, Germany
1922 to date
Founders: Georg and Johann Einfalt
Specialty: Oversized penny toys; comic and erratic action tin
wind-ups. Prior to 1930s, toys can be identified by initials "G.E."
or "G.E.N." Assumed the mark "Technofix" after 1935.

Ellis, Britton & Eaton, Springfield, Vermont
1859–early 1900s
Founder: Joel Ellis
Specialty: Wooden dolls, sleds, pianos, rolling hoops, toy carriages. In 1873, Ellis patented his most popular toy, the Jointed
Wood Doll, made of maple with cast-iron hands and feet. Two
nearby firms, Cooperative Mfg. Co. and Vermont Novelty Works,
continued the patent.

Enterprise Manufacturing Co., Philadelphia, Pennsylvania
1876–1888
Specialty: Hardware manufacturer specializing in coffee grind-
ers, turned out a series of still banks commemorating the U.S.
Centennial Exposition held in that city (i.e., Independence Hall
Globe Bank). Also produced such mechanical banks as Elephant
with pop-out man and Memorial Money Bank (Liberty Bell).

J. Falk, Nuremberg, Germany
Late 1890s–1940
Founder: J. Falk
Specialty: Stationary steam engines, optical projectors, and
steam-propelled boats.

James Fallows & Sons, Philadelphia, Pennsylvania
1870 (Organized under name "C.B. Porter Company")
Founder: Firm was continuation of Francis, Field and Francis,
  of which Fallows was designer, inventor, and official overseer.
  Firm began carrying his name about 1880. Principals were
  James Fallows and his sons, Henry, Charles, and David. In
  1894, name was changed to Frederick & Henry Fallows Toys.
Specialty: Painted and stenciled tin horse-drawn, wheeled vehicles, trains, and river boats. Highly prized toys often carried
mark "IXL," said to be based on word-play "I Excel." (Some
feel that it signifies the date of Fallows' arrival in Philadelphia,
from the old country.) Fallows' demise coincided with the advent of lithographed tin toys in the 1880s.

Georg Fischer, Nuremberg, Germany
Early 1900s–1914
Specialty: Tin penny toys and other novelties. Trademark:
"G.F."

H. Fischer & Co., Nuremberg, Germany
1908–early 1930s
Founder: H. Fischer
Specialty: Produced line of comic/character toys for jobber,
George Borgfeldt of New York City, under "Nifty" trademark;
also line of erratic action tin toys with Fischer's own logo of fish
swimming through letter "A."

Fisher Price Toys, East Aurora, New York
1930 to date
Founders: Irving L. Price, Herman G. Fisher, and Helen M.
  Schelle. Herman Fisher, who was first president, resigned in
  1966 and was succeeded by Henry H. Coords. Quaker Oats
  Company acquired the firm in 1969.
Specialty: Lithographed paper applied over wooden and plastic
pull toys, including the early Doctor Doodle, Lookee Monk, Dizzy
Dino, and Woodsy-Wee Toys. Mickey Mouse, Donald, Goofy,
Snow White, and scores of other Disney characters were featured in the 1930s and 1940s. To date Fisher Price, any toy
featuring the vertical white reverse out of black logo predates
1962; any item containing any or all plastic parts was made
after 1949.

Gebruder Fleischmann, Nuremberg, Germany
1887 to date
Founder: J. Fleischmann
Specialty: Quality tinplate boats in the 1920s, as well as automotive replicas. Took over Doll et Cie just before World War II
and has concentrated on model railroads to this day.

Francis Field & Francis, Philadelphia, Pennsylvania
1838–1870
Founders: Henry and Thomas Francis
Specialty: Line of tinplate clockwork toys which went by name

of Philadelphia Tin Toy in the late 1840s. James Fallows joined the firm in 1870, and in 1880 the name was changed to Fallows.

Gibbs Mfg. Co., Canton, Ohio
1884 to date
Founder: Lewis E. Gibbs
Specialty: Originally manufactured plows. Added toys in 1886. Mechanical spinning tops, wagons, and lithographed paper-on-wood, metal, and advertising toys.

A.C. Gilbert Co., New Haven, Connecticut
1908–1966
Founder: Albert C. Gilbert
Specialty: Began as manufacturer of boxed magic sets. Introduced Erector Sets in 1913, an instant success (30 million would be sold over next 40 years). Bought out Richter Anchor Block, an American affiliate of Meccano, at beginning of World War I. Pressed-steel autos and trucks were added to line in 1914, plus a variety of scientific toys. Purchased American Flyer in 1938 and retained only the name for a line of trains. Gilbert subsequently had financial woes of its own and the toy train line was sold to Lionel in 1966.

Girard Model Works, Inc.
1919–1922
Girard Mfg. Co.
1922–1935
The Toy Works, Girard, Pennsylvania
1935–1975 (Spinning tops, skates, banks, trains, military toys)
Founder: Frank E. Wood
Specialty: In the late 1920s, Girard made Louis Marx a commission agent and for several years produced toys under the Marx label, along with its own line of steel autos, trucks, and trains, which were produced at Girard Model Works. Marx and Girard toys are for all intents indistinguishable (a few of the Girard toys bore the slogan "Making Childhood's Hour Happier"). Girard declared bankruptcy in 1934, although toy production continued until 1975. Quaker Oats had bought out Marx's interest in Girard when they bought Marx's American and English toy division in 1972.

Gong Bell Mfg. Co., East Hampton, Connecticut
1886–late 1930s
Specialty: Hardware bells and cast-metal bell pull and push toys.

Greppert & Kelch (Gundka, G.&K.), Brandenberg, Germany
Circa 1912–1930
Specialty: Small lithographed tin mechanical toys; mid–1920s
appears to have been the height of their popularity. Often
marked "Gundka Werke," or with "G.&K."

Grey Iron Co., Mount Joy, Pennsylvania
1900 (Under name Brady Machine Shop) to date. (First produced
  toys in 1903)
Specialty: Grey Klip Army toy soldiers (1917–1941) in cast iron,
nickel plated. "Iron Men" series, 1936; "Uncle Sam's De-
fender," 1938. The firm produced miniatures under the name
"Greyklip Armies"; also an "American Family" series just prior
to World War II. Still operating today as John Wright division
of Cons co.

S.G. Günthermann, Nuremberg, Germany
1877–1965
Founder: Sigfried Günthermann. When founder died in 1890,
  his widow married Adolph Weigel; toys from that period on
  bore maker's mark with shield inside circle and initials
  A.S.G.W. Weigel's initials were removed following his death
  in 1919. Company was acquired by Siemens in 1965.
Specialty: Began producing tinplate mechanical cars in 1898;
also a number of comic and character wind-ups in the early
1960s.

Gutmann, Paris, France
1945 to date
Specialty: Lightweight tin motor vehicles. Trademark: MEMO.

Hafner Mfg. Co., Chicago, Illinois
1900–1950
Founder. W. F. Hafner
Specialty: Joined with Edmunds-Metzel Co. in 1907 to manufacture trains and mechanical toys. Became American Flyer Manufacturing in 1910 and was sold to Wyandotte in 1950. When Wyandotte closed its doors, Marx acquired Hafner dies.

Hardware and Woodenware Mfg. Co., New York City, New York
1907–1912
Founder: Consortium
Specialty: Consortium purchased Grey Iron Casting, Jones and Bixler, Stevens, Kenton, and eleven other toy companies, but went into bankruptcy two years later.

John Harper & Co., Ltd., Willenhall, England
1790–1940
Founder: John Harper
Specialty: Produced banks in the 1880s. Cast-iron still/mechanical banks and toys. Noted banks include: "Wimbleton Bank," "Grenadier," "I Always Did Spise a Mule," "Football Bank," and "Giant on Tower."

Harris Toy Co., Toledo, Ohio
Circa 1887–1913
Specialty: Produced cast-iron toys in the 1880s. Harris also acted as jobber for Dent, Hubley, and Wilkins. Financial difficulties forced them out of toy production by 1913.

Hasbro Mfg., Pawtucket, Rhode Island
1923 to date
Founders: The Hassenfeld brothers
Specialty: Makers of plastic and wood toys, including Super Weeble, Potato Head, and G.I. Joe series, which has gone through several transformations. The articulated plastic figures in cloth uniforms were originally 11 ½ inches tall; the new G.I. Joes, recalled to active duty in 1982, measured a mere 4 inches. In 1987, G.I. Joe was the number one selling toy in America.

O. & M. Hausser, Stuttgart (Ludwigsburg), Germany
1904–1983
Founders: Otto and Max Hausser
Specialty: Dolls, toys, and military miniatures of composition

sawdust and glue, manufactured under name "Elastolin." Made
still banks from 1929–1939.

Ernst Heinrichsen Miniatures, Nuremberg, Germany
1839–1950
Founder: Ernst Heinrichsen
Specialty: Military flats. Heinrichsen instituted the "Nuremberg" scale with 30 mm standardization in tin soldier battlefields, circa 1848. Ernst's son, Wilhelm, who took reins in 1869,
and grandson, Ernst Wilhelm, who assumed the helm in 1908,
carried on the Heinrichsen tradition until after World War II.
Toys identified by "E.H." or with first initial and full surname.

J.L. Hess, Nuremberg, Germany
1826–mid–1930s
Specialty: Tinplate pull-along trains and various other parlor
toys; toy autos bore trademark "Hessmobil."

Heyde Miniatures, Dresden, Germany
1872–1945
Specialty: Full-round solid military miniatures. Decidedly topical, Heyde produced new sets of replications of soldiers whenever a war broke out, in a variety of sizes from 40 to 145 mm.
Highly prized are the special sets (i.e., "Buffalo Bill," "North
Pole Expedition," "Tiger Hunting in India"). Heyde's factory was

wiped out by Dresden firebombing in 1945. Heydes usually bear
no trademarks, but can be distinguished by their highly stylized, thin, and fragile appearance.

N.N. Hill Brass Co., New Jersey
Circa 1889–1960
Specialty: Branch of National Novelty for four years ending in
1907. In 1905, merged with Watrous Mfg. Co., another bell toy
maker. Specialized in cast-iron and pressed-steel bell push and
pull toys, toy telephones, and target games.

Johann Gottfried Hilpert, Nuremberg, Germany
1770s–1801
Founders: Johann Hilpert, Johann Georg, Johann Wolfgang Hil-
 pert
Specialty: The firm was the first identified manufacturer of tin
soldiers. In addition to military (Frederick the Great's Potsdam
Guards are a stunning example), Hilpert also produced a variety
of flat figures depicting hunting, farming, and theatrical life.
Identifying marks: "H.," "JH," "JGH," or "Hilpert" on base.
Figures were often dated.

Hoge Mfg. Co., New York City, New York
1920s–mid 1930s
Specialty: Pressed-steel cars and trucks closely resemble Marx
and Girard toys (reportedly manufactured by Girard and distributed by Henry Katz). Best known for Popeye Tru-To-Life Mechanical Rowboat, produced in 1935.

Hubley Mfg. Co., Lancaster, Pennsylvania
1894 to date
Slogan: "They're Different"
Brand Name: Lancaster Brand Iron Toys
Founder: John E. Hubley
Specialty: Originally manufactured electric toy train equipment
and parts. Purchased Safety Buggy Co. factory and moved to
site in 1909. First manufactured cast-iron toys, horse-drawn
wagons and fire engines, circus trains, and cap guns. Toy autos
became the headliners in the 1930s. By quickly converting to
cheaper small toys during the Depression, they avoided financial woes experienced by many other toy companies. Iron shor-
tages in World War II and commitments to fill war contracts did
spell the demise of Hubley's toy division in 1942. The name was

later changed to Gabriel Industries and still existed as a division of CBS as of 1978.

Hull & Stafford, Clinton, Connecticut
1860s–1880s (Established as Hull & Wright; acquired Union Mfg. Co. in 1869)
Specialty: Intricate, enameled tin toys.

Ideal, Brooklyn, New York
1903 to date
Founders: Rose and Morris Michtom
Specialty: Stuffed toys and dolls, anchored by the original Teddy Bear. Ideal still ranks as one of the top producers of stuffed toys and dolls.

Industria Nazionale Giocattoli Automatica, Padova, Padua, Italy
1920–?
Specialty: Tin mechanical trains, cars, airplanes. Trademark: INGAP.

Ives Corp., Bridgeport, Connecticut
1868–1932
E.R. Ives & Co., Plymouth, Connecticut
1868–1870
Founder: Edward R. Ives
Specialty: Originally made baskets and hot air toys.
Ives and Blakeslee & Co., Bridgeport, Connecticut
1872–1931
Specialty: Ives joined partner Cornelius Blakeslee, a brother-in-law. Ives moved to Bridgeport in 1870; by the 1880s, they were leaders in superb clockwork toys designed by Jerome Secor, Nathan Warner, and Arthur Hotchkiss. Ives also acted as jobber for other manufacturers' toys. The firm filed for bankruptcy in 1929, another victim of the Depression. Lionel took over the company at that time, and the names Ives and Blakeslee remained until 1931.

Jeanette Toy & Novelty Co., Jeanette, Pennsylvania
1898–?
Specialty: Lithographed tin toys, including trays, tea sets, and figural glass candy containers.

JEP (Jouets en Paris), Paris, France
1899–1965
Founder: Known originally as the Société Industriel de Ferblan-
teriel, the firm underwent a name change to J de P in 1928;
its contemporary name came about in 1932.
Specialty: Lithographed, tin, clockwork toy automobiles, motorcycles, aircraft, and other motor miniatures. JEP cars tradition-
ally carried a trademark on the radiator of the particular vehicle
replicated.

John Hill & Co. (Johillco), London, England
1900–1960
Founder: Wood (first name unknown), a former Britains' em-
ployee.
Specialty: Primarily 54 mm hollowcast toy soldiers in Britains' tradition, but in most cases lacking the quality and refinement of the
latter. Never really recovered following destruction of its Totten-
ham factory in the London blitz; Johillco closed doors in 1960.

Jones & Bixler, Co., Freemansburg, Pennsylvania
1899–1914
Founders: Charles A. Jones and Louis S. Bixler
Specialty: "Red Devil Line" of cast-iron auto toys (introduced in
1903, when J & B became part of National Novelty Corp.). From
1909–1913, J & B and Kenton Hardware (which also became
part of National Novelty toy trust) produced toys that were indistinguishable from each other.

Jones (Metal Art Miniature Co.), Chicago, Illinois
Circa 1925–1941
Founder: J. Edward Jones
Specialty: 3 ¼ inch military miniatures; primarily a dimestore
line.

Judd Mfg. Co., Wallingford, Connecticut
1830–?
Originally known as H.L. Judd Co. when founded in 1830 in
New Britain; changed name to M. Judd & Sons in 1855; Judd
Mfg. in 1870.
Founder: Morton Judd
Specialty: Cast-iron mechanical banks, including "Peg-Leg Beg-
gar," "Ticket Collector," and "Standing Giant."

Jumeau, Paris and Montreil-sous-Bois, France
1842–1899
Founder: Emile Jumeau
Specialty: Bisque head, composition body dolls, including exquisite bébé.

> *Note:* Date 1878 often appears on back of doll; refers to winning gold medal at Paris Exposition, not date of manufacture.

Georg G. Kellermann, Nuremberg, Germany
1910 to date
Founder: Georg Kellermann
Specialty: Clockwork tin motorcycles and penny toys. Trademark: C.K.O. Son Willy took over firm following death of his father in 1931.

Kelmet Corp., New York City, New York
1923–late 1920s
Specialty: Large pressed-steel trucks under name "Kelmet" and "Trumodel." Parts were frequently subcontracted and A. C. Gilbert assembled the finished product. A further designation was "Big Boy," modeled after the White Truck.

Kenner Products, Cincinnati, Ohio
1947 to date
Founders: Al, Phil, and Joe Steiner
Specialty: First toy was "Bubble Gun" in 1947. "Six Million Dollar Man" and "Bionic Woman" were mid-1970s favorites, but most spectacular success was line of "Star Wars" toys.

Kenton Hardware Co., Kenton, Ohio
1890–1952
"The Real Thing in Everything but Size"

Founder: F.M. Perkins (Patented line of refrigerator hardware)
Specialty: Toy production began in 1894 with line of horse-drawn fire equipment, banks, and toy stoves. Renamed Kenton Hardware in 1900. Became part of mammoth National Novelty Corp. merger in 1903, it continued its toy line under the name Wing Mfg. Co. Involved in several unsuccessful takeovers, it eventually emerged as a separate unit, the Kenton Hardware Co., and again produced toys successfully from 1920–1935. Kenton ceased production in 1952 and assets were sold in 1953. The Littlestown Hardware & Foundry acquired many Kenton toy designs and marketed them under the brand "Utexiqual." Littlestown folded in 1982.

Keystone Mfg. Co., Boston, Massachusetts
Circa 1920
Specialty: Originally produced toy motion picture machines and children's comedy films (Keystone Moviegraph). Gained permission from Packard Motor Co. in mid-1920s to market pressed-steel riding trucks copied from full-size Packard models, including famous radiator design and logo. Keystone, in competing with Buddy "L," added such refinements as nickeled hub-caps and radiator caps, transparent celluloid windshield, and engine crank. For 50 cents extra you could get rubber tires and headlamps. Keystone trucks also featured steering and signal arms for "stop" and "go." Keystone introduced line of "Siren Riding Toys" in 1934 with saddle riding seat and handlebars for steering. In 1936, one of its big sellers was a "Ride-Em" mail plane. In the post-World War II years, most of Keystone's toy output was based on tools and dies purchased from the defunct Kingsbury toy division.

Kienberger & Co., Nuremberg, Germany
1910 to date
Founder: Hubert Kienberger
Specialty: Penny toys; simple mechanical motor toys and wheel-mounted animals. One of the most popular exports to the United States was the Billiard Player marble toy. Trademark: HUKI.

Kilgore Mfg. Co., Westerville, Ohio
1920s–possibly late 1940s
Specialty: Slogan was "Toys That Last." Originated in 1925 with purchase of George D. Wanner Co., makers of "E-Z-Fly" kites. In 1928, Kilgore introduced cast-iron trucks, cars, and fire en-

gines, along with cast-iron cap guns, cannons, and toy paper
caps (after its merger with Andes Foundry and the Federal Toy
Co. under the aegis of American Toy Co.). Butler Brothers became its biggest distributor. Later, Kilgore would fall back on
its cap pistol and toy paper cap line, and the company remained
in business until 1944.

Kingsbury Mfg. Co., Keene, New Hampshire
1919–1942 (see also *Wilkins Toy Co.*)
Specialty: Harry T. Kingsbury bought Wilkins in 1895 and combined with the Clipper Machine Works, which specialized in farm
equipment. In the early 1900s, toy automobiles were introduced
to the company line. The Wilkins name was dropped following
World War I in favor of Kingsbury, by now an established name
in the field. Kingsbury specialized in copying famous models of
aircraft and assembly-line roadsters, trucks, and buses. World
War II saw Kingsbury shifting to war contracts and never returning again to toy production. All production equipment was
sold to Keystone in Boston. The company still exists, but as
Kingsbury Machine Tool Division, a subcontractor for such giants as IBM, General Motors, and GE.

Kingston Products Corp., Kokomo, Indiana
1890s
Founders: Charles T. Byrne and James F. Ryan
Specialty: Byrne and Ryan started the Kokomo Brass Works to
produce brass castings for the plumbing industry. Kingston soon
became an alliance of many kindred companies. Their line of
toys, under the name of Kokomo Toys, came into prominence
in the 1920s and 1930s with racers, trucks, fire engines, and
transportation toys a specialty. Electrically run racers were an
ingenious addition, though so expensive for Depression times
that Kingston dropped them in 1931. Kingston today is part of
Scott & Fetzer Co., and makes components for auto manufacturers.

Kirchoff Patent Co., Newark, New Jersey
1852 to date
Founder: Charles Kirchoff, a German builder of weaving looms
    and other weaving machinery
Specialty: Small metal toys, noisemakers, Christmas ornaments
and novelties. Kirchoff essentially was a developer of patents

and in addition to toys produced Braille printers and ticker-tape machines. (Although no longer in business under the Kirchoff name, the company did undergo a number of changes in ownership over the years and was still recorded as being active up to the 1950s.)

Knapp Electric Novelty Co., New York City, New York
1899 to date
Specialty: One of our earliest manufacturers of transportation toys powered by wet cell batteries. Carlisle & Finch, noted for electric toy trains and other novelty toys, served as Knapp's distributor.

Kohnstam, Furth, Germany
Circa 1875–1959 (Became part of Lesney)
Founder: Moses Kohnstam
Specialty: European distributor of German-made toys, under the Moko trademark. J. Kohnstam Ltd. was established in London in early 1920 and helped launch Lesney Products.

Kyser & Rex, Philadelphia, Pennsylvania
1880–1884
Founders: L. Kyser and Alfred Rex
Specialty: Cast-iron toys and mechanical banks. Among their highly desirable banks are: Hindu with Turban, Uncle Tom, Chimpanzee, The Organ Bank, Lion and Monkeys.

Lefkowitz Toy Co., Brooklyn, New York
Early 1900s–?
Specialty: Ingenious Rube Goldberg-type mechanical tin toys (i.e., The Flying Cupid).

Ernest Lehmann Co., Brandenberg, Germany
1881 (Re-established in 1951 in Nuremberg and still producing
   toys)
Founder: Ernest P. Lehmann
Specialty: Lehmann exported vast quantities of toys to the
United States from 1895 to 1929 (excluding years of World War
I). Specialized in lithographed tinplate, mechanical transporta-
tion toys, and figures known for colorful patina. Some of the
most desirable Lehmann's include: Mr. and Mrs. Lehmann,
Dancing Sailor, Icarus, and Autobus.

Lenci, Turin, Italy
1920 to date
Founders: Enrico and Elena Scavini
Specialty: Seamless stuffed felt dolls. The Lenci trademark was
registered in Europe in 1922; in the United States in 1924. (Lenci
was Elena Scavini's pet name.)

Le Rapide, Paris, France
1920s–1954
Founder: Louis Rouissy
Specialty: Electric and clockwork "O" gauge model trains; toy
racers on oval tracks.

Lesney ("Matchbox"), London, England
1947–1982
Founders: Jack Odell and Leslie and Robert Smith
Slogan: "Models of Yesteryear"
Specialty: Die-cast miniature cars and transportation vehicles,
many of which were copies of real-life models.

Georg Levy, Nuremberg, Germany
Circa 1920–1971
Founder: Georg Levy ("Gely" trademark)
Specialty: Produced automotive tin toys under Kienberger name ("Kico") until 1920, then launched his own firm. Sold out and left Germany in the 1930s, but factory resumed under name of Nuremberg Tin Toys Factory.

Lindstrom Tool & Toy Co., Bridgeport, Connecticut
1913–early 1940s (Resumed toy production after World War II)
Specialty: Mechanical toys and games of pressed steel and tin. Included stoves, sewing machines; amusement park-type auto, the "Doodlebug."

Lineol, Brandenberg/Havel, Germany
1905 to date
Founder: Oskar Wiederholz
Specialty: Tinplate military toys and trenchworks; also composition armies, barnyard scenes, zoo menageries, Christmas crèches, cooking and tea sets, wooden toys. Lineol's 7.5 cm military miniatures are deemed superior to Elastolin. Lineol was nationalized in 1949 and moved to Dresden. It still produces miniatures today under the name VEB Lineol-Plastik Dresden.

Lines Brothers Ltd., London, England
1919–1971
Specialty: Small clockwork tin motor toys; "Minic" series, 1930. "Spot-On" series of die-cast models, 1959; "Triangtois" on wooden toys, circa 1927. Lines closed its doors in 1971 following financial woes.

Lucotte Miniatures, Paris, France
1780s–1825 (acquired by Mignot)
Specialty: One of the earliest toy makers; many miniatures fea-

ture "L.C.," the Lucotte trademark, as well as the Imperial Bee of Napoleon. Many of the figures replicated Napoleon's army members. Known for anatomical detail and meticulous painting. Early Lucottes can be distinguished by their separate removable parts.

Gebruder Maerklin, Göppingen, Germany
1859 to date
Founders: Theodor and his wife, Caroline Maerklin
Specialty: Originated as maker of doll-size tinplate kitchenware. When sons took over in 1888, firm name was changed to Gebruder Maerklin. Branched out to variety of enameled tinplate boats, carousels, aeronautical toys. Unsurpassed in production of clockwork, steam, and electric trains. Introduced first standardized tinplate tracks in 1891. Maerklin switched to plastic train sets in the late 1950s.

Manoil Mfg. Co., New York City, New York, and Waverly, New York
1937–1941
Specialty: Hollowcast toy soldiers (sometimes called dimestore soldiers).

Fernand Martin, Paris, France
1887–1919
Specialty: Widely copied maker of amusing double-action tin mechanicals, including *Le Clochard* (Tramp) and *Ivrogne* (Toper or Drunk).

Martin & Runyan, New York City, New York
1860s–?
Specialty: Manufacturer of the earliest known clockwork toy, "Autoperipatetikos," designed by Enoch Morrison, in 1862; soon followed by "Walking Zouave."

Louis Marx & Company, New York, New York
1919–1979
Founder: Louis Marx, formerly with the toy firm of Ferdinand Strauss. Originally placed large orders with Girard Model Works, Strauss, and C. G. Wood, who produced toys under the Marx trademark. Acquired Girard in 1935 and Haffner Trains in 1955. Quaker Oats acquired Marx in 1972 and later

sold it at a loss to the European firm of Dunbee-Combex. The Marx division declared bankruptcy in 1979, following a fantastic auction of their stock from 1920–1960.
Specialty: Lithographed, tin wind-up toys; Marx successfully revived the Yo-Yo in 1928; it sold well even through the Depression. Marx was one of the big four among American electric train manufacturers.

Mason & Parker, Winchendon, Massachusetts
1899–1966
Founders: H.N. Parker and Orlando Mason
Specialty: Pressed-steel transportation toys. Later (1907), Mason & Parker switched to wood products, including the proven standard, Boy's Tool Chest.

MADE IN JAPAP

Masutoku Toys, Tokyo, Japan
1945 to date
Specialty: Mechanical and battery-operated tin toys. Trademark: "MT."

McLoughlin Brothers, New York City, New York
1850s–1920 (Milton Bradley acquired McLoughlin in 1920)
Specialty: Known early on for "revamping" popular European juvenile games, McLoughlin also created such staples as "Pilgrim's Progress," "Fish Pond," "Peter Coddle," and "Jack Straws." Lithograph paper-on-wood construction toys included the Palmer Cox Brownie series; also alphabet blocks and numerous educational toys.

Meccano (Dinky Toys), Liverpool, England
1901–1964 (Taken over by Lines Bros. in 1964)
Founder: Frank Hornby
Specialty: Metal construction sets (à la Erector). First produced miniatures called Dinky Toys in 1933.

Mechanical Novelty Works, New Britain, Connecticut
Early 1800s–?
Founders: Andrew Turnbull, James A. Swanson, George Eddy
Specialty: Cast-iron mechanical banks, including "Initiation
Bank" (1st and 2nd degree models), "Squirrel and Tree Stump."

Johann Philipp Meier, Nuremberg, Germany
1879–1917
Specialty: One of the more prolific penny toy manufacturers at
the turn of the century. Meier also produced painted tin mechanical toys. Trademark: Dog pulling cart.

Merriam Mfg. Co., Durham, Connecticut
1856–1880s
Specialty: Enameled tinplate clockwork toys. Continues today
as box manufacturer; ceased toy production in 1880s. Known
for such classics as "Horse on Sculptured Base," ptd. by William A. Harwood, Brooklyn, New York, plus "Rabbit in Hoop."

Metalcast, New York City, New York
1899 (as S. Sachs Toy Mfg. Co.; subsequently The Toy Soldier
   Mfg. Co.; name changed to Metalcast in 1929)
Founder: H. Sachs
Specialty: 2 ½ inch hollowcast soldiers, cowboys, and Indians;
later, 3 ¼ inch hollowcast soldiers.

Metalcraft Corp., St. Louis, Missouri
1920–1937
Specialty: Playground equipment such as teeter-totters. Produced pressed-steel trucks in 1928 and acquired rights to
pressed-steel airplane in kit of Lindbergh's "Spirit of St. Louis."
Produced millions of toy truck premiums known as "Business
Leaders."

Metalgraf, Milan, Italy
1910–1930s
Specialty: Exquisite handpainted tin clockwork automobiles.

Mettoy Co., Ltd., Great Britain
1934–1984
Founder: Philip Ulmann, dispossessed owner of Tipp & Co., who
   was forced to flee Nazi Germany.
Specialty: Tinplate automotive mechanicals and novelties; after

1945, Mettoy converted to plastic toys. Introduced Corgi Toys in 1959. Went into liquidation in 1984.

C.B.G. Mignot Miniatures, Paris, France
1900–?
Founders: A partnership between Messrs. Cuperly, Blondel, and Gerbeau (hence the initials C.B.G.) and Henri Mignot, the chief stockholder.
Specialty: Produced their own miniatures as well as limited editions using Lucotte molds acquired in 1825. (See Lucotte Miniatures.) Later Mignot examples differ from Lucotte in that they were singly cast, without separate removable parts and accessories. Mignot boasted over 20,000 molds of warriors from Ancient Rome to World War II.

Milton Bradley, East Longmeadow and Springfield, Massachusetts
1860 to date
Slogan: "Maker of the World's Best Games"
Founder: Milton Bradley; James Shea, Sr. took over firm in 1911, following Bradley's death. Hasbro Industries, Inc. of Pawtucket, Rhode Island, bought out Bradley in 1984. (Bradley had acquired McLoughlin Bros. in 1920.)
Specialty: Games, puzzles, blocks, optical toys, kindergarten aids. Noted Bradley games included, "Babe Ruth Baseball," "Checkered Game of Life," "Game of Mail Express & Accommodation." Logos at various stages identified firm as Milton Bradley Company, Milton Bradley & Co., Milton Bradley Co.

Moline (see Buddy "L")

Muller & Kadeder (M.&K.), Nuremberg, Germany
Circa 1900 to date
Specialty: Lithographed tin wind-ups; aeronautical toys includ-

ing zeppelins and a fanciful balloon with parachute; also carousels and character toys (i.e., "Buster Brown With Poodle," "Tailor Riding Buck," and "Clown on Pig"). In the post–World War I years, turned to lithographed tin automobiles.

National Novelty Corp., New Jersey (see *N.N. Hill Brass Co.*)
1903–1907
Specialty: A trust or consortium of over 30 leading manufacturers of cast-iron and wood toys, formed to cut costs and stifle competition. Poorly managed, the "Toy Trust" soon failed. A number of participating toy makers reorganized under the aegis of Hardware & Woodenware Manufacturing Co., but it, too, soon faded.

Neff-Moon Toy Co., Sandusky, Ohio
1920–1925
Specialty: Pressed-steel automotive toys with interchangeable bodies packaged with single chassis.

Nonpareil Toy & Novelty Co., Newark, New Jersey
Post-World War I–late 1940s
Specialty: Lithographed tin toy trucks and wagons, mostly of the penny toy or tiny prize package toy variety.

North & Judd, New Britain, Connecticut
1812 to date
Specialty: Originally in saddlery parts. Started small line of cast-iron toys in 1930s, but could not compete with the "giants" and discontinued line after one year. Now part of a Gulf & Western conglomerate.

Parker Brothers, Salem, Massachusetts
1883 to date
Founder: George S. Parker
Specialty: Created first card game, "Banking," in 1883. World renowned for producing board game "Monopoly" beginning in 1934. Another game, "Chivalry," later updated under the name "Camelot," has been regarded by many board game experts as a more challenging game. Acquired the rights of a number of smaller makers, including W. & S. B. Ives and the U. S. Playing Card Co.

Paya, Alicante, Spain
Dates unknown
Specialty: Tin clockwork and steam motor toys; also "O" gauge
model railroads.

Peco (Product Engineering Co.), Tigard, Oregon
1952–1956
Founder: John Benneth
Specialty: Realistic military figures, first made of a clay-like material called Pyrocon, and, later, Vinylite. Most popular in line:
cowboys and Indians.

Philadelphia Tin Toy Co., Philadelphia, Pennsylvania
Toy firm of Francis Field and Francis carried this name in Phil-
    adelphia area in late 1840s.

Ernst Plank, Nuremberg, Germany
1866–1930s
Founder; Ernst Plank
Specialty: Tin trains, airplanes, boats, automobiles.

Pratt & Letchworth, Buffalo, New York
1880–1900
Founders: Pascal P. Pratt and William P. Letchworth
Specialty: Cast-iron toy trains, horse-drawn hansom cabs,
pumpers, artillery wagons. Originally known (1870s) as Buffalo

Malleable Iron Works. Francis Carpenter's stock and patent rights were acquired by Pratt & Letchworth in 1890.

W.S. Reed Toy Co., Leominster, Massachusetts
1875–1897
Founder: Whitney S. Reed
Specialty: Lithographed paper-on-wood toys and construction sets. Patented one mechanical bank, "The Old Lady In the Shoe."

Richter (Anchor Blocks), Rudolstadt, Germany
1508–1920s (Reputedly the oldest toy company, with a 16th-century founding date)
Specialty: Anchor Toy Building Bricks, alphabet and puzzle blocks. A.C. Gilbert, the Erector Set people, bought the American interest of Anchor Blocks in 1913.

Rico, Alicante, Spain
Late 1930s–1950s
Specialty: Tin mechanical autos and airplanes. Trademark: RSA.

Riemann, Seabrey Co., Inc., New York City, New York
1920s–1944
Specialty: Manufacturers' representatives acting as sole sales agents for Kenton, Grey Iron, N.N. Hill Brass, J. & E. Stevens, and other leading cast-iron toy makers.

William Rissmann Co. (RI-CO) Nuremberg, Germany
1907–?
Founder: William Rissmann
Specialty: Toy trains and tin mechanical motor toys. Not to be confused with Spanish firm, Rico. Look for additional word, "Germany," to differentiate from the two.

Karl Rohrseitz, Zindorf, Germany
1890s–?
Specialty: Tinplate novelties.

Charles Rossignol, Paris, France
1868–1962
Founder: Charles Rossignol
Specialty: Painted tin clockwork vehicles. Logo is of entwined letters "C" and "R." Made first automotive toy, a Renault taxi, in 1905. Parisian buses, produced by Rossignol in the 1920s, are highly prized.

Schieble Toy & Novelty Co., Dayton, Ohio
1909–1931
Specialty: Carried on line of "Hill Climber" friction toys, initiated by D.P. Clark & Co.

Leo Schlesinger Co., New York City, New York
1880s–1900
Founder: Leo Schlesinger
Specialty: Painted and stenciled tinplate horse-drawn vehicles, producing as many as 6 million annually. Later, Schlesinger produced open-front tinplate miniature kitchens, complete with utensils.

A. Schoenhut & Company, Philadelphia, Pennsylvania
1872–1935
Founder: Albert Schoenhut, a German emigrant, who originally worked for a Philadelphia toy importer, John Deiser & Sons
Specialty: Began manufacturing toy pianos in 1872. Featured a series of over 20 different Living Pictures in the 1890s, which were framed cardboard figures animated by a clockwork mechanism. Schoenhut is best known, however, for high-quality dolls and wood-jointed circus and comic strip characters, including

Felix, Maggie & Jiggs, Barney Google, and Sparkplug. In the
1950s, the firm of Delvan, Seneca Falls, New York, bought the
patent rights to Schoenhut wood-jointed figures and again produced a series of circus animals. These toys received a luke-
warm reception and are not up to the quality and charm of their
predecessors. Schoenhut doll houses hit the assembly line from
1917 to 1934 and doll house furniture from 1928 to 1934.
Schoenhut circus tents were known to have been reproduced in
the 1970s.

Schuco Toy Co., Nuremberg, Germany
1912–1970
Founders: Heinrich Müller and Heinrich Schreyer (Schuco is an
   abbreviation of Schreyer u. Co.; following World War I,
   Schreyer Müller formed a new partnership with Kahn.)
Specialty: Mohair-covered mechanical toys. An independent
Schuco Toy Co. with import rights to the German toys was
formed in the United States in 1947 by Adolf Kahn's son, Eric.
Schuco declared bankruptcy in 1970.

Jerome Secor Manufacturing, Bridgeport, Connecticut
1872–mid–1880s
Founder: Jerome B. Secor
Specialty: Introduced a line of sewing machines plus mechanical singing birds at the 1873 World's Fair, Vienna. One of the
first patented toys: a sheet brass whistling bird, the American

Songster. His ingenious clockwork creations included: "Brudder Bones, the Banjo Player," "Sister Lucinda at the Play," and the rarest and most coveted of all mechanicals "The Freedman's Bank." Secor sold his business to Ives in the mid-1880s. He continued to design and manufacture clockwork toys through Ives.

Selchow and Righter, New York City, New York
1860s–present
Founder: Elish G. Selchow (John H. Righter later became partner)
Specialty: Board games and puzzles. Best known for SCRABBLE, the crossword game.

Selwyn Miniatures, London, England
1951–1952
Founder: Roy Selwyn-Smith
Specialty: Composition toy soldiers of pumice and glue. Firm lasted only seven months with death of Smith's backer, Otto Gottstein. Smith joined toy business of a Pole, M. Zang, to produce Herald Series of toy soldiers with an exquisite set of Smith's plastic figures re-issued as Knights of Agincourt. Later, the talented designer was hired by Britains.

C.G. Shepard and Co., Buffalo, New York
1866–1892
Founders: Walter J. and Charles G. Shepard
Specialty: Tin horns; still and mechanical banks (beginning in 1882). Sold mechanical bank business in 1892; three Shepard banks were later reissued by J. & E. Stevens.

William Shimer & Son Co., Freemansburg, Pennsylvania
1875–1913
Founder: William Shimer
Specialty: Cast-iron toys, banks, trains for several years prior to World War I.

J.H. Singer, New York City, New York
1893–1895
Founder: Jasper Singer
Specialty: Primarily a jobber of games and novelties in lithographed paper on wood. Included toy theaters and popular

games (i.e., "Authors," "Cuckoo," "Jumping Frog"). Lines once
sold by George S. Parker.

> *Note:* Box or novelty often identified by initials: J.H.S.N.Y. or
> J.H.S.

Smith-Miller Toy Co., Los Angeles, California
1944–1958
Specialty: Pressed-steel motor toys. Fred Thompson, Canoga
Park, California, acquired the Smith-Miller name as well as ex-
isting stock in the late 1970s, and still operates under that
name.

SON-NY (see *Dayton Toy & Specialty Company*)

Stadden Miniatures, London, England
Late 1940s to date
Founder: Charles Stadden
Specialty: Military miniatures targeted to the connoisseur col-
lector as display specimens; sized 30 to 54 mm.

Star Collectibles (Marlborough, a toy firm in Wales)
1950s–early 1960
Founder: Michael Curley and his wife, Star, formed a distribu-
   torship out of the Midwest, importing miniatures cast by Frank
   and Jan Scroby in Wales. Following Curley's death, his wife
   continued the business, offering limited editions of 50 and later
   100 sets, with Highland Black Watch Band and Grenadier
   Guard figures among the most popular.

Margarete Steiff, Giengen, Germany
1877 to date
Founder: Margarete Steiff
Specialty: Stuffed toy animals and character dolls. The founder's nephew, Richard Steiff, designed the first Teddy Bear in
1903. Steiff button and label identification is stamped in one ear
or on clothing, with white and black lettering and blank button
signifying a 1903–1904 manufacture.

J. & E. Stevens, Cromwell, Connecticut
1843–1930s
Founders: John and Elisha Stevens
Specialty: Cast-iron mechanical banks from 1870 to the turn of

the century. Elisha Stevens later joined George Brown to establish the Stevens & Brown toy firm. J. & E. Stevens supplied Gong Bell and Watrous with castings for their bell toys.

Stevens & Brown, New York City, New York
1869–1880
Founders: Elisha Stevens and George Brown (who pooled their tin and cast-iron lines and also distributed for other toy makers)

Walter Stock, Solingen, Germany
1905–1930s
Founder: Walter Stock
Specialty: Lithographed tin mechanical toys much similar to Lehmann line; also penny toys exported to America.

Ferdinand Strauss Corporation, New York City, New York
Circa 1900s–mid–1940s
Founder: Ferdinand Strauss
Specialty: Major producer of tin mechanical toys from 1914 to 1927.

Structo Mfg. Co., Freeport, Illinois
1908 to date
Founders: Louis and Edward Strohacker and C.C. Thompson. In late 1920s, A.C. Gilbert distributed Structo's line of stamped steel push toys. Structo was then partnered with American Flyer. In 1935, Strohackers sold most of business to J.G. Gokey. In 1975, firm was acquired by F. Ertel, Dyersville, Iowa.
Specialty: Erector construction kits, ready-built and construction kit toy autos.

The Sturdy Corporation—Sturditoys, Providence, Rhode Island (Sales Offices)
Factory: Pawtucket
1929–1933
Founders: Victor C. Wetzel and Charles I. Bigney
Specialty: Child-size, pressed-steel trucks, closely akin to Buddy "L" and Keystone, but generic rather than replicating real life truck models.

S.A.E. (Swedish South African Engineers) Capetown, South
    Africa
1952–1960s
Founders: An offshoot of Comet/Authenticast, which went out
    of business in the early 1950s. A Swede, Holger Eriksson, re-
    sumed casting these miniatures, imported from South Africa
    by distributors Curt Wennberg and Fred Winkler.
Specialties: 30 mm scale miniatures.

Tipp & Co., Nuremberg, Germany
1912–1971
Founders: Tipp and Carstans
Specialty: Military line of tin toys

Tommy Toy, Union City, New Jersey
1935–1938 or 1939
Founders: Dr. Albert Greene, Charles Weldon, and several other
    partners
Specialty: Miniature soldiers and nursery rhyme figures and vehicles under name, "Tommy Toy." Sculpted and designed by
Olive Kooken and Margaret Cloninger. Tommy Toy was acquired by Barclay following financial difficulties.

Tower (Guild), South Hingham, Massachusetts
1830s–1850s
Founder: William S. Tower
Specialty: Founded Tower Guild, a marketing cooperative for
woodworkers and carpenters, who fashioned much prized
wooden toys.

Trix, Mangold, Nuremberg, Germany
1930s to date
Specialty: "OO" gauge locomotives and railroad accessories under "TTR" trademark. Set up British subsidiary with Bassett-Locke as agent.

John C. Turner Co., Wapakoneta, Ohio
1915–1948
Founder: John Turner
Specialty: Known for line of "Victory is Won" flywheel toys sold by direct mail.

Union Manufacturing Co., Clinton, Connecticut
1853–1869
Hull & Stratford acquired this small tin toy-producing firm in 1869.

Unique Art Mfg. Co., Newark, New Jersey
1940s–?
Specialty: Comic/character tin mechanicals, including "Li'l Abner Dogpatch Band" and "Gertie, The Galloping Goose," 1940s.

U.S. Hardware Co., New Haven, Connecticut
1896–1901
Specialty: Cast-iron toys (i.e., "Marine Oarsmen," "Fairy Rubber Balls").

Warren Lines, New York City, New York
1936–1940
Founder: John Warren, Jr.
Specialty: Upscale quality 60 mm solid cast and hollowcast soldiers, including U.S. infantry, cavalry, and horse artillery lead figures. Some of the more limited production models included the Scout Car and Staff Car. Horses were designed by Margaret Cloninger, one of Tommy Toy's specialists. Most figures feature two movable arms and plug heads.

Watrous Mfg. Co., East Hampton, Connecticut (Branch of the National Novelty Co., New York City. Merged with N.H. Hill in early 1890s)
1880s–1930s
Specialty: Bell toys.

Weeden Mfg. Co., New Bedford, Massachusetts
1883–1939
Founder: William N. Weeden
Specialty: Produced working toy steam engine in 1884; also
steamboats, fire engines, and automobiles in miniature with
steam as motor power. Manufactured several ultimate rarities
among clockwork tin mechanical banks, including "Ding Dong
Bell" and "Japanese Ball Tosser."

Welker & Crosby, Brooklyn, New York
1883–1888
Founder: M. Crosby
Specialties: Meticulously detailed cast-iron, animal-drawn toys,
featuring distinctive swivel wheel.

> *Note:* Pratt & Letchworth adopted Crosby's patents and designs
> when he joined that firm in 1889.

Wells Brimtoy, Hollyhead, Wales, and Wells, London, England
1920 to date
1922–Acquired Brimtoy Co.
Specialty: Tinplate automotive toys; Wells Brimtoy also ven-
tured into die-cast motor toys. Most popular are the post–World
War II tinplate buses.

Wilkins Toy Co., Keene, New Hampshire
1890–1919 (see also *Kingsbury*)
Founder: James S. Wilkins
Specialty: One of the earliest manufacturers to produce toy automobiles, circa 1895. Another Keene, New Hampshire, firm,

headed by Henry T. Kingsbury, bought out Wilkins that same year, but the toy line carried the Wilkins name and trademark until 1919.

A. C. Williams Co., Ravenna, Ohio
1886 to date
Founder: John W. Williams
Specialty: Produced cast-iron, horse-drawn rigs, autos, airplane, and tractor toys from 1893 to 1923; line included mostly miniatures distributed through Woolworth, Kresge's, and other five-and-dime emporiums.

Wyandotte Toys (All Metal Products Co.), Wyandotte, Michigan
1920–1956 (Toy production began in 1921)
Founders: George Stallings and William F. Schmidt
Specialty: Toy guns, rifles, targets, pressed-steel airplanes, and other motor toys with baked-enamel finish and battery-operated headlights. Biggest year was 1935 with 5½ million dollars in toy guns. Acquired Haffner Trains (1950–1955) (see *Haffner*).

The Importance
of Condition

✳ ✳ ✳

Of all the factors that help determine the value of a given toy, *Condition* with a capital C *has* to rate at the top of the list. Toys in mint condition ("mint" is a term borrowed from our philatelist friends, connoting "fresh, superb, as new") can often command prices double that of toys in average condition. Most major toy auction houses make it a point to grade all cataloged examples as to condition, based on a scale of 1–10. In reviewing auction catalogs from a number of galleries over the past five years, it was amazing how consistently the prices realized reflected the condition ratings.

Toys in their original boxes also exact a premium price. The lithography on such popular 1930s Marx toys as the Fresh Air Taxicab of "Amos 'n' Andy" or "Walking Sandy" from the comic strip "Orphan Annie," for example, is as graphically appealing as the toys themselves. In the case of the "Sandy" toy, the original box is assembled to form a doghouse that serves as a colorful display for Sandy. In a recent toy auction, two "Li'l Abner Dogpatch Bands" by Unique Art went on the block; both were graded in excellent condition. The version with a rather shop-worn box sold for $325, while the boxless toy realized $200. The "Dogpatch Band" with box commanded a 62.5% higher bid! Even when only one panel or two of an original box is still intact, collectors are eager to salvage remnants, and some will frame these portions. In addition to their strong graphic appeal, an original box invariably reveals additional information regarding the toy contained therein (i.e., full name of manufacturer, patent date, year of copyright). Robert Lesser of New York City, a leading collector of comic art and memorabilia writes in *A Celebration of Comic Art and Memorabilia* (Hawthorn Books, Inc., New York, 1975): "Try to collect [toys] in mint condition in the original boxes. Yes, it is an impossible dream today, but by establishing this internal discipline you will be amazed that dealers recognize you as a mint collector and will therefore offer you their finest pieces, and you will be paying more, but getting the best of their wares."

The Undesirable Three "Rs"—Reproductions, Repaints (Retouches), Repairs (Replaced Parts)

GRADING SCALE

The following is a grading scale that might prove helpful in future communications regarding toys, banks, and trains.

About Mint: No chips, scratches, fading; no rust; fully operable. (10 points on grading system)

Pristine: May have minor paint or litho wear, but 98% plus is still perfect. (8–9 points)

Fine: Still excellent, with 90% considered perfect. (6–8 points)

Good: Average condition with 70% litho or paint intact. (4–6 points)

Fair: Below average with only 50% coverage. (2–4 points)

Poor: Example has less than 30% coverage and is barely salvageable. (0–2 points)

HOW TO COPE WITH REPRODUCTIONS

One of the first toys to enter our possession some 20 years ago was a cast-iron pull toy on wheels of a lady in a large sunbonnet riding sidesaddle on a donkey. The only problem with "Sunbonnet Sue," as she came to be affectionately known, was that she was an out-and-out fake. (Sue has even managed to fool certain toy book people; we've seen it pictured as an original and guided in the $100 range. Actually, purists would argue that she qualifies as a "fantasy," created from scratch and not intended to replicate an earlier, original toy.)

While it came as a severe blow to our egos as well as our pocketbooks, we kept "Sue" on display with our collection for a number of years as a reminder to keep our acquisitive emotions under control, while remaining ever alert and cautious.

Unfortunately, "Sunbonnet Sue" runs in fast company with an untold number of cast-iron reproductions that plague the hobby today. Some questionable banks and toys are merely an attempt by certain manufacturers to provide promotional or commemorative items to our nostalgia-conscious society. A good example are the *World Book Encyclopedia* replications of early mechanical banks. World Book made no pretense of the fact that the banks were repros; they cast their logotype on the underside of the base of each bank. This did not deter unscrupulous tricksters from grinding off the World Book mark and passing a bank off as a 19th-century original. A few years ago, a number of horse-drawn and automotive Kenton molds were purchased and marketed clearly as reproductions by Sears and Roebuck. These toys appear frequently at flea markets and auctions, priced right up there with the originals. Many reproductions appear on the market today that are so crudely cast and poorly finished that few people are fooled by the deception. The trouble lies with reproductions that are fiendishly clever.

The following story was related to us a few years ago by a very reliable source in the hobby: a gentleman approached a toy auctioneer and one of the leading cast-iron toy and bank collectors with two seemingly identical examples. "One of these is the real McCoy and the other is a copy; which is which?" Both auctioneer and collector picked the bogus piece over the original! Apocryphal or not, this poses a real dilemma facing not only fledgling collectors but real pros. Fortunately, of the tens of thousands of cast-iron circus wagons, fire rigs, carriages, and walking horses manufactured from 1870 until World War II, only a minuscule percentage have been reproduced. There are certain dead giveaways and here are some ways to avoid getting stung:

1. One of the most common categories to be reproduced is that of still banks. Learn which ones have been faked. (Our listing of still banks and mechanical banks reveals many of the more commonly copied examples.) Actually, there are very few scarce still banks that are being passed off as old (i.e., Bear Stealing Pig, Polish Rooster, Baby in

the Cradle, Nesting Hen, and Two-Faced Devil). By learning as much as you can about each specimen you will know, for example, that the repro pig in Bear Stealing Pig is cast in brass, while the original is in iron (a magnet will quickly detect the deception). We know many collectors who wouldn't be without a magnet, loupe or magnifying glass, and a black light whenever they're out "prospecting." Some repro banks are heavier than the originals, as is the case with the Polish Rooster. In the case of the North Pole Bank fake, the pole itself is not nickel-plated like the original.

2. Other telltale repro signs are bright shiny paint, dead black or shiny gold finish, and no signs of wear except in suspicious places where a repro identification may have been obliterated.

3. Most figural toys and banks were cast in two parts, mated and assembled with bolts or screws. Watch for mismating, where parts do not fit together snugly; new screws are also easily detected.

4. Following the sand-casting process, cast-iron repros usually aren't tumbled smoothly; the finish has a tough, pebbly feel, a bit like cement; in the modern product, most makers have yet to duplicate the smooth, almost soapstone-like feel of the oldtimers.

5. Normally, re-cast toys and banks tend to be heavier, thicker, and slightly smaller than the original. The latter occurs due to the iron shrinking in the mold as it cools. In the case of mechanical banks, a number of helpful books are available that contain base tracings of originals for comparison purposes.

6. Watch the price. A lowball price, while it may appeal to your baser instincts to close a deal on a toy that is far below market value, more often is the first indication that its pedigree is spurious.

7. Don't be shy about questioning the seller about *his* knowledge of the toy; and don't hesitate about seeking a second opinion.

8. Deal with only reputable people—dealers, auctioneers, and fellow collectors who, without hesitation, back up everything they sell.

9. Train yourself to become almost instinctive in the selection process. Meyric Rogers, a leading authority on an-

tiques, would first walk through the American wing of the Metropolitan Museum of Art to get his eye attuned to quality authentic pieces before going shopping so that he would possess a higher degree of perception. While there may not always be access to great collections of toys, there is certainly a treasure-trove of reference books, early toy catalogs, flyers, and clipping files to consult.

10. Above all, know your specialty. In *Antique Toy World*, noted motortoy collector Lillian Gottschalk offered this advice: "If you're a diamond collector, you better know your diamonds or find someone who does—at least until you gain the knowledge and experience to work alone. This comes with time and handling toys. There should be no fears."

Note: Within the last several years, a number of leading toy show promoters have taken positive steps by policing their exhibitors' wares to make doubly certain that reproductions are not being offered for sale. As a result, the situation has vastly improved, although there is still evidence of toys being offered that exemplify the other two dreaded "Rs," Repairs and Repaints.

A number of leading antique and collectible trade publications keep tabs on the latest reproductions as they come on the market, as a service to their subscribers.

There *is* a law on the books that requires that imitations of various kinds of Americana be marked "Reproduction," or with a similar term, in a prominent place and in a nonremovable manner. Signed into law by Congress as the Hobby Protection Act (Public Law 93–167), it was ironically the last action by President Richard M. Nixon just prior to his resignation. Unfortunately, some manufacturers and entrepreneurs are unaware of the law or choose to ignore it. More collectors, dealers, show promoters, and auctioneers should be alerted to the fact that this law can be enforced. There is, of course, no substitute for sound knowledge.

To be ever alert to these unfortunate incursions, it is important to clarify certain terms:

Reproduction: Item similar in most aspects to originally produced item, but issued subsequent to the period in which original was distributed.

Fantasy: An original item, not a copy of a pre-existing artifact, giving every appearance of dating back to a specific era or expo, but issued much later. Most fantasies are not intentionally deceptive, but commemorative in nature.

Rerun: An item completely re-manufactured at a date subsequent to original issue; sole motive seems to be based on exploiting the collector market.

Altered: A recognized artifact, "doctored" or transformed into another incarnation or state, putting it in a rarer classification.

REPAINTS (RETOUCHES)

Lithographed or decaled toys are less likely to fall victim to the retouch artists since their finish is so difficult to duplicate. Even if possible, it would be prohibitively expensive. It is with the classic early enameled tin mechanicals and cast-iron toys and banks where we see the most evidence of cosmetic trickery. Look for old paint characteristics as follows:

1. Generally shows evidence of crazing (tiny hairline cracks).
2. Shows wear and chipping in normal wear areas (i.e., next to key wind) and around moving parts (i.e., where legs and arms connect to torso on animal and human figures).
3. Has a harder finish than new paint; will not scratch easily.
4. Will appear a different color than new paint under black light test (i.e., original red will appear olive green under ultraviolet light; newer red may come out as bright orange).

New paint may be detected as follows:

1. Often betrays its presence by odor.
2. Easily scratches because of softness of paint.
3. Parts of same color match up and change color uniformly under black light test.
4. By using cotton swab tip on obscure part of toy. Applied with xylene or acetone agents, new paint quickly dissolves while old paint remains unaffected.

Any one or a combination of the above tests may be employed to expose new paint-altered examples.

In addition, seeking the advice of an authority on paint can

lead to a quick, precise resolution to the mystery of new paint
vs. old paint. I am fortunate to have as a father-in-law a chemical
engineer who worked with the Pigments Department of E.I.
DuPont. A few years ago, I showed my father-in-law a cast-iron
Toonerville Trolley that had been resurrected from the old Dent
Toy works in Fullerton, Pennsylvania. An enterprising collector/
dealer had assembled parts from remaining stock and ostensibly
used original paint that was found on-site still good in the cans.
In effect, the toy then appeared to be as original as those that
came off the assembly line when the toy was actually in production in the late 1920s. Taking a tiny sliver of paint from under the trolley, my father-in-law subjected it to a battery of tests.
He was able to determine that the paint purported to be ger-
mane to the toy had not been introduced until some 30 years
later.

Someone might well ask, "What difference does this make?"
Obviously, from an aesthetic point of view, very little. There are
many collectors who have no intent to deceive, but simply want
to present or exhibit their toys in the best possible light. It is
when a repainted toy is *resold* that the ethical question arises.
It is a general rule-of-thumb that a repainted specimen is worth
about 50% that of an all-original. When confronted with such a
dilemma, it is well worth considering this fact and revising the
amount you are willing to pay for a reprint, since it is obviously
in a devalued state. Obviously, if it is an extremely rare or unique
toy and the quality of the restoration is A-one, one should have
fewer qualms about the matter.

On cast-iron toys and banks, and even on paint that has remained permanently bonded, it is advisable not to clean the item
in soap or detergent solutions or even water. Use a clean cloth
with a few drops of light machine oil and exert very little pressure when cleaning the iron object. Items such as advertising
and commemorative tin containers, tin signs, and tin toys—all
of them lithographed—normally can be cleaned safely with water and a mild detergent. Many dealers and collectors recommend Murphy Oil Soap Household Cleaner, an item available at
your nearest supermarket. If there is ever any doubt about a
lithographed tin, use a cotton swab dipped in cleaner and test it
on the bottom of the item or some other inconspicuous place
before cleaning the entire tin. Murphy's has also proven effec-
tive in cleaning early lithographed game boxes, boards, and paper on wood. Here again, extreme caution should be exercised.

REPAIRS (REPLACED PARTS)

On a recent visit to the Allentown Toy Show & Sale, we spotted a familiar dealer transacting business in one of the back rows of Agricultural Hall. Arranged on his table were boxes and boxes of wheels, axles, headlamps, drivers—literally thousands of spare parts. "These are all original spare parts from my own collection," we overheard him tell a prospective customer. We remember this dealer well; years ago, in a transaction with this writer, he tried to pass off an Arcade cast-iron Andy Gump roadster as an original unadulterated toy. The retouch job was the worst I'd ever encountered and he'd even painted white polka dots on Andy's driving gloves! Chances were that the license plate, the front grille, and even the Andy figure itself were repros. There are all manner of sources for repro parts cast in zinc, lead, brass, and cast iron. The quality ranges from excellent to fairly crude, but collectors eagerly grab them up. There is a whole universe of miniature junkyards with toy vehicles missing spare wheels, steering columns, headlights, etc., that are ripe for restoration. Here again, the majority of purchases are made to transform the toy whole again, to make it presentable in the collection. Only a small percentage are added with intent to pass off as originals. Replacing parts leads to retouching and repainting. To quote Sir Walter Scott, "Oh, what a tangled web we weave who only practice to deceive."

The best advice on combating these pesky "doctored" toys with replaced parts and repaints is to know your craft or rely on someone who does. Use your second sense or "third eye" to determine if the toy is "right." Again, it pays to deal with only those whom you can trust and who will guarantee the originality of the toy.

The Value of a Missing Figure

Ray Holland, a few years ago, was in search of a missing main figure for a lithographed tin toy in his collection. He found a toy intact with the main figure and paid $350 for it. A few months later, the same toy, minus the key main figure, brought a whopping $11 at auction!

Inoperable Toys

The survival rate of toys with wind-up mechanisms capable of activating a toy is suspect, often as erratic as the crazy erratic motions they intend to convey. Rust and overwinding of spring mechanisms are major culprits, as well as the flimsiness or built-in obsolescence inherent with certain manufacturers.

A surprisingly sizable group of collectors is caring less about a toy's ability to operate and more about its facility for showing well in one's collection. Even if operable, certain purists would not think of turning the key, as if winding would endanger the toy's mortality.

In selling a toy that is inoperable, however, there is no doubt that your bargaining position as seller is substantially weakened. We pass along this advice from a leading tin toy practitioner: if the toy is pre-20th century and is of the type where mated halves have been soldered or braised together, to obtain access to the mechanism by softening the closures would char the finish. It would be best to leave well enough alone. On toys made after 1900, however, with the familiar tab closures, it is relatively easy to take the toy apart and have the spring mechanism rewound or shortened. (We've had this done by jewelers and watch repairmen for a nominal fee.) In instances where cams, cogs, and other movable parts are missing or have been damaged, we suggest the services of a toy restoration specialist. The best advice is to avoid attempting any of these delicate operations yourself.

Buying and Selling
at Auction

✳ ✳ ✳

In buying at auction, the following suggestions may prove helpful:

Always get to the preview as early as possible so that you can give any entries of interest a thorough inspection, without being rushed or distracted by the crowd. If you have any questions regarding condition or provenance, or wish to have the item put up at a certain time (providing it is not a cataloged sale), you will have time to discuss it with the auction manager.

Be sure to find a seat or a place to sit or stand where you can be readily spotted by the auctioneer. Make positive bidding motions. Some bidders we know go through all manner of method-acting machinations, such as eye twitchings, shoulder tics, and head scratchings, to indicate a bid (as if to disguise their identity from others while bidding). What generally happens is that the auctioneer is the one who misses your bid and you may be "out" a very desirable toy.

Try to contain your excitement by taking a few deep breaths between bids and don't raise your own bid. Most auctioneers are charitable about this, but we do know of a few who will have you up there well beyond what you should be paying. If you are not certain who has the high bid, don't be shy about asking the auctioneer. This advice is easier to give than to follow, but decide *beforehand* the very maximum you'd be willing to pay, and hold to it.

Above all, don't be intimidated by any bidding "pool" that may be working in the audience. Remember, those involved in the pool are usually dealers who have yet to hold their little "side auction" and still be able to resell the item at a profit. As long as they are bidding with you, in all probability the toy remains within the realm of reason.

The consignor's role in an auction is often clouded in mystique and most auction goers find it more complex to comprehend than the buyer's role. Usually this is because the seller is the silent partner in the auction process. Once the would-be seller has consigned his property to the auction house, his participation ends. Unless a single item is of significant value, an auction house usually elects not to accept one item, preferring, of course, sizable lots of items. The latter tends to balance things out; an item might go disappointingly low, but the law of averages dictates that other items will correspondingly top-off beyond expectations.

Auction houses charge varying rates to consignors and for different services, including transportation, insurance, photography, advertising, and repairs. There is also a seller's commission to be exacted. Rates vary from house to house, according to how the contract is negotiated. You pay the house a 10–21% fee, depending upon whether there is a buyer's premium. There have been, of course, auction houses who have accepted extremely coveted properties without charging a seller's fee.

Before choosing an auction house, it pays to check out their commission arrangement thoroughly. Also, most houses assume complete responsibility as to how the consignments are described in the catalog or advertisements. Be certain to touch bases with your auction house to make sure that the item will be described accurately. Resolve any differences before committing yourself to anything.

To protect your investment, you may also want to discuss selling your consignment subject to reserve. This price is usually determined by the seller and ranges from 50–80% of the low estimate. On items of higher value, the reserve is usually mid-range between the low and high estimate. If, perchance, your consignment fails to meet reserves, you still may be money-out-of-pocket. At many big auction houses, the contract stipulates that the consignor authorize the house to act as exclusive agent for 60 days following the auction to sell the property privately for the previously agreed reserve price.

Consignors can expect to be paid, minus seller's commission and set fees, as soon as the buyers have paid *them*. Usually this is 35 days after the gavel falls.

This may sound like an awful headache, considering the negotiating that is required, but there are those who swear by selling at auction as the best way to get their maximum return on investment.

Housing and Preserving
Your Toy Collection

✳ ✳ ✳

If ever there was a group of collectors who fails to conform to any mold or pattern, it is the maverick group that pursues playthings from the past. How a given collection should be housed and displayed is strictly a matter of one's taste, personality, imagination, or creative flair.

We know of individuals who, as compulsive accumulators or "pack rats," will stash their treasures away in crates and boxes for some inderminate rainy day. Conversely, there is the toy enthusiast who "lives" his hobby, going to the extreme in some cases of transforming his or her home into a veritable museum or shrine.

Toys, banks, and games were obviously created with every intention of being displayed, admired, and examined periodically to remind us of bygone days when so much care, ingenuity, and obvious affection were directed to the creation of a toy.

There are, of course, certain constraints to exposing ones collection to daily scrutiny in open display areas. Being exposed to excessive handling, dust, humidity, insects, and direct sunlight all will take their toll and can lead to not only a loss of aesthetic appeal, but a marked depreciation in value as well. Lithographed paper on wood toys are particularly vulnerable to overexposure. To avoid all this, many collectors wisely rotate their toys, keeping those not on display in special drawers, packing crates, and vaults.

As for display areas, those special little knick-knack shelves and open armoires are less desirable than fully glass enclosed bookshelves, shelving units, or custom-built display cases. A source for a number of attractive display units can usually be found in hobby publications or in the *Yellow Pages*.

To avoid the harmful glare of ultraviolet rays in these special display cases, most conservators and dealers recommend using low wattage, mini shelf lights, arranged in tandem. This shows off your treasures to best advantage without distorting colors and tones, and makes it easy to distinguish variations. Fluorescent lighting would be second choice, but it will give a slightly different cast to objects. Treated plexiglass will also block out harmful ultraviolet rays that readily cause fading. It also pays to place your display in a part of the room where it will be in the shade during the day.

STORAGE AND DISPLAY DO'S AND DON'TS

- Fragile objects, particularly those litho on wood toys, as well as painted objects, should remain in small heated rooms in the winter.
- Minimize contact with acidic wood or paper; many collectors pack their toys in newspaper, which has a particularly high acidic content. A plastic bubble wrap or styrofoam would be far more expedient.
- Paper toys and most wood toys like about 50% humidity, much as people do.
- Define a specific area for each category.
- Catalog each object using an identifying number and a corresponding card with basic data, including description, type of material, specifications, and sources. (You may prefer to mark with an archival ink, or old-fashioned lead pencil. The latter can easily be removed with a vinyl eraser, if you so desire.)
- Make a seasonal cleaning schedule and stick to it.
- Survey your collection at least once a year. Be on the lookout for signs of trouble and immediately take steps to remedy the situation.

COLLECTIBLE TOYS

Banks

MECHANICAL BANKS

Mechanical banks date back as early as 1793 in the United States, but full-scale production of banks with intricate, highly complex coin-activated mechanisms had their inception in the 1870s and extended to the end of World War I. Actually, mechanical banks are still being produced today in limited editions. Leading makers include J. & E. Stevens, W.J. Shepard, Kyser & Rex, and J. Hall. Oddly enough, Ives produced only a few mechanicals, The Boy and Bulldog bank being an obvious exception. John Harper Ltd. was the leading toy bank maker from Great Britain. German and French toy makers stuck to their tin and never entered the cast-iron mechanical bank arena. Mechanical banks are coveted by an ever-widening circle of enthusiasts, attributable to cleverness of animation as well as being almost exclusively American phenomena.

Perelman Toy Museum Sale

Cast-iron

Afghanistan, Mechanical Novelty Works, New Britain, Connecticut, circa 1885, Bear (Russia) and Lion (G.B.) pivot toward Herat Gate, to city of Afghanistan, when activated by coin.   *$4,500*

Alligator in Tin Trough, manufacturer unknown, circa 1880.
$20,000

Jerome B. Secor, of Bridgeport, CT, a sewing machine manufacturer, produced but one mechanical bank, and it proved to be the most coveted mechanical of all time, the Freedman bank, 1878–1883. One of the hobby's foremost collectors, the late Andrew Emerine, is said to have acquired his Freedman bank from a Mexico City librarian who had read his advertisement in quest of mechanicals. The asking price (read it and weep) at the time was $11.

"American," American Sewing Machine Co., Inc., Massachusetts, semi-mechanical, crank turn will rotate sewing machine wheel, probably a promotional item, black with gilt, red, blue trim.   *$15,000*

Arab Figure, Pelican Series, Trenton Lock & Hardware, Trenton, New Jersey, patented 1878 by John Gerard, Arab emerges from pelican's bill.   *$2,200*

Artillery, Shepard Hardware, Buffalo, New York, 1892, bronze plated, Civil War commander, cannon and pillbox, a nickel-plated version may possibly be a bank by J. & E. Stevens.   *$750*

Atlas, manufacturer unknown, 1880s, cast-iron base, white metal Atlas, paper-covered wood globe, globe spins when activated.   *$4,500*

Baby Elephant, Charles A. Bailey, Middletown, Connecticut, patented 1880, elephant rears up, sticks out tongue, and lifts up baby to save from alligators. *$22,000*

Bad Accident, J. & E. Stevens, Charles Bailey patent, circa 1890s, boy jumps in road, donkey rears as cart and driver are upended. *$3,500*

Bank Teller, J. & E. Stevens, Arthur Gould, Brookline, Massachusetts, patented 1876, teller's arm and head lower and coin slides in bank as he returns to original position, black, white, gilt. *$30,000*

Beggin' Bear, collectible fake, manufacturer unknown, 1890s(?). *$250*

Three popular favorites among mechanical banks: Darktown Battery, J.H. Bowen, 1888, $400–$600; Bad Accident, J. & E. Stevens, 1890s, $500–$700; Girl Skipping Rope, J. & E. Stevens, 1890, $5,000 ($19,800 at Bernard Barenholtz Auction in 1989).

Bill E. Grin, J. & E. Stevens, John W. Schmitt, New York City, patented 1915, sticks out tongue and rolls eyes, white, red trim.   *$850*

Billy Goat, J. & E. Stevens, Charles Frisbie patented, 1910, goat butts forward when coin activated (orig. sold as Goat Bank).
$4,000

Bird on Roof, Elisha Stevens, Cromwell, Connecticut, patented 1878, bird tilts forward, sending coin down chimney, japanned, 4³/₁₆″ base. Also came in uncommon silver finish.   *$1,250*

Bismark Pig, J. & E. Stevens, Charles Bailey patent, circa 1883, originally known as "Pig Bank"; Chancellor Bismark pops up out of pig, base length 4⅛″, black, white.   *$3,200*

Bowling Alley, Kyser & Rex, Frankford, Pennsylvania, patented 1879, bowler releases ball, knocks over pins, and rings bell when activated, multicolor.   *$35,000*

Boy Charging Dog, Judd Mfg. Co., Wallingford, Connecticut, boy moves forward to put coin in bank as dog retreats, purple, japanning, the most uncommon version is multicolor.   *$850*

Boy on Trapeze, J. Barton & Smith Co., Philadelphia, Pennsylvania, circa 1891 (also known as "French's Automatic Toy Bank"), boy revolves around trapeze once for a penny, six times for half-dollar, multicolor.   *$2,000*

Boy Robbing Nest, J. & E. Stevens, Charles Bailey patent, circa 1906, when spring is released, limb of tree falls and pushes coin in trunk, originally known as "Tree Bank."   *$4,000*

Boy Scout Camp, J. & E. Stevens, Charles Bailey patent, circa 1915, scout raises flag when coin is inserted, 9⅞″ base length.
$2,500

Boys Stealing Watermelons, Kyser & Rex, circa 1894, "Watermelon Bank," dog emerges from doghouse to protect watermelon, boy hastily withdraws hand from melon, came with single-color outfits on boys (rare) and two-color outfits (2nd casting).   *$500*

Breadwinner's Bank, J. & E. Stevens, Charles Bailey patent, circa 1886, coin activates hammer to strike as Labor smites Monopoly, sending "the rascals up."   *$15,000*

Bull and Bear, J. & E. Stevens, Charles Bailey patent, circa 1880s, slot in pedestal above stump pivots either in direction of bear or bull and deposits coin in that figure, multicolor.

$65,000

Bulldog Savings, Ives Blakeslee & Williams Co., Bridgeport, Connecticut, patented 1878 by Enoch Morrison and Joseph Walter, bulldog jumps up and seizes coin from man's hand, clockwork mechanism. $2,500

Butting Buffalo, Kyser & Rex, Frankford, Pennsylvania, patented 1888 by Alfred C. Rex, buffalo butts boy and lifts up stump, as if to view raccoon peering out of stump top, base length 7^{11}/$_{16}$″. $4,500

Calamity, J. & E. Stevens, James H. Bowen patent, 1904, originally known as "Football Bank," two tackles converge on fullback when coin is inserted, base length 7^7/$_{16}$″, multicolor, with original wooden box. $32,000

Camera, Wrightsville Hardware, Mount Joy, Pennsylvania, 1890s, semi-mechanical, "Kodak" appears on sides, picture of babies pops up when lever is rotated. $4,500

Cat and Mouse, J. & E. Stevens, James Bowen patent, 1891, kitten appears in fancy dress, turns somersault, holding mouse and ball, cat balancing version. $2,200

Cat and Mouse Type II, with cat standing. $5,000

Chimpanzee, Kyser & Rex, patented 1880 by Louis Kaiser and Alfred Rex, moving slide toward Chimp's log book causes him to lower head and bell rings, signifying deposit, base length 5^{15}/$_{16}$″, various color combinations (red or blue are most uncommon). $3,500

Chinaman in Boat, Charles Bailey, Middletown Connecticut, patented 1881, menu reads, "Dinner 1 cent in Advance," press Chinaman's pigtail and arm flips over trap with serving of dead rat, note reads, "Dinner is Ready," multicolor, japanning.

$35,000

Chronometer, manufacturer unknown, 1890s $8,500

Circus, Shepard Hardware, patented by Charles Shepard and Peter Adams, clown in pony-drawn cart goes around ring as clown's arms move up and down. $7,500

Circus Ticket Collector (orig. "Money Barrel Bank"), Judd Mfg., man nods head in thanks as coin is inserted, came in three versions: japanned, multicolor, bronze plated.   *$2,000*

Clown and Harlequin (Harlequin), J. & E. Stevens, circa 1907, James Bowen patent (also attributed to J. Le Blanc or Charles Bailey), clown twirls dancer, harlequin turns, base length 7³/₁₆".   *$90,000*

Clown on Bar, C.G. Bush & Co., Providence, Rhode Island, circa 1890s, coin placed between pair of rings in clown's hand causes him to rotate forward and coin is deposited when he's upside down, clown figure is white with red-striped tin, base is cast-iron latticework in brown.   *$45,000*

Clown on Globe, J. & E. Stevens, James Bowen patent, circa 1890s, known as "Funny Clown," globe with clown straddling whirls around, came with yellow or tan (scarce) base, red, yellow, blue, white.   *$1,000*

Confectionary, Kyser & Rex, patented 1881 by Lewis Kyser and Alfred Rex, when knob at counter is pressed, saleslady gives candy (believed to be a Chase Lozenge, a popular candy treat of the period), part of Bust Bank Series, multicolor.   *$6,500*

Cupola, Diedrich Diekmann, New York City, patented 1872, pushing doorbell lever reveals top of cupola, which pops up, exposing cashier, some figures are bearded and resemble Lincoln, numerous colors, one of the choicest of the building banks.   *$11,000*

Darktown Battery, J. & E. Stevens, 1888, $1,000–$2,000.

Darktown Battery, J. & E. Stevens, patented 1888 by James H. Bowen (''Baseball Bat''), pitcher tosses coin at batter who misses as it is deposited by catcher, base length 9⅞".   *$1,800*

Darky Watermelon (''Football Bank''), J. & E. Stevens, Charles Bailey patent, 1888, coin placed in football activates darky's leg, sending ball over watermelon and depositing itself, part of Pedestal Series marketed by Ives Blakeslee.   *$245,000*

Dentist, J. & E. Stevens, Charles Bailey patent, circa 1880s, dentist pulls darky's tooth, both collapse from impact and coin is deposited in dentist's gas bag, base length 9½", marketed by Ives, Blakeslee as part of Pedestal Series.   *$8,500*

Elephant With Tusks, J. & E. Stevens, designer unknown, circa 1886, dark gray elephant on green wheeled platform, red blanket, moves head.   *$5,500*

English Clown Bust, Chamberlin & Hill, Ltd., Walsall, Staffordshire, England, circa 1925, clown raises arm and swallows coin as eyes roll and tongue glides in.   *$7,500*

English Football, John Harper Co., Ltd., 1895, soccer kicker sends coin into goal net, uniform comes in various colors.   *$2,500*

Freedman (see Mechanical Banks, Wood)

Germania Exchange, J. & E. Stevens, Charles Bailey patent, late 1880s, coin placed on lead goat's tail and turning spigot, activates goat to deposit money and present a glass of beer.   *$15,000*

Giant (Standing), Judd Mfg. Co., 1880s, giant's arms raise, jaw opens, and tongue sticks out, in electroplated or gilt versions.   *$22,000*

Giant in Tower, John Harper & Co., Ltd., patented 1892, giant wielding club leans forward when coin is deposited, red club, black giant, orange tower with yellow trim.   *$10,000*

Girl Skipping Rope (a.k.a. Jumping Rope Bank), J. & E. Stevens, James Bowen patent, 1890, girl skips rope activated by small motor, in yellow, blue, light blue, or pink dress. *$12,500*

Girl in Victorian Chair, W.S. Reed Toy Co., Leominister, Massachusetts, 1880s, coin inserted in bank's top sends dog (in girl's arms) pitching forward as coin falls, yellow-haired girl comes in a red or blue dress.   *$6,000*

Guessing Bank, McLaughlin Brothers, Springfield, Massachusetts, patented 1877 by Edward McLaughlin, male figure with arms resting on pedestal marked "Guessing Bank," when coin is dropped, guessing hand moves around dial and stops at random number, believed to be a gaming device, figure of white metal, bank is bronzed with black base.   *$3,500*

Hen and Chick (a.k.a. Hen and Chicken Bank), J. & E. Stevens, Charles Bailey patent, 1889, coin in slot at front, with lever raised, prompts hen to call and chick to pop out from under her, base length 9¾".   *$4,000*

Hold the Fort, Five Holes, manufacturer unknown, coin placed in fort is struck by cannonball, propelling into bank, also produced in seven-hole model.   *$6,500*

Horse Race, J. & E. Stevens, patented 1869 by John D. Hall, horse assemblies are tin (a.k.a. Race-Course Bank).
   straight base version: *$8,000*
   flanged base version: *$6,000*

Initiating Bank, First Degree ("Eddy's" on base), Mechanical Novelty Works, New Britain, Connecticut, patented by George Eddy, John Turnbull, and James Swanston, 1880, goat butts boy forward, frog springs forward as coin slides from tray to its mouth.   *$11,000*

Initiating Bank, Second Degree (a.k.a. Goat, Frog, and Old Man Bank), same as above, 1880s, coin on plate in bearded rider's hand, touching goat's tail springs him forward and slings coin down frog's throat.   *$7,500*

Japanese Ball Tosser (see Mechanical Banks, Tin)

John Bull's Money Box, Sydenham & McOustra, Walsall, Staffordshire, England, patented 1909, John Bull watches as bull dog jumps forward to deposit coin in barrel.   *$15,000*

Jonah and Whale, Shepard Hardware, Peter Adams patent, 1890, man tosses Jonah forward as if to throw him out of boat, as whale opens mouth to receive coin, base length 10¼".   *$1,500*

Jonah and Whale, Pedestal Version (a.k.a. The Jonah Bank), J. & E. Stevens, Charles Bailey patent, circa 1880s, Jonah appears from whale's mouth when coin is inserted in whale's side, marketed by Ives Blakeslee.   *$33,000*

> *Note:* In 1978, at a Bob, Chuck, and Rich Roan auction in Cogan Station, Pennsylvania, a Jonah pedestal bank sold at $18,500, then the highest price ever paid for a mechanical bank.

King Aqua, German, manufacturer unknown, circa 1900, German soldier in spiked helmet fires gun toward open mouth of African King Aqua, coin entering mouth, trips window in Aqua's back to reveal the king's comely wife, commemorates the capture of the Cameroons in W. Africa by the Germans.   *$95,000*

Light of Asia, J. & E. Stevens, designer unknown, 1890s, light gray elephant on wheeled platform with gilded spokes, moves head.   *$5,000*

Lion Hunter, J. & E. Stevens, patented by Charles Bailey, 1911, coin placed in barrel of Big Game Hunter, Teddy Roosevelt, strikes crouched lion and falls into receptacle, patent assigned to A.E. Cudworth and F.W. Crandall, receivers for Hardware & Woodenware Mfg., New York City.   *$7,500*

Little Hi-Hat (often listed as a John Harper bank, but may have been by U.S. maker), 1920s, similar to "Jolly Sambo" and "Little Joe" as he raises arm, swallows coin, eyes roll, and tongue flips in, made in cast-iron or brass.   *$2,500*

Little Jocko Musical Bank, Ferdinand Strauss Corp., circa 1912, monkey does jig as music sounds.   *$4,000*

Mama Katzenjammer, Kenton Hardware, Kenton, Ohio, 1900s, Mama with youngsters Hans and Fritz straining in her grasp, her eyes roll when coin drops.   *$7,500*

Mama Katzenjammer Reproduction, 3/32 of an inch smaller than original.   *$1,200*

Mammy and Child, Kyser & Rex, patented 1884 by Alfred Rex, (a.k.a. Baby Mine), Mammy spoons as if feeding baby whose legs rise at coin drop.   *$4,000*

Man Thumbs Nose, Pelican Series, Trenton Lock & Hardware, Trenton, New Jersey, patented 1878 by John Gerard, pelican's mouth opens to expose man.   *$2,400*

Mason, Shepard Hardware, patented 1887 by Charles Shepard and Peter Adams, mason raises and lowers trowel and brick while carrier moves forward with coin in hod.   *$5,500*

Mason Bank, Shepard Hardware, 1887, $4,000–$5,000.

Merry-Go-Round, Kyser & Rex, 1880s, patented by R.M. Hunter, red, white, blue canopy, attendant with four carousel figures, when coin is inserted, handle cranks and bell chimes ring.
$20,000

Milking Cow (a.k.a. Kicking Cow), J. & E. Stevens, Charles Bailey patent, circa 1880s, one of Stevens' pedestal series, coin placed in cow's back with lever pressed causes cow to kick up hind legs, upsetting boy and milk pail. $6,000

Motor Bank, Kyser & Rex, Alfred Rex patent, 1889, cast-iron wind-up activated by coin, bell rings, red and blue-sided trolley. $8,500

Octangle Fort, American, manufacturer unknown, circa 1890 (a.k.a. Fort Sumter Bank), coin fired from cannon propels into tower. $3,500

Organ Grinder and Bear (a.k.a. Dancing Bear), Kyser & Rex, 1890s, Italian plays organ while bear does jig, internal ringing bell. $5,500

Panorama, James Butler, Lancaster, Massachusetts, jobbed to J. & E. Stevens by Selchow & Righter, patented 1876, coin inserted produces various scenes in picture window. $2,500

Patronize the Blindman, J. & E. Stevens, William Lutz patent, Chicago, 1878, coin in hands of blindman is retrieved by springing dog and deposited, red, black, and yellow (a.k.a. Faithful Dog Bank). *$5,000*

Pistol, Richard Eliot, Chicago, Illinois, patented 1909 by James Bevington, small book pops out of barrel end when coin drops. *$2,500*

Professor Pug Frog's Great Bicycle Feat, J. & E. Stevens, patented by Charles Bailey, circa 1886, bicycle moves forward in full circle and slings coin into barrel held by clown. *$3,500*

Pump and Bucket, U.S., manufacturer unknown, (a.k.a. Pump Registering Bank), circa 1892, combination mechanical and registering bank, drop coin, pump handle up and down, and coin goes in bucket, cast iron and tinplate. *$2,200*

Punch and Judy, Harry James Banks & Sons, Ltd., Handsworth, England, 1929 patent, cast-iron front, tin back, figures appear when lever is pressed, drop back as coin drops. *$8,500*

Queen Victoria Bust, English, manufacturer unknown, circa 1887, coin inserted creates up and down eye movement, cast iron (a brass version is also known). *$22,000*

Red Riding Hood, W.S. Reed Toy Co., circa 1880s, when coin is inserted in slot in pillow, grandma's mask slides forward exposing the wolf's face, Red Riding Hood's head turns upward, as if frightened. *$32,000*

Paddy and the Pig, J. & E. Stevens, 1890s, $800–$1,200.

Rival, J. & E. Stevens, patented 1878 by Danial James McLean, Reading, Pennsylvania, house with monkey, which springs up with coin and deposits into open dormer, japanned, multicolor.
$17,500

Robot, Starkie's, Lancaster, England, patented 1910 by Robert and Nellie Starkie, coin put in postman's raised envelope is deposited in mail slot of building marked "The Robot," with "10" on door, possible reference to No. 10 Downing Street, Prime Minister's residence, cast iron.   *$5,000*

Schley Bottling Up Cevera, manufacturer unknown, circa 1899, Spanish American War hero, Admiral Schley, or his Spanish adversary, Pascual Cervera. Either portrait appears in circular opening at bank's top when coin is dropped. Shake bank and image changes.   *$27,500*

Seek Him Frisk, manufacturer unknown, patented 1881 by John Murray, New York City, dog chases cat, which escapes to tree when coin is dropped.   *$55,000*

Shoot the Chute, Second Casting (a.k.a. Buster Brown & Tige in Boat), J. & E. Stevens, patent assigned National Novelty Corp., Westfield, New York, 1906, boat speeds down sharp incline when coin is inserted, base length 9 13/16", 6 5/8" height.   *$18,500*

Smyth X-Ray, Henry Hart, Detroit, Michigan, patented 1899 by Charles Smith, nickel-plated, semi-mechanical, coin inserted in middle of x-ray, look through eyepiece, see through coin and out the opposite end, optical illusion.   *$2,000*

Sportsman (a.k.a. Fowler's Bank), J. & E. Stevens, Edwin I. Pyle patent, 1892, when lever is pushed, coin disappears, bird rises in air as sportsman fires paper caps.   *22,000*

Stump Speaker, Shepard Hardware, patented 1886, black man deposits coin in satchel.   *$2,200*

> *Note:* Price shown is that paid at Skinner Christmas Auction, 1988.

The Old Woman in the Shoe, W.S. Reed Toy Co., patented 1883 by William S. Reed, little boy drops in coin as mother raises arms threateningly.   *$245,000*

> *Note:* Price given is estimated price paid by collector Stan Sax for an example from the Hagerty collection.

Time Lock Savings, Louis Mfg. Co., New York City, patented 1892 by Leroy Baldwin, semi-mechanical, wind-up clock is set for pre-determined time and coin trap pops up when time expires, chrome and gold finish. **$12,000**

Tommy, John Harper Ltd., 1914, World War I soldier fires coin into tree. **$5,500**

Turtle, Kilgore Mfg., Westerville, Ohio, designed by M. Elizabeth Cook, early 1920s, Pokey's head extends, then disappears in shell when coin drops. **$30,000**

Uncle Remus, Kyser & Rex, 1890s, Remus, the chicken thief, slams door of coop as cop moves in for arrest. **$3.800**

U.S. and Spain, J. & E. Stevens, patent by Charles Bailey, 1898, hammer on cannon fires paper cap, coin knocks down Spanish ship's mast and disappears, base length 8⅜". **$10,000**

U.S. Building, J. & E. Stevens, patent by Anthony Smith, Brooklyn, New York, circa 1890, push on knob reveals coin slot, boy's face and dog's face appear at opposite windows. **$6,500**

Wimbleton, John Harper Ltd., patented 1885, British soldier lying on ground firing coin in slot of pillbox, cast iron with brass coin launcher. **$7,500**

Zoo, Kyser & Rex, circa 1894, put coin in slot, shutters fly open in building and monkey, then a lion and tiger face appear, then shutter closes. **$1,400**

Tin and Aluminum

African Native, Selhumer & Strauss, 1910–1920s, part of set of seven tin banks, jaw drops for big grin when lever is pressed. **$4,000**

British Clown, Selhumer & Strauss 1910–1920s, part of set of seven tin banks (same action as above). **$650**

British Lion, Selhumer & Strauss, Germany, circa 1910–1920, mouth opens, tongue sticks out, eyes lower when lever is pulled. **$3,500**

Harold Lloyd, Selhumer & Strauss, 1910–1920s, one of set of seven, jaw action when lever is pressed. **$10,000**

Indian Bust, English or possibly Australian; manufacturer unknown, 1890s, aluminum, coin placed in hand moves up into Chief's mouth as tongue flips back to swallow.   *$25,000*

Japanese Ball Tosser, Weeden Mfg., New Bedford, Massachusetts, clockwork mechanism, ball tosser juggles when activated.   *$85,000*

Lion, Selhumer & Strauss, 1910–1920s, one of set of seven tin banks, lower jaw action when lever is pressed.   *$3,500*

London Tower, Lehman, German, patented 1925, drop coin and towerman hoists, then lowers, British flag, lithographed tin. (A Berlin Tower version was also produced.)   *$8,000*

Mickey Mouse (Hand's Apart version), possibly Selhumer & Strauss, tin Mickey sticks out tongue when lever is pressed.   *$18,000*

Snake and Frog in Pond, German, manufacturer unknown, early 1900s, coin placed in snake's mouth is deposited in frog's open mouth, multicolored tin bank.   *$7,500*

Springing Cat, Charles Bailey, patented 1882, cat tries to pounce on mouse, but it disappears.   *$16,500*

Starkie's Airplane, Starkies, Lancaster, England, circa late 1930s, aluminum British fighter plane spirals on shaft, as it descends it drops bomb inside mountain.   *$5,000*

Toad in Den (Toad On Stump), J. & E. Stevens, 1880s, mouth opens when lever is pressed to toss in coin, in dark green or chartreuse (the rarer version).   *$10.000*

William Tell Crossbow, Australian, maker unknown, aluminum with tin tower, Tell launches coin with crossbow, knocking apple off head of son.   *$1,750*

World's Banker, German, manufacturer unknown, 1890s, when John Bull's hat is pressed, globe spins and coin is deposited in his chest, lithographed tin.   *$8,500*

Wood and Tin

Barking Dog, National Co., Boston, Massachusetts, 1880s, wood and tin, dog springs forward as coin is inserted.   *$4,000*

Freedman's, Jerome Secor, Bridgeport, Connecticut, 1879, white metal head, cloth outfit, wood desk, black figure sweeps coin into slot in desk, thumbs nose, and wiggles hands disdainfully. $250,000

Freedman's Bureau, Jerome Secor, Bridgeport, Connecticut, circa 1882, dark black satin with stenciled flowers and "Now You See It & Now You Don't," (works on disappearing coin, trick door principle). $3,500

Frog on Arched Track, tin, James Fallows, Philadelphia, patented 1871, leaping frog goes for coin, swings backwards and drops coin in receptacle. $35,000

Give Me a Penny, manufacturer unknown, 1880s, when drawer is opened, sign pops up out of slot, illustrating monkey with tin cup and above words, carved lion's head in front in bas relief. $4,500

L.E. Wando's Savings Bureau, manufacturer unknown, circa 1880s. $2,000

Mailbox Bureau, manufacturer unknown, circa 1880s. $750

Presto Savings (Mouse on Roof), Frederick & Charles, Montrose, Pennsylvania, patented by Charles Crandall, 1884, as assignor to Crandall and Benjamin Baldwin, coin is deposited, when knob turns, mouse cleverly emerges from hiding place as coin disappears into bank building, lithopaper on wood. $22,000

Serrill's Bureau, James A. Serrill, Philadelphia, patented 1869— the first patented Old Mechanical Bank, came in five-knob and three-knob versions with plain or ribbed border. $1,750

Woodpecker, Gebruder Bing, patented 1896, musical tin and wood bank, bird sticks head outside hole in house, picks up coin from perch as crank is wound. $6,000

STILL BANKS

Outsiders often consider the term "still" in still banks misleading, feeling that it connotes something to do with Prohibition. The term merely distinguishes banks with no mechanical motion involved when a penny is inserted. Tinplate banks predominated from the end of the Civil War to the 1890s, with Schlesingers, George Brown, William Fallows, and Althof Bergmann as the principal makers. Mass-produced cast-iron stills, using highly detailed molds, delighted youngsters and taught them the virtue of saving. From the late 19th century to the 1930's, A.C. Williams, J. & E. Stevens, Hubley, and Kenton were the leaders in their field.

Animals

Bears

Bear (Teddy), 1900s, has word "Teddy" on side, 4″ wide (331) (see "Political and Patriotic Toys" listing).

Bear Stealing Pig, classic pose in finite detail makes this the most desirable of still banks, 5½″ height (246).   *$1,000–plus*

Board of Trade, bear and bull vie for sack of grain, black figures, silver sack, green base, 4¾″ height (264).   *$9,000–$1,100*

Small Bear Eating Honey, 2½″ height.   *$200–$300*

A pyramid of nice, early still banks, mechanicals, and pull toys. The safe banks (bottom left) are priced in the $50–$75 range; Independence Hall bank at very top, $350–$400. Columbian cast-iron pull toy in cast iron (third shelf down) rates a $450–$550 price tag.

Camels

Camel With Pack is on all fours with pack on back, 2 ½ " height (256). $300–$400

Camel With Saddle, light brown with red, yellow trim, 7 ¼ " height, 6 ¼ " width (201). $350–$450

Camel With Saddle, light brown with red, yellow trim, 4 ¾ " height, 4 " width (202). $100–$200

Oriental Camel With Young Camel on Rockers, "Oriental" appears on rockers, one of the most uncommon animal banks, 4 " height (263). $900–$1,000

Cats

Cat With Ball, green cat is sprawled out to pounce on gold ball, 2 ½ " height (247). $200–$300

Cat With Bow Tie, sits primly with nicely curled tail, gold finish (244). $100–$200

Cat Standing, believed to be a Tom, bronze finish, 4 ½ " height (245). $100–$150

Deer

Elk, A. C. Williams, 1934, 6 ¼ " height (195), large version is 9 " height (196). $100–$150

Dogs

Basset Hound, long-eared little fellow with oversized head, a tough bank to find, 3 " height (261). $450–$550

Bulldog, seated, 4 ⅜ " height (102), Hubley, 1920–1930 (105). $50–$60

Dog With Pack, St. Bernard, A. C. Williams, 1905, black finish, 5 ½ " height, 8 " width (113). $75–$150

Dog With Pack, St. Bernard, A. C. Williams, 1905, black finish, 3 ¾ " height, 5 ½ " width (106). $50–$100

Lost Dog, undetermined breed, sits on haunches with mouth open and appears to be baying, 5 ½ " height. $350–$450

Pup on Cushion, one of numerous wide-eyed puppy versions from the 1920s, has "Fido" on collar, sits on flowered cushion, 5″ height (337). $35–$50

Spitz, Hubley, 1920–1930, 4¼″ height (103). $100–$150

Ducks

Duck, white with orange bill, preening, 5″ height (332).
                                                       $50–$100

Duck on Tub, wears red top hat with umbrella tucked under wing, "Save For A Rainy Day" embossed on gold tub, 5¼″ height (323). $35–$50

Elephants

Elephant, the largest of a vast herd of elephant still banks, also probably the best detailed, live gray finish, 4¾″ height, 7″ width (62). $100–$150

Elephant With Chariot, bright red and yellow chariot, 3½″ height, 5½″ width (62). $300–$400

Elephant With Howdah, gold finish, 4″ height, 6½″ width.
                                                       $75–$150

Elephant on Tub, gilded elephant with elaborate blanket stands erect on circus platform, 5¼″ height (60). $75–$150

Seated Elephant, nice stylized features, looks like Babar, 4½″ height (66). $75–$150

Horses

Horse, prancing, on oblong base, black horse on gold platform rears on hind legs, 7½″ height (78). $75–$150

Horse, small, black with red harness, 2¾″ height. $50–$100

Horse With Fly Net, gilded horse looks like it is wearing medieval armor, 4″ height (80). $200–$300

Lions

Green Lion, A.C. Williams, circa 1935, offered in blue, red, green, or gold in two sizes, 2½″ height (94). $75–$100

Lion, gilded king of beasts with wide stance as if confronting an enemy, 3″ height (92).　　　　　*$100–$150*

Lion, standing, Dent Hardware, 1935, gilded, 5½″ height.
　　　　　$100–$150

Lion on Wheels, made by Dent or Hubley, 1920s, the common standing version on wheeled platform, becomes pull toy, gilded with nickeled wheels, 5″ height (95).　　　　　*$75–$150*

Pigs

Bismark Pig, believed to be identical pig to one used in mechanical bank by same name, 3½″ height.　　　　　*$150–$250*

Decker's Iowana Pig, advertising slogan (probably for hog mash) appears on both sides of gilded porker, 2½″ height.　*$75–$150*

Pig, very uncommon miniature black piglet, 1¾″ height.
　　　　　$250–$350

Pig, bears words "I Made Chicago Famous," black finish, has nice primitive look about it, 2¼″ height (177).　　*$100–$150*

Pig, nickeled finish, "A Christmas Roast," 7″ width.
　　　　　$100–$200

Seated Pig, the most colorful of all porkers is also one of the more common still banks, black pig wears yellow outfit trimmed at collar in red, 3″ height (178).　　　　　*$100–$150*

Thrifty Pig, gilded with verse on silver box hanging from pig's neck, "Thrifty" appears at base, 6½″ height (175).　*$50–$100*

Rabbits

Rabbit Standing, upright gilded figure, 5¼″ height (98).
　　　　　$100–$125

White Rabbit, nicely detailed rabbit on green base, word "bank" appears on one side, "1884" on the other (97).　　*$350–$450*

Roosters

Rooster, black Polish breed with red, silver, and gold trim, 5½″ height.　　　　　*$200–$300*

Rooster, gilt with red trim, 4¾″ height (187).　　*$75–$100*

Miscellaneous

Bird on Stump, excellent detail, 4¾″ height (209). *$200–$300*

Buffalo, "Amherst Stoves," 5″ height (207).   *$75–$150*

Bull, aluminum alloy, embossing on inside bank reads "There is Money in Aberdeen Angus," 4½″ height, 7½″ length (190).
$100–$150

Cow, underfed little dogie is hard to find, 2½″ height (188).
$100–$200

Cow, bright red finish, 3½″ (200).   *$75–$150*

Donkey, gilt with red saddle, 6¼″ height (198).   *$75–$125*

Hen, black layer has soapstonelike feel, 6″ height. *$50–$100*

Hen on Nest, gilt, 3″ height (253).   *$350–$450*

Hippopotamus, gilt with incredible detail, 2½″ height (251).
$300–$400

Lamb, same lamb accompanied nursery rhyme Mary bank, 3″ height (192).   *$75–$100*

Opossum, gilt, 2½″ height (205).   *$100–$200*

Pecking Duck, short little waddler, gilt, 4″ height (213).
$100–$200

Red Goose, "Red Goose Shoes" slogan, 4½″ height.
$100–$200

Rhino, 2″ height (252).   *$400–$500*

Seal, black sea lion sits on gray rock, 3½″ height (199).
$150–$250

Squirrel, holds pecan, gilt, 4″ height.   *$250–$350*

Steer, long horns, white, 4″ height (189).   *$75–$125*

Three Monkeys, traditional "See No Evil" trio, brown, 3¼″ height (236).   *$100–$200*

Turkey, magnificent Tom, black with red wattles, 4½″ height (194).   *$150–$250*

Two Kids, pair of goats butting each other over tree stump, black goats, silver stump, gold "Two Kids" embossed on green base, 4¼″ height (262).   *$500–$600*

Buildings, Cast Iron

Old South Church, famous old Boston landmark, features roof with multiple slots for coins, gray with green roof, one of largest and rarest of building banks, 13″ height.   *$800–$900*

Victorian House, George Brown design, 1870s, tin, ornate gingerbread with four gables and three chimneys, white with blue chimneys, red roof, gold stenciling, 6¼″ height.   *$1,000–plus*

Woolworth Building, rendering of New York City skyscraper, gold finish, 8″ height, also a 5¾″ height version.   *$75–$100*

World's Fair Administration Building, a white with gold and red trim replica of building from Colombian Exposition in 1893, Chicago, small red safe in main entrance.   *$100–$125*

Fictional Figures

Andy Gump, Arcade, 4½″ height (see "Comic and Character Toys" listing).   *$500–$600*

Billiken, A. C. Williams, 1902, 4½″ height.   *$50–$100*

Billy Can, A. C. Williams, 5″ height.   *$300–$400*

Black Beauty Horse, 4″ height.   *$50–$100*

Buster Brown and Tige, A. C. Williams, 1900s (see "Comic and Character Toys" listing).   *$100–$200*

Campbell Kids, 3¼″ height, 4″ width.   *$150–$250*

Captain Kidd, 5½″ height, 4″ width.   *$250–$350*

Devil, Two-Faced, 4¼″ height.   *$350–$450*

Foxy Grandpa, 5¾″ height (see "Comic and Character Toys" listing).   *$300–$400*

Gollywog (English doll character), 6¼″ height.   *$200–$300*

King Midas, 5½″ height.   *$200–$300*

Little Red Riding Hood, Harper, English.   *$1,000–plus*

Mary Had a Little Lamb, 4½″ height.   *$500–$600*

Mermaid in Boat, 4½″ height.   *$500–$600*

Mutt and Jeff, A. C. Williams, 5¼″ height (see "Comic and Character Toys" listing).   *$200–$250*

Porky Pig, 5¾″ height (see "Comic and Character Toys" listing). $100–$200

Professor Pug Frog, 3¾″ height. $250–$350

Rumplestiltskin, "Do You Know Me?" on base, 6½″ height.
                                                     $300–$400

Santa Claus With Tree. $2,000–$2,500

Sunbonnet Girl, 1940s, 4″ height. $75–$150

Historic Figures and Landmarks

American Eagle, nice detail with shield of stars and stripes, 4″ height. $300–$400

Benjamin Franklin, bronze finish, cast metal, 5″ height.
                                                      $50–$100

Boss Tweed Bank, based on cartoon representation of Tammany Hall figure by Thomas Nast, "Savings Bank" embossed on lapels of Tweed's coat, 3¾″ height (see "Political and Patriotic Toys" listing). $1,000–$2,000

Bunker Hill Monument, 7½″ height. $75–$150

Charles Lindbergh, bust figure. $150–$250

Coronation Bank, heads of King George V and Queen Mary in relief, English, 6¾″ height, 7¼″ width. $175–$250

Dreadnought Bank, two clasped hands and two British flags, English, 6¾″ height, 7¼″ width. $350–$450

General Pershing, 1918, 8″ height. $100–$200

General Sheridan, Arcade, 5½″ height. $500–$600

George Washington, magnificent bust on gold pedestal, in colorful colonial mufti, 8″ height. $550–$650

Independence Hall, 10¼″ height, 8″ width. $700–$800

Liberty Bell, musical bank, eagle embossed on front, "Centennial 1776–1886," the rarest of any number of Liberty Bell still banks, 5¾″ height. $800–$900

Moody and Sanky, oval photograph of Civil War Revivalists, 4½″ height, 4½″ width (see "Political and Patriotic Toys" listing). $1,000–plus

Cast-Iron Still Banks: Teddy Bear, $100–$125; Prosperity Elephant, $1,200–$1,500; Teddy Rough Rider, $100–$150.

Old South Church, 9¾" height. $700–$800

Smiling Jim and Peaceful Bill, Taft-Sherman campaign bank, 1908, bronze finish, caricature face back-to-back, 4" height.
$600–$700

Statue of Liberty, 6" height. $50–$75

Statue of Liberty, 9½" height. $200–$300

Teddy Roosevelt, bust of T. Roosevelt in Rough Rider uniform (see "Political and Patriotic Toys" listing). $100–$200

Transvaal (Paul Kruger), John Harper Ltd., 1885–1900, 6" height. $700–$800

Washington Monument, 6" height. $100–$200

Household and Personal Effects

Clothes Basket, two doves on top of cover, gilt, 2½" height (339). $75–$125

Cook Stove, advertises "Oak" kitchen stove, 2½" height (134).
$75–$125

Cradle, baby sleeps in rocker-type cradle with small dove perched on headboard, 3½" height (231). $150–$250

Furnace, "Gem" advertising on front, black, cast by A. Bendroth Bros., New York, 4½" height (131). $50–$100

Gas Stove, white enamel range advertising "Roper," 3¾" height. $50–$100

Grandfather's Clock, "Grandfather's Clock" embossed, dark finish, 5½" height (222). $150–$250

Ice Cream Freezer, "North Pole" slogan embossed on bucket with "Save Your Money and Freeze It," 4" height (156). $75–$125

Kodak Bank, one of Kodak's early Brownies in nickel finish with handsome scrollwork, 4½" height. $150–$250

Mailbox, green, eagle with "U.S. Mail" embossed on face, 3½" height (123). $75–$125

Mailbox, one of the largest of many mailbox banks, wide-based pedestal, eagle perched atop, padlock closure, red with gilt patina, 9½" height (119). $150–$250

Pump and Bucket, painted cast metal, 4½" height (235). $35–$50

Purse, black coin purse with "Put Money in Thy Purse" on side, as plain as it is rare, 2¾" height. $300–$400

Radio, floor model GE from the late 1920s, 4" height. $35–$50

Radio, a No. 70 Crosley in green, 4½" height. $35–$50

Refrigerator, top has honeycomb unit popularized by GE, 3¾" height (237). $50–$75

Rocking Chair, dark finish, seat is bank, patented 1898, comprises six separately cast pieces, an intricate rarity, 7" height. $550–$650

Sundial, nice example on gilt column, 4¼" height (153). $250–$350

Wood Parlor Stove, decorative black column stove with silver finial, 7" height. $75–$125

"Little People" Figures

Barrel With Arms, caricature figure of barrel with arms, legs, and man-in-the-moon's face, key slot is in stomach of barrel, 3½" height (151). $150–$200

Baseball Player, A. C. Williams, 1909, 5¾" height (10).
$300–$400

Billy, 4¾" height (22). $200–$300

Boy Scout, A.C. Williams, 6" height (14). $200–$300

Butler, A. C. Williams, 5¾" height (4). $300–$400

Capitalist, 4¾" height (21). $450–$550

Clown, 6½" height (29). $75–$150

Clown, with crooked hat, 6¾" height (28). $400–$500

Cop (Mulligan the Cop), 5¾" height (8). $100–$200

Doughboy (World War I), 6⅞" height (15). $250–$350

Dutch Boy, 6½" height (25). $350–$450

Dutch Girl, 6½" height (24). $600–$700

Fireman, 5½" height (9). $200–$300

Football Player, with large football aloft, 5" height.
$600–$700

Football Player, gold finish, 5¾" height (11). $200–$300

Indian, Hubley, 1920s, 6" height (39). $100–$200

Indian Family, chief, squaw, papoose, 3¾" height.
$750–$850

Mammy, holds spoon, 5¾" height (17). $75–$150

Mammy, 5" height. $75–$150

Man on Bale of Cotton (Coon Bank)(37). $700–$800

Middy, 5¼" height (26). $100–$200

Sailor With Oar, Hubley, circa 1926, 5¾" height (16).
$250–$350

Save and Smile, moonfaced girl with sunbonnet, 4" height (46). $450–$500

Share Cropper (18). $100–$200

Two-faced Indian, chief in full headdress, 4½" height (291).
$600–$700

Two-faced Woman, 4" height (43). $150–$250

Woman With Bustle, English pottery bank, 1890s, 18″ height.
$2,000–plus

Military

Armored Car, red, World War I vehicle, 3½″ height, 6½″ length (160).   *$500–$600*

Battleship Maine, "Maine" embossed midships, gold and black, 4½″ length (142).   *$200–$300*

Battleship Massachusetts, battleship gray, rides green waves, 6″ height, 10″ length (143).   *$250–$350*

Battleship Oregon, green, 5″ height, 6″ width (146).
$100–$200

Battleship Oregon, green, 4″ height, 6″ width (144).
$75–$100

Cannon, black cannon with red wheels, 3″ height, 7″ length (165).   *$400–$500*

Doughboy, World War I soldier, khaki uniform, one knee flexed, 8½″ height.   *$200–$300*

Doughboy Hat, brim, American shield on crown, 3¾″ diameter.   *$100–$150*

Shell, deactivated World War I bullet shell, brass finish, 8″ height (385).   *$50–$75*

Soldier, sometimes called "Minuteman" but uniform looks more like Spanish-American War era, 6″ height (15).   *$150–$200*

Tank, "U.S. Tank Bank," turretless, dark finish, 1¾″ height, 4″ length.   *$50–$100*

Tank, "Tank Bank U.S.A. 1918," red with turret, 3¼″ height, 6″ length (161).   *$100–$200*

Transportation

Auto, red coupe with passengers, 3″ height, 5½″ length (157).
$200–$300

Auto, four-door Model A, dark green, 3½″ height, 7″ length (159).   *$200–$300*

Dirigible, "Graf Zeppelin" on side, silver, 6¾" length (171).
$200–$300

Ferry Boat, sidewheeler, believed to be by Dent, 2½" height, 7¾" length (148).
$100–$200

Ferry Boat, sidewheeler, silver, believed to be by Dent, 2½" height, 8" length (150).
$100–$200

Monoplane, tin, 8" length.
$50–$100

Small Sailboat, dark red, "When My Fortune Ship Comes In," 4" height (249).
$300–$400

Steamship Bank, tin twin-stack vessel on wheeled base, circa 1900s.
$1,000–$1,100

Street Car, gilt trolley with passengers, 3" height, 6½" length (164).
$200–$300

Trolley Car, yellow and red with black wheels, 2½" height, 4½" length (265).
$200–$300

Tug Boat, has wheels, red and black, 3½" height, 5½" length.
$1,200–$1,300

Yellow Cab, yellow and black, "Yellow Cab Co." on door, 4" height (158).
$700–$800

Miscellaneous

Alphabet, 26-sided gilt bank with letter of alphabet embossed on each facet, 3½" height.
$1,000–$2,000

Apple With Bumblebee, juicy red apple with green twig and leaf, bumble rests on top, another candidate for "Number One" among stills (299).
$700–$800

Chimney Sweep, figure on roof ready to clean chimney, cast metal, thought to be English, 4" height.
$100–$200

Money Bag, sack tied with cord, "100,000" on sack, 3½" height (295).
$300–$400

Noah's Ark, red and black with five separated flat-cast animals (elephant, lion, cow, hippo, and camel), 4½" height, 7½" length (290).
$1,000–plus

Old Volunteer Fire Department, octangular-shaped hydrant with gold raised letters, 1890s, 6" height.
$400–$500

"Pingree" Potato, World War I victory garden promotion by Mayor Pingree of Detroit, 5 ½" length (301).   *$200–$300*

Seashell, white conch shell on round base, "Shell Out" appears on outer lip, 2 ½" height, 5" length (293).   *$500–$600*

Street Clock, red with gold face, "Bank Clock" on face, 6" height.   *$300–$400*

Dime Register Banks, Tin

Intriguing offshoots for still bank enthusiasts are the tin daily dime register banks produced in the United States in the 1930s and 1940s, with some versions as recent as the late 1960s. Generally, these banks are 2 ½" square, with rounded corners, and feature a small window where the total amount appears as each dime is inserted. Usually, the appealing little banks held 50 dimes ($5) and provided a real incentive to save, as the bank opened automatically when the $5 goal was reached.

TOP ROW (LEFT TO RIGHT):

"Dopey," from Snow White and The Seven Dwarfs, 1938, $50–$60

"Superman," King Features Synd., 1940, $45–$55

Comic characters dominate this group of Dime Register banks.

"Popeye," 1950s, silver version, King Features Synd., $25–$30
"Popeye," 1950s, full color, King Features Synd., $25–$30
"Popeye," 1929–1930s, silver, King Features Synd., $30–$50
"Clown," 1950s (with monkey playing saxophone), $25–$30

MIDDLE ROW (LEFT TO RIGHT):

"Snow White and The Seven Dwarfs," 1930–1940, $50–$75
"Captain Marvel," Fawcett Pub., 1944–1946, $75–$85
"Astronaut," early 1960s, $35–$45
"P-40 Fighter Plane," 1940s, $35–$45
"Little Orphan Annie," Famous Artists Synd., 1936, $60–$70
"New York World's Fair," 1964–1965, $15–$20

THIRD ROW (LEFT TO RIGHT):

"Jackie Robinson," early 1940s, $75–$100
"Elf," 1950s, $10–$15
"Mickey Mouse," Walt Disney Prod., 1939 (Mickey teaches nephews to save), $75–$100
"Piggy," 1960s (smiling head of pig), $25–$30
"Little Girl," with pet rabbit and duck, titled "Vacation" bank, 1960s, $15–$20
"Young Cowboy" (little boy in cowboy suit with two bags of money), $15–$20

Perelman Toy Museum Sale, Cast Iron and Tin

Alphabet Octangular Bank, U.S., cast iron, 3 7/8″. $2,500

American Ambulance Bank. $1,500

Andy Gump on Barrel, pot metal. $5,000

Andy Gump Reading Newspaper, Arcade, cast iron, 4 3/8″ height, painted red, yellow, white, black. $1,500

Apple, Kyser & Rex, 1882, classic bank has bee on it. $850

Bear Stealing Pig, 5 1/2″ height, gilt. $1,000

Black Cab, Flat Top, Arcade, 1921, cast iron painted black, steel wheels. $1,000

Coon Bank (Man on Cotton Bale), U.S. Hardware, 1898, 4 7/8″ height. $850

Doc Yak (Conversion), Arcade, circa 1917, comic strip figure.
$1,000

General Grant Safe Bank, Harper, 1903, 5⅝″ height.   *$2,000*

Hippo Bank, U.S., 5³⁄₁₆″ length, gilt.   *$1,500*

"I Luv a Copper" Bank, Chamberlin & Hill (or possibly Sydenham & McOustra), England, circa 1910, visual pun, cherubic British Bobby.   *$1,500*

Independence Hall Bank, Enterprise Mfg., 1876, 9½″ height, gilt finish.   *$900*

Indian Family Bank, J. M. Harper, England, cast iron, 1905, 5⅛″.   *$950*

Jester Bank, cast iron (information unavailable).   *$4,500*

Lloyd George Bank, England, 1910, 5¾″ height, cast iron w/ bronze finish.   *$1,500*

Mickey Mouse Dancing on Drum.   *$,1500*

Mickey Mouse Treasure Chest, Automatic Recording Safe Co., Chicago, 1935, 2⅝″ height × 3¼″ width, brightly lithographed tin with images of Mickey, Minnie, Pluto, Donald, Three Pigs, etc.   *$1,500*

Musical Savings Bank, 1924 Swiss patent by Madam Alice Reuge of St. Croix, tin mechanical, featured various medallions (i.e:, dog, stag).   *$10,000*

Old South Church, U.S., 13½″ height, white with brown trim, cast iron.   *$1,000*

Old South Church, with slotted roof, 9¾″ height, cast iron, bronze finish.   *$1,200*

Orange Cab, Flat Top, Arcade, 1921, cast iron with orange paint, rubber tires.   *$1,200*

Oriental Camel on Rocker, U.S., manufacturer unknown, 1910, 3¾″ length × 5⅜″ height.   *$1,200*

Peaceful Bill and Smiling Jim (William Taft and running mate, James Sherman), bronze finish, 4″ height.   *$850*

Potato Bank, Mary A. Martin designer, U.S., 1897, 5¼″ width, brown finish.   *$1,000*

Santa Claus Bank, Harper, England, painted cast iron. *$4,000*

Santa Claus Bank, cast iron, Ives, 1890s, 7 ¼ ″ height, w/holder for wire Christmas tree. *$3,200*

Steamship on Tin Base, maker unknown, 1890s, ship and base of single construction. *$2,750*

Stork Safe Bank, Harper, 1903. *$1,000*

Taft Bank, "Eggman" caricature of William Howard Taft, Arcade, 1910–1913, 4″ height. *$1,500*

Toboggan Bank (information unavailable). *$3,500*

Battery-Operated Toys

Often considered an offspring of contemporary electronics wizardry, battery-operated toys originated as early as the mid-1920s, following the inception of the self-contained dry cell battery. These fledgling attempts, however, were readily susceptible to corrosion and not really affordable in the face of competition from wind-up versions, particularly during the Depression. Battery-operated toys made their greatest inroads in the post-World War II years, as the occupied zones of Germany and Japan began to flood the market. Today, highly sophisticated remote control robots and space toys are already being trumpeted as collectible "futures." Whether justified or not, only time will determine if they merit the attention as the hottest collectible category in the hobby today.

CARTOON, MOVIE, AND TELEVISION PERSONALITIES

Barney Rubble and Dino, Marx, 1963, litho tin mech, plastic, 8 1/8″ length. $75–$100

Blushing Frankenstein, Rosko, Japan, 1960s, litho tin, plastic, sways, makes roaring sound, arms move, pants drop, face reddens. $50–$75

Charlie Weaver Bartender, Rosko, 1960s, litho tin, plastic, Jack Parr's "Tonight Show" celebrity, smoke emits from ears. $35–$50

Dennis the Menace Xylophone Player, Marx, litho tin, plastic musical, plays "London Bridge." $100–$125

Frankenstein Monster, T-N, Japan, 1960s, six actions, 14″ height. $150–$250

Fred Astaire, Tap Dancer, Alps, Occupied Japan, 1950s celluloid, tin. $200–$300

Fred Flintstone and Dino, Marx, 1960s, plush-dressed tin, vinyl, Fred rides dinosaur, 22″ length. $75–$100

Howdy Doody Electric Doodler, 1950–1955, litho question-and-answer game, 9″ × 13″. $50–$60

James Bond 007 Car, M101, Daiwa, Japan, 1960s, seven actions, ejectable driver, 11″ length. $75–$100

Louis Armstrong, Rosko, Japan, 1960s, litho tin, vinyl, cloth mechanical, 9½″ height. $125–$150

Mighty Kong, Marx, 1950s, five actions, litho tin, plastic, 12″ height. $100–$125

Mother Goose, Japan, late 1940s, plush-covered tin, celluloid beak, big red tin shoes, waddles, tail vibrates. $35–$50

Mr. Magoo Car, Hubley, circa 1961, litho tin, cloth roof, vinyl head, bump-and-go action. $50–$75

Pinocchio Playing "London Bridge," Marx, 1960s, litho tin, plastic, three actions, 10″ length. $75–$100

Tarzan, San Co., Japan, 1960s, litho tin, vinyl head, cloth dressed (loin cloth), Tarzan walks, 13″ height. $100–$125

SPACE AND ROBOT BATTERY-OPERATED TOYS, POST–WORLD WAR II

Apollo, U.S.A., N.A.S.A., K. K. Masutoku Toy Factory, Japan, 1960s litho tin, rubber wheels, 9⅝″ length. $100–$150

Apollo Spacecraft, Alps Shop Ltd., Japan, 1960s, litho tin, plastic, 9½″ length. $100–$125

Apollo-X Moon Challenger, Nomura Toys Ltd., Japan, 1960s, litho tin, plastic, 15¾″ length. $100–$150

One of the earliest, and more primitive, robots produced in Occupied Japan in the 1950s, $150–$250.

Atomic Robot Man, Japan, late 1940s, litho tin, 5″ height.
$350–$450

Big Loo, Marx, 1961, litho tin, plastic, 3″ height. $250–$300

C3PO, GM FGI, Hong Kong, plastic, late 1970s, 12½″ height.
$100–$125

Cape Canaveral Series 2000 Kit, Marx, 1960s, contains four-stage rocket, flying saucer, missile, and NASA personnel figures. $125–$150

Chief Robotman, K.O. Co., Japan, 1950s, four actions, 12″ height. $125–$150

Dino Robot, S.H. Co., Japan, 1960s, five actions, 11″ height.
$75–$100

Fighting Robot, Horikawa Toys, 1966, litho tin, plastic, 9⅝″ height.
$75–$125

Flying Saucer, Cragston, Japan, 1960s, hatch opens and closes as astronaut enters, siren, 10″ diameter.
$125–$150

Friendship 7, Modern Toys, Japan, 1960s, astronaut's space capsule, 6½″ height.
$25–$35

Great Garloo, Marx, 1961, litho tin, plastic.
$150–$200

King Flying Saucer, Japan, circa 1950, litho tin, plastic, tilt-and-roll motion, 7¼″ diameter.
$125–$150

Laser 008, Japan, 1960s, plastic, 7″ height.
$100–$125

Man in Space Astronaut, Alps, circa 1960, litho tin, plastic, 6″ height.
$75–$100

Mars Explorer Car, EXECO, Japan, 1950s, light and dark green tin litho, astronauts are in twin plastic bubbles, simulated exhaust flame in red plastic.
$150–$200

Mars Explorer Robot, S.H. Co., Japan, circa 1950s, litho tin, plastic, seven actions, 9½″ height.
$50–$75

Martian Robot, S.J.M. Co., 1970s, litho tin, plastic, four actions, 12″ height.
$50–$75

Mechanical Jumping Rocket, S.H. Co., Japan, litho tin, plastic, robot astride rocket, rocks and rolls when activated, 6″ height.
$100–$150

Mechanized Robot, F.N. Co., Japan, circa 1950s, four actions, 13½″ height.
$100–$150

Mr. Atomic, Cragston, Japan, 1960s, litho tin. $1,500–$2,000

Mystery Universe Car, Taiwan, ME #089, 1960s, litho tin with plastic fins, oval dome, makes noise, 4″ height × 10″ length.
$75–$100

N.A.S.A. Space Center Saucer, Hong Kong, 1960s, plastic and rubber, bumps and turns.
$50–$75

Office Rex Mars Planet Patrol, Marx, 1930s, 10″ length.
$150–$200

Omni Robot, Hong Kong, 1970, litho tin, plastic, 10 ⅛ ″ height.
$50–$75

Piston Robot, Linemar, 1950s, 5 ½ ″ height. $75–$100

Robot, K.O. Co., Japan, 1950s, tin and plastic, lights, bumps and turns. $100–$150

Robot Cosmic Raider Force, Taiwan, 1970s, plastic, blinking lights, 14 ½ ″ length. $50–$60

Robot 2500, Hong Kong (for Durham Industries, New York), plastic, 9 ¾ ″ height. $50–$60

Rocket Launcher T-12, Daiya, Japan, 1960s, 10 ″ length.
$100–$150

Roto Robot, maker unknown, 1960s, litho tin, plastic, 8 ½ ″ height. $35–$50

Saturn Robot, Taiwan, 1970s, plastic, lighted eyes, TV screen, 11 ⅝ ″ height. $50–$75

Silver Robot, maker unknown, 1960s, red circle lights up in robot's "heart" area, 9 ½ ″ height. $30–$50

Son of Garloo, Marx, 1960s, litho tin, offspring of Great Garloo (two versions: one has Son of Garloo medallion as part of design; other wears medallion on chain around neck). $100–$150

Space Capsule, Horikawa, Japan, 1960s, tin, plastic, and rubber, 9 ⁵⁄₁₆ ″ length. $50–$75

Space Explorer, Horikawa, Japan, 1960s, litho tin, plastic, TV monitor. $75–$100

Space Patrol Car, VW-Rosko, litho tin silver body with red and silver trim, coiled wire bumpers, clear plastic panel with light, 12 ″ length. $150–$200

Space Rocket Solar X, T-N Co., Japan, 1960s, litho tin, plastic wings retract. $50–$75

Space Saucer, maker unknown, 1960s, plastic, rubber, 4 ″ length. $25–$50

Space Scooter, M-T Co., Japan, circa 1960s, plastic, litho tin, three actions, 8 ″ length. $50–$75

Space Tank, K.O. Co., Japan, 1960s, litho tin, plastic, tilt-and-roll motion, 8″ length. $50–$75

Sparky Robot, K.O. Co., Japan, 1960s, tin, lights beam from eyes, 9½″ height. $75–$100

Strange Explorer, Horikawa, 1950, litho tin, plastic, 8″ length. $75–$100

Super Space Capsule, maker unknown, 1960s, litho tin, blinking lights, body revolves, door opens and astronaut pops out, 9½″ length. $35–$50

Super Space Commander, Horikawa, 1960s, litho tin, plastic, 9⅝″ length. $75–$100

Talking Robot, Cragston, Japan, 1960s, litho tin, plastic, 12″ height. $125–$150

Televison Space Man, maker unknown, 1950s, litho tin, revolving antenna, TV monitor. $35–$50

UFO-XO5, M-T Co., Japan, circa 1960s, plastic, litho tin, three actions, 7½″ diameter. $15–$25

Universe Televibot, Taiwan, circa 1960s, litho tin, plastic, rubber wheels, 13½″ length. $50–$75

Bell Toys

Bell toys were some of the most engaging and popular of Victorian toys. They were pushed, pulled by a string, and, in some instances, propelled along the floor with a long wooden handle.

The fanciful push-pull toy ranges from a simple bell mounted between a pair of wheels to a figure or group of figures mounted on a platform to which a bell is attached. As the toy moves across the floor, a clapper strikes the bell. Half bells, joined at the center, were sounded by a floating steel striker that rolled around inside the toy; a wire loop was attached loosely to the axle between the bell and wheels, which were cast iron or brass.

The earliest bell toys were made in Connecticut between 1865 and 1875, with the leading manufacturers being Watrous, Gong Bell, N.N. Hill (which later merged with Watrous), and J. & E. Stevens. All but Stevens operated out of East Hampton, Connecticut, and all also produced house and carriage bells.

Initially, bell toys were fashioned of painted tinplate; in the last quarter of the 19th century, makers switched to brass or cast iron. Some bell toys featured stationary bells of either one half-pound section with exterior clapper or two half-round sections encasing an interior clapper. Another version featured free-swinging bells with interior clappers.

Most of the cast-metal bell toys were produced between 1890 and 1910. Gong Bell, which produced bell toys as early as 1866, made wooden, and then plastic, versions until it ceased operation in 1960.

Bell toys of wood and plastic are still popular today, with Playskool, Gong Bell, and Fisher-Price among the industry leaders.

Mingling of folk art and manufactured toys at Allentown Toy Show, November 1988, includes a Red Church (*top left*), a Fisherman Bell Toy (*2nd row, center*), and a Lady Churning Butter by Ives. (Similar toys sold at $2,500, $2,750, and $4,000 at Perelman; photo of display in Bob Schneider's booth.)

PERELMAN MUSEUM SALE PRICES REALIZED

Acrobats Bell Toy, Gong Bell, 1903, figures perform various maneuvers, each with bell in hand, 6¾". $1,500

Airplane Bell Toy, Watrous, early 1900s. $950

Baby Quieter Bell Toy, J. & E. Stevens, 1893, bell rings when toy is pulled and baby rises up on dad's knee, 7 ½ " length.
$2,750

Bell Ringing Pistol, J. & E. Stevens, 1890s. $1,250

Billy's Bell Toy, Gong Bell, 1890s. $2,750

Boy Fishing Bell Toy, N.H. Hill Brass Co., 1905, boy lifts up pole with fish on line, 6 ½ " length. $2,750

Boy on Alligator, Gong Bell, 1890s. $2,750

Cat and Negro Boy, N.H. Hill Brass Co., 1905, boy pulls cat's tail as bell rings, 6" length. $3,500

Charlie Chaplin Bell Toy, Watrous, 1900. $3,500

Cinderella Bell Toy, Gong Bell, 1900s. $875

Cinderella Chariot Bell Toy, Gong Bell, 1900s. $875

Clown and Poodle Dog Bell Ringer, Gong Bell, 1903, poodle jumps and rings bell. $3,500

Clown and Tumbler Bell Toy, Hubley Mfg., early 1900s.
$1,200

Columbus Landing Bell Toy, Gong Bell, 1892 (see "World's Exposition Toys") listing. $900

Daisy Bell Toy, Gong Bell, 1893, girl hugging doll on sleigh, 8 ¼ " length. $1,000

Darky Riding Alligator, N.H. Hill Brass Co., circa 1905, 6" length. $2,750

Ding Dong Bell (Puss's Not in the Well), Gong Bell, circa 1900, two nursery rhyme characters and cat, wheel house, 9" length. $2,200

Dog and Cat Bell Toy, Gong Bell, 1872, cat bluffs dog who retreats into his house, 9" length. $3,200

Donkey and Rider, Gong Bell, 1900s. $3,500

Drummer Boy Bell Toy, J. & E. Stevens, early 1900s. $7,500

Eagle Bell Ringer, Gong Bell, 1903, eagle swings bell in beak.
$1,250

Daisy Bell Toy, Gong Bell, 1893, $1,000–$1,500.

Elephant Bell Ringer, N.H. Hill Brass Co., 1905, elephant swings bell in trunk, 7″ length. $650

Eskimo and Bear Bell Toy, Watrous, 1890s. $1,250

Foxy Grandpa Bell Toy, Gong Bell, 1911. $2,750

Gator-Baiter Seesaw, Gong Bell. $6,000

Improved Fish Toy, Gong Bell, circa 1900, boy dangles bell as bait above fish's head. $2,000

John Bull and Uncle Sam, Watrous, 1905, 7″ length. $2,250

Jonah and the Whale Bell Toy, N.H. Hill Brass Co., 1905, whale swallows Jonah and bell rings with each revolution of wheels. $1,250

Liberty Bell Toy, Kyser & Rex, 1890s, cast iron. $6,500

Little Nemo and Mr. Flip, Watrous. $3,500

May Queen Bell Toy, U.S. Hardware, 1890s. $1,200

Monkey and Chariot Bell Toy, J. & E. Stevens, 1890s. $2,750

Monkey on Tricycle, J. & E. Stevens, 1890s. $3,500

Monkey Bellringer, N.H. Hill Brass Co., 1905, $700–$800.

Punch and Judy Bell Toy, J. & E. Stevens, 1890s, ranks supreme among bell ringers, Punch hits Judy over head and she vanishes into well.   **$28,000**

Rough Riders Bell Toy, Watrous, 1905, double riders on horseback.   **$650**

Running Monkey Bell Toy, Gong Bell, early 1900.   **$1,350**

Saratoga Chimes Bell Toy, J. & E. Stevens, 1890s, cast iron.
                                                              $3,500

Soldier and Sailor Bell Toy, Watrous.   **$1,200**

Suffragette Bell Toy, maker unknown, 1890s.   **$6,500**

Swan Chariot, J. & E. Stevens, circa 1890s, cast iron with bellows voice box, one of the very few cast-iron mechanical toys, patented by C.M. Henn, Chicago.   **$9,000**

The Two Coons, Gong Bell, 1903, raccoon and darky peek at opposite ends of hollow log with bell attached below.   **$2,750**

Uncle Sam and the Don Bell Toy, Gong Bell, 1903, the pair engage in lively set-to, U.S. flag ornamented platform, 7 ½" length.   **$4,500**

Two Coons Bell Toy, Gong Bell, 1903, $2,750 at Perelman Toy Museum Sale in 1988.

Watermelon Bell Toy, N.H. Hill Brass Co., 1905, darkies slice melon with crosscut saw as bell rings, 9″ length.   *$4,500*

Whoa Dere Caesar Bell Toys, Ives, Blakeslee, 1890s.   *$1,750*

Circus Toys

Few collecting categories evoke more nostalgia or amusement than circus and fairground toys. Any number of toy makers have outdone themselves in terms of creativity to produce their finest work. Prime examples include Schoenhut with their Humpty Dumpty Circus; Hubley and the Róyal Circus cast-iron menagerie (owning the entire entourage has been likened to holding a royal flush in poker); Kenton's more recent Overland Circus wagons, and, not to be overlooked, the ingenious animated bell ringer pull toys featuring cavorting clowns and tumbling acrobats by Gong Bell and Watrous from the turn of the century.

CIRCUS AND FAIRGROUNDS AMUSEMENT RIDES

Aerial Carousel, Chein, 1930s, lithographed tin mechanical, four rocket-shaped rides with propellors, two passengers in each, 18″ height. $200–$250

Carousel, German, circa 1910, handpainted tin mechanical and musical, with five swings, 13″ height. $700–$800

Carousel, German, circa 1915, lithographed tin mechanical, three swings with three blown figures, 13″ height. $400–$500

Carousel, German, early 1930s, imported by Gibbs, painted tin clockwork, 8″ height. $300–$400

Three classic circus toys. *Top left:* maker unknown, late 1890s, painted tin mechanical, canvas tent, $650–$750. *Bottom left:* Crandall's Lively Horseman wooden pull toy, 1880s, $550–$650. *Right:* "Jumbo" gravity string toy, maker unknown, early 1900s, $350–$450.

Double-Action Revolving Observation Swing, French, 1910, tower with twin American flags atop, six cars suspended from three double swings, each with two passengers, 13″ height.

$500–$600

Double Ferris Swing, French, 1910, double-revolving swings on twin columns, passengers ride in tiny gondolas, bright painted colors on tin, mechanical, 13½″ length. $350–$400

Ferris Wheel, German, circa 1915, handpainted tin mechanical with blown figures, 16″ height. $300–$350

Ferris Wheel, German, circa 1915, handpainted tin with crank, composition figures, two-color flat atop small roof over wheel, very ornate, 15½″ height. $400–$500

Ferris Wheel, German, 1915, lithographed tin, steam attachment, four seats with passengers, 13″ height. $350–$400

Ferris Wheel, Chein, 1930s, lithographed tin mechanical, 12″ height. $100–$150

Midget Roller Coaster, maker unknown, 1930s, tiny car runs down incline and raised by chute to starting point. $75–$100

Musical Carousel, French, 1910, painted tin mechanical, three children on goats on revolving platform, six children in swings suspend from revolving canopy as music plays, 11½″ height.

$350–$450

Musical Russian Carousel, German, circa 1900, painted tin, hand-crank mechanical, three horses and riders revolve around single hub while music plays. $450–$500

CIRCUS WAGONS, CAGES, AND OTHER ASSEMBLAGES

Cage Wagon, Schoenhut (from Humpty Dumpty Circus), 1920s, paper lithographed on wood, tops lift off to reveal cages, on wooden wheels, minus animals. $1,200–$2,200

Circus Platform Pull Toy, from Oscar Strasburger Catalog, circa 1890, painted tin with cast-iron wheels, features musicians, two horses with feet on drum, smaller figure with pony jumping through hoop, painted tin, 13½″ length. $1,000–$2,000

Revolving Monkey Cage Wagon, circa 1919–1926, rarest of all cast-iron toys. Sold at $19,000 at Bill Holland Collection, Sotheby's, NYC, in 1985; second example sold at Perelman, 1988, for $30,000.

Circus Train, Cole Bros. and Wardie Jay, 1930s, for O gauge railroads, a kit featuring Britains cast-metal figures, includes over a dozen cars, including cage cars and a calliope.

$700–$800

Circus and Two Poodles, Muller & Kadeder, circa 1900, painted tin mechanical, revolving carousel on small stand with jutting rod that has poodles jumping over each other on one end, spinning prop on other.

$500–$600

Circus Wagon, Wyandotte, 1920s, pressed steel and tin, truck with attached trailer cage, cardboard lithographed animals, 20" length.

$200–$300

Polar Bear Cage Wagon, Bliss, 1915, lithographed paper-on-wood, pair horses pull wagon with mechanical bear.

$800–$900

Pony Circus Wagon, Gibbs, 1920s, paper lithographed on wood and tin, cast-iron wheels.

$300–$400

"Ring-A-Ling" Circus, L. Marx, 1927, ringmaster snaps whip, clown turns somersault, elephant, lion, and monkey do stunts, lithographed tin mechanical, 9½" diameter.

$300–$400

Trained Circus Horses, German, 1904, painted tin clockwork, ringmaster on barrel, clown holds hoop on edge of platform, horses dance around ring on hind feet, 11 ½ " height.
                                                    $1,000–$2,000

Turning Circus, German, double-tiered spinning round platform, flagstaff and large bannerette in center, four circus horseback riders move in one direction, two riders in another when clockwork mechanism is activated, while music plays, 9 " diameter.   *$1,000–$2,000*

AMUSEMENT RIDES

Acrobat Wheel, Wilkins, circa 1900s, five acrobats perform on Ferris wheel-type rig on four-wheeled platform pull toy, painted cast iron, 9 ½ " length.   *$600–$700*

Aerial Merry-Go-Round, maker unknown, 1910, painted tin, battery operated or electrical, flies American flag atop canopy, six suspended cars, 18 " height.   *$1,200–$1,400*

Bath House, maker unknown, 1929, lithographed tin mechanical, green celluloid swimming tank, painted swimming suits on steel bar, 5 ¼ " height, 5 ½ " width.   *$100–$200*

Carousel, Four Horses, German, circa 1910, painted tin mechanical, nice filagreed canopy topped by bannerette, 13 " height.   *$650–$750*

Coney Island Carousel, maker unknown, circa 1910, three horses with riders circle as music plays, high platform, painted tin mechanical, 9 ½ " height.   *$300–$400*

The Giant Dip, Coney Island, maker unknown, 1929, lithographed tin mechanical, with four passengers, double-action spring, airplane revolves above, amusement booths and other attractions lithographed on base, 18 " length, tower, 13 " height, car, 1 ¾ " length.   *$300–$400*

Hy and Lo, maker unknown, 1924, lithographed tin mechanical, cars run on double-inclined runway, drop to lower track and glide back to starting point where spring mechanism sets it on its way again, 9 ¾ " length.   *$100–$150*

Musical Carousel, Converse, 1915, lithographed paper on wood, five seats (five pair of horses), music box in base, 36″ diameter. **$1,500–$2,500**

Reindeer Circus Train, Milton Bradley, circa 1890, lithographed on wood, engine tender and four cage cars, animals include rhino, bear, bison, tiger, 45″ length. **$800–$900**

Roundabout, German, 1910, painted tin mechanical zeppelin and early bi-wing revolve around pylon, 15″ height. **$600–$700**

CIRCUS RIGS, CAST IRON

Hubley Royal Circus Series: 1919–1926

Animal Cage, 1920, drawn by four horses, includes driver, two caged animals, painted cast iron, 23″ length. **$1,000–$2,000**

Band Wagon, 1920, painted cast iron, four horses, driver, six or eight musicians, 30″ length. **$2,000–$3,000**

Bear Cage, 1920, two horses with balance wheels, driver, pair caged bears, painted cast iron, 15¾″ length. **$1,000–$2,000**

Bear (Tiger, Rhino, or Lion) Circus Wagon, 1924, painted cast iron, Hubley produced a less elaborate Royal Circus Series, only 12¼″ long, minus the ornate embossing, with an option of four wild animals. **$800–$1,000**

Buffalo Van, 1920, has buffalo embossed in oval on cage, painted cast iron, two horses with driver, 13¼″ length. **$1,000–$1,200**

Calliope, 1920, two horses, painted cast iron, some models featured chimes, boiler, sizes 9¼″, 12¾″, 16″ length. **$2,000–$3,000**

Chariot, 1920, painted cast iron, less elaborate standing clown driver, only 5½″ length. **$700–$800**

Chariot With Clown, 1920, painted cast iron, standing clown holds reins of three black horses, 9½″ or 12½″ length. **$1,000–$2,000**

Clown Van, 1920, painted blue cast iron, similar to Monkey Van, with clown's head and trapeze projecting from top of van, also with oval mirror, sliding doors, embossed angels' trumpets in gold, 16½" length.   *$1,000–$2,000*

Eagle Van, 1920, painted cast iron, eagle embossed in gold in oval on enclosed cage wagon, sizes: 6", 7", 8½" length (also featured lion variation).   *$900–$1,000*

Farmer Van, 1920, pair draft horses, hauling wagon with pressed-steel floor and roof, painted cast iron, cast aluminum, bearded farmer with straw hat and spectacles projects from top of cage, embossed rhino appears in gold on cage against deep green background, wheels are bright red with gold starburst centers, farmer's head revolves as toy is pulled, 16¼".
                              $2,000–$3,000

Giraffe Cage, 1920, caged mother giraffe (whose head projects out of top of cage) and baby, horses wear plumes on harness, painted cast iron and sheet metal, cast lead, sizes available of two horses 16½" length or four horses 24½" length.
                              $1,500–$2,500

Lion Circus Wagon, 1924, two horses, driver, two caged lions, painted cast iron, 15¾" length, Hubley produced a slightly longer (16¼" length) version of the same wagon in 1924.
                              $900–$1,000

Monkey Van, 1920, painted cast-iron van, pair horses and driver, monkey's head projects from top of van, with trapeze, large oval mirror on each side of van, 13" length.   *$1,000–$2,000*

Rhino Cage, 1920, two horses, two caged rhinos (in open cage), plus driver, painted cast iron and pressed steel, 16" length.
                              $1,000–$1,200

Tiger Van, 1920, has tiger embossed in oval on side of fully enclosed cage, painted cast iron, two horses with driver, 12¼" length.   *$900–$1,000*

Other Manufacturers (See Schoenhut Auction and Sales Prices Realized under "Litho-Painted Wooden Toys" Heading)

Band Wagon, Ives, 1900s, painted cast iron (similar to Hubley example except for more ornate wheels), 31" length.
                              $3,000–$4,000

Band Wagon, Kenton, 1950, painted cast iron and sheet metal, features driver, six musicians, two men riding white horses, rubber balance wheel, 15 ½ ″ length.   *$300–$350*

"Big Six" Circus Wagon, Arcade, 1920s, painted and stenciled wood and cast iron, head of cowboy and words "Big Six Circus—Wild West" on side of wagon, 14 ½ ″ length.   *$250–$300*

Circus Band Wagon, Schoenhut Humpty Dumpty Circus, 1910, embossed and painted wood, four dappled horses, eight bandsmen, one driver in felt outfits, leather harnesses on horses, 40 ″ length.   *$10,000–$12,000*

Circus Band Wagon Wind-up Phonograph, Charles Belknap Manufacturing, circa 1910, painted red wood with gold trim, plays miniature 78-RPM record as wagon is pulled, plywood musicians atop wagon, 15 ″ length.   *$500–$600*

Circus Calliope, Kenton, 1940s, cast iron and sheet metal, two horses, driver, musician playing calliope, unlike Hubley calliope, there is no boiler, 14 ″ length.   *$550–$650*

Circus Set, Schoenhut Humpty Dumpty Circus, 1924, seven pieces, three clowns, two ladders, barrel and chair, columns 8 ″ height (also available in 4-, 5-, 8- and 10-piece sets). *$400–$500*

Circus With Tent, Schoenhut Humpty Dumpty Circus, 1910, painted wood figures, cloth tent, 18 pieces include ringmaster, lady bareback rider, clown, each 6 ½ ″ height, animals: elephant 6 ¼ ″ height, donkey and horse 8 ″ height, trapeze, two ladders 8 ½ ″ height, two chairs, barrel, hoop, two whips, tent, and flags.   *$1,000–$2,000*

Circus Wagon, Arcade, 1928, painted cast iron, two horses, driver is a large lion in elaborate cage, partially of pressed steel, approximately 14 ″ length.   *$1,500–$2,500*

Elephant With Clown in Cart, Harris, 1903, painted cast iron, seated clown holds reins of elephant, 7 ½ ″ length.   *$700–$800*

Horse-Drawn Cage Wagon, Schoenhut Humpty Dumpty Circus, 1910, painted wood, tin, and embossed cardboard, two dappled horses, driver, and caged leopard, 29 ″ length.   *$2,000–plus*

Polar Bear Cage, Kenton, 1940, painted cast iron and sheet metal, small, nonfunctional wheel on left leg of pair of white horses (later Kenton models feature movable balance wheel), 14 ″ length.   *$300–$350*

Show Wagon, Schoenhut Humpty Dumpty Circus, circa 1910, painted and embossed cardboard and wood, decorated panels depict bareback rider, tiger, and elephant, canopy top.
$1,000–$2,000

Teddy's Adventures in Africa, Schoenhut, 1910, painted wood animals and safari figures, 15 figures include Teddy Roosevelt, photographer, two native bearers, rhino, giraffe, elephant, alligator, hippo, zebra, and gorilla, box marked "T.R. Mombasa" (the gorilla is probably the most difficult Schoenhut animal figure to find).
$8,000–$10,000

CIRCUS CLOWNS

Balancing Clown, German, 1910, handpainted tin cloth-dressed clown on wood platform with balancing bar.
$600–$650

Balancing Toy Clown, German, 1915, handpainted composition wood, iron-weighted balancing bar, 11" height.
$550–$650

Carnival Strong Man, German, 1920s, clown hits gong on strength machine with large hammer, 4½" length.
$100–$150

Cirko Clown Cyclist, maker unknown, 1924, lithographed circus figure appears on large wheel of high-wheeler, clown wears high peaked cap, 8½" height.
$300–$400

Clown and Black on See-Saw, Watrous Mfg., Co., 1905, tin and cast-iron bell pull toy, 5¾" length.
$300–$500

Clown and Goat, German, 1920s, lithographed tin mechanical with cloth clown outfit, clown has whip, goat butts cart from behind.
$200–$250

Clown Balancing Bears, German, 1900s, painted and stenciled tin, clown is on back, resting on platform with feet in air balancing a spinning ball with bar, at each end of bar is a bear suspended in a swing, small bells at each end of bar ring as toy is activated, 11½" height.
$1,000–$2,000

Clown Barrel Walker, Chein, 1940s, lithographed tin mechanical (variation of Chein's Popeye and Barnacle Bill toys), 7¾" height.
$150–$200

Clown Bell Toy, gong bell, 1910, clown rides in cart pulled by pig.
$350–$450

Clown Cello Player, maker unknown, 1920s, clown saws away at cello, music comes from seven-note disc under chair, 8″ height. $400–$450

Clown Circling Flag, maker unknown, circa 1900, double-motion painted tin mechanical, clowns on three-wheeler circle flag as toy runs erratically across floor. $300–$350

Clown Dog Trainer, French, circa 1914, clown has switch, small dog rides in swing, poodle dog dances on hind feet, 8″ height. $300–$350

Clown Doing Handstand, German, circa 1915, painted tin, cloth costume, mechanical, 9″ height. $350–$400

Clown Drummer, German, 1900s, handpainted tin mechanical of dressed clown beating on large drum (with actual drum skin), hand-crank mechanical, 6″ height. $200–$250

Clown Four-Piece Set, Schoenhut, 1924, painted wood, jointed, 8″ height, clown with chair, 5″ height, ladder, 12″ height, barrel, 2¾″ height, full-size figures. $75–$125

Clown Hand Car ("Hoky Poky"), Wyandotte, 1920s, two clowns pump handle, key-wind mechanical, lithographed tin, 5¾″ length. $100–$150

Clown Hoop Toy, German, circa 1910, tin mechanical, figure revolves inside hoop, 6½″ height. $550–$600

Clown on Horse Rocker, German, 1900s, clockwork mechanical, papier-mâché, cloth dressed, wood rockers, 8″ height. $250–$300

Clown on Ladder, German, 1900s, composition tin, wood, and cloth, crank activated, beats cymbals together, 11½″ height. $300–$350

Clown on Ladder, maker unknown, circa 1915, composition wood with cloth costume, hand crank brings cymbals together as clown tumbles on ladder, 11½″ height. $250–$300

Clowns on Mechanical See-Saw, maker unknown, 1910, painted tin, cloth outfits. $200–$250

Clowns With Merry-Go-Round, German, 1920s, lithographed tin mechanical, pull toy, clown rings gong and small carousel revolves. $500–$600

Clown With Monkey on Railroad Baggage Truck, maker unknown, 1904, painted tin mechanical, clown pushes truck and monkey bangs cymbals. $450–$500

Clown With Pig, German, circa 1910, painted tin mechanical, 8″ length. $350–$400

Clown on Pig Rocker, German, late 1890s, painted tin clockwork, mechanical, activates clown to wave arms, pig to wiggle ears, has swinging pendulum weight, 6″ length. $700–$800

Clown Playing Harp, German, 1910, painted tin, cloth outfit, head and arms move as if strumming harp, 8″ height.
                    $500–$600

Clown and Poodle, Gong Bell, 1903, clown swings dog who rings bell attached to muzzle, cast metal, painted, 8 1/4″ length.
                    $350–$450

Clown Push Chime Toy, Watrous Mfg. Co., 1905, tin and nickeled wheels and bells, on wooden stick, 5″ length. $250–$300

Clown Pushing Another Clown in Wheelbarrow, German, 1920s, lithographed tin mechanical, 4 1/2″ length. $450–$550

Clown Quartette, German (possibly Guntermann), circa 1915, painted clockwork mechanical, musicians wear red, green, yellow, blue on yellow base, 11 3/4″ length. $1,200–$1,400

Clown Riding Bareback, Ives, 1893, tin painted clown with cloth outfit stands up in saddle of horse, clockwork mechanical.
                    $2,000–plus

Clown Riding Hog, Muller & Kadeder, circa 1900, painted tin mechanical, figures ride on small three-wheeled platform, clown holds on for dear life by grabbing pig's ears. $450–$500

Clown Roly-Poly, Schoenhut, 1920s, papier-mâché, handpainted, 15″ height. $350–$400

Clown With Stubborn Pig, German, circa 1914, painted tin mechanical, clown attempts to lead pig (on pair of wheels) by ears, other versions of toy appeared in 1920s, 7 1/2″ length.
                    $250–$300

Clowns Throwing Ball, German, 1920s, two clowns seated on platform toss ball back and forth (may be penny toy), 3 1/2″ length. $150–$200

Clown With Trained Poodle, German circa 1900, painted tin, clockwork mechanical, clown rides poodle which is on heavy cast-iron wheels. $400–$450

Clown With Trick Dogs, German, 1904, painted tin mechanical on platform, clown and poodle turn rope as smaller terrier type jumps rope. $300–$350

Clown Trick Mule Target Game, W. S. Reed, 1915, lithographed paper-on-wood, rolling balls at target activates mule to unseat clown, 22″ length. $1,000–$2,000

Clown With Trick Poodle, maker unknown (possibly Guntermann), 1904, figures on platform, painted tin mechanical, clown in cloth outfit, seated in tilted chair, is pushed back and forth by poodle wearing peaked clown's cap, clown tosses celluloid ball, 8 ½″ length. $350–$400

Clown Violinist, Schuco, 1920s, cloth covered tin mechanical, 4 ½″ height. $150–$200

Clown on Wheels With Monkey, maker unknown, 1910, painted tin mechanical, clown on small cart pursued by monkey.
                              $250–$300

Comical Clowns in Roadster, maker unknown, 1920s, lithographed tin mechanical, three clowns, one drives, the other pair beat each other on head with umbrellas. $250–$300

Dandy Jim Clown, Strauss, 1920s, 10″ height, clown dances on roof and plays cymbals. $250–$300

Donkey-Drawn Clown Chariot, Schoenhut, 1920s, wood, 16″ length. $1,400–$1,600

Forepaugh's Trained Elephants, maker unknown, 1904, clown on unicycle moves whip as elephants, also on wheels, move along floor on hind legs, approximately 8″ height. $500–$600

Hanging Dancing Clown, Ives, 1900s, cloth costume, lead tin, wood figure (Ives box is marked No. 22–11, ''Mechanical Hanging Dancer''), 10 ½″ length. $2,000–$3,000

Le Clown Orchestra, Fernand Martin (French), circa 1900, clown wears bells on hands, feet, and head. $500–$600

Mule Clowns, possibly Ives, tin clockwork figures on wooden base, clowns riding mules on opposite ends of wire shaft, lots of bucking and rearing. $2,000–$3,000

Pair Clowns With Instruments, Guntermann, circa 1915, hand-painted tin, larger clown plays trombone, smaller figure in barrel toots trumpet, 9 ½″ height.   *$600–$700*

Tom Twist, F. Strauss, 1920s, lithographed tin mechanical, painted clown with bells for earrings, flat cap (variation of Boob McNut comic toy by Strauss) so toy can be turned upside down and Tom dances on head.   *$200–$300*

Tumbling Clowns, German, circa 1910, painted tin mechanical, front clown grabs barbell, back clown holds his partner's feet in the air and pushes along, 5⅞″ height.   *$800–$1,000*

Unique Artie, Unique Art, 1920s, lithographed tin mechanical, clown rides crazy car, small dog sits on hood, 9 ½″ height.

$200–$300

"What's It?," F. Strauss, 1927, lithographed tin, clown with high peaked hat pilots speedboat on wheels (two large center wheels, two small pivoting wheels at each end), 9 ½″ length.

$200–$300

Comic and Character Toys

* * *

Four visionaries are credited with launching the comic art form that inspired a legion of lovable, laughable toys and games in their images. James Swinnerton created a jolly menagerie of animal characters in "Little Bears and Tigers." Richard Outcault made the first real comic strip breakthrough in America with "The Yellow Kid" in *The New York Sunday World* in 1896. Rudolph Dirks originated "The Katzenjammer Kids" for the Hearst Syndicate a year later. Fred B. Opper introduced the eternal scapegoat, "Happy Hooligan," via the color comics section of the *New York Journal* in 1896. Outcault's artistry with the pen was soon matched by his marketing acumen. At the 1904 St. Louis World's Fair, Outcault set up shop with the express purpose of merchandising the services of his latest creation, "Buster Brown," and succeeded in signing up hundreds of licensees. Fontaine Fox, also a marketing innovator, laid the foundation for numerous franchises when he created "Toonerville Folks" in 1915. The transformation from the comic pages to exceptional, colorful lithographed and painted tin and cast iron has continued uninterrupted to this day. The advent of the Golden Age of Radio in the 1920s and 1930s inspired another toy parade recreating actual real-life personalities in their various roles, including Joe "Wanna Buy a Duck?" Penner, Ed "Fire Chief" Wynn, and the irrepressible "Amos 'n' Andy," created by Freeman Gosden and Charles Correll. From the movie lots of Hollywood would emerge Charlie Chaplin, W. C. Fields, Felix the Movie Cat, Betty Boop, and Shirley Temple. The 1940s and

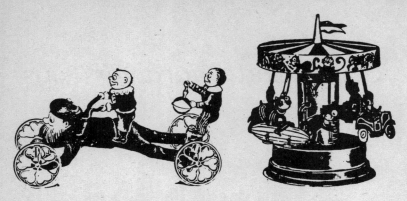

Two "Inner Circle" comic toys: "Captain and the Kids" bell toy, Gong Bell Manufacturing Co., $2,000 plus; Felix musical carousel, German (probably Nifty), 1927, $1,500–$2,000.

1950s were dominated by Edgar Bergen (and his sidekicks, Charlie McCarthy and Mortimer Snerd), "The Lone Ranger," "Tom Corbett, Space Cadet," "Radio Orphan Annie," and "Sky King." TV in the 1950s spawned its "Captain Video," "Uncle Miltie," "The Honeymooners," and "Howdy Doody"—all making the transition from the tube to tin, composition, and plastic playthings. The super heroes, "Buck Rogers," "Flash Gordon," "Superman," and "Captain Marvel," may be upstaged today by Han Solo, Luke Skywalker, Captain Kirk, and He-Man, but the early movie serial characters and comic heroes were the prototypes of what we have today. Comic toys are assured some form of immortality as nearly three generations of toy collectors keep steadfastly on their trail.

AGGIE

A comic strip moppet from "Reg'lar Fellers" by Gene Byrnes in 1923.

Aggie, lithograph tin, Nifty, 1925–1926.   *$400–$500*

Reg'lar Fellers Bowling Game, Selchow & Righter, 1920s, figures of heavy cardboard with wood base, 10″ height.

$200–$300

Alphonse "The Nodders" Donkey Cart, Kenton, 1911, $600–$700.

ALPHONSE AND GASTON

Comic strip characters created by Fred B. Opper in 1896, whose names became synonymous with exaggerated politeness. ("After you, my dear Gaston. No, after *you*, my dear Alphonse.")

Alphonse and Gaston Auto, Kenton, 1910, cast iron, yellow and orange with gold trim, 8″ length.   *$1,000–$1,200*

Alphonse Nodder in Circus Cart, cast iron, bright colors, figure is interchangeable with Happy Hooligan, another Opper character. *Note:* Both the figures and cart have been recast in recent years, the repro version has the name "Nodders" cast on the donkey pulling cart, original version has "The Nodders."
                                                   $800–$900

AMOS 'N' ANDY

Two radio characters created by Freeman Gosden and Charles Correll in 1928. Amos 'n' Andy also appeared in a comic strip, movies, and TV (1950–1955).

Amos 'n' Andy Walkers, $400–$500 each.

Andrew H. Brown Wood-Jointed Figure, 1930s, manufacturer unknown, Andy wears orange derby and smokes a cigar.
$40–$50

Fresh Air Taxicab, Dent Hardware, cast iron, 1930, 6″ length, this toy has sparked considerable controversy among collectors, as it probably never advanced past prototype stage; samples of the toy were assembled from married parts a few years ago after a "find" in Dent's factory. $500–$600

Fresh Air Taxicab, Marx, 1930, litho tin, wind-up, cab runs with erratic, jerky motion, 8″ length (two versions: one with head-

Amos 'n' Andy Fresh Air Taxicab, Marx, 1930, $600–$700.

lights, one without headlights but with inscription, "Andy Brown Prez, Amos Jones Driver" on door); make certain that hand crank, meter flag, and horseshoe radiator cap are intact and all three are there for toy to be complete.   *$600–$700*

Sparklers, German, early 1930s, litho tin with glass eyes that light up when squeezing plunger, each.   *$1,500–$2,000*

Walking Toys, Marx, 1930, litho tin wind-ups, 12″ height (deluxe models featured rolling eyes and command 10–20% higher prices), each.   *$500–$600*

BARNACLE BILL

A comic figure inspired by the 1920s song hit, "I'm Barnacle Bill the Sailor."

Barnacle Bill in the Barrel, Chein, 1930s, litho, 6″ height (both this toy and the Barnacle Bill Walking Figure, by Chein, incorporated the same dies for Popeye versions, which are more highly prized by comic collectors).   *$100–$200*

Barnacle Bill in a Rowboat, manufacturer unknown, 1930s, tin litho wind-up.   *$700–$800*

Barnacle Bill Walking Figure, Chein, 1930s, litho tin wind-up, 6″ height.   *$150–$250*

BARNEY GOOGLE

A cartoon character that first appeared in syndication in 1919 and was created by Billy DeBeck. Also inspired the Billy Rose song hit in the 1920s, "Barney Google With the Goo-Goo-Googly Eyes."

Barney Google Riding Sparkplug, Nifty, 1924, litho tin wind-up, 7½″ height.   *$1,000–$2,000*

Barney Google Scooter Race, German, 1924, litho tin wind-up, Barney on scooter, Sunshine is jockey aboard Sparkplug.   *$2,000–$2,500*

Barney Google and Sparkplug, Schoenhut, late 1920s, wood-jointed figures with cloth outfit and horse blanket, each.   *$300–$400*

Barney Google Riding Sparkplug, Nifty, 1920s, $1,500–$2,000.

Barney Google and Sparkplug Platform Toy, Nifty, 1924, litho tin wind-up, variation of racing toy, Barney rides up front on scooter, Sparkplug's barn in rear shows Snowflake drawing water, Rudy eating oats, and Sparkplug trying to jump over Dutch doors, only one known example, 9¼" length.   *$3,000–$4,000*

Rudy the Ostrich, Nifty, 1924, tin wind-up, litho body with handpainted tail, neck, and body, Rudy was Barney's pesky little friend, 9" height.   *$1,000–$1,200*

Sparkplug Platform Pull Toy, manufacturer unknown, 1930s, wood toy hinged in two places to create greater animation, 9" length.   *$100–$200*

BETTY BOOP

In the early 1930s this pixy-like character starred in animated movie cartoons created by Max Fleischer. Later she appeared in a comic strip as a movie queen. A contemporary wooden and plexiglass Betty Boop, 5 feet high, sold for $1,100 at the Atlanta Toy Museum Auction in October 1986.

Betty Boop and Bimbo Racer, Keeneye, Inc., 1932. *$600–$700*

Betty Boop, CK, Japan, design and copyright by Fleischer Studios, celluloid w/tin base, 7 ½ " height, $250–$300.

Betty Boop Standing Figure, CK, Japan, 1930, celluloid figure on tin base, 7 " height. $500–$600

Betty Boop Wood-Jointed Figure, manufacturer unknown, 1930s. $300–$400

BLONDIE

In the early 1930s Chic Young created this long running family comic strip; later "Blondie" was adapted to radio, a movie series in the 1940s, and a TV series in the 1950s.

Blondie's Jalopy, Marx, late 1930s, litho tin wind-up, open sedan with Dagwood and Baby Dumpling in front seat (variation of Marx's Mortimer Snerd Private Car), 15 " length. $650–$750

Dagwood Musical Sandwich, Midwest Corp., Milwaukee, 1947, 5 " length. $50–$75

Dagwood the Driver, Marx, 1935, tin litho wind-up, pictures of Blondie, Daisy the dog, and Cookie are litho'd on side panels of auto, 8″ length (copyright dates appear on the car as 1930, 1934, 1935, but since new baby Cookie didn't arrive in the Bumstead household until 1935, we assume the latter date to be the manufacture date). $450–$550

Dagwood the Pilot, Marx, late 1930s, tin litho wind-up, 7″ length (variation of Marx's Popeye the Pilot, but Dagwood is not as easy to come by). $650–$750

BOOB McNUTT

Rube Goldberg, who is best remembered for his wacky, complicated cartoon inventions, created Boob McNutt in a syndicated strip in 1918.

Boob McNutt, Schoenhut, mid-1920s, wood-jointed, cloth outfit, 9″ height. $800–$900

Boob McNutt Walker, Strauss, 1925, litho tin wind-up, 9½″ height, there are two variations of this toy: one shows him with tiny hat atop his head, another has hat upside down so that Boob could perform on his head. $500–$600

BONZO

A clever little spotted Boston bulldog appearing in a Hearst syndicated comic strip created by an English cartoonist, G.E. Studdy.

Bonzo on Scooter, S.G. (a German manufacturer), circa 1930s, litho tin wind-up. $400–$500

BRINGING UP FATHER

Maggie and Jiggs, the stars of this comic strip created by George McManus in 1913.

Jiggs and His Jazz Car, Nifty, 1924, litho tin wind-up, King Features Service, Inc., copyright on side of auto, 6½″ length. $800–$900

Maggie and Jiggs Family Squabble, Gebruder Einfalt (Nifty), 1924, litho tin wind-up, figures joined by 2″ connecting strip which undulates when toy is activated to give illusion of Maggie and Jiggs attacking each other, 7″ length. $1,000–$2,000

Maggie and Jiggs Squeeze Toy, German, late 1920s, tin with steel handles, squeeze handles and couple seems to be fighting. $400–$500

Maggie and Jiggs Standing Figures, Schoenhut, mid-1920s, wood-jointed with cloth outfits, Maggie has a rolling pin and Jiggs a bucket of his favorite corned beef and cabbage, each. $400–$500

BUCK ROGERS

The first of the great science fiction cartoon characters stepped into the 25th century in 1929. Buck was created by John Dille, drawn by Lt. Dick Calkins, and written by Phil Nowlan. Buck, Wilma, and their fellow astronauts also provided their share of thrills in movie serials and in the 1970s on TV.

Buck Rogers Rocket Police Patrol Ship, Marx, 1939, litho tin wind-up, shoots sparks. $300–$400

Rocket Ship, Marx, 1934, litho tin wind-up, shoots sparks, 12″ length. $200–$300

Rocket Ships, Tootsietoys, 1930s, series of three pot metal models: Venus Duo Destroyer, Battlecruiser, and Flash Blast Attack Ship with names embossed on painted metal, 5″ length, each. $200–$250

BUSTER BROWN

One of the earliest comic characters, Buster Brown was created by Richard Outcault in 1902; his faithful companion was a somewhat mean-looking talking bulldog named Tige. Although they've been funny page dropouts since just after World War I, they continue to be popular advertising spokesmen for a variety of products.

Bob and Bruno (a knockoff version), Gong Bell, pull toy, cast iron. $800–$1,200

Buster Brown in Cart (variation), manufacturer unknown, believed 1920s, cast-iron figures and sheet metal cart, hand-painted in bright colors. $600–$700

Buster Brown in Cart Pulled by Tige, manufacturer unknown, 1910, cast-iron two-piece casting, painted all silver, 7″ length. $600–$700

Buster Brown With Dog, Muller & Kadeder, 1906, tin litho wind-up, figures pull one another up on string-pulley mechanism, 13″ height. $1,000–$2,000

Buster Brown and Monkey on Seesaw, German, handpainted tin rocking toy, 1909, figures roll celluloid ball to each other, 9¼″ height. $1,000–$2,000

Buster With Poodle, Muller & Kadeder, 1900s, litho tin wind-up, figures ring bell attached to lantern post, 7½″ height.
                                                    $2,000–plus

Buster Brown Roly-Poly, Schoenhut, 1910, papier-mâché, turning head, 17″ height. $450–$550

Buster Brown and Tige, A.C. Williams, early 1900s, cast-iron still bank, gold finish, 5″ height. $100–$200

Buster Brown and Tige, Watrous, 1905, cast-iron bell toy, nickeled wheels, 7¼″ length. $1,000–$2,000

Buster Brown and Tige Cashier Bank, Buster appears as cashier at one window, Tige appears at the other three windows, words "Security," "Paying Teller," and "Fidelity" appear under Tige, green, gold, with white dial for registering coin input, 5″ height. $600–$700

Horseshoe, black horse framed by gold horseshoe, bust of Buster Brown appears above arch in horse's neck, Tige sits at base of horseshoe, 4″ height. $300–$400

BUTTERCUP

This cartoon character was pride and joy of the comic strip couple "Toots and Casper," created by Jimmy Murphy in 1918.

Buttercup and Spare Ribs Platform Toy, Nifty, mid-1920s, litho tin wind-up, a kneeling Buttercup seems to be grooming, with a whisk broom, her pet dog Spare Ribs, 8″ length.   *$600–$700*

Crawling Buttercup, German (no manufacturer name), painted tin wind-up, has Jimmy Murphy copyright, 8″ length.   *$700–$800*

CAPTAIN MARVEL

Billy Batson, who was transformed into crime fighter Captain Marvel upon uttering the magic word "Shazam" and invoking a lightning bolt, first appeared with Fawcett Publications comic books in 1941 and continued until 1953, when National Comics brought legal action, claiming that the Captain infringed on their Superman copyrights. Charles C. Beck created Captain Marvel and Otto Binder authored the feature.

Captain Marvel Lightning Racing Cars, copyright Fawcett Publications, 1948, set of four racing cars with the Captain in flight litho'd on cars, for the complete set.   *$100–$200*

CHARLIE CHAPLIN

The Little Tramp achieved his greatest fame in the movies, beginning with the Keystone Studio in 1913 and spanning over 50 years. Charlie also inspired a comic strip which first appeared in 1915 and was drawn by several cartoonists, including Elzie Segar of "Popeye" fame, Ed Carey, and Gus Mager.

Charlie Chaplin, litho paper-on-wood figure, on wood stand, German, 1917, swings with outstretched arms on post.
$450–$550

Charlie Chaplin Bell Ringer, believed Gong Bell, 1917, cast-iron figure with sheet metal three-wheel vehicle.   *$800–$900*

Charlie Chaplin Boxer Champion, 1915, tin with felt covering on face, inspired by movie "The Champion" made with Essanay in 1915.   *$1,000–$2,000*

Charlie Chaplin Dancing Toy, German, 1920s, 5½″ × 7″ paper over tin box with jointed figure of Charlie simulating dancing.   *$400–$500*

Charlie Chaplin Squeak Toy, German, 1917, composition head with cloth body, squeaks when bellows is pressed. *$500–$600*

Charlie Chaplin Squeeze Toy, German, early 1920s, litho tin, when plunger is pushed, arm raises and cymbals strike, Charlie holds a cat in left hand.   *$400–$500*

Charlie Chaplin Standing Figure, German, 1920s, celluloid, Chaplin assumes famous stance with one hand on hip, the other holding a cane.   *$300–$400*

Charlie Chaplin Standing Figure, German, 1920s, litho tin with cast-iron feet wind-up, rocks back and forth at waist, carries little wire cane, 8¾″ height.   *$700–$800*

Charlie Chaplin Wooden Figure, French, 1920s.   *$300–$350*

Standing Charlie Chaplin Spinning Cane, Schuco, 1920s, tin with felt covering on face, cloth outfit, 6½″ height. *$750–$850*

Whistling Charlie Chaplin Carved Wooden Figure, German, 1920s, Charlie whistles "How Dry I Am."   *$600–$700*

CHARLIE McCARTHY

An unlikely duo of a ventriloquist named Edgar Bergen and his wooden sidekick, Charlie McCarthy, dominated the airwaves beginning in 1936 to 1948 on the "Chase and Sanborn Hour" on NBC (they switched to CBS with Coca Cola as sponsor for another eight years before calling it quits in 1956). In 1939, Bergen added a companion for Charlie, the country bumpkin Mortimer Snerd. The pair starred in numerous movies, a syndicated comic strip drawn by Ben Batsford, and Whitman Big Little Books.

Many comic toy collections include a variety of Charlie and Mortimer marionettes, with composition heads and cloth bodies (in various sizes from 17″ to 20″) at $200–$250. The best of these, by Effenbee Doll Co., featured Charlie as Sherlock Holmes, a cowboy, or a French legionnaire.

Effenbee also produced a W.C. Fields doll, inspired by his frequent guest appearances on the show ($450–$500). Ideal Co. produced a Mortimer Doll that featured flexible hands and feet ($250–$300). A McCarthy endorsed hand-puppet with composition head sells in the $35–$50 range.

Charlie McCarthy Benzine Buggy, Marx, 1940s.   *$300–$400*

Charlie McCarthy Drummer, Marx, 1940s, litho tin wind-up, pushes bass drum on three-wheel car, 8″ height.   *$500–$600*

Charlie McCarthy and Mortimer Snerd Private Car, Marx, 1939, striped roadster with big bumpers (see also Blondie Jalopie, a Marx variant), Charlie's favorite saying, "We'll mow you down," appears on driver's door, 15″ length; in 1983, this toy with original box sold for $1,400 at a Lloyd Ralston Auction, then a record for any toy of 1940s vintage.   *$900–$1,100*

Charlie McCarthy Still Bank, manufacturer unknown, 1940s, slush-cast painted, this is a knockoff version, as there is no indication on the bank that this was one of Edgar Bergen's Charlie McCarthy, Inc., endorsed toys.   *$100–$200*

"Charlie Strut," Marx, 1940s, litho tin wind-up, mouth goes up and down as he waddles, 8″ height.   *$100–$200*

Mortimer Snerd Benzine Buggy, Marx, 1940s, litho tin wind-up.   *$200–$300*

Mortimer Snerd Drummer, Marx, 1940s, litho tin wind-up, pushes bass drum on three-wheel cart, 8″ height.   *$350–$450*

"Mortimer Strut," Marx, 1940s, litho tin wind-up, hat moves up and down when activated, 8″ height.   *$200–$300*

DICK TRACY

Created by Chester Gould in 1931, "Dick Tracy" has the distinction of being the first comic strip to introduce blood and gore to its legions of readers.

B.O. Plenty Standing Figure, Marx, 1940s, litho tin wind-up, shuffles along and cap tilts—a variation of Mortimer Snerd Strut wind-up, another weird character from the strip, B.O. holds his baby Sparkle Plenty in one arm, 8½″ height.   *$75–$100*

Dick Tracy Automatic Police Station, Marx, 1940s, tin litho with swinging doors, 8½″ length, includes 7½″ length friction squad car which shoots sparks.   *$75–$100*

Dick Tracy Bonnie Braids Game, Charmore Co., Paterson, N.J., "Watch the Nursemaid Take Bonnie Braids for a Ride," United Artists Synd., 1951, after two decades of courtship, Tracy finally married Tess Trueheart and Bonnie Braids was their progeny.   *$70–$80*

Dick Tracy Riot Car, Marx, 1939, tin litho wind-up with battery-operated probe light and siren, 11″ length, also a 7″ length size. $100–$200

> *Note:* A 16″ length Riot Car, which featured plastic figures of Tracy and his partner, Sam Ketchum, was manufactured by Marx in the 1950s ($100–$125 range).

ED WYNN

Wynn was an old-time vaudevillian, billed as "The Perfect Fool," who made a successful transition to radio in 1932 as "The Texaco Fire Chief."

Ed Wynn Firehouse, Schoenhut, 1933–1934, litho cardboard and wood, rubber-band-powered horse-drawn toy driven by Chief Wynn, shoots vehicle out of firehouse when lever is pressed, 9½″ length (this toy, in pristine condition, sold for $375 at the Atlanta Toy Museum Auction in October 1986). $200–$300

FELIX THE CAT

Originated as Felix the Movie Cat, a star in animated movie cartoons in 1920, his creator was Pat Sullivan. Three years later, Felix had his own comic strip syndicated by King Features. Often mistaken for the more cerebral Krazy Kat. Nifty made several toys for both Felix and Krazy using identical dies, further adding to the confusion.

Felix on the Scooter, Nifty, 1931, $350–$500; Happy Hooligan Police Patrol, Kenton, 1911, cast iron, $2,000 plus.

Felix the Bowler, Nifty, 1931, tin litho, miniature alley with pins. $700–$800

Felix Hood Ornament on Roadster, Carl Bubb, 1930s, litho tin wind-up, 6″ length. $1,000–$2,000

Felix and Mice Platform on Wheel Toy, Nifty, 1931, pull toy, 7 ½″ length. $500–$600

Felix the Movie Cat Sparkler, Nifty, 1931, 5″ height.
$300–$350

Felix Musical Carousel, German, manufacturer unknown, 1927, litho tin, little Felixes ride in miniature autos, zeppelins, 7 ½″ height, 5 ½″ diameter. $1,500–$2,000

Felix on the Scooter, Nifty, 1931, tin litho wind-up.
$350–$500

Felix With Umbrella, manufacturer unknown, cast-iron, painted figure with nodder head attached with spring steel.
$400–$500

Felix Wagon, Nifty, 1931, tin litho, Felix pulls two-wheeler.
$500–$600

Jointed Felix, Nifty, 1931, wood two-dimensional figure.
$200–$300

Speedy Felix, Roadster Pull Toy, Nifty, 1931, litho wood.
$200–$300

Walking Felix, German, 1930s, has name, copyright dates, and Sullivan's name on band around waist, painted tin, walks with swaying motion, a rather crude visualization of Felix.
$200–$300

> Note: A knockoff version of this toy was produced by Gama in Germany, 6 ½″ height, circa 1929, featured arms raised rather than folded. It was marketed as "Comical Cat." $200–$300

Wood-Jointed Felix Three-Dimensional Figures, Schoenhut, 1932, sizes from 4″ height to 12″ height:
smaller versions. $75–$100
larger versions. $100–$250

Worried Felix, German, late 1920s, manufacturer unknown, celluloid figure. $400–$500

FLASH GORDON

Along with Prince Valiant, this 1934 strip by Alex Raymond has been acknowledged as one of the best drawn of all comic strips. Raymond also created Secret Agent X-O, Jungle Jim, and Rip Kirby before his untimely death in 1956. Flash Gordon emerged as a TV show in the early 1950s starring Buster Crabbe.

Flash Gordon Radio Repeater Pistol, Marx, 1936, tin litho.
$100–$150

Flash Gordon Rocket Fighter, Marx, 1939, 12″ length, tin litho, shoots sparks. $250–$350

Flash Gordon Signal (Space) Pistol, Marx, 1936, tin litho.
$100–$200

FOXY GRANDPA

One of the earliest comic strips in the American idiom, along with "Buster Brown," "The Yellow Kid," and the "Katzenjammer Kids." Created by Carl Schultze, he began in the *New York Herald* in 1900 and was finally discontinued in 1927.

Foxy Grandpa Bell Ringer, manufacturer unknown, early 1900s, cast iron, Foxy sits sedately at reins of three-wheeled cart featuring two figures of running boys on front wheel.
$1,200–$1,400

Foxy Grandpa Hat Flipper Toy, manufacturer unknown, early 1900s, cast iron with tin hat, lever is pushed to attempt putting hat on Foxy. $1,000–$2,000

Foxy Grandpa Still Bank, Wing, Chicago, Foxy is in black suit and wears derby, cast iron, originally marketed as "Grandpa Bank," 5¾″ height. $200–$300

Foxy in Horse-Drawn Cart, Harris, cast iron, there are matching versions with figures of Gloomy Gus and Happy Hooligan standing in cart, 7¼″ length. $1,000–$2,000

Foxy Nodder, Kenton, 1910, cast-iron painted nodder in cart, a companion piece to Kenton's Happy Hooligan and Alphonse

Nodders, the words "The Nodders" appear on horse's blanket, 7″ length. $700–$800

Foxy Nodder, Kenton, 1910, circus cart, also features Alphonse and Gloomy Gus, 11½″ length. $1,000–$2,000

Foxy Walker, German, early 1900s, handpainted, wheels on feet, tin wind-up action allows Foxy to simultaneously raise and lower arms as hinged legs open and close as toy moves across floor, 8″ height. $1,000–$2,000

Twin Nodder Toy, Foxy and Happy Hooligan cart, driven by Gloomy Gus, Kenton Mfg. Co., 1900s, drawn by two horses, 16″ length. $2,000–plus

GASOLINE ALLEY

A strip that mirrors small town life in the U.S.A. was launched on Valentine's Day, 1921, by Frank King. The main characters were Uncle Walt and Auntie Blossom. Skeezix, who later became the main focus of this longrunning strip (it continues to this day), was found abandoned on Walt's doorstep.

Uncle Walt in Roadster, Dowst (Tootsietoy), 1932, one of series of five comic miniatures, cast metal, painted in red. $200–$300

GLOOMY GUS

Another Fred Opper creation, Gloomy appeared in a number of "Happy Hooligan" strips opposite his hapless brother.

Gloomy Gus Cart, Harris, 1903, cast iron, this version with Gloomy standing also featured Happy and Foxy, 7¼″ length. $1,000–$2,000

Gloomy Gus Cast-Iron Cart, Harris, 1903, Gloomy is standing in horse-drawn cart, 14″ length. $1,000–$2,000

Gloomy and Happy, Harris, 1903, in cast-iron cart with driver, 18″ length. $2,000–plus

THE GUMPS

This was the first comic strip to tell a serialized story and the first to deal with real people in real-life situations. Launched in 1917 by Joseph Medill Patterson, one of the owners of the *Chicago Tribune*, it was drawn by a *Tribune* staff artist, Robert Sidney Smith, who later became the first cartoonist to sign a million dollar contract.

A rather crudely drawn strip about a goat named Doc Yak and his son Yutch was the predecessor to the Andy Gump series. Sidney Smith had drawn Doc Yak from 1915–1917, a few years prior to the directive to create The Gumps. The only legacy from the Yak saga was the 348 license plate; Doc Yak had a little roadster that he bought for $3.48, which he considered such a bargain that the price became his plate number and a popular landmark of the strip.

Andy Gump Still Bank, Arcade, 1928, cast iron, same figure as used in Arcade's Andy Gump 348 Car, Andy sits on tree stump in two-piece casting, 4¼″ height.   *$1,000–$2,000*

Andy Gump Still Bank, manufacturer unknown, late 1920s, tin litho.   *$600–$700*

Andy Gump in 348 Car, Arcade, 1924, cast iron, there were three variations of this model: (1) nickel-plated figure, wheels, and 348 grill; (2) painted figure with green wheel covers and red hubs; (3) Andy wears a number of colors (as opposed to dark green in figure 2), including dark blue suit, wheels are white with green center and red hubs, red car chassis is trimmed in green, there is a 348 rear plate, painted like front grille, plus red crank, 6″ height, 7¼″ length.   *$600–$700*

Andy Gump 348 Car, Dowst (Tootsietoy), 1932, cast metal, one of six toys in Tootsietoy Funnies Series, figures moved up and down with deluxe models, also painted in bright colors, standard models were nonaction with simple color scheme, 2¾″ length (20% higher for deluxe version).   *$200–$300*

Andy Gump Wood-Jointed Standing Figure, Sidney Smith copyright.   *$100–$125*

Chester Gump in Pony Cart, Arcade, 1924, cast iron, 8″ length.   *$600–$700*

Old Doc Yak Still Bank (conversion), by Arcade, 1920s, cast iron, 6½" height. $1,000–plus

HAPPY HOOLIGAN

Another silly saga by Fred B. Opper (Alphonse and Gaston, Maude the Mule, Happy's brother Gloomy Gus). Happy Hooligan, with the red tin can hat, symbolized the eternal scapegoat. Introduced in new color comics section of the *New York Journal* in 1896.

Happy Hooligan Automobile Toy, N.N. Hill Brass, early 1900s, cast iron, bell-ringing open roadster (the rear end features what looks like a wood stove with stove pipe elbow), perhaps the most uncommon, highly prized of all comic toys, car is painted red, Happy wears yellow jacket with blue pants, 6½" length. $2,500–plus

Happy Hooligan Cast-Iron Cart, Harris, 1903, Happy stands in horse-drawn cart, 14" length. $1,000–$2,000

Happy Hooligan on Ladder, Schoenhut, 1924, wood jointed with cloth outfit. $600–$700

Happy Hooligan Nodder in Cart, Harris, 1903, cast iron (matching versions included Gloomy Gus and Foxy Grandpa), 7¼" length. $1,000–$1,200

Happy Hooligan Police Patrol, Kenton, 1911, cast iron, wagon is driven by Gloomy Gus, animated cop raps Happy on noggin with nightstick as toy is pulled along, one of the rarest classic comic toys, 17½" length. $2,000–plus

Happy Hooligan Roly-Poly, F. Opper copyright, manufacturer unknown, 1920s. $400–$500

Happy Hooligan Standing Figure, Schoenhut, 1924, wood jointed with cloth outfit. $700–$800

Happy Hooligan Walker, Chein, 1932, litho tin wind-up, Happy wears bright green coat with light green trousers and orange oversize shoes, 6" height. $500–$600

HAROLD LLOYD

This star of the silent film era made millions portraying a meek, mild-mannered character with large hornrimmed glasses who overcame obstacles that made strong men quail.

Harold Lloyd on the Telephone, German, 1920s, litho tin squeeze toy, by pushing plunger, as with sparkler versions, the same type of facial action is produced as with the Marx walker, 6″ height. $300–$400

Harold Lloyd Walker, Marx, 1925, litho tin wind-up, as toy waddles, top part of face moves up and down, creating smiles or frowns; although the toy does not bear Lloyd's name, the image is unmistakably his, 11″ height. $300–$400

Harold Lloyd Wind-Up, manufacturer unknown, 1920s, celluloid, vibrates when wound, holds straw hat in hand, 5″ height.
                                                                         $500–$600

HENRY

This comic strip by Carl Anderson began in the early 1930s, first in the *Saturday Evening Post* with sporadic appearances, then with King Features Syndicate. It violated all the rules by its complete absence of dialogue. (Henry was not only speechless, but expressionless.)

Henry the Acrobat, C.K., Japan, 1930s, celluloid, with steel swinging apparatus, wind-up. $400–$500

Henry and Henrietta Travelers, C.K., Japan, 1934, celluloid, with tin suitcase wind-up, 7¼″ height. $500–$600*

Henry and His Brother, C.K., Japan, celluloid with each figure on tin platform with wheels, wind-up. $400–$500

Henry Riding on Elephant's Trunk, C.K., Japan, 1930s, celluloid wind-up. $500–$600

HI-WAY HENRY

A bearded old gentleman and his rather hefty wife were featured in this comic strip drawn by Oscar Hitt in the early 1920s. Many consider Hi-Way Henry to be the most desirable of all comic toys.

*Sold for $575 at the Atlanta Toy Museum Auction.

Hi-Way Henry Auto, German, 1928, litho tin wind-up, front of car rears up as it travels, whirls about, and re-starts; Henry IV, a dog appearing in radiator, bobs in and out; a very delicate toy with many loose-fitting or removable parts; be sure the following are intact: stove, stove pipe, wash tub and board, clothesline; a tiny string runs from tiny hole in clothesline to headphones Mrs. Henry is wearing.   *$1,000–$2,000*

Hi-Way Henry Cross-Country Auto Game, late 1920s, litho cardboard.   *$200–$300*

HOPALONG CASSIDY

A popular cowboy movie idol played by William Boyd in over 50 feature films in the 1950s. Later, Hopalong inspired a TV series also starring Boyd.

Hopalong Cassidy Rocking Horse, Marx, early 1950s, litho tin wind-up, toy rocks when activated and Hoppy swings lariat astride his white horse, Topper, 11″ length.   *$200–$300*

HOWDY DOODY

This show reigned supreme among Saturday morning kiddie's TV fare from 1947–1960. Emceed by the show's orginator, Buffalo Bob Smith, "Howdy Doody" featured its namesake as a marionette, along with Phineas T. Bluster, Dilly Dally, Flub-a-Dub, and other Doodyville denizens. (Clarabelle the Clown was played by Bob Keeshan, who went on to fame in "Captain Kangaroo.")

To help date Howdy items (over 600 manufacturers received permission to license and distribute), use the following rule-of-thumb:

1948–1951, items marked Bob Smith or Martin Stone Associates
1951–1956, items marked Kagran Corp.
1956–1960, items marked California National Products (an NBC marketing division)
1960 to date, items marked NBC

Many collections also include the marionettes: Howdy Doody, Clarabelle, Phineas T. Bluster, Dilly Dally, Flub-a-Dub, Princess

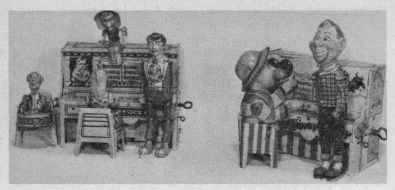

Dogpatch Band (*left*) and Howdy Doody Band, both by Unique Art,
1950s, $400–$500 each.

Summer-Fall-Winter-Spring, and Heidi Doody, with the latter
possibly the rarest of the seven. Price range: $100–$150.

Howdy Doody Band, Unique Art, early 1950s, litho tin wind-up
(variation of a host of piano toys by Unique as well as Marx).
$300–$400

Note: A smaller version of the Howdy Band appeared in the 1950s,
manufacturer unknown, $100–$150.

Howdy Doody Clock-a-Doodle, Japan, 1950s, marketed by Kagran Corp., distributed by Bengor Products, New York City, litho
on wood and plastic, features Howdy, Flub-a-Dub, the Princess,
and Clarabelle. $100–$200

Howdy Doody Phone-a-Doodle, Japan, 1950s, litho on wood and
plastic, features many of Doodyville gang. $100–$200

Howdy Doody Standing Figure, manufacturer unknown, 1950s,
wood jointed, 12½" height. $50–$100

JOE PALOOKA

The heavyweight boxing champion with heart of gold was
launched by Ham Fisher for the McNaught Syndicate in 1927.
Ironically, to our knowledge, there was no toy based on Palooka
himself, although there exists a small (4" height) wood-jointed
figure of the Champ ($35–$50).

Humphrey Mobile, Wyandotte, 1948, litho tin wind-up, Palooh-ka's best pal, Humphrey, pedals an ''outhouse-like'' version of a mobile home, 9″ length (be sure plastic smokestack is intact on this toy). $300–$350

Little Max Speshul #1, Sal Metal Prod., litho tin wind-up, Max rides scooter with shoeshine box, pictures of Palooka and Knobby, his manager, appear on side of box, 7″ length (Max was another admiring pal of Joe). $200–$300

JOE PENNER

This ex-burlesque comedian emerged as one of the most popular stars in early radio in the 1920s. Although perhaps the most obscure of the comics who inspired toys, Joe Penner was a household name across the United States until his untimely death in the early 1930s.

Joe Penner Astride Duck, manufacturer unknown, early 1930s, heavy die-cut litho'ed cardboard, rocks back and forth.
                                        $100–$125

Joe Penner and Goo Goo the Duck, Marx, early 1930s, litho tin wind-up, a variation of Marx's Popeye and the Parrot Cages wind-up with several ingenious additions, Penner's hat flips up as he waddles and a cigar moves around in his mouth, the famous Penner line, ''Wanna buy a duck?'' is litho'ed on a cage with three ducks, 8″ height. $250–$350

KATZENJAMMER KIDS

Providing perfect counterpoint to the prissy little Buster Brown were two devilish offspring, Hans and Fritz, created by Rudolph Dirks in 1897 for the Hearst syndicate. Dirks left Hearst's *New York Journal* in 1912 and was forced to leave the title to his strip. While another cartoonist, H.H. Knerr, picked up the strip at the *Journal*, Dirks resumed at the *World* with his own version called ''The Captain and The Kids.'' Both strips co-existed for over 80 years. Dirks' characters often made guest appearances in the ''Alphonse and Gaston'' strip and vice versa.

Captain and The Kids Bellringer, Gong Bell, 1912, painted cast iron, Fritz moves back and forth, ringing bell as toy is pulled, the captain is sprawled out and Hans rides his backside.

$10,000–plus

Katzenjammer Nodders, German, 1910, papier-mâché and wood, Mama and Fritz figures, 9 ½ " height, each. $500–$600

Mama Katzenjammer in Donkey Cart, believed made by Kenton, early 1900s, painted cast iron, donkey kicks up hind legs.

$900–$1,000

Mama Katzenjammer Standing Figure, German, 1910, papier-mâché with cloth dress and apron, 11 ½ " height. $400–$500

KRAZY KAT

In perhaps the most literate of all comic strips, Krazy Kat, Ignatz the mouse, and Offisa B. Pupp acted out one of our culture's most macabre love triangles against a surreal backdrop of Arizona desert country. Created by George Harriman in 1901, the strip continued until the cartoonist's death in 1944.

Many Krazy Kat collections often include the stuffed dolls Krazy and Ignatz, created by Knickerbocker Toy Co., New York

Little Orphan Annie Skipping Rope, Marx, 1930s, $400–$500; Ignatz Mouse on Tricycle, Chein, 1932, $350–$500; Mutt and Jeff Playing Leapfrog, German, 1920s, $2,000 plus.

City, in 1931. Ignatz bears a striking resemblance to Mickey Mouse. These price between $200–$250 each.

Ignatz Mouse on Tricycle, Chein, 1932, litho tin pull toy; Ignatz bangs cymbals as toy is pulled. *$300–$400*

Ignatz Standing Figure, manufacturer unknown, 1930s, wood-jointed toy. *$100–$200*

Krazy Kat on a Scooter, Nifty, 1927 or 1928, painted tin wind-up (variation of Nifty's Felix the Cat toy), 8″ length.
$400–$500

Krazy Kat Wheeled Platform Toy, Nifty, early 1930s, litho tin, toy features noisemaker which emits squeaking sound when pulled, two Ignatz mice appear in front of platform, 7½″ length. *$500–$600*

LI'L ABNER

This comic strip dealing with a hillbilly family, the Yokums, was created by Al Capp in 1934. The sharply satirical strip that absorbed Sadie Hawkins Day into our American folklore produced a rich gallery of characters—from Moonbeam McSwine to Stupifyin' Jones, Jack S. Phogbound, and Joanie Phoanie (a takeoff on Joan Baez). Transferred to the Broadway stage in the early 1950s, it quickly became a hit.

Li'l Abner Band, Unique Art, Newark, New Jersey, litho tin wind-up, features Daisy Mae at piano, Pappy on drums, Mammy sits atop piano with drumstick and Abner dances a jig.
$400–$500

Shmoo Wooden Figure, manufacturer unknown, 1940s, 6″ height. *$50–$100*

LITTLE KING

Otto Soglow's "Little King" first ran as a series of cartoons in the *New Yorker* in the early 1930s before emerging as a syndicated strip in the daily newspaper.

Little King, Marx, 1935, painted wooden figure, pulling a string in his crown spun the toy forward, 4″ height. *$200–$250*

LITTLE ORPHAN ANNIE

This wide-eyed moppet with orange hair made a dramatic debut in the *New York Daily News* in 1924 with Harold Gray as her creator. The ageless little orphan girl is still active in the 1980s. In the late 1970s she inspired a broadway hit, "Annie," followed by a full-length movie.

Andy and Sandy on the Road, C.K., Japan, 1930s, celluloid and tin wind-up, both figures move on little wheeled platforms as with Henry and Henrietta toys by C.K.   *$600–$700*

Orphan Annie Cart, Trixy Toys, 1933, litho on wood.
                                                $75–$100

Orphan Annie Dime Bank, 1930s, tin.   *$75–$100*

Orphan Annie Skipping Rope, Marx, 1930s, litho tin wind-up, Annie skips rope, small gears under her feet allow wire rope to pass around her with this ingenious mechanism, 5″ height.
                                                $400–$500

Orphan Annie Standing Figure, manufacturer unknown, 1930s, wood jointed.   *$100–$125*

Sandy Crawler, Marx, 1930s, spring-loaded toy activated by lowering tail, litho tin, Sandy's name on collar.   *$100–$150*

Walking Sandy, Marx, 1930s, litho tin wind-up, Sandy carries valise with Annie's name on it, 4″ height; original box is highly prized, as it assembles to become Sandy's doghouse.
                                                $400–$500

LONE RANGER

The masked rider first appeared on radio in 1933 over station WXYZ, Detroit. First conceived by a motion picture tycoon, George Trendle, who teamed with writer Fran Striker, the show was tested with a premium offer of a free souvenir program and 25,000 letters immediately poured in. Striker also wrote a best-selling series of Lone Ranger novels. "The Lone Ranger" premiered on TV in 1949; a cartoon series was produced by CBS in 1966; in 1981 a full-length feature film, "The Legend of the Lone

Ranger,'' was produced by Universal City, Jack Wrather Productions.

Lone Ranger collections frequently include a pair of dolls of the masked rider with Tonto, 20″ height, circa 1938. The pair pack cast-iron pistols. There is also a hand-puppet of the Lone Ranger from the same era.

Hi-Yo Silver Lone Ranger Target Game, Marx, 1938, tin stand with metal gun and plunger darts (three sizes), nice litho inset illustrative of Lone Ranger and Tonto. $50–$75

Lone Ranger Riding Silver, Marx, 1938, litho tin wind-up, Silver stands on hind legs and vibrates with winding as Lone Ranger spins lariat, 8″ height. $200–$300

MAX AND MORITZ

Wilhelm Busch, one of the best loved creators of illustrated light verse in the German language, created a juvenile history of two malevolent little tykes, Max and Moritz, in the latter part of the 19th century. Undoubtedly, Rudolph later used these mischief-makers as models for his Hans and Fritz characters, The Katzenjammer Kids.

Max and Moritz Standing Figures, Schoenhut, 1914–1915, wood jointed with cloth outfits and artificial hair, approximately 9″ height. $1,000–plus for pair

MICKEY MOUSE (SEE DISNEYANA)

MILTON BERLE

Milton Berle, a practitioner of broad, brassy buffoonery, earned the title of ''Mr. Television'' during his 1948–1956 stint. His ''Texaco Star Theater'' on NBC was the first big production variety show.

Milton Berle Car, Marx, late 1940s, litho tin and plastic wind-up, another variation of Marx's crazy cars, 6½″ length.
     $100–$200

MOON MULLINS

Arguably the biggest con artist and lowbrow in all of comicdom, Moonshine Mullins (his full name) has been on the scene since 1923, with Frank Willard the creator.

Kayo on Ice Truck, Dowst (Tootsietoy), 1932, cast metal, comic series, Kayo sits on cake of ice, 2¾" length. *$100–$200*

Moon Mullins and Kayo with Railroad Handcar, Marx, early 1930s; two versions: 1st, with Kayo on dynamite box and runs on simple barrel spring; 2nd, deluxe version with clockwork spring and bell which rings as handcar moves around track, body of heavy gauge steel vs. tin on cheaper version, 6" length. *$300–$400*

Moon Mullins in Police Patrol Wagon, Dowst (Tootsietoy), 1932, cast metal (one of six in comic series), policeman drives Moon (holding hat) off to hoosegow, 2¾" length. *$100–$200*

Moon Mullins Standing Figure, manufacturer unknown, 1930s, wood jointed, Moon wears his famous derby and smokes cigar. *$75–$100*

Uncle Willie and Mamie in Motor Boat, Dowst (Tootsietoy), 1932, cast metal, comic series, 2¾" length. *$100–$200*

MUTT AND JEFF

Tall slim Augustus Mutt was a carefree bachelor who loved to "play the ponies." His friend, Jeff, was an exact opposite—short, on the plump side, married, and with a son, an eternal victim of Mutt's pranks. The first strip to run in daily papers, it was created by ex-sports cartoonist Bud Fisher beginning in 1907 and continuing to this day. Mutt and Jeff were the subject of a Broadway musical in the late 1920s.

Mechanical Mutt and Jeff, German, 1920s, litho tin wind-up, Jeff appears to be playing leapfrog over his buddy Mutt, except that he faces in the wrong direction, 6" length. *$2,000–plus*

Mutt and Jeff Standing Figures, Switzerland, late 1940s, metal-jointed figures with plaster and attired in felt clothing, Mutt 8" height, Jeff 6½" height. *$100–$200*

Mutt and Jeff Still Bank, A.C. Williams, Ravenna, Ohio, 1915, cast iron, gold finish, also appeared in bright colors, 5 ¼ " height. $100–$200*

POPEYE

Elzie Seger, one-time apprentice to Richard Outcault of "Buster Brown" and "The Yellow Kid" fame, sold the idea of his "Thimble Theater" to King Features in 1929. Originally focused on Olive and the rest of the Oyl family, a squint-eyed sailor smoking a corncob pipe soon stole the show and the strip was renamed "Popeye" several years later. The strip later inspired many movie cartoons and a full-length screenplay by Jules Feiffer in 1980. Along with Mickey Mouse, Popeye is the most universally recognized of all cartoon characters. The sailor man may well hold the record for having the most toys created in his image.

Juggling Popeye and Olive, Linemar, early 1950s, litho tin wind-up. $300–$400

Popeye in the Barrel, Chein, 1932, litho tin wind-up, 7 " height. $200–$300

Popeye the Champ, Marx, 1937, litho tin with celluloid boxers, winding-up produces furious action and bell rings signaling round's end. $750–$850

Popeye Cowboy, Fisher Price, 1937, wheeled platform pull toy, litho on wood, Popeye rides old plug horse as wheels make clicking sound. $200–$300

Popeye Drummer Boy, Fisher Price, 1937, platform pull toy, Popeye beats on drum as wheels turn. $200–$300

Popeye Express With Airplane, Marx, 1937, litho tin wind-up, Popeye soars overhead in tiny plane while Wimpy, Olive, Sappo, and Swee' Pea circle in Union Pacific train below, 9 " diameter. $1,000–$2,000

Popeye the Flyer, Marx, 1937, litho tin wind-up, Olive and Popeye circle tower in planes, lithographing varies on a number of versions, 9 " diameter. $700–$800

*As much as 20% higher in bright colors.

Popeye the Heavy Hitter, Chein, 1930s, litho tin wind-up, Popeye wields a mallet to ring the gong on carnival strength tester, 9¾" height. $1,000–$2,000

Popeye in Horse Cart, manufacturer unknown, 1930s, celluloid Popeye figure in steel cart, 7½" length. $300–$400

Popeye Jigger on Roof, Marx, 1936, litho tin wind-up.

     $300–$400

Popeye Knockout Bank, Marx, late 1940s and early 1950s, litho tin, coin drop produces action. $700–$800

Popeye on Motorcycle, Hubley, 1938, cast iron, "Spinach Delivery" embossed on sidecar, many are found with reproduced figure which is removable, 5½" length. $1,000–$1,500

Popeye and Olive Ball Toss, Linemar, early 1950s, tin wind-up, 19" length. $600–$700

Popeye and Olive Handcar, Hercules Metal Line (distributed by Marx), 1935, heavy-gauge steel body (similar to Moon Mullins deluxe version handcar), with figures in rubber.

     $1,500–$2,000

Popeye and Olive Oyl Jiggers on the Roof, Marx, 1935, $600–$800.

Popeye and Olive Jiggers on the Roof, Marx, 1935, litho tin wind-up, Popeye dances and Olive plays the accordion.
$500–$600

Popeye Paddle Wagon, Corgi, 1969–1972, cast metal push toy, Swee' Pea, Bluto, Olive, Wimpy, and Popeye appear as rubber figures, there are several variations of this toy, 6″ length.
$35–$50

Popeye and the Parrot Cages, Marx, 1930, litho tin wind-up, 8¼″ height. $300–$400

Popeye Patrol, Hubley, 1938, cast iron, Popeye figure and motorcycle are cast separately, 9″ length. $700–$800

Popeye the Pilot, Marx, 1937, litho tin wind-up, 7″ length, Marx produced two versions, the earlier model had a wider fuselage and wings. $400–$500

Popeye Pirate Pistol, Marx, 1950s, litho tin click gun, 10″ length. $100–$150

Popeye and the Punching Bag, Chein, 1932, litho tin wind-up, punching bag is on spring coming from floor vs. a second overhead Chein version, 7½″ height. $400–$500

Popeye and the Punching Bag, Chein, 1932, litho tin wind-up with overhead bag (an uncommon version that's tough to come by), 9¾″ height. $1,000–$1,500

Popeye the Sailor in a Rowboat, Hoge Mfg., New York City, 1935, litho tin wind-up, the most uncommon of all Popeye toys, 15½″ length. $2,000–$3,000

Popeye Sparkler, German, 1932, litho tin, die-cut head of Popeye, sparks appear in hole in one eye and nose. $250–$300

Popeye Sparkler, Chein, 1959, litho tin, round-shaped, with picture of Popeye's head. $75–$100

Popeye Standing Figure, manufacturer unknown, 1930s, cast iron, this may have well been cast as a door stop, 8″ height.
$900–$1,000

Popeye on a String, manufacturer unknown, 1930s, variation of any number of toys featuring monkeys and clowns which climb up and down string when figure is in vertical position and cord is pulled taut, 6″ height. $75–$100

Popeye and Swee' Pea, Fisher Price, 1937, wheeled platform pull toy, litho on wood, Popeye is at helm of ship-shaped platform. $200–$250

Popeye and the Wheelbarrow (a.k.a. "Popeye Express"), Marx, 1937, litho tin wind-up, 8 ¼″ height (deluxe model has parrot that pops up out of wheelbarrow). $300–$400

Popeye Wood-Jointed Figure, Chein, 1932, litho wood. $200–$300

Standing Popeye, Chein, 1932, litho tin wind-up, they call this toy a "walker," but it mostly just vibrates when wound up, 6″ height. $300–$350

Wood-Jointed and Hard Rubber Figures, made in various sizes of Popeye, Olive, Wimpy, Swee' Pea, and Jeep. $35–$70

PORKY PIG

Leon Schlesinger Productions, which began in 1930 as the producer of Looney Tunes and Merry Melodies, introduced their first important cartoon character, a stuttering, bewildered porker known as Porky Pig. Later, Porky was overshadowed by a nemesis who appeared in his film, "Porky's Hare Hunt," Bugs Bunny, who became the number one animated animal of the 1940s.

Porky Pig with Umbrella, Marx, 1935, litho tin wind-up, 6″ height. $300–$350

SMITTY

Smitty, a young office "go-fer" created by Walter Berndt in 1922, aspired to be a big tycoon like his boss, Mr. Bailey. (With orange hair and empty circles for eyes, he'd have made a great match for Orphan Annie.)

Smitty and Herby on Motorcycle, Dowst (Tootsietoy), 1932, cartoon series, cast metal, Smitty drives the motorcycle and brother Herby rides in side car. $200–$300

Smitty on the Scooter, Marx, 1930, litho tin wind-up, figure is detachable, 5″ length, 8″ height. $1,000–$2,000

SNOWFLAKE AND SWIPES

Oscar Hitt, of Hi-Way Henry fame, created "Snowflake and Swipes" in the mid-1920s. The strip was based on the adventures of a small black boy, Snowflake, and his dog Swipes, a scrappy little fellow who seemed to always get the worst of it.

Snowflake and Swipes, Nifty, 1929, platform pull toy, litho tin, Snowflake runs when toy is pulled; Swipes, who has apparently lost a recent dogfight (he is all bandaged), brings up the rear.
$500–$600

SUPERMAN

The man of steel was the creation of Jerry Siegel and Joe Shuster in 1938. His instant climb to fame quickly earned him his "Superman Comics" by the following year, a radio show in 1940, movies in 1941, and TV by the early 1950s. In the 1980s there have been no less than four full-length Superman movies.

Superman Fighting Tank, Linemar, 1960s, litho tin wind-up (several variations), this was a very disappointing toy as Superman was simply lithographed on a small flat piece of tin, when wound, Superman seemed to be dazed by a dose of Kryptonite, as he rarely flipped the tank over. *$125–$150*

Superman Figure, manufacturer unknown, 1940s, wood jointed, 12″ height. *$200–$250*

Superman Racing the Airplane, Marx, 1940, litho tin wind-up (one of the last quality made toys prior to World War II), Superman spins around airplane on steel wire and turns it over, 5″ length. *$500–$600*

THE TOONERVILLE TROLLEY

Fontaine Fox started the Toonerville Folks in 1908, and the beloved saga that centered around a run-down old trolley entertained readers for over 40 years. A number of small wood-jointed Toonerville folk appeared in the 1930s ($75–$100 range).

Aunt Eppie Hogg on Flatbed Truck, Nifty, 1923–1945, litho tin wind-up. Rotund Aunt Eppie slides back and forth on flatbed,

Toonerville Trolley, Nifty, 1922, lithographed tin mechanical, $450–
$550; "Katrinka," Jimmy, and wheelbarrow, Nifty, 1924, lithographed
tin mechanical, $750–$850.

when she reaches back end, it sends front of 7″ length truck in
the air. Dark green, blue, and orange. Captain is the driver. This
ingenious toy is rarely found with all its figures intact.

$5,000–plus*

Mickey McGuire Figure, manufacturer unknown, wood wind-up
with felt clothing, Mickey wears hat and scarf and smokes
cigar. $300–$400

Powerful Katrinka With Jimmy, Nifty, 1924, red and blue litho
tin wind-up, Katrinka hoists Jimmy with one hand as she moves
across floor, 6¾″ height. $800–$900

Powerful Katrinka With Jimmy and Wheelbarrow, Nifty, copyright by Fontaine Fox, 1924, red and blue litho tin wind-up,
Katrinka raises and lowers Jimmy in wheelbarrow as she moves
across floor, 6¾″ height. $1,000–$1,500

Tin Miniature Toonerville Trolley, German, 1922, 1¾″ height,
1½″ length (Crackerjack collectors claim this as one of the sur-
prise giveaways from the popcorn firm; we've also seen it classified as an English penny toy). $450–$500

*At the Ray Holland Toy Auction at Sotheby's in spring of 1985, an
Eppie Hogg toy *minus* the Captain failed to meet reserves of $6,000–
$8,000.

Toonerville Trolley, Dent Hardware, 1929, cast iron, two-color variation green with orange; red with yellow trimmed with gold, 4″ length, 6″ height. $500–$600

Toonerville Trolley, copyright by Fontaine Fox, manufacturer unknown, 1923, slush-cast metal, painted, available in yellow, red, or green with trim, 4″ height. $500–$600

Toonerville Trolley, Kemtron, 1938; HO gauge electric, brass, unpainted, featured tiny working headlight, 2½″ height.
$500–$600

UNCLE WIGGILY

Howard Garis created this long-eared friend of countless millions of youngsters at the turn of the century. In addition to story books, Uncle Wiggily appeared in a daily comic strip in the 1930s, making his debut in New Jersey's *Newark Evening News.*

Uncle Wiggily Car, German, early 1920s, litho tin wind-up, auto decorated in bright pastel patches, Uncle Wiggily holds valise in one hand, a red, white, and blue cane in the other, Howard R. Garis' name appears across lower edge of radiator panel, 10″ length. $750–$800

Uncle Wiggily Car, Marx, early 1935, litho tin wind-up, one of earliest Marx crazy cars, rabbit's head spins around, 6½″ length. $300–$400

YELLOW KID

There were a number of earlier beginnings, but the first real breakthrough in American comic strips occurred in 1896 with the creation of "The Yellow Kid" by Richard Outcault. An unpleasant little baldheaded street urchin with floppy ears, the Kid wore an oversized yellow nightshirt which was used as a placard upon which dialogue appeared. Format was page-size single panel. When William Randolph Hearst stole Outcault away from bitter rival Joseph Pulitzer (giving birth to the phrase "yellow journalism"), Pulitzer hired George Luks to draw "The Yellow Kid" for *his* paper. Ironically, both versions proved to be short-lived as the violent, foul-mouthed little imp proved not to be the role model that parents had anticipated.

Yellow Kid, manufacturer unknown, early 1900s, lever-operated, wood, lead, cloth. $500–$600

Yellow Kid Cap Bomb, cast iron, cap is placed in Kid's mouth. $75–$100

Yellow Kid on Easter Egg, licensed by Richard Outcault, papier-mâché, arms move on metal shaft. $700–$800

Yellow Kid Goat Cart, Kenton, early 1900s, 7 ½ ″ length (cast-iron figure is usually painted all yellow); there is a version in which the Kid is black with a red nightshirt. $300–$400

Yellow Kid Squeeze Toy, manufacturer unknown, scissor action, papier-mâché, wood, and cloth. $300–$400

MISCELLANEOUS COMIC AND NOVELTY TOYS

American Newsboy, Nikko Kogyo, Occupied Japan, 1950s, celluloid; boy rings bell and holds "Extra" newspaper (red, white, and blue outfit). $100–$200

Archie "Ronson," 1920s, litho tin head with sparkling action, 4″ height. $75–$100

Auto Race, Jeannette, 1930s, litho tin mechanical, course layout where tiny autos race on track through tunnels, 9″ diameter. $200–$300

Baggage Carrier, Unique Art, 1950s, litho tin mechanical, figure pulling large cart stacked with baggage, 13″ length. $100–$150

Ballet Dancer, Marx, 1930s, litho tin mechanical, 5 ¾″ height. $200–$300

Beetle, German, 1930s, painted tin mechanical, 7″ length. $100–$125

Bird in Cage, German, 1920s, litho tin mechanical with bellows, 8″ height. $200–$250

Bird Cage on Stand, Ges. Gesch (German), 1920s, painted tin and steel, 7 ½″ height. $100–$200

Birds on Swing, German, 1920s, painted tin mechanical, 14 ¼″ height. $650–$750

Bird in Tree, German, circa 1910, painted tin mechanical with bellows, 6 ½″ height. $100–$150

Blue Bird, German, circa 1910, handpainted tin mechanical with paper propellers. $100–$200

"Bombo," Unique Art, 1950s, litho tin mechanical, 9 ½″ height. $100–$125

Boy and Girl Dancing, Schuco, 1930s, cloth-dressed tin mechanical, 5″ height. $100–$200

Boy Riding St. Bernard, Rocker, German, 1910, painted tin, 5″ length. $200–$300

Bus, Gunthermann, 1920s, litho tin mechanical with man boarding, 8 ¾″ length. $200–$300

Busy Bridge, Marx, 1940s, litho tin mechanical with battery-operated street lights. $100–$200

Busy Lizzie, German, 1920s, litho tin wind-up, 7 ½″ height. $300–$400

Busy Lizzie Cleaning Woman, German, 1920s, litho tin mechanical. $100–$200

Busy Miners, Marx, 1930s, litho tin mechanical, coal cars on track course, 16 ½″ length. $100–$125

Butter and Egg Man, Marx, 1930s, litho tin mechanical, 7 ½″ height (variation of Joe Penner comic toy by Marx). $200–$250

Cat Barber, Toply, Japan, 1950s, litho tin mechanical, cat lathers up to shave kitten in barber chair. $100–$200

Cat With Glasses, German, 1920s, painted tin mechanical, 6 ½″ height (similar to Krazy Kat toy, but without any identifying mark). $100–$200

Cat on Scooter, Chein, 1920s, litho tin spring action, 7 ¼″ length (very similar to Felix and Krazy Kat Nifty versions). $150–$200

Chef on Rollerskates, Japan, 1960s, litho tin mechanical, 6 ½″ height. $100–$125

Clarinetist, German, circa 1910, handpainted tin mechanical, 8″ height.   *$300–$350*

Coo-Coo Car, Marx, 1930s, litho tin mechanical, 8″ length.
                                                   $200–$250

Crawling Baby, German, circa 1910, painted tin mechanical, 5 ½″ length.   *$100–$200*

Dancing Couple, F. Martin, circa 1915, painted tin mechanical, 7 ½″ height.   *$500–$600**

Dancing Couple, German, 1915, painted tin mechanical, 6¾″ height.   *$250–$300*

Dog Chase, Stock, German, 1920s, litho tin mechanical, high-hatted driver on three wheeler pursued by white dog, 7″ length.   *$400–$500*

Dog Chasing Monkey, Stock, German, 1920s, litho tin mechanical, 6 ½″ length.   *$400–$500*

Dragon With Riders, maker unknown, Japan, celluloid mechanical.   *$100–$125*

Drinker, Schuco, 1930s, tin and plastic mechanical, 5″ height.
                                                   $100–$125

Drinking Man, F. Martin (French), 1915, painted and cloth-dressed tin mechanical, man in high hat tipples from bottle, 8 ¼″ height (one of a series of comic toys by Martin from this era).   *$500–$600*

Drinking Pig, Schuco, 1930s, cloth-dressed tin mechanical, 5″ height.   *$100–$200*

Drum Major, Marx, 1930s, litho tin mechanical, with rolling eyes.   *$75–$100*

Drum Major, Wolverine, 1930s, litho tin mechanical, 13 ½″ length.   *$75–$100*

Drummer Boy, Marx, 1930s, litho tin mechanical, 9″ length.
                                                   $75–$100

Drummer Boy, Marx, 1950s, litho tin mechanical, eyes roll, 9″ height.   *$35–$50*

*Brought $850 at Atlanta Toy Museum Auction, October 1986.

Drumming Monkey, German, 1930s, litho tin mechanical, 8″ height. $250–$300

Drunkard, manufacturer unknown, Japan, 1930s, celluloid mechanical, 280mm height (clever imitation of F. Martin's version of drinking man toy holding bottle in one hand). $100–$200

Duck, German, circa 1910, painted tin mechanical, with paper props, 6″ length. $200–$250

Dude Nodder, German, 1915, painted tin mechanical, 7¾″ height. $100–$150

Elephant in Evening Attire, manufacturer unknown, 1930s, tin with felt covering, paper hat, figure has cane and top hat, 8¾″ height. $100–$150

Express Boy, German, 1920s, litho tin mechanical and composition. $75–$100

Fish, German, 1915, handpainted tin, on three wheels, 10″ length. $350–$450

Funny Harry, Gama, German, litho tin with composition head, 5¼″ length. $100–$150

Girl and Donkey, German, circa 1915, handpainted tin mechanical, girl on two wheels holds whip over donkey, 7½″ length. $150–$200

Girl Pulling Cart, French, circa 1910, stained tin friction, 5″ length. $250–$300

Grinder Steam Toy, Fleischmann, 1920s, live steam attachment, 3¼″ square. $50–$75

Hee-Haw, Marx, 1950s, litho tin mechanical, milkman driving donkey cart, 10½″ length. $50–$75

Ho-Bo Train, Unique Art, 1930s, litho tin wind-up, hobo runs across freight car with dog biting pants, 8″ length. $200–$300

Honeymoon Express, Marx, 1940s, litho tin mechanical train circles around tracked course. $100–$200

Horse Cart, Gibbs, 1920s, paper litho and wood, pair of horses pull cart, 16″ length. $100–$200

Ice Cream Vendor, Courtland, 1940s, litho tin mechanical, 6″ length. $100–$125

Jackie the Hornpipe Dancer, F. Strauss, 1920s, litho tin wind-up, 9″ height. $200–$250

Jenny Balking Mule, Strauss, 1920s, litho tin mechanical, farmer in cart, mule kicks up heels, 8″ length. $200–$250

Jolly Pals, Stock, German, 1920s, litho tin mechanical, monkey in cart pulled by small dog, 8″ length. $100–$125

Joy Rider, Marx, 1930s, litho tin mechanical (crazy car), 7″ length. $200–$300*

Jumpin' Jeep, Marx, 1940s, litho tin mechanical, four helmeted passengers in crazy car variant, 6″ length. $200–$300

Kiddie Cyclist, Unique Art, 1920s, litho tin mechanical, 8½″ height. $100–$125

Lady in Three-Wheel Auto, Stock, 1920s, litho tin wind-up, 4¾″ length. $300–$400

Leaping Lena, Strauss, 1920s, litho tin mechanical, 8″ length. $200–$250

Merrymakers, Marx, 1931, stylized band toy wind-up, $800–$1,000.

*Reached high of $425 at Atlanta Toy Museum Auction, October 1986.

Let's Go Happy, manufacturer unknown, 1920s, litho tin crank toy of character balancing atop cymbals on large drum, 9″ height. $150–$200

Man With Baggage, Distler, German, 1920s, litho tin mechanical, 7 ½″ height. $250–$300

Monkey, Schuco, 1930s, cloth on tin mechanical, monkey with steamer trunk, 5″ height. $100–$150

Monkey and Crab, NPK, Knarit, Japan, 1920s, litho tin, manually activated, monkey climbs up seesaw and drops ball down chute for direct hit on crab, lithographed on base, 225mm height. $200–$300

Mother Duck and Ducklings, German, 1915, painted tin mechanical, 8″ length. $100–$200

Musical Camel, manufacturer unknown, 1920s, crank-operated musical toy, cloth-covered tin. $150–$200

Native With Hippopotamus, Toply, Japan, 1950s, litho tin mechanical, native rides hippo and leads hippo along by dangling bunch of bananas. $100–$200

Native on Turtle, Japan, 1950s, litho tin mechanical, 8 ½″ length. $100–$200

Nursemaid with Baby, German, 1910, painted tin mechanical, 7 ½″ height. $350–$450

Oh Boy, Fisher, 1920s, litho tin mechanical, boy rides on scooter in this nicely detailed German wind-up, 8″ height. $300–$400

Old Jalopy, Marx, 1950s, litho tin mechanical, another Marx crazy car, 5 ½″ length. $50–$100

Oriental Woman, German, circa 1915, handpainted tin mechanical, figure has fan and parasol, 8 ½″ height. $150–$200

Peacock, EBO, Pao-Pao, German, 1910, painted tin mechanical with bellows squeaker, 9 ½″ length. $200–$300

Penguin Skier, Nomura, Japan, 1950s, litho tin mechanical. $75–$100

Pianist, Yoshiya, Japan, 1930s, litho tin and celluloid mechanical, little girl plays while overhead parasol with little balls spins when activated, 170mm height. $100–$200

Pike, Bing, German, 1890s, handpainted tin mechanical, fish on wheels, 14 ½" length.   *$350–$450*

Pinched, Marx, 1930s, litho tin mechanical, 10" length (another Marx laid-out course where smaller figures [i.e., police cars and other vehicles] chase each other around a tracked mechanism).
$200–$300

Pony Cart, Gibbs, 1920s, litho wood and tin, steel wire.
$100–$200

Porter, German, 1920s, litho tin mechanical, porter obviously tries to close stuffed trunk by lying on it, 2" height.
$100–$200

Rabbit Violinist, Kuramochi, 1930s, celluloid mechanical.
$100–$200

Rangerider, Marx, 1930s, litho tin mechanical, rocker-type with steel lariat (variation of Hopalong Cassidy toy).   *$100–$125*

Revolving Monkey, Gesenia, German, 1890s, hand-painted tin mechanical, 6 ¼" height.   *$150–$200*

Rocking Horse, Gibbs, 1920s, litho wood and tin, rider waves hat as horse rocks, 9" length.   *$100–$200*

Rodeo Joe, Marx, 1940s, tin litho, plastic mechanical, 6" length (another Marx variation of the crazy car).   *$200–$250*

Rookie Pilot, Marx, 1940s, litho tin mechanical, variation of Popeye and Dagwood airplane wind-ups by Marx, 6¾" length.
$175–$200

Running Pig, German, 1920s, painted tin mechanical, 6" length.   *$200–$250*

Sailor, manufacturer unknown, 1920s, painted tin string climbing toy, 7" height.   *$50–$75*

Sailor Playing Squeezebox, manufacturer unknown, circa 1915, papier-mâché, cloth dressed, 8" height.   *$100–$150*

School Boy (at Blackboard), Tippco, circa 1910, painted tin mechanical, 7 ½" height.   *$500–$600*

Scottie Dog and Shoe, German, 1940s, tin and celluloid mechanical, 8" length.   *$50–$75*

Sheriff Sam Patrol Car, Marx, 1949, litho tin mechanical.
$100–$125

Skidoodle, Nifty, 1920s, litho tin mechanical, family in back of open-bed truck, bright colored cartoon characters, 10½" length.
$400–$500

Sky Bird Flyer, Marx, 1940s, litho tin mechanical, 9" height.
$75–$100

Snoopy-Gus, believed made by Marx, 1950s, litho tin mechanical, man with dog are passengers in fire-truck contrivance, another figure is on raised ladder, 8" length.
$300–$350

Speedy Boy Delivery, Marx, 1940s, litho tin mechanical.
$25–$50

Steam Locomotive, manufacturer unknown, Japan, early 1900s, litho tin friction with heavy cast-metal wheels, passengers look out from third-class coach behind steam engine, a classic toy noted for its simplicity and excellent lithography.
$400–$500

Teddy Bear and Boy Three-Wheel Cart, CKO, German, 1920s, litho tin mechanical, 5½" length.
$300–$400

Tidy Tim, Marx, 1930s, litho tin mechanical, street cleaner with barrel on wheels, 8" length (variation of Popeye and Wheelbarrow wind-up by Marx).
$200–$250

Tom Twist, Strauss, 1930s, litho tin mechanical, paint-faced character with flat hat, 7" (variation of Boob McNutt wind-up by Strauss).
$100–$200

Topsy Turvy Tom, H.E. Nurenburg, 1920s, litho tin mechanical, ingenious car rolls over and rights itself, clown driver, 10¼" length.
$600–$700

Train Station, Arnold, German, 1920s, litho tin mechanical, tiny train runs from station to roundhouse, 15" length. $100–$125

Traveler, German, 1920s, handpainted tin, cloth-dressed mechanical, dapper-looking man in straw hat, checked suit, small valise, 8½" height.
$200–$250

Unique Artie, Unique Art, 1930s, litho tin mechanical, 7" length.
$100–$200

Violinist, Martin, 1915, handpainted tin mechanical, cloth, 8″ height.   *$500–$600*

Waltzing Lady, German, circa 1910, painted tin mechanical, 4″ height.   *$400–$500*

What's Wrong Car, German, 1920s, tin litho and painted mechanical, 7″ length.   *$100–$200*

Whoopee Car, Marx, 1930s, girl with pigtails driver, litho tin and plastic mechanical, 6″ length.   *$100–$200*

Woman With Basket, German, circa 1915, painted tin mechanical, 7″ height.   *$200–$300*

Woman Pulling Cart, German, 1920s, litho tin, friction, 6″ length.   *$200–$300*

Woman Vendor Pushing Orange Cart, Martin, circa 1915, handpainted tin mechanical, 6½″ length.   *$800–$900*

Zylotone, Wolverine, 1920s, litho tin mechanical, musical toy with discs.   *$400–$500*

PERELMAN TOY MUSEUM SALE

Comic and Character Toys (See also "Banks, Mechanical and Still" and "Bell Toys")

Amos 'n' Andy Fresh Air Taxicab, Marx, 1930.   *$750*

Amos 'n' Andy Walkers, Marx, 1930–1931, pair.   *$900*

Brownie on Horse Pull Toy, Hubley Mfg., cast iron.   *$4,500*

Brownie Patrol, Wilkins Toy Co., Brownie policemen on horse-drawn wagon, cast iron.   *$4,500*

Brownie Sleigh, Hubley Mfg., late 1890s, drawn by pair of reindeer, oversize, 14″ length, 6½″ width, Mutt (of Mutt and Jeff) and Buster Brown passengers.   *$14,000*

Buster Brown Chime Toy, Watrous Mfg. Co.   *$1,500*

Captain and The Kids, Gong Bell Mfg., 1912, bell toy with Hans and Fritz atop a sprawled-out Captain, Fritz rocks back and forth ringing bell.   *$15,000*

Charlie Chaplin, Schuco, 1920s. $675

Charlie Chaplin Clockwork Toy, German, 1920s. $2,200

Charlie Chaplin Walker, German, 1920s, tin, cast-iron feet. $1,000

Comic Funnies Set, Tootsietoy, 1932, set of six includes: Moon Mullins in Police Patrol Wagon, Andy Gump 348 Car, Smitty and Herby on Motorcycle, Uncle Willie and Mamie in Motorboat, Uncle Walt in Roadster, and Kayo on Ice Truck. $2,500

Double Eagle Chariot w/Nodders, Kenton Hardware, circa 1910, cast iron, with Happy Hooligan and Foxy Grandpa, as interchangeable nodder figures, with Gloomy Gus as driver, two horses, 16″. $40,000

Elves on Seesaw (a.k.a. Mamma Katzenjammer and Professor), Kenton Hardware, 1910–1911, figures on three-wheeled platform. $1,250

Gloomy Gus Plantation Wagon, Harris Toy Co., 1912. $11,000

Happy Hooligan Dog Cart, Harris Toy Co., 1911. $800

Happy Hooligan and Gloomy Gus Plantation Wagon, Harris Toy Co., 1912. $10,000

Happy Hooligan Goat Cart, Harris Toy Co., 1911. $500

Happy Hooligan Nodder in Horse-Drawn Rig, Kenton Hardware, 1911, cast-iron three-wheeler, 17″ length. $2,000

Happy Hooligan Phaeton, Hubley Mfg., 1910, cast iron. $13,500

Happy's Police Patrol, Kenton Hardware, 1911, double horse-drawn paddy wagon, policeman conks Happy Hooligan on noggin as toy is pulled. $2,500

Highway Henry, German, 1928, lithographed tin mechanical. $3,000

Maggie and Jiggs on Rollerskates, Nifty, 1924. $1,400

Mamma Katzenjammer Spanker, Kenton Hardware, 1911, cast-iron donkey-drawn cart, Uncle Heine holds reins, Mamma spanks Fritz over knee as Hans looks on. $11,500

Mickey Mouse Airplane, Marx. $2,200

Mickey Mouse Drummer, Nifty Toys, 1931, litho tin wind-up.
$4,000

Mickey Mouse Hurdy Gurdy, German (probably Distler), 1931, litho tin, 7″ height, Mickey cranks, while Minnie dances atop the toy. $9,500

Popeye "Spinach Delivery" Motorcycle w/Sidecar, Hubley Mfg., 1938, cast iron. $2,500

Powerful Katrinka (twirls Jimmy in wheelbarrow), Nifty, 1924, lithographed tin. $1,500

Seeing New York Auto Car #899, Kenton Hardware, 1911, same passengers as in Sightseeing version, except auto is orange.
$8,500

Sightseeing Auto Car #899, Kenton Hardware, 1911, open roadster, cast iron, with comic figures Happy Hooligan, Alfonse, Gaston, Mamma Katzenjammer, and sailor as passengers, white auto, 10½″ length. $18,000

Yellow Kid Board, manufacturer unknown, circa 1896, wooden, multicolored, gravity toy, characters from the comic strip go click-click down the nails of board, 34″ height × 3½″ width.
$467.50*

Yellow Kid in Goat Cart, Harris, 1911. $800

Miscellaneous Character Toys, Painted and Lithographed Tin

Fernand Martin, Paris, France.

Barber.	$1,200
Boy w/Chair.	$1,750
Dancing Couple.	$600–$700
Delivery Boy, 1910.	$700–$800
Drunkard.	$500–$600
Dutch Girl.	$600
Little Salesgirl.	$1,000–$2,000
Little Salesgirl w/Orange Cart.	$1,200–$1,500
Madeleine w/Dishes.	$800–$900
The Top Man, 1900.	$700–$800

*The Game Preserve Auction, 1988.

Note: An ingenious La Conquete du Nord toy by F. Martin, cele-
brating Robert Peary's journey to the North Pole in 1909, sold for
$2,290 at Christie's in 1988.

Musicians and Character Toys, Clockwork Tin, Early 20th Century

Sigfried Gunthermann, Nuremberg, Germany.

Banjo Player and Dancer.	$1,250
Donkey and Clown.	$1,850
Flute Ballerina.	$1,750
Flying Angel.	$3,500
Three Musicians on Bench.	$2,500
Two Musicians: Fiddler and Flutist.	$1,000

Note: Gunthermann and Martin toys are of painted tin. They tend
to flake easily and wind-up mechanisms are very fragile. These
factors greatly influence price.

Disneyana

The debut of a little pie-eyed rodent named Mickey Mouse on November 18, 1928, the eve of the Great Depression, took place in "Steamboat Willie," the first sound-animated cartoon, at New York's Colony Theater. The legacy of Mickey, his pals Minnie, Donald, Goofy, Dumbo, Bambi, Snow White and the Seven Dwarfs, and all the beloved cartoon characters are not only enshrined in films, videos, comic strips, books, and world-famous tourist attractions, but in the countless products created in their image for well over 50 years—products created by over 400 licensees in the United States, Canada, Great Britain, Japan, Germany, and Taiwan. Walter Ewing Disney's cartoon characters have inspired more toys, in numerous variations, than all other cartoonists combined. Many collectors stick strictly to the vast field of Disneyana.

CLARA CLUCK

This operatic hen was introduced in the Disney short "The Orphan's Benefit" in 1934.

Clara Cluck Pull Toy, Fisher Price, 1934, litho and wood platform toy, 8″ length. $100–$200

DONALD DUCK

Donald, who in recent years may well have overshadowed his sidekick, Mickey, made his first appearance in a cameo role in

Margarete Steiff began producing Mickey, Minnie, and Donald stuffed dolls in the early 1930s. Highly prized, they can command $2,000 and up.

"The Wise Little Hen" in 1934. He was his usual, obstreperous self in Mickey's first color cartoon, "The Band Concert," 1935. His first starring role did not come until 1937 in "Donald's Ostrich."

"Disney Flivver," Line Mar, 1940s, litho tin friction car, Donald at wheel, lithographs of Dopey, Donald's nephews on chassis, 6″ length. $200–$300

Donald Duck on Bicycle, Line Mar, 1940s, litho wind-up, 4″ height. $100–$150

Donald Duck Car, Paperino Politoys, Italy, 1960s, litho tin, Donald drives with nephews in rumble seat. $150–$200

Donald Duck Drummer, Line Mar, 1950s, litho tin wind-up, 6″ height. $100–$150

Donald Duck Fireman on Ladder, Line Mar, 1950s. $100–$200

Donald the Bubble Duck, Morris Plastics, 1960s, squeeze toy, 8″ height, $75–$100.

Donald With Nephew, Line Mar, 1945, litho tin wind-up, 5″ length.   *$100–$150*

Donald Duck in Open Roadster, Sun Rubber, 1933–1934, hard rubber, painted push toy, 6½″ length.   *$75–$125*

Donald Duck and Pluto Rail Car, Lionel, 1936. Pluto is in dog-house while Donald stands in rear, composition and metal, 10″ length.   *$800–$900*

Donald Duck and Pluto Roadster, Sun Rubber, 1930s, 7″ length.   *$75–$100*

Donald in the Rowboat, Sun Rubber, 1940s, hard rubber, 6″ length.   *$100–$150*

Donald Duck Walker, Shuco, early 1930s, tin, cast iron, and felt cloth, 5½″ height.   *$800–$900*

Donald Duck Xylophone, Fisher Price, 1939, lithographed wood, 7½″ length.   *$200–$250*

DUMBO THE ELEPHANT

A feature film by RKO Radio Pictures released in 1941.

Dumbo Walker, Marx, 1940s, lithograph tin wind-up, Walt Disney's "Dumbo" appears on left ear, 6″ height.   *$100–$125*

ELMER ELEPHANT

Elmer Elephant Pull Toy, Fisher Price, 1936, litho and wood, 7½″ length.   *$100–$125*

FERDINAND THE BULL

Disney adapted the book *The Story of Ferdinand*, by Munro Leaf and Robert Lawson, to a special short feature film in 1938.

Ferdinand the Bull, Marx, 1938, litho tin wind-up (tail spins), 7½″ length.   *$200–$250*

Ferdinand Composition-Jointed Figure, Ideal, 1938, 9″ length.   *$100–$150*

GOOFY

Goofy Gardiner, Line Mar, 1940s (see also Donald Duck Duet, with Goofy playing bass fiddle).   *$75–$100*

Goofy Walker, Line Mar, 1940s, tin litho wind-up, 7″ height.   *$50–$100*

LUDWIG VON DRAKE

Ludwig Von Drake, Line Mar, 1950s, litho tin wind-up, 6″ height.   *$50–$100*

MICKEY AND MINNIE MOUSE

Climbing Mickey, Dolly Toy Co., Dayton, Ohio, early 1930s, copyrighted by Walt Disney Enterprises, die-cut pasteboard, 9″ height.   *$200–$225*

Dancing Mickey and Minnie, Japan, 1930s, celluloid wind-up, variations include Minnie and Elmer the Elephant, Donald and Elmer dancers, 3 ½ " height. $800–$900

Fun-E-Flex Mickey and Minnie on Dog Sled Pulled by Pluto, George Borgfeldt, wood and composition, 10 ¾ " length.
$350–$400

Fun-E-Flex Minnie and Mickey, 1931, distributed by George Borgfeldt, wood-jointed bodies with composition heads, figures produced separately for Minnie, Mickey, and Pluto, ears were leatherette or felt, 7 " height, each. $300–$350

Mickey With Banjo, Japan, 1935–1936, copyrighted by Walt Disney, litho tin base with celluloid figure of Mickey, rubber band mechanical (see Betty Boop for similar version).
$400–$500

Mickey in Bathing Suit, Japan, 1930s, celluloid, 5 ½ " height.
$400–$500

Mickey on Bicycle, Japan, 1940s, celluloid and tin wind-up, with metal bell behind seat, 5 ¾ " height. $1,000–$1,500*

Mickey and Donald Acrobats, Line Mar, 1950s, litho tin, steel with celluloid figures (also Minnie and Mickey Acrobats versions), 17 " height. $500–$600

Mickey and Donald in Rowboat, Japan, 1930s, celluloid, 6 " length. $1,000–$2,000**

Mickey and Felix Picnic Basket, Isla, Spain, circa 1930, litho tin spring action, lid pops up to reveal Felix the Cat, 4 ½ " height.
$900–$1,000

Mickey and Felix Sparkler, Isla, Spain, circa 1930s, litho tin spring action, Mickey and Felix light up cigars on sparks ignited by friction of flint on sandpaper, action is seen through die-cut hole in candle's flame, 5 ½ " height. $800–$900

Mickey Jack-in-the-Box, Japan, 1930s, celluloid Mickey figure, box is paper-covered wood, 6 " height. $350–$400

Mickey in Life Preserver, Japan, 1930s, hard rubber, 4 ½ " height (serves as both toy and baby rattle). $300–$350

---

*Sold for $1,125 at same Lloyd Ralston Auction as previous Mickey toy.
**Sold for $1,175 at Lloyd Ralston Auction, April 1981.

Mickey and Minnie Circus Pull Toy, Nifty, distributed by George Borgfeldt, 1930s, litho and wood, wood composition figures of pair, paper bellows emits squeaking sound.   *$1,000–$2,000*

Mickey and Minnie on Motorcycle, Tipp, Germany, early 1930s, litho tin wind-up, Tip logo appears on gas tank, "Dunlop Cord" lithographed on wheels, Mickey and Minnie are five fingered, as was typical of early 1930s versions, 10″ length (this toy intended for export to Great Britain).   *$2,000–$3,000*

Mickey and Minnie Motoring, Japan, 1930s, litho tin three-wheel cart, celluloid figures, 5½″ length.   *$300–$400*

Mickey and Minnie Mouse Handcar, Lionel, 1934, litho tin, composition figures of Mickey and Minnie, made in red, green, orange, or maroon (the latter is rarest), 8″ length. *Note:* Orders for over $350 of the $1 handcars saved Lionel from bankruptcy.   *$600–$700*

Mickey and Minnie Riding Elephant, Japan, distributed by George Borgfeldt, 1935, celluloid, wind-up vibrates, head bobs and ears flap when activated, elephants appeared in both red and white variations, 8″ height, 10″ length.   *$1,000–plus*

Mickey and Minnie Seesaw, Japan, 1930s, copyrighted by Walt Disney, distributed by George Borgfeldt, celluloid and tin, pendulum and rubber band mechanism, 6″ length.   *$2,000–plus*

Mickey and Minnie Standing Figures, Japan, 1930s, celluoid, heads attached by elastic, nonanimated, each.   *$300–$400*

Mickey Mouse Baby Grand Piano, mail order, Sears, 1935, dark oak with Mickey decal on top.   *$250–$300*

Mickey Mouse Balancer, Japan, 1940s, celluloid wind-up, Mickey with umbrella balances on ball, 9½″ height.
$700–$800*

Mickey Mouse Ball Trap Game, Migra, France, 1934.
$500–$600

Mickey Mouse Band, Fisher Price, 1935, litho wood pull toy, Mickey bangs cymbal on Pluto's backside, 12″ length.
$100–$200

*Sold for $900 at Lloyd Ralston Auction, November 1980.

Mickey Mouse Cast-Iron Still Bank, French, 1930s, hand-painted, Mickey stands with arms akimbo. Possibly unique; owner is said to have turned down offers for as high as $15,000.   *Price Indeterminate*

Mickey Mouse Cast-Iron Still Bank, manufacturer unknown, 1970s, Mickey leans against book.   *$75–$100*

Mickey Mouse Circus Tent, Wells O'London, England, 1935, made to accompany the Circus Train Set, litho tin, magnificent lithography, 5½″ height, 8″ diameter.   *$1,000–$1,500*

Mickey Mouse Circus Train, Lionel, 1935, lithographed tin and steel with 7″ length Commodore Vanderbilt engine, Mickey sits in tender, five cars in all, 30″ long, 84″ of track (originally sold for $1.79).   *$700–$1,000*

Mickey Mouse Circus Train Set, Wells O'London, England, Brimtoy Brand, 1935, features Silver Link engine No. 2509, "Mickey the Stoker" composition figure in coal car (swivel action allows him to shovel coal), circus car, Mickey Mouse Band car, circus dining car, engine 7½″ long, tender 4″ long, cars 6″ long, made to run on 0 gauge track.   *$1,000–$2,000*

Mickey Mouse Crazy Car, Line Mar, mid-1950s, litho tin wind-up, plastic figure, see Donald Duck companion version, 5½″ length.   *$300–$400*

Mickey Mouse Dime Register Bank, copyrighted by Walt Disney Productions, 1939, Mickey at blackboard with nephews.   *$300–$400*

Mickey Mouse Drummer, Nifty, distributed by George Borgfeldt, 1931, litho tin, lever activated, 7″ height.   *$1,000–$2,000*

Mickey Mouse Express, Marx, 1940s, litho tin, shows Disneyville train depot, small streamliner goes around track as Mickey circles in airplane (on wire) overhead, variation of Popeye Express, 9½″ diameter.   *$800–$900*

Mickey Mouse Handcar, Wells O'London, England, 1935–1936, litho tin with celluloid figures of pair, features bell, 7½″ length.   *$300–$400*

Mickey Mouse Locomotive, Fisher Price (Choo-Choo No. 432), 1938, copyrighted by Walt Disney Enterprises, litho wood with tin bell on locomotive, Mickey doffs engineer's cap, 8½″ length. $200–$300

Mickey Mouse Meteor Train Set, Marx, 1930s, litho tin, five cars, 43″ length. $600–$700

Mickey Mouse Paddle Boat, licensed by Walt Disney Enterprises, distributed under Macy's label, litho tin and wood, 12″ length. $2,000–plus

Mickey Mouse Play Piano, Marx Bros., Boston, 1935, wood, glass, and cardboard; as keys are depressed, cardboard cutout figures of Mickey and Minnie dance in front of colorful lithographed panel atop piano, 10″ height, 9″ width (variations featured Big Bad Wolf and Three Pigs). $600–$700

Mickey Mouse Rocking Horse, copyrighted by Walt Disney, Japan, 1930s, celluloid Mickey on wooden horse, 7½″ height.
$2,000–plus

Mickey Mouse Saxophone Player, German, early 1930s, litho tin, pressing metal wire activates arms and legs and crashes cymbals attached to Mickey's heels, 6″ height. $1,000–$2,000

Mickey Mouse Slate Dancer, Johann Distler, Nuremberg, 1930–1931, litho tin, handcrank mechanism has Mickey tapping lively tune, 6½″ height (has registration number 508041).
$2,000–$4,000

Mickey Mouse Sparkler, Nifty, 1931, litho tin, spring activated, 4½″ height. $500–$600

Mickey Mouse Tin Still Bank, Great Britain, "Happynak Series," 1940s. $100–$200

Mickey Mouse Walker, Japan, 1940s, celluloid wind-up, 7⅜″ height. $1,000–$2,000*

Mickey the Musical Mouse, Distler, litho tin, distributed by George Borgfeldt with exclusive arrangement with Ideal Films, lower half has three Mickey torsos playing fiddle, dancing, and playing cymbals, top half has Mickey heads that pivot as handle is turned to play tune. $1,000–$2,000**

*Sold for $1,350 at Lloyd Ralston Auction cited earlier.
**A second version shows Minnie pushing carriage at left, while Mickey grinds organ.

Mickey and Pluto in Three-Wheel Cart, Japan, litho tin and celluloid, 4 ½ ″ length. $500–$600

Mickey in Roadster Pull Toy, licensed by Walt Disney, Japan, 1934, roadster is tinted celluloid, Mickey figure is string-jointed wooden beads, 12 ″ length. $600–$700

Mickey's Musical Money Box, still bank, Combex, England, tin, 6 ″ height. $75–$100

Mickey Walker, Distler, 1930–1931, litho tin with rubber tail, wind-up features big orange pointed feet and decidedly rodent-like countenance, handpainted, 9 ″ height, only a few of this example are known to exist. $2,000

Minnie Mouse Pushing Baby Carriage (Pram), Wells O'London, England, early 1930s, litho tin with Minnie figure in composition, wind-up features dimensional tin figures of Pluto (sitting in front) with two baby mice in pram. $2,000–$3,000

Minnie Mouse and Seated Felix in Carriage, Isla, Spain, early 1930's, Minnie pushes carriage while Felix sits under umbrella, 7 ½ ″ height. $600–$700

Pluto Pulling Mickey on Tricycle, Japan, 1933, copyrighted by Walt Disney, litho tin and celluloid, approximately 6 ″ long. $600–$700

Rambling Mickey, Japan (for George Borgfeldt), 1934, celluloid wind-up, steel tail provides balance, 7 ″ height. $900–$1,000

Running Mickey Bell Toy, N. N. Hill Brass Co., 1935, litho wood with large pressed-steel back wheels, 13 ″ length, other versions depicted Donald and Pluto. $200–$300

Santa Handcar, No. 1105, Lionel, 1935, litho tin with composition figures of Santa, a Christmas tree, and a Mickey Mouse in Santa's sack, 11 ″ length, 6 ½ ″ height (all Lionel handcars were for 0 gauge track; 72 ″ track included in set). $1,000–$1,500

Standing Mickey, Rhenische Rubber and Celluloid Fabric Co., Germany, late 1920s or early 1930s, celluloid wind-up, vibrates when activated, 6 ″ height. $1,000–$2,000

The Toy Peddler, German, 1935, litho tin, man rolls eyes and jiggles string of toys, including Mickey Mouse and monkeys, 6 ½ ″ height. $350–$450

Mickey Mouse Santa Handcar, Lionel, 1935, 11″ length, $1,000–$1,500.

PINOCCHIO

This was the second full-length animated technicolor film produced by Disney Studios. It was released in February 1940, and regarded by many critics as Disney's most brilliant technical extravaganza.

Jiminy Cricket Composition-Jointed Figure, Knickerbocker Toy Co., 1940s. *$100–$200*

Joe Carioca Walker, VB and Cie, France, celluloid wind-up.
$100–$200

Pinocchio the Acrobat, Marx, early 1940s, litho tin wind-up, puppet swings high up on platform as toy rocks below, 16½″ height. *$200–$250*

Pinocchio Walker, George Borgfeldt, 1940s, litho tin wind-up, 10½″ height. *$300–$400*

Pinocchio Walker, Marx, early 1940s, litho tin wind-up, 8″ height. *$200–$250*

Pinocchio Walker, VB and Cie, France, celluloid wind-up.
$600–$700

Pinocchio Wood-Jointed Figure, Ideal, 1940s, 11" height.
$100–$125

PLUTO

Pluto, after playing second banana in a number of Disney productions, assumed a starring role in "Pluto The Pup" in 1938.

Pluto, Marx, 1939, pressed steel with leatherette ears, push tail to activate.
$75–$100

Pluto Roll Over, Marx, 1939, litho tin wind-up, 7" length.
$100–$150

Stretchy Pluto, Line Mar, 1940s, litho tin on wheels, front and back halves of Pluto are joined by large coiled spring.
$75–$100

Top-Hatted Pluto Blowing Horn, Line Mar, 1950s, litho tin wind-up, 6½" height.
$75–$100

   Note: See also Pluto toys listed under Donald Duck and Mickey Mouse headings.

SNOW WHITE AND THE SEVEN DWARFS

The first full-length animated technicolor opus by Disney debuted in 1938, a masterful retelling of Grimm's fairy tale.

Doc and Dopey, Fisher Price, 1940s, litho wood pull toy, 10" length.
$200–$250

Dopey Walker, Marx, 1940, litho tin wind-up, 7" height.
$200–$250

Snow White and Dwarfs Figures, Sieberling, 1940s, handcolored hard rubber, 6" height.
$50–$60

Snow White and Dwarfs Marionettes, Alexander Doll Co., New York City, 1940s.
$300–$400

Snow White and Dwarfs Wood Pull Toy, N.N. Hill Brass Co., 1940s, with large pressed-steel back wheels (variation of Mickey Mouse toy).
$250–$300

Snow White Piano, Marx Bros., Boston, 1940s, variation of Mickey Mouse Piano with animated figures of Snow White.

$200–$250

THREE LITTLE PIGS

Another Grimm's fairy tale-based film, ''The Three Little Pigs,'' came to the screen in 1933, the most famous of all Disney's Silly Symphonies.

Big Bad Wolf Walker, Line Mar, late 1940s, litho tin wind-up, 6″ height.　　　　　　　　　　　$100–$125

Drummer Pig, Fiddler Pig, and Fifer Pig, Schuco, mid-1930s, felt on tin wind-ups, 6″ height.　　　　　　$400–$500

Fiddler Pig Walker, Line Mar, late 1940s, litho tin wind-up, 6″ height.　　　　　　　　　　　$75–$125

Three Little Pigs Acrobats, Line Mar, 1950s, celluloid and metal (variation of Mickey and Donald Acrobat toy).　$450–$500

Educational Toys

One of the first toy categories specifically designed to be educational was that of alphabet blocks. It was described as early as 1653 in *The Jewel House of Art and Nature*, published in London. It was not until the second half of the 18th century, however, that alphabet blocks were manufactured on any scale for children. By the 1860s in the United States, S.L. Hill Co., New York City, McLoughlin Bros., also of New York, and Jesse Crandall (with his nested blocks), all were producing richly decorated alphabet blocks. Milton Bradley followed with his Kindergarten Alphabet and Building Blocks in 1872; raised-letter blocks were introduced by the Embossing Co. in 1879. Throughout the latter half of the 19th century, F. Richter Co. produced their famous Anchor Box of building stones in three colors.

Construction toys made their appearance as early as the 1860s, when Ellis, Britton, and Eaton of Springfield, Vermont, manufactured hardwood logs with simple locking devices. Charles Crandall developed several toys employing an ingenious finger joint—his building blocks and acrobats. W.E. Crandall, another member of the famous toy-making clan, devised toy building blocks which were the forerunner of the Lego units developed in plastic by Gottfried Christianson in Denmark, some 60 years ago. The big three—Meccano, A.C. Gilbert, and Tinkertoy—were early 20th-century innovators. The Meccano system originated in England in 1901; A.C. Gilbert designed his first Erector Set in 1913; Tinkertoy sets were first sold in 1914. Take-apart toys, including lithograph paper-on-wood trains, boats, and tiny buildings, were popular children's fare in the late 19th century as W.S. Reed and R. Bliss sought to satisfy a primal urge among youngsters to dismantle and reassemble toys.

Card games were common in the early colonies by the 18th century, although they took a strong moralistic tone and were not intended for amusement. In the mid-19th century, things lightened up with such popular card games as Dr. Busby, Yankee Pedlar, and Old Maid. Board games originated with the sole purpose of instructing the child, as in the 1804 "Game of Science and the Sport of Astronomy," or H. and S.B. Ives' "The Mansion of Happiness" in 1843, although the entire family generally participated. George Parker of Parker Brothers produced his first game, "Banking," in 1883. It not only taught youngsters the value of money but had the added benefit of interaction between family members of various ages.

Puzzles in shapes of squares and cubes were brightly lithographed and offered countless combinations. A popular puzzle of the late 19th century cut images of famous Americans into three sections, creating obviously humorous combinations titled "Prominent Americans Sliced." Early picture puzzles were best exemplified as dissected maps. John Wallis, a prominent English cartographer, first produced pictured map puzzles in the 18th century. Ironically, these early picture puzzles were confined primarily to teenagers and adults. It was not until the 1920s, when Playskool began turning out wooden puzzles with few pieces, that younger children could also participate.

An instructional toy category that bears special mention because of its inherent graphic appeal is the Historoscope, an elegant chromolith panorama of famous historic events by which pictures on rollers were moved by turning tiny wooden knobs. Any number of panoramas were available, but one of the most popular dealt with George Washington riding his white charger into battle against the British. The real trick is to find these unusual treasures in presentable condition.

Wind, water, sand, gravity—all natural forces—have powered toys for centuries. Among the most popular of these playthings were optical toys, such as the kaleidoscope, rediscovered by Englishman David Brewster in 1817. The persistence of vision, the principle on which motion pictures are based, was exemplified by the Zoetrope, Phenikistiscope, Praxinoscope, Thaumatrope, and the stereoptican—all designed for family viewing and enjoying. The Zoetrope was perfected in 1867 by Milton Bradley from the Wheel of Life, patented in Britain some seven years earlier. Various interchangeable disks, when spun, taught children color mixing with light.

Electro-magnetic toys and chemistry sets were introduced in America in the late 1890s, with chemistry sets having their heyday in the 1920s.

Within the present time frame, plastic blocks made by Halsam and Kiddiecraft during the 1960s, soft blocks by Creative Playthings and Galt, Fisher Price Activity Centers, and plastic modular kits by Leggo and Playmobile all qualify as educational toy collectibles of the future.

The following is a brief sampling of the hundreds of highly collectible educational toys.

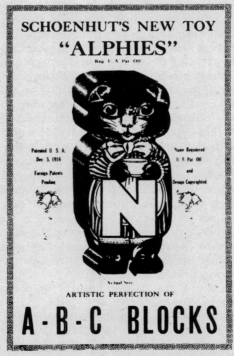

Advertisement for "Alphies" ABC Blocks by Schoenhut, dated 1916. These whimsical educational toys range from $600 to $700 for a set of 26 blocks.

Alphabet of Country Scenes, McLoughlin, 1887, color litho paper on wood. $150–$200

Alphie's ABC Blocks, A. Schoenhut, 1916. $200–$300

Around the World Trunk, R. Bliss, 1911, litho paper-on-wood trunk with ABC blocks. $200–$250

Beasts and Birds Novelty Blocks, Lyman Whitney Publishers, Leominster and Boston, Massachusetts, 1874, printed paper on wood. $200–$250

Boy Contractor, Cruver, Chicago, circa 1900, metal forms, sandstone, cement, plaster. $100–$150

Boy's Union Tool Chests #725 B, Bliss, 1911. $100–$150

Cardhouse, designed by Charles Eames, late 1950s. $50–$75

Chemistry Lab, A.C. Gilbert, 1950s. $100–$125

Chiromagica, McLoughlin, circa 1870, wood, glass, printed cardboard. $250–$300

Cob House Blocks, McLoughlin, circa 1887, litho paper on wood. $100–$150

Crandall's Acrobats, Charles Crandall, circa 1875, painted wood. $350–$400

Crandall's Building Blocks, Charles Crandall, 1867. $300–$350

Crandall's Wide-Awake Alphabet, Charles Crandall, 1867. $200–$300

Deluxe Erector Set, A.C. Gilbert, metal, magnet. $50–$75

Farmyard Puzzles, Milton Bradley, circa 1900, color litho paper on cardboard. $75–$100

Goodie Two Shoes Spelling Game, McLoughlin, 1870, wood stenciled with letters and numbers. $200–$225

Great East River Suspension Bridge, Stirn and Lyons, New York, wood, metal, circa 1880s. $300–$400

Illustrated Cubes Spelling Blocks, Embossing Co., Albany, New York, 1870. $100–$150

Jackstraws, Bone, handmade, 1820s. $150–$200

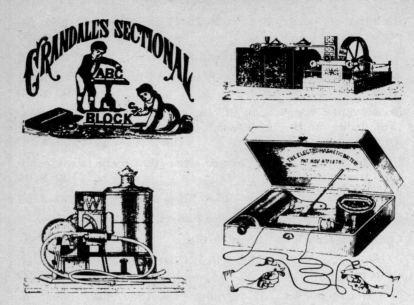

Educational toys, 1890s, Crandall's Sectional ABC Blocks, $250–$300 a set; Weeden Steam Engines, double is $200–$250, single is $150–$200; Electric Battery, $75–$85.

Junior Printing House, Baumgarten, Baltimore, 1883, wood, rubber letter and number stamps.   *$100–$125*

Kaleidoscope, McLoughlin, circa 1870, wood, glass, metal.
                                                                   $250–$300

Life of George Washington Puzzle, manufacturer unknown, circa 1860, handpainted paper-on-wood picture puzzle.
                                                                   $100–$150

Lincoln Logs, John Lloyd Wright Design, 1930s.   *$75–$100*

Log Cabin Playhouse, Ellis, Britton, and Eaton, circa 1865.
                                                                   $200–$300

Marriage of Jenny Wren to Cock Robin Story Blocks, J.A. Crandall, 1881.   *$200–$250*

Masquerade Blocks, Charles Crandall, circa 1870. *$100–$200*

Meccano Set, Mecanno Ltd., Liverpool, England, designed by Frank Hornby, 1901. $75–$125

Mr. Machine Plastic Figure, Ideal Toys, 1950s. $20–$25

Nest of Pictures and ABC Blocks, McLoughlin Bros., circa 1885. $200–$300

Ninth "Gift" Rings For Ring Laying, Friedrich Froebel, 1826. $125–$150

Organ of Constructiveness, Edward Wallis, London, 1820s, construction toy. $200–$225

Playtime Animal Object and Alphabet Blocks, Milton Bradley, 1910, cardboard litho pictures. $100–$200

Praxinoscope, ER, Paris, circa 1880, litho paper strips. $500–$600

Prominent Americans, patented by Walter Stranders, 1881 litho paper on cardboard. $100–$150

Roman Architect Wood Cubes, German, 1870s. $100–$150

Scrabble, Selchow and Righter, New York, 1953. $15–$25

S.L. Hill's Kindergarten Building Blocks, 1860s, printed paper on wood. $150–$200

Steam Engine, manufacturer unknown, 1870s, brass, tin, glass. $100–$150

Tinkertoy, designed by Charles A. Pajeau, 1914. $75–$100

Utopian School Master, manufacturer unknown, circa 1840, wood litho paper-on-cardboard spelling aid. $175–$200

Victorian Hand Shadow, manufacturer unknown, projector, 1870s. $110–$125

Zoetrope, Milton Bradley, circa 1870. $350–$400

Ethnic Toys

For a number of years ethnic toys, black toys in particular, were kept under wraps by dealers and collectors for fear that patrons might be offended by the derogatory names and roles associated with them. More recently, however, with the TV mini-series *Roots* and the inception of the Institute of Black Studies, black collectibles are regarded in a new light, as artifacts of history. The fact of their existence is undeniable, despite the controversy over their aesthetic presentation. Some of the leading collectors, dealers, and authorities in this field are themselves blacks. (Ron Rooks of Baltimore and P.J. Gibbs of Nashville, Tennessee, are two names that immediately come to mind.) Ms. Gibbs has recently published a fine comprehensive book, *Black Collectibles Sold in America*. A monthly *Guide to Buyers, Sellers, and Traders of Black Collectibles* is also available. Write CGL, Box 158472, Nashville, Tennessee 37215, for information.

Often overlooked in the ethnic toy field are those toys, largely from the late 19th century, that depicted Irish, German, and Chinese immigrants in anything but a flattering manner. From 1850 on, Chinese laborers flooded into California; their cheap labor was much in demand in those days to work on the first transcontinental railroad. When hard times came in the late 1870s, strong anti-Chinese sentiment prevailed, leading to the Chinese Exclusion Act of 1882. An Ives cap pistol, "Chinese Must Go," shows a Coolie being pulled by his pigtail and booted out of the country by an immigration official—typical of the defamatory nature of a number of like toys and banks. The Irish-

Three minstrel-inspired clockwork toys: Brudder Bones, Fiddler, and the Banjo Player (Poor Old Joe), all three attributed to J.B. Secor, and all from the late 1870s. The three clockwork toys are extremely rare, $5,000 plus; the Crandall Donkey and Rider are $800–$1,000.

man, too, did not escape the satirical barbs of toy makers, as witness the Ives "Irish Woodchopper" clockwork toy, featuring a woodsman with decidedly simian features. "Paddy and His Pig," clearly a lampoon of the company kept by the shanty Irish, was replicated by Lehmann, Stock, and F. Strauss over the years. It depicts a crude-looking bumpkin astride a pig. Many toys showed Germans performing the most menial of tasks and

Two humorous black toys produced over 30 years apart. *Left:* Unfortunate African, maker unknown, 1885, wood, tin and cloth pull toy, $1,200–$1,400. *Right:* "Oh My" (or Alabama Coon Jigger), Lehmann, 1914; Strauss made an identical toy called "Tap Tap" which apparently Lehmann produced for them. "Oh My" is $450–$550.

the famed "Katzenjammer Kids" comic toys portrayed Hans and Fritz as nasty little brats.

What may have been lacking in taste was often redeemed by clever and amusing animation. Ethnic toys reflect a fascinating part of our culture and are increasingly in demand these days.

BLACKS

Alabama Coon Jigger, Strauss, 1910, lithographed tin, windup, also known as Tombo, a variation of the Lehmann jigger "Oh My" (Lehmann made the toy for Strauss).   *$300–$350*

Alligator With Rider, patented by Edward Ives and Joseph Pilkington, 1893, cloth-covered tin, black rides jointed gator, 22″ length.   *$5,000–plus*

Amos 'n' Andy (see "Comic and Character Toys").

Automatic Toy Boxers, patented by Maguire & Gallot, New Jersey and New York, 1876, painted tin with cloth clockwork on wood platform box, fighters give realistic sparring motion.

    $2,000–plus

Automatic Toy Dancers, patented by H. L. Brower, 1873, painted tin with cloth, clockwork, scenic backdrop in wood.
$2,000–plus

Banjo Player (Poor Old Joe), Secor, 1880s, clockwork, painted tin with cloth.
$2,000–plus

Black Couple, German, 1910–1912, lithographed tin, 8″ height, each.
$200–$250

Black Dancers, German, 1910, clockwork musical lithographed painted tin, 6″ height.
$350–$400

Black Dandy Dancing Toy, German, 1900s.
$300–$350

Black Dude, German, 1900s, with moving glass eyes, lithographed tin wind-up, 6¾″ height.
$300–$400

Black Girl Leading Elephant, German, 1910, 4½″ length.
$300–$400

Black Man Playing Bass, Gunthermann, 1900s, painted tin clockwork, man in big hat seated on stool plays violin with both hands and feet, bright colors, 8½″ height.
$500–$600

Black Man Pushing Cart, German, 1900s, 6½″ height.
$150–$200

Black Musicians, Gunthermann (German), banjo and tambourine men, 8¾″ width, 8″ height.
$700–$800

Black Driver and Donkey Cart, $600–$800.

Black Squeeze Toy, maker unknown, 1920s, bellows activates mouth, $300–$400.

Black One-Man Band, German, 1910, lithographed tin, wind-up, 8½" height. $300–$350

Black "Yellow Kid" in Goat Cart, early 1900s, identical to Yellow Kid version by Kenton except for black color and red vs. yellow nightshirt, 7½" length. $250–$350

Brudder Bones, Secor, 1882, painted tin, clockwork.
$3,000–plus

Busy Bootblack, German, early 1900s, painted tin wind-up, 6" height. $600–$700

Cakewalk Dancer (Hero of the Cakewalk), variation of J. M. Cromwell patent, 1879, dapper "gentleman of color" in swallowtail coat dances on platform that has hanging backdrop overhead, 9½" height (see also "Shoo Fly Champion Dancers").
$2,000–plus

Charleston Trio, Marx, 1920s, lithographed tin wind-up, includes dancer, violinist, and performing poodle. $350–$450

Colored Dancers, German, circa 1910, painted tin mechanical, couple appears to be waltzing in circles. $450–$550

Crow's Patent American Negro Dancing Toy, German, 1910, 9″ height. $400–$500

Dancer With Fan, H. P. German, 1910, lithographed tin, black lady, 7″ height. $400–$500

Dapper Dan (The Jigging Porter), Marx, 1920s, lithographed tin wind-up, Dan wears porter's cap. $400–$500

Darktown Battery (see "Mechanical Banks" listing).

Darktown Dude, German, 1910, painted tin mechanical. $500–$600

Darky With Alligator, Gong Bell, 1903, cast-iron pull toy, black pulls bell on chain with alligator at opposite end, 7½″ length. $1,500–$2,500

Darky Ball Toss, German, 1900s, handpainted composition and cloth, ball toss with darky's mouth open as target, 20″ height. $2,500–$3,000*

Darky Banjo Player, German, 1910, painted tin wind-up, 6¾″ height. $450–$550

Darky Boy and Dog, German, 1924, painted tin. $300–$400

Boy with Dog, German, 1920s, 6¾″ height (missing chicken), $75–$100.

*Sold for $3,300 at Opfer Christmas Auction, December 1985.

Darky in Rocking Chair, German, 1900s, painted tin, known for scary, distorted features of man who rocks back and forth.
                                                                    $300–$400

Disappearing Darky (Jack-in-Box), German, 1910, composition and wood, black thumbs nose as he pops up out of chimney, 4 ½″ height. $250–$300

Female Driver With Large Earrings Driving Car, George Levy, German, 1920s, lithographed tin wind-up, celluloid windshield, 6 ½″ length. $300–$400

Freedman's Bank (see "Banks, Mechanical, Perelman Toy Museum Sale" listing).

Frightened Coon, German, 1910, black riding pig, painted tin wind-up. $650–$750

Funny Fire Fighters, Marx, 1920s, lithographed tin and celluloid, pair black fighters with boxing gloves in crazy car type with ladder, 8″ length. $200–$250

Ham and Sam, Struss, 1920s, one of scores of piano toys produced by Strauss and arch competitor, Louis Marx, lithographed tin wind-up, Ham is at piano while Sam plays banjo, 8 ½″ height. $300–$400

Ham and Sam, Line Mar, 1950s, pair behind blackboard, 5″ height. $400–$450

Happy Jack and Happy James Dancers, W.K., German, 6 ½″ height. $400–$500

Happy Jack Dancer, W.K., German, tin crank lithographed, 8″ height. $300–$350

Hercules Jazz Band, Chein, 1920s, lithographed tin wind-up, group of four black musicians, 11 ½″ height. 12″ width.
                                                                    $150–$200

Hey Hey the Chicken Snatcher, Marx, 1920s, lithographed tin wind-up, 8 ½″ height. $350–$400

Hot n'Tott, Strauss, 1925, lithographed tin wind-up, more uncommon variation of above, 8″ height, 7 ¾″ width. $500–$600

Initiation First Degree, Stevens, 1890 (see "Banks, Mechanical, Perelman Toy Museum Sale").

Jazzbo Jim, Strauss, 1920s, lithographed tin wind-up, 10″ height. $300–$350

Jazzbo Jim Dancer on Roof, Unique Art, 1920s, 8″ height. $400–$500

Jazzbo Jim and His Friends, Strauss, 1925. $400–$450

Jolly Nigger Mechanical Bank, England, 1900s, cast metal. $300–$400

Lady With Basket, German, 1910, painted tin mechanical, 7½″ height. $300–$350

Lenox Avenue and 125th Street, Japanese, 1950s, lithographed tin wind-up with celluloid and cloth, black man dances in front of street sign (the Savoy, Cotton Club, and Lenox Club were all located on this celebrated avenue in New York's Harlem). $200–$250

Male Evangelist, Ives, 1880s, composition, tin, cloth clockwork. $2,000–plus

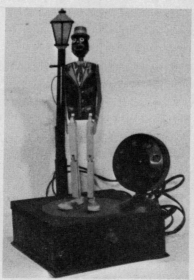

Microphone Dancer, National Co., 1920s, painted wood figure, metal base, battery operated, 11″ height, $650–$700.

Mammy's Boy, German, 1929, lithographed tin mechanical, 11″ height. $200–$250

Maude and Sam, All Fair Toys, 1920s, lawn cart, lithographed tin, 9″ height. $300–$400

Microphone Dancer, National Comp. Inc., 1920s, composition and tin, black leans against lamp post, toy is activated by speaking through small attached microphone, 12″ height.
                                                                              $650–$700

Negro Boy and Cat, N.N. Hill, 1905, cast-iron bell toy, boy pulls cat's tail, 6½″ length. $650–$700

Negro Nursemaid With White Child, Excelsior Toy Co., 1880s, painted composition with cloth. $2,000–plus

Negro With Three-Wheeler, German, 1910, painted tin, rider doffs hat in greeting motion as vehicle moves. $800–$900

Negro Woman Shopper, German, 1910, painted tin mechanical, 6½″ height. $400–$500

"Oh My" (Lehmann version of Alabama Coon Jigger).
                                                                              $450–$550

"Old Aunt Chloe," Ives, 1880s, composition with cloth, clockwork, scrubs over washboard. $8,000–plus

"Old Black Joe," Ives, 1880s, clockwork, painted composition with cloth. $7,000–plus

"Old Susannah" Musical Crank Toy, German, 1910, plays tune when cranked, black strumming banjo pictured, 4½″ height.
                                                                              $350–$450

One-Man Band, Muller & Kadeder, drummer with cymbals, painted tin mechanical, 7½″. $700–$800

Plantation Mechanical Bank, Weeden, 1888, dancer and banjo player. $1,000–plus

Porter With Rollo Chair (see "Lehmann Toys" listing).

Pushcart With Black, Fernand Martin, French, 1920s, painted tin clockwork, black leans into pushcart loaded with fruit and pushes from rear. $5,000–plus

Rastus and His Mother, Gong Bell, 1903, mammy and son hold bell between them on chain, bell pull toy, 7½″ length.
                                                                              $2,000–plus

Red Cap Porter, Strauss, 1930s, 6½″ height, $100–$150.

Red Cap Porter, Strauss, 1927, lithographed tin mechanical, 6½″ height. $300–$350

Red Cap Porter With Handcart, Strauss, 1920s, lithographed tin mechanical, dog leaps out of steamer trunk as porter pushes, 6½″ length. $400–$500

Sambo Special, manufacturer unknown, 1920s, lithographed wood, painted toy, 8″ height. $100–$125

Seesaw With Clown and Darky, Gong Bell, 1903, cast-iron pull toy, 6½″ length. $800–$900

Shoo Fly Champion Dancers, patented by J. M. Cromwell, late 1870s, tin clockwork, figures advance, retreat, pousette, and perform variety of antics, 9½″ height. $5,000–plus

Sister Lucinda at the Play, Secor, 1880s, composition clockwork with cloth, fans self and shakes head and body from side to side. $10,000–plus

Spic and Span, Strauss, 1935–1936, lithographed tin wind-up, another jigger toy, 10″ height. $500–$600

Stump Speaker, Stevens, 1900s, cast-iron mechanical bank. $1,000–plus

Spic and Span, Strauss, 1935–1936, 10″ height, $500–$600.

Sweeping Mammy, Lingstrom, 1920s, lithographed tin mechanical, 9″ height. $200–$300

Tom Bones Marionette, maker unknown, painted wood, minstrel dummy, 13″ height. $2,500–$3,000*

"Two Coons," Gong Bell, 1903, cast-iron bell pull toy, black and possum gaze at each other from opposite ends of hollow log, 8½″ length. $2,000–plus

Watermelon Bell Toy, N.N. Hill, 1905, cast-metal pull toy, black boys slice watermelon on platform with cross-cut saw as toy is pulled across floor. $1,000–plus

Women's Rights or Suffragette Clockwork Toy. $5,000–plus

OTHERS

Automated Tea Drinker, manufacturer unknown, early 1900s, Mandarin raises cup to lip, clockwork, tin mechanical.
                                                       $2,000–plus

*Sold for $3,850 at Riba-Mobley Auction in November 1986.

Chinaman in Boat, possibly James Bailey, lead, mechanical bank, place coin on tray and raise Chinaman's pigtail, he raises arm and flips coin, 4½" height.   *$2,000–plus*

The Chinaman Walker, patented by Arthur Hotchkiss, Ives, 1876, composition with cloth clockwork (toy inspired by movement begun in 1850s to exclude Chinese from immigrating to the United States).   *$6,000–plus*

Chinese Boxers, early 1900s, possibly German, 4 boxers in each corner of ring, 5th is tossed in blanket, pair of dice and ball also accompanied toy (may well have been used as gambling game, see also Lehmann version of toy).   *$2,000–plus*

Chinese Roly-Poly, Schoenhut, 1910, composition, with turning head, 15" height (Schoenhut made toy in several other sizes).
                    $400–$500

Dancing Dutch Couple, Martin, 1910, painted tin mechanical, 6½" height.   *$500–$600*

Dutch Boy Roly-Poly, Schoenhut, 1910, papier-mâché.
                    $400–$500

Dutch Girl Roly-Poly, Schoenhut, 1910, papier-mâché.
                    $400–$500

Dutch Jolly Jiggers, Schoenhut, papier-mâché, wood, and cloth, jiggers are on bent wires and dance when platform below is squeezed, 16" height, 22" length.   *$1,200–$1,400**

Indian Bust Still Bank, manufacturer unknown, 1910, cast iron, 3¾" height.   *$300–$400*

Indian (Hindu) Roly-Poly, Schoenhut, 1910.   *$600–$700***

Indian on Horse, German, 1920s, two-dimensional handoperated squeeze action, tin, Indian has sharp, stylized features, 6½" length.   *$300–$400*

Indian Rowing Canoe, manufacturer unknown, 1920s, painted tin wind-up, 8" length.   *$300–$400*

Irish Woodchopper, Ives, 1882, composition clockwork, Irishman with pipe chops log.   *$3,000–plus*

*Sold for $2,800 at Atlanta Toy Museum Auction, October 1986.
**Sold for $1,100 at Atlanta Toy Museum Auction, October 1986.

Irish Woodcutter, Ives, 1880s, clockwork mechanical, possibly unique, sold for $22,500 at Bernard Barenholtz Sale at Acevedo's, New York City, in 1989.

Irishman With Pigs, German, 1914, painted tin mechanical, chases two pigs with stick, 7 ½" length.   *$400–$500*

Jiggs in His Jazz Car, Maggie and Jiggs (see "Comic and Character Toys" listing).

Polite Chinaman, German, early 1900s, painted tin clockwork, Mandarin with pigtails seesaws on high pole, 13" height.

$400–$500

Sax Player, German, 1930s, lithographed tin squeeze toy, cymbals on feet, eyes roll, arms move and cymbals clash, 6½" height.   *$150–$200*

Scotchman on Scooter, Nifty, 1929, lithographed tin mechanical, 8" length.   *$300–$400*

Squaw and Papoose, in bas relief bust, dark finish with gold trim.   *$350–$450*

Two-faced Indian, manufacturer unknown, 1900s, cast-iron still bank, chief with full headdress back-to-back bust figure, 4¼" height.   *$250–$350*

CRANDALL'S
TWO JOLLY BLACKS.

Top: A pair of clockwork toys from the 1880s. "Old Nursemaid and
Child" is made by Excelsior Toy Company. The doll's head is of Ger-
man China, the maid's head is composition, Double Dancers by Ives.
Both are rarities, and clearly belong in the $2,000 plus range.

Games

W.B. and S.B. Ives made the first moves on these shores to bring board games into the social milieu in 1843 with the highly moralistic "Mansion of Happiness" (see "Educational Toys" listing for additional background). The real triumvirate among game board manufacturers, however, proved to be McLoughlin Brothers, Parker Brothers, and Milton Bradley (with Selchow and Righter a not too distant fourth). The exciting and colorful chromolithography that typifies late 19th-century mass-produced board games has caught the eye of a growing legion of games people. Noel Barrett, co-manager of the Atlanta Toy Museum series of auctions, cites board games as one of the most active categories in the hobby today, and prices realized from their October 1986 auction clearly bear him out.

COMIC STRIP GAMES

Andy Gump, His Game, licensed by Sidney Smith Corp., 1924. $100–$125

Beetle Bailey, The Old Army Game, Milton Bradley, 1963. $25–$35

Charlie McCarthy Question and Answer Game, Whitman Pub., 1938. $25–$35

Charlie McCarthy Topper Game, Whitman Pub., 1938. $35–$40

Dick Tracy Detective Game, Whitman Pub., 1937. $35–$50

Dick Tracy Playing Card Game, Whitman Pub., 1937.
$25–$35

Donald Duck's Party Game for Young Folks, Parker Bros.
$50–$75

Eddie Cantor's Tell It to the Judge, Parker Bros., 1938.
$35–$50

Ed Wynn, the Fire Chief, Selchow and Righter, 1937.
$35–$50

Fibber McGee and the Wistful Vista Mystery Game, Milton Bradley. $25–$35

High Spirits, With Calvin and the Colonial, Milton Bradley, 1920s. $25–$35

Hi-Way Henry Cross-Country Auto Race, circa late 1920s.
$250–$300

Little Orphan Annie Game, Milton Bradley, 1927. $75–$100

The Nebbs, Adventures of, Milton Bradley, 1925–1927.
$35–$50

Oh Blondie, 1940, Whitman Pub., game (played like Bingo).
$25–$35

Popeye Playing Card Game, circa 1934, Whitman Pub.
$15–$25

Smitty Game, Milton Bradley, circa 1930. $50–$75

Snow White and the Seven Dwarfs, Milton Bradley, 1937.
$100–$150

Toonerville Trolley Game, Milton Bradley, 1927. $100–$200

Uncle Remus Game, Zip, Parker Bros., circa 1930. $100–$125

Uncle Wiggily, Milton Bradley, 1918. $75–$100

Walt and Skeezix Gasoline Alley Game, Milton Bradley, circa 1920. $50–$75

Yellow Kid, maker unknown, late 1890s. $125–$150

GAME PRESERVE SALE, SKINNER, BOLTON, MASSACHUSETTS

The sale of the Game Preserve Collection at Skinner Auctions in Bolton, Massachusetts, on September 17, 1988, was truly a landmark event. The Game Preserve proprietors, Lee and Rally Dennis of Peterborough, New Hampshire, had been collecting vintage board games for the past 35 years. A total of 315 lots came under the hammer, and group lots pushed the total to over 1,500 games. Highlighted here are some of the prime specimens from that sale. Additional examples appear under the "Sports Games" heading. The 10% buyer's premium is included in the figures quoted below.

Babe Ruth's Baseball Game, Milton Bradley, in conjunction with Christy Walsh Syndicate, circa 1926–1928, 85 cards, 12 round wooden counters, multicolored lithographed board. *$770*

Black-Related Board Games, Lot of 6, "Game of Hitchhiker," Whitman Pub.; "Alabama Coon," by Spears; "Conversation Cards," J. Ottmann; "Game of Snap," "Ten Little Niggers," Parker Bros.; "Black Sambo," S. Gabriel & Sons. *$1,430*

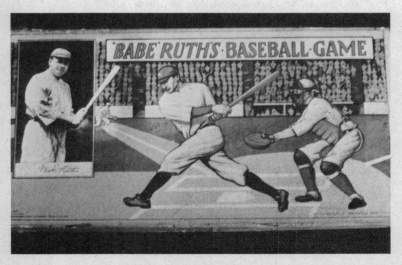

Babe Ruth's Baseball Game, Milton Bradley, 1926, $770. (The Game Preserve Sale, 1988; Skinner Auctions photo.)

Boys Own Football Game, McLoughlin Bros., circa 1901, 24 pieces, cardboard indicator, wooden piece representing football, 11 wooden round counters (red) and 11 counters (white) representing teams, multicolored lithographed board with football field layout. $550

Checkered Game of Life, Milton Bradley, 1866, Bradley's first game, red, black, and white lithography on card stock, framed. $1,045

Chiromagica, McLoughlin Bros., circa 1870, wooden box with slide cover, mechanical hand pointer revolves in circle to answer questions, also an answer sheet with three matching question disks to set in center, answers are magnetically keyed to questions. $825

Enchanted Table and Bewitched People, McLoughlin Bros., 1875, wooden box, glass table with wooden and felt "rubbing tool," 5 handcolored rice paper dancers. $770

Errand Boy or Failure and Success, McLoughlin Bros., circa 1891, wooden box, five pieces: four wooden colored counters and cardboard spinner, errand boy pictured in center of board, Horatio Alger theme track game. $770

Game of Balloon, R. Bliss, 1889, pair of rackets, hoop with stand and balloons. $500

Game of Baseball, McLoughlin Bros., circa 1896, 21 pieces, including nine lead players, lithographed board of baseball diamond. $2,530

> *Note:* Another example, in similar condition, brought $550 a few months later at a Riba Auction in Wethersfield, Connecticut.

Game of Bicycle Race, McLoughlin Bros., circa 1891, 11 pieces, including six colored numbered wheelmen, track game. $605

Game of Cat, Chafee & Selchow, circa 1900, wooden box, spinner, and six wooden counters, multicolored lithographed board forms bottom of box, shows 11 children at play. $220

Game of Cats and Mice, Merry Christmas Series, McLoughlin Bros., circa 1890–1901, five pieces, large wooden "cat" counter, three small wooden "mice" counters, double-arrow spinners, board has litho of cats chasing mice; track game. $880

Mail Express or Accommodations, McLoughlin Bros., 1895, $1,100. (Sold at The Game Preserve Auction, 1988; Skinner photo.)

Game of Golf, McLoughlin Bros., circa 1896, wooden box, 23 pieces including players, counters, and spinner, board depicts golf course layout.   *$825*

Game of Mail Express or Accommodations, McLoughlin Bros., 1895, wooden box, 45 pieces including four lead trains, pair of dice cups, lithographed board depicts map of the U.S., engraved by Bradley & Poates, New York City.   *$1,100*

Game of Man in the Moon, McLoughlin Bros., circa 1901, wooden box, 24 round counters, lithographed multicolored checkerboard showing phases of the moon, strategy game.
                                                                   $5,060

Game of Playing Department Store, McLoughlin Bros., 1898, wooden box, 54 counters including numerous cards representing money, multicolored lithograph shows all kinds of store merchandise for sale.   *$1,320*

Game of the Races, William Crosby, 1844, Bouvre & Sharp, Boston lithographers, oval track, game pieces, teetotum and ivory markers, forms book when closed, framed.   *$1,210*

Game of Red Riding Hood, Parker Bros., circa 1895, spinner and two colored wooden markers, colorful lithographed board shows Red Riding Hood, Big Bad Wolf, lumberman, and long track winding through forest. $440

Game of Stars and Stripes or Red, White, and Blue, McLoughlin Bros., circa 1900, wooden box, 53 pieces, two dice cups, 44 small silver stars, one large star and four lead soldiers carrying U.S. flag, red, white, blue checkerboard with field of stars in center. $990

Game of the Telegraph Boy, McLoughlin Bros., circa 1888, wooden box, four messenger boys, metal arrow, scenes of training schools, applicant's office, and prison, track game to reach goal of "President." $1,100

Game of Tobogganing at Christmas, McLoughlin Bros., circa 1899, four lead Santas driving sleigh, a reindeer and spinner, track game similar to Chutes & Ladders. $770

Game of Topsy Turvy, McLoughlin Bros., circa 1899, wooden box, 26 pieces, four wooden men, four smaller men, 17 round counters and spinner, Parchesi-type track game. $605

Game of Trip Around the World, McLoughlin Bros., circa 1897, wooden box, 14 pieces including dice cups, six lead pieces shaped like yachts, multicolored board of map of the globe.
$1,320

Game of the Visit of Santa Claus, #605, McLoughlin Bros., circa 1899, 38 pieces including 36 cards, spinner, and a wooden counter, multicolored board shows Santa with vignettes of Santa in his workshop. $2,090

Game of a Visit to the Old Homestead, McLoughlin Bros., 1902, wooden box, 19 pieces including spinner, four colored wooden tokens, 14 flat wooden round counters, track game. $1,210

Game of War at Sea, McLoughlin Bros., circa 1898, wooden box, 8 painted metal battleships, multicolored litho on box cover shows giant warship with "Don't Give Up the Ship" (Spanish American War inspired). $715

Majestic Game of the Asiatic Ostrich, William Darton, London, circa 1812, multicolored lithograph on parchment, hand-painted, 19½" × 23" framed. $650

Major League Baseball Game, Philadelphia Game Mfg. Co., circa 1912, back of box cover features baseball diamond framed by oak, 20 pegged players, six wooden score pegs, two small red boxes, nine packets of line-up cards, Honus Wagner, Ty Cobb listed on line-up cards. $715

Mansion of Happiness, W. & S.B. Ives, 1843, oval track, lithographed and handpainted, S.W. Chandler lithographer, Boston, closed like book and buckled, game pieces, teetotum, and ivory markers, framed. $990

Milton Bradley Table Games (10 Assorted), Little Orphan Annie, Adventure of the Nebs, Andy Gump, His Game, Parker Bros.; The Woggle Bug Game, Balancing the Budget, The Embossing Company; The Game of the Hour Quick Kit, The Elkin Game Co.; Bottoms Up, All-Fair Cities, Hareh-Gilmar, Inc.; Storyland Puzzle Wizard of Oz. $1,760

Monopoly, Charles B. Darrow, circa 1934, 187 pieces, believed to be one of Darrow's 25,000 games manufactured privately by the inventor before Parker Bros. purchased rights. $2,640

Monopoly Memorabilia, including another game invented by Charles Darrow, "Bulls & Bears, A Stock Exchange Game," other games, books, photos relating to Darrow. $3,740

The Naturalist, E. Wallis, London, 1820, circular track, lithographed on linen, handpainted, various exotic fauna, illustrated, framed. $1,650

New Game of Aesop, H.M. Francis, 1861, multicolored lithographed and handpainted board, framed. $770

New Game of Hunting, McLoughlin Bros., circa 1904, wooden box, 20 pieces, four colored lead dogs, spinner, 14 round lithographed game pieces, board depicts country vista with brook and mountains. $990

New National Snake Game, Charles Magnus, circa 1855, political game, multicolored lithograph and handpainted, framed.
                                                           $1,210

North Pole Game, Milton Bradley, circa 1907, six pieces, two dice cups, pair dice, two wooden counters, multicolored scenes of Arctic depicted on board, track game. $522.50

Reward of Virtue, W. & S.B. Ives, J. H. Bufford & Co., Boston lithographer, invented by Anne Abbot, framed. $1,760

New National Snake Game, Charles Magnus, circa 1855, $1,210. (The Game Preserve Sale, Skinner, 1988.)

Rival Policemen, McLoughlin Bros., circa 1896, wooden box, two wooden dice cups, 23 pieces, four lead policemen in maze, framed. **$2,200**

Running the Blockade, Charles Magnus, lithographer, circa 1861–1865, handpainted, Civil War scenes, 13 wooden counters representing crooks, board pictures streets of a city, track game. **$1,760**

Siege of Havana, Parker Bros., circa 1898, wooden box, four metal colored battleships, dice cup and dice, numerous colored wooden "shots" and "shells," pull-out drawer for playing pieces, board has cameo views of Havana, Morro Castle, batteries, cannon, and ships, track game. **$522.50**

The Susceptibles, McLoughlin Bros., 1891, wooden box, 48 pieces, one wooden "leader," four "companions," five colored wooden aids, eight checker "susceptibles," board depicts 1890s scenes around perimeter, starred square in center of board, strategy game. **$605**

Train for Boston, Parker Bros., circa 1900, $990. (Sold at The Game
Preserve Auction, 1988; Skinner photo.)

Train for Boston, Parker Bros., circa 1900, wooden box, five
pieces, four colored wooden counters, board shows train depots
of Washington, St. Louis, Chicago, New York in each corner,
Boston is right of center, track game.   *$990*

Wonderful World of Oz, Parker Bros., circa 1921, 11 pieces, dice
cup, six wooden "Wizard" cubes, four pewter figures of Dorothy
and friends, lithographed map track game.   *$1,045*

Yankee Doodle, Parker Bros., circa 1895, wooden box, five (plus)
pieces, four colored wooden counters, red and yellow cardboard
disks, board shows cameos of historic naval battles in U.S.
history.   *$715*

Zippy Zepps, Alderman Fairchild, circa 1925, 31 pieces, 25
cards, five painted metal zeppelins, folding lithographed board
shows airship flying over ocean to London, Berlin, and Paris,
track game.   *$357.50*

HISTORICAL GAMES

Admiral Byrd's South Pole Game, Parker Bros., 1934.
                                                     $100–$200

American History in Pictures, Interstate School Educational
Game.   *$20–$25*

Captain Kidd Treasure Game, Parker Bros., 1890s.
$100–$125

Columbus Puzzle, Milton Bradley, 1890s. $35–$50

Comical History of America, Parker Bros., 1920s. $25–$35

Defenders of the Flag, Noble and Noble Pub., 1920s. $50–$75

Dewey's Victory, Parker Bros., 1900. $250–$300

Flag Game, McLoughlin Bros., 1880s. $350–$400

Flight to Paris, Milton Bradley, 1927. $150–$200

Game of American History, Parker Bros., 1890s. $35–$50

Game of Buffalo Bill, Parker Bros., 1980s $25–$35

Game of Politics (see "Political and Patriotic Toys" listing).

Game of Rough Riders, Clark and Sowdon, early 1900s.
$200–$250

Game of '76 (or The Lion and the Eagle), Noyes and Snow, 1876. $100–$125

Game of the Transatlantic Flight, circa 1924, Milton Bradley.
$200–$250

Game of World's Fair, Star Pub., card game, 1923. $100–$125

George Washington's Dream Reading Game, Parker Bros., late 1890s. $35–$50

Heroes of America, Games of Nations Series, Paul Educational Games, card game, 1920s. $25–$30

Historical Game of Cards, A. Flanagan, 1800s. $25–$30

History of Up To Date, Parker Bros., card game, early 1900s.
$25–$30

Home History Game for Boys and Girls, Milton Bradley, card game, 1910. $35–$40

Hood's War Game, C. I. Hood, Spanish-American War, circa 1900. $30–$50

In the White House, Fireside Game Co., card game, 1896.
$50–$75

Lindy Flying Game, Parker Bros., card game, 1927. $25–$50

Mayflower, Cincinnati Game Co., card game, 1890s.   *$25–$30*

Naval Engagement, McLoughlin Bros., Civil War, 1870.
      $100–$125

North Pole Game, Milton Bradley, 1907.   *$300–$350*

Panama Canal Puzzle Game, U. S. Playing Cards Co., 1910.
      $75–$100

Pyramids, Knapp Electric, 1930s.   *$25–$35*

Race for the North Pole, Milton Bradley, 1900s.   *$100–$150*

Royal Game of Kings and Queens, McLoughlin Bros., 1890s.
      $50–$75

Siege of Havana, Parker Bros., late 1890s.   *$300–$400*

Strat: The Great War Game, Strat Game Co., World War I, 1915.   *$50–$100*

War of Nations, Milton Bradley, World War I, 1915.   *$50–$75*

The Way to the White House, Electing the President, All-Fair.
      $25–$50

Yankee Doodle, Cadaco-Ellis, circa 1940.   *$15–25*

NURSERY RHYME GAMES

Aesop's Fables Cube Puzzles, McLoughlin Bros., 1800s.
      $200–$250

Beauty and the Beast, Milton Bradley, 1900s.   *$50–$100*

Black Sambo, Samuel Gabriel and Sons, circa 1939.
      $125–$150

Bo Peep, McLoughlin Bros., 1890s.   *$350–$400*

Cinderella, Milton Bradley, card game, 1900s.   *$25–$50*

Cinderella/Hunt the Slipper, McLoughlin Bros., variation of Old Maid, 1887.   *$25–$50*

Cock Robin and His Tragical Death, McLoughlin Bros., card game, 1880s.   *$25–$50*

Dr. Busby St. Nicholas Series Game, J. Ottmann Lithograph Co., 1890s.   *$15–$25*

Game of Fox and Geese, J. H. Singer, card game, 1870s.
$20–$25

Game of Little Jack Horner, McLoughlin Bros., card game, 1880s.
$25–$50

Game of Old King Cole, McLoughlin Bros., card game, 1880s.
$25–$35

Game of Old Mother Hubbard, Milton Bradley, board game, 1890s.
$50–$75

Game of Red Riding Hood, Adventure Series, Parker Bros., board game, 1895.
$250–$300

Game of Robinson Crusoe, Parker Bros., card game, 1895.
$25–$50

Game of Sambo, Parker Bros., target game, 1920s. $75–$100

Game of Three Blind Mice, Milton Bradley, board game, 1920s.
$75–$100

Game of Tom Sawyer, Milton Bradley, board game, 1930s.
$125–$150

Game of Treasure Island, Gem Publishing Co., board game, 1920s.
$75–$100

Game of Visit of Santa Claus, McLoughlin Bros., board game, 1899.
$500–$600

Hickety-Pickety, Parker Bros., board game, 1920s. $50–$100

Ivanhoe, Parker Bros., card game, 1890s. $35–$50

Jack and the Beanstalk, Parker Bros., board game, 1890s.
$200–$250

Jack and Jill, Milton Bradley, board game, 1909. $35–$50

Little Bo Peep, Parker Bros., card game, 1895. $15–$25

Little Boy Blue, Milton Bradley, board game, 1900s.
$175–$200

Little Jack Horner, Milton Bradley, board game, 1900s.
$175–$200

Little Mother Goose, Parker Bros., card game, 1890. $50–$75

Old Woman Who Lived in a Shoe, Parker Bros., board game.
$350–$400

Owl and Pussycat, E. O. Clark, board game, 1890s.
$300–$350

Peter Rabbit, Milton Bradley, board game, 1910. $200–$250

Pollyanna, The Glad Game, Parker Bros., board game, circa 1914. $75–$100

Raggedy Ann's Magic Pebble Game, Milton Bradley, board game, 1940. $50–$75

Red Riding Hood and the World, McLoughlin Bros., board game, 1890s. $200–$250

Robinson Crusoe, McLoughlin Bros., board game, 1890s.
$200–$250

Santa Claus Game, Milton Bradley, board game, 1920s.
$200–$300

Santa Claus Puzzle Box, Milton Bradley, picture puzzles, 1920s. $150–$200

Tortoise and the Hare, U.S. Playing Card Co., board game, 1900s. $100–$150

Winnie the Pooh, Steven Slesinger, Inc., board game, 1933.
$75–$100

Wonderful Game of Oz, Parker Bros., board game, 1921.
$300–$350

SPORTS GAMES

Amateur Golf, Parker Bros., 1928. $150–$200

Babe Ruth's Baseball Game, Milton Bradley, 1926.
$500–$600

Baseball, J. Otmann Lith. Co., New York City, exciting graphics of batter and catcher from early 1900s. $300–$350

Baseball Game, Parker Bros., 1913, card game. $50–$75

Big Six: Christy Mathewson, Indoor Baseball Game, Piroxloid Products Corp., 1922. $400–$500

Bobby Shantz Baseball Game, Realistic Games, mid-1950s.
$50–$100

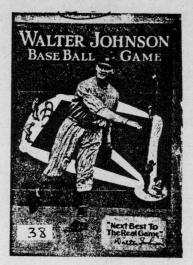

Walter Johnson Baseball Game, 1915, $418. (Riba Auctions, 1988.)

Bob Feller's Big League Baseball, Saalfield Pub., 1950s, bust portrait of Cleveland fireballer on box cover. $200–$250

Bowling, Parker Bros., 1896, board game. $250–$300

Boy's Own Football Game, McLoughlin Bros., 1800s.
$450–$500

Carl Hubbell's Mechanical Baseball, Gotham Pressed Steel Corp., New York City, 1950s, action game between pitcher and catcher. $125–$150

Carl Yastrzemski Action Baseball, Pressman, 1960s, all-metal diamond, automatic scoreboard, umpire. $50–$100
  Featuring Tom Seaver. $50–$100
  Featuring Roger Maris. $75–$120

Casey on the Mound, A. J. Kamms, 1930s, action game with box as part of diamond layout, portrait of pitcher on box lid (perhaps Hugh Casey of the Brooklyn Dodgers?). $100–$200

Championship Baseball Parlor Game, Grebnelle Novelty Co., circa 1914, 30 pieces, 20 yellow and blue players' position disks, photograph of 1914 Boston Braves, booklet listing all 16 leagues and 120 clubs, board is laid out as baseball diamond, invented by Henry Ellenberg, Jr. $1,430

Classic Derby, Doremus-Schoen Co., circa 1930s, race track board. $75–$100

Cross-Country Marathon, Milton Bradley, 1930s. $100–$150

Danny MacFadden's Stove League Baseball Game, National Games, Newtonville, Massachusetts, 1930s (McFadden was a so-so Yankee pitcher). $200–$250

Derby Day, Parker Bros., circa 1900, card game. $50–$75

Derby Steeplechase, McLoughlin Bros., 1890. $200–$250

Diamond Game of Baseball, McLoughlin Bros., circa 1885.
                                                       $350–$400

Dog Race, Transogram Co., Inc., circa 1930s. $50–$75

Favorite Steeplechase, J.H. Singer, circa 1895. $200–$250

Foot Race, Parker Bros., circa 1900. $200–$250

Fox Hunt, Milton Bradley, 1905. $175–$200

Game of Baseball, McLoughlin Bros., 1886. $1,000–plus

Game of Bicycle Race, McLoughlin Bros., 1891. $350–$450

Game of Football, George Childs, Brattleboro, Vermont, 1895.
                                                       $400–$500

Game of Gold, Clark and Snowdon, circa 1900s. $100–$150

Game of Steeple Chase, Milton Bradley, circa 1910.
                                                       $150–$200

Game of Tobogganing at Christmas, McLoughlin Bros., 1899.
                                                       $500–$600

Gil Hodges Pennant Fever, RGI, mid-1960s, Hodges in Met's uniform. $75–$125

Grande Auto Race, U.S. Playing Card Co., circa 1910.
                                                       $100–$125

The Great American Game, Baseball, Frantz Co., mid-1920s, lithographed tin, diamond layout skill game. $75–$100

Hank Aaron Baseball Game, Ideal, 1970s, plastic diamond lay-out and miniature pitching machine. $25–$50

Hank Bauer's "Be a Manager Game," National League Edition, Barco Games, 1960s. $50–$100

Hialeah Racing Game, Milton Bradley, 1940. $75–$100

Home Run King, Selrite Products, New York City, 1930s, wind-up batter (The Banbino) hits ball off batting tee, lithographed tin. $300–$400

Horse Race Game, Marx Bros. Co., circa 1930, Belmont Park. $75–$100

Hurdle Race, Milton Bradley, 1905. $200–$225

Joe "Ducky" Medwick's Big League Baseball Game, Johnson-Brier Co., mid-1930s. $175–$250

Kentucky Derby Racing Game, Whitman Pub., 1930s. $75–$100

Lou Gehrig's Official Play Ball, Christy Walsh, 1930s, metal diamond. $300–$400

Major League Baseball Game, Philadelphia Game Co., circa 1910, spinner skill game. $500–$600

Micky Mantle's Big League Baseball, Gardner & Co., late 1950s, includes portrait of Mantle on box, autographed photo and instructional record. $200–$300

National-American Baseball Game, Parker Bros., 1930s. $100–$125

New Game of Hunting, McLoughlin Bros., 1904. $500–$600

Official Baseball Game, Milton Bradley, late 1960s, includes 300 black and white playing cards, box cover shows nine major league stars including Mays, Aaron, Maglie, Frank Robinson, Ernie Banks. $100–$150

Official Radio Basketball Game, Toy Creations, 1930s. $50–$75

Official Radio Football Game, Toy Creations, 1939. $35–$50

Open Championship Golf Game, Beacon Hudson Co., 1920s. $75–$100

Outboard Motor Race, Milton Bradley, 1920s. $50–$75

Par Golf Card Game, National Golf Service Co., 1920s. $75–$100

Pat Moran's Own Ball Game, Smith, Kline, & French, early 1920s, portrait of Cincinnati Red's player on box cover.

$150–$200

Peg Baseball, Parker Bros., early 1900s, very ornate diamond layout with peg holes at each base, portrait of batter in middle of diamond. $250–$300

Races, Milton Bradley, circa 1880. $200–$250

Robin Roberts Sports Club Baseball Game, Dexter Wayne Co., 1950s, large cover portrait of Phillies' ace with autograph on ball. $100–$150

Saratoga Race Horse Game, Milton Bradley, 1920s.

$100–$125

Speedboat Race, Milton Bradley, 1930s. $100–$125

Speedem Auto Race, Alderman-Fairchild, 1922. $75–$100

Star Basketball, Star Paper Box Co., circa 1920s, bagatelle game. $75–$100

Steeplechase, C.M. Clark, 1910. $250–$300

Steeplechase, J.H. Singer, circa 1890s. $200–$250

Strike Three by Carl Hubbell, Tone Products, late 1940s, illustration of bat and ball on box cover. $100–$125

Table Croquet, Milton Bradley, circa 1890s, skill game.

$75–$100

Traps and Bunkers, A Game of Golf, Milton Bradley, circa 1930. $75–$100

Willie Mays "Say Hey" Baseball Game, Centennial Games, late 1950s. $200–$250

World's Championship Baseball Game, National Indoor Game and Novelty Co., 1900s. $100–$125

Yacht Race, Milton Bradley, circa 1905. $100–$125

Yachting, Parker Bros., circa 1895. $200–$250

TARGET GAMES

Big Game Hunters, Schoenhut, 1924, target game featuring large buffalo (five variations) with Buffalo Bill-type hunters who spring up when target is hit, varnished natural colors, wood base, 12″ width × 10¼″ height, other combinations: rhino and Hindu, bear and Indian, lion and deer with jungle hunters, 13½″ length gun included with eight wood cartridges.

$600–$700

Brownie Nine Pins, McLoughlin Bros., 1892, Palmer Cox Brownies including Uncle Sam, policeman, Eskimo, Dutchman, lithograph on wood, 11¾″ height. $500–$600

Buster Brown Beanbag Toss, Bliss, 1900s, lithograph on wood, Buster, Tige, and Buster's girl friend, 24″ wide. $500–$600

Columbia Ring Toss Game, maker unknown, 1890s, lithograph paper on wood, three metal hoops, 19½″ height.

$500–$600

Columbus Marble Pool Game, believed made by Bliss, circa 1893 (in celebration of Columbian Exposition), lithograph paper on wood, coiled metal spiral tower with lithograph alphabet blocks, Columbus figure with Spanish flag stands atop tower, 58″ height. $1,000–$2,000

Darky Ring Toss Game, maker unknown, 1890s, painted cast-iron stained wood, seven black figures, 8⅝″ wide. $300–$400

French Boy Marble Game, maker unknown, 1890s, lithograph paper on wood, boy is 8½″ length wide hole in stomach from which marble rolls toward recessed target area, 22″ length.

$500–$600

Jolly Marble Game, W. S. Reed, 1892, lithograph paper on wood, tivoli game, four of five clowns with animated legs which kick when activated, 21″ height. $500–$600

Le Moulin Game, French, 1890s, lithograph paper on cardboard, marble target game, two painted tin carts with boy drivers alternately climb ramp to retrieve marble, then roll back down to dump in scoring field as windmill turns. $500–$700

Le Nouveau Toboggan Game, French, 1890s, lithograph paper on wood and cardboard, spring-activated tin cars move down ramp in tower to tip trays, releasing marbles into scoring field, 25½″ height. $1,000–$2,000

Mother Goose Target Game, maker unknown, 1890s, lithograph paper on wood, ball roll target game; when knobs are hit, five targets pop up, 18¼″ wide. $700–$800

Old Guard Ten Pins, Ives, 1890s, lithograph paper on wood, 10 soldiers, 14″ height.   *$1,000–plus*

Punch and Judy Skittles, maker unknown, 1900s, painted wood and papier-mâché, nine figural skittles in shapes of Punch and Judy and other brightly painted characters, on weighted wooden bases, two wooden balls.   *$2,000–plus*

Pussy Cat Bean Bag Game, maker unknown, 1890s, lithograph on wood, wire stand, 15″ height.   *$300–$400*

Rubber Ball Shooting Gallery, Schoenhut, 1920s, lithograph paper on wood, popgun and nine targets include clowns, Negro, rabbit, and clay pipes.   *$350–$400*

Three Blacks Target Game, maker unknown, 1800s, paper lithograph on wood, rubber band gun, rubber missile spins black figures on wood dowels, 9½″ wide.   *$400–$500*

Trick Mule Target Game, W. S. Reed, lithograph on wood, clown rides mule on wood platform, roll ball to hit target and unseat clown, 22″ length.   *$1,200–$1,400*

Uncle Sam and John Bull Marble Roll, lithograph paper on wood, figures have movable arms, uses regular marbles, 15″ height.   *$450–$500*

Shooting Game, Strauss, 1920s, with original box, $300–$400.

TRAVEL GAMES

Account of Peter Coddle's Visit to New York, Milton Bradley, 1890s. $20–$25

Across the Continent, Parker Brothers, circa 1935. $50–$75

Across the Yalu, Milton Bradley, circa 1905. $100–$125

Aeroplane Race, McDowell Mfg. Co. (No. 60), 1930s. $75–$100

Airship Card Game, Parker Bros., 1916. $75–$100

Amusing Game of Innocence Abroad, Parker Bros., 1888. $200–$250

Auto Game, Milton Bradley, 1906. $100–$125

Billy Bumps' Visit to Boston, George S. Parker, circa 1887. $25–$50

Cousin Peter's Trip to New York (Game of), McLoughlin Bros., 1898. $15–$25

Crazy Travelers, Parker Bros., circa 1920, skill game. $35–$50

Crossing the Ocean, Parker Bros., circa 1893. $50–$75

Down the Pike With Mrs. Wiggs at the St. Louis Exposition, Milton Bradley, 1904. $50–$75

Excursion to Coney Island, Milton Bradley, circa 1880s. $200–$250

Fast Mail, Milton Bradley, circa 1900s. $300–$350

North Pole by Airship (Game of), McLoughlin Bros., 1897. $300–$400

Ocean to Ocean Flight Game, Wilder Mfg., circa 1927. $125–$150

Peter Coddle and His First Trip to New York, Milton Bradley, circa 1925 (there were several offshoots of this game). $15–$25

Pike's Peak or Bust, Parker Bros., circa 1895.   *$100–$125*

Round the World With Nelly Bly (Game of), McLoughlin Bros., circa 1890.   *$275–$300*

Street Car Game, Parker Bros., 1892.   *$250–$275*

Through the Locks to the Golden Gate, Milton Bradley, circa 1905.   *$175–$200*

Toll Gate (Game of), McLoughlin Bros., circa 1890.
          $250–$300

Touring, automobile card game, Wallie Dorr Co., 1926.
          $25–$50

Tourist, railroad game, Milton Bradley, circa 1900.   *$50–$75*

Train for Boston, Parker Bros., circa 1900.   *$350–$450*

Transatlantic Flight (Game of), Milton Bradley, circa 1924.
          $150–$200

Travel (Game of), Parker Bros., circa 1894.   *$150–$200*

Trip Around the World, Parker Bros., circa 1920.   *$50–$75*

Trip Around the World (Game of), McLoughlin Bros., 1897.
          $400–$500

Trip Through Our National Parks, Game of Yellowstone, Cincinnati Game Co., circa 1910.   *$125–$150*

Trips of Japhet Jenkens and Sam Slick, Milton Bradley, circa 1871.   *$35–$50*

Trips Railroad Game, Trips Card Co., 1905.   *$50–$75*

Trolley Ride (Game of), Hamilton-Myers Co. Pub., 1890s.
          $35–$50

Voyage Around the World (Game of), Milton Bradley, circa 1930s.   *$100–$125*

Wide World Game, Parker Bros., 1933.   *$50–$75*

Glass Figural
Candy Containers

✳ ✳ ✳

More and more toy collectors are encroaching on the sacred soil
of glass collectors in recent years in quest of fascinating figural
candy containers in shapes of animals, transportation vehicles,
household items, and comic characters. Although candy containers have enjoyed a recent revival in certain gift shops and
confectionaries, it is the pre–World War II vintage containers
that are so eagerly pursued, particularly varieties dating back
as early as 1912.

Considering their rarefied standing today, it is difficult to con-
ceive of containers as mere trinkets, available for 10 to 12 cents
at any local five-and-dime store. Once emptied of their treasure
of tiny hard candy pellets, a surprisingly large quantity of these
containers were preserved as decorative objects. Most containers were of clear glass, although there are examples in ruby,
blue, and even milk glass. Frequently, they were painted in vivid
colors. The value of the glass toy is enhanced if it has the original paper or tin closure, and if it has retained the original paint.
Chips and cracks, of course, quickly send the value plummet-
ing.

Most of the following candy containers were offered in one of
the largest collections of such items to be offered in recent memory, that of Florence Main, at the Lloyd W. Ralston Auction in
Fairfield, Connecticut. We've included descriptive material on
each lot. The price estimates given are a partial reflection of
gaveled prices. To list actual prices realized would be misleading, since all types of grading variations came into play that
profoundly affected bidding.

Where available, references are given to two authoritative guides in this highly esoteric specialty. For example, (AE577) on the Upright Piano Bank refers to *American Glass Candy Containers* or *More American Glass Containers*, both by George Eikelberner and Serge Agadjanian, 1967 and 1970. Reference two (S778) is *A Century of Glass Toys* by Mary Louise Stanley, 1971.

Alligator Purse (AE599–S550), 4 ¼ ″ length. $250–$300

American Locomotive With Tin Lithographed Closure (AE496–S712), 4 ⅛ ″ length. $25–$50

Amos 'n' Andy (AE21–S1257), 4 ½ ″ length. $450–$500

Anchor Condiment Set (AE385–S353), 5 ¾ ″ height. $15–$25

Armored Tank (AE721–S1137), 4 ¼ ″ length. $50–$66

Army Bomber With Paper Propeller (AE6–S27), 4 ⅛ ″ length, each. $15–$25

Auto Lamp (AE396–S637), 5 ¾ ″ overall. $50–$75

Babe Ruth on the Bag (AE78–S315), 4 ⅛ ″ height. $600–$650

Baby Ben Alarm Clock (AE161–S259), 3 ½ ″ height.
$100–$125

Barney Google, 3 ⅝ ″ height. $150–$200

Barney Google With Apple (AE72–S294), 3 ⅞ ″ height, no paint; *Spark Plug* (AE699–S295), 4 ⅛ ″ length, each. $150–$200

Baseball Player and Bat Barrel Bank (AE77), 3 ¼ ″ height.
$500–$550

Battleship (AE97–S221), original paper closure, C6, 3 ⅝ ″ length. $50–$75

Battleship on Waves, (AE96–S220), 5 ¼ ″ length. $75–$100

Boston Kettle (AE355), leather handle, 2 ″ height. $50–$75

Br'er Rabbit (AE614), 5 ⅛ ″ height. $50–$60

Bugle With Tin Whistle (AE312–S762), 6 ¾ ″ height.
$75–$100

Bull Dog (S404), 4 ¼ ″ height. $50–$75

Camera on Tripod (AE121–S590), original bulb, 4 ½ ″ height.
$150–$200

Candy Swing (AE69–S13), 6¾" width overall.   *$500–$600*

Cannon on Golden Tin Carriage (AE124–S270), 4¾" length; *Cannon on Red Tin Carriage* (AE123–S274), 3¾" length, each.   *$225–$250*

Carrot (AE609–S850), 4½" height, each.   *$25–$50*

C.D. Kenny Co., dime savings bank with slotted tin top, 2¾" height.   *$35–$50*

Charlie Chaplin, Borgfeldt, 2⅞" length.   *$150–200*

Charlie Chaplin Barrel Bank (AE137–S307), 3¾" height.
     $150–200

Charlie Chaplin Barrel Bank, Smith (AE138–S308), 4⅛" height.   *$250–$300*

Chevrolet (AE34–S65), 5" length, each.   *$20–$30*

Chick in Cracked Eggshell Driving Auto (AE144–S186), 4¼" length.   *$250–$300*

Chicken on Nest (AE149–S187), 5" length.   *$50–$75*

Chicken on Rope Top Basket (AE147–S189), 3½" length.
     $50–$75

Chrysler Airflow (AE57–S49), 5" length.   *$75–$100*

Clambroth Coupe (AE51–S36), 5¼" length.   *$50–$70*

Convertible Auto 10 Cents (AE640–S92), 3¾" length.
     $20–$30

Cottage (AE324–S446), chipped chimney, 2¾" length.
     $200–$250

Crowing Rooster (AE151–S201), 5½" height.   *$100–$150*

Dirigible Los Angeles (AE176–S20), 6" length.   *$100–$125*

Dog by Barrel, screw cap, missing eyes, painted, 4" length.
     $100–$125

Dolly Sweeper (AE133–S517), 6½" height, C3; *Baby Sweeper* (AE132–S3), 7¾" height, each.   *$250–$300*

Don't Park Here Traffic Sign (AE196–S1147), 4⅝" height.
     $100–$150

Drinking Mug (S790), 4⅛" height.   *$15–$25*

Duck (AE198–S194), 3 ¾ " length.   *$50–$60*

Duck With Large Bill (AE199–S193), 4 ⅝ " length.   *$75–$100*

Duck on Sagging Basket (AE197–S192), rough edges on base,
C4, 3 ¾ " length.   *$75–$100*

Dutch Windmill (AE843–S1150), 4 ⅞ " height.   *$75–$100*

880 Locomotive (AE482–S725), 5 " length.   *$150–$200*

888 Locomotive (AE485–S708), 5 " length.   *15–$25*

Electric Car (AE48–S67), 3 ⅜ " length.   *$35–$50*

Electric Car (AE48–S68), 3 ½ " length; *Ford Hearse* (AE39–S79),
4 ⅜ " length, each.   *$75–$100*

Electric Car (AE49–S69), 3 ⅜ " length.   *$25–$50*

Electric Coupe No. 1, embossed under running boards, stamped
tin closure, 2 ⅝ " height.   *$50–$75*

Electric Iron(AE343–S520), 4 ⅜ " length.   *$15–$25*

Embossed Baby Jumbo Pencil (AE567), 6 " length.   *$15–$25*

Essex (AE38–S66), 4 ¾ " length.   *$100–$125*

Felix the Cat Barrel Bank (AE211–S268), 3 ½ " height.
                                                               $450–$500

Fire Engine (AE217), 4 ¼ " length.   *$15–$25*

Fire Engine (AE220), 5 ¼ " length.   *$15–$25*

Fire Engine (AE223), 5 " length.   *$35–$50*

Fire Engine #2 (AE212–S436), 4 ¾ " length.   *$15–25*

Fire Truck (AE215–S426), 5 " length.   *$15–$25*

Flossie Fisher's Bureau (AE237), litho tin, 3 " width.
                                                               $300–$350

Ford, high rounded hood (AE59–S767), 4 ⅛ " length.
                                                                $50–$60

Ford Hearse, (AE40–S77), corrugated hood, 4 ¼ " length.
                                                               $75–$100

Gas Pump (AE240–S1130), 4 ½ " height.   *$150–$200*

Gobbler Turkey Standing (AE790–S206), 3 ½ " height.
                                                               $75–$100

Gold Drum Mug (AE543–S784), 2 ³/₈ ″ height. $15–$20

Green Taxi (AE46), lithographed tin roof, 4 ¹/₈ ″ length.
$100–$125

Greyhound Bus (AE113–S44), 5 ″ length. $100–$150

Happy Fats on Drum (AE208–S301), 4 ¹/₂ ″ height. $150–$200

Hen on Sagging Basket (AE148–S183), 3 ¹/₂ ″ length. $50–$75

Horn (AE313–S763), Dutchboy, opal glass, 5 ¹/₂ ″ height.
$75–$100

Horn Trumpet, milk glass with painted-on bears, screw closure, 5 ¹/₂ ″ height. $50–$75

Hurricane Lamp (AE371–S586), 4 ⁵/₈ ″ height. $15–$25

Independence Hall Bank (AE342–S441), 7 ¹/₄ ″ height.
$250–$300

Indian Motorcycle With Sidecar (AE522–S1269), 5 ″ length.
$350–$400

Jack O'Lantern (AE349–S470), wire bale, 3 ⁷/₈ ″ height.
$25–$50

Jackie Coogan (AE345–S313), clear glass, 5 ″ height.
$850–$900

Jitney Bus (AE114–S1134), 4 ¹/₄ ″ length. $200–$250

Jolly Santa Claus (AE674–S892), plastic head, 5 ³/₄ ″ height.
$15–$25

Kewpie Doll Barrel Bank (AE359–S303), 3 ¹/₈ ″ height.
$75–$100

Kiddie Car (AE360–S503), hobbyhorse head, 4 ¹/₂ ″ length.
$75–$100

Knapp Pig, missing cap, 4 ″ length. $75–$100

Ladder Fire Truck (AE216–S45), 5 ″ length. $100–$150

Lantern, ruby flashed with gold trim, twist on closure, 4 ³/₈ ″ height. $50–$75

Lantern With Chain (AE438–S645), 3 ¹/₈ ″ height. $35–$50

Large Suitcase (AE707–S538), painted opal glass, C5, 4 ″ height. $75–$100

Letters U.S. Mail (AE521–S486), 3¼″ height. $100–$125

Liberty Bell (AE85), pink champagne, wire bale, 3⅜″ height.
$50–$60

Limousine (AE42–S39), 4⅛″ length. $75–$100

Lindbergh Spirit of Good Will (AE8–S18), 4⅞″ length.
$50–$75

Lynne Type Telephone (AE740), 4¾″ height. $25–$35

Mantel Clock Bank (AE164–S258), 3⅞″ height. $75–$100

Miniature Dial Telephone (AE739–S922). $75–$100

Miniature Fire Engine (AE213–S427), 5″ length; *Fire Truck, Chemical Bottles* (AE214–S439), 5¼″ length. $25–$50

Miniature Locomotive (AE489), 3⅞″ length; 888 Locomotive (AE482–S710), 4⅞″. $25–$35

Miniature Railroad Lantern (AE394), ribbed base, C6, 4½″ height. $50–$60

Miniature Streamline Auto, cardboard push closure, 3⅝″ length. $35–$50

Miniature War Tank (AE724–S1138), 4⅛″ length. $15–$20

Mutt Dog Barrel Bank (AE190–S405), 3¼″ height. $75–$100

999 American Locomotive (AE487–S7419), 4⅝″ length.
$100–$125

Nursery Lamp, Pair (AE374–S1267), waxed paper shades, 4⅝″ height. $300–$325

1028 Locomotive (AE492–S740), 5⅛″ length. $15–$25

1028 Locomotive (AE492–S748), 5⅛″ length. $15–$25

Opera Glasses (AE558–S535), 3″ height. $75–$100

Opera Glasses With Brass Frame, 3½″ height. $35–$50

Owl Perched on Branch (AE566–S176), 4½″ height.
$100–$150

Peep Peep Baby Chick (AE145–S185), 3½″ height. $50–$75

Penny Trust Co. Safe (AE661–S511), clear, 2⅞″ height.
$25–$35

Peter Rabbit (AE618–S844), 6½″ height.   *$50–$60*

Phonograph (AE574–S776), glass record, tin horn, 4½″ height.   *$250–$300*

Pierced Metal Lantern (AE449–S627), 5¾″ height.   *$15–$25*

Pocket Watch (AE823), leather strap with American eagle fob, 2¾″ height.   *$250–$300*

Policeman With Search Light and Billy Club (AE592–S471), 4⅞″ height.   *$550–$600*

Powder Horn (AE589–S1223), plain glass, 5″ length; *Six Shooter*, 5½″ length; *Space Gun*, 3¾″ length; each.   *$20–$30*

Pumpkin-Head Witch, original paint with closure, 4⅜″ height.   *$100–$125*

Rabbit, basket on arm, painted, screw closure, 4½″ height.   *$75–$100*

Rabbit Carrying Basket (AE606–S854), 4½″ height.   *$15–$25*

Rabbit With Collar, screw-type closure, 5½″ height.   *$75–$100*

Rabbit Crouching, slide closure, body smooth, 3″ height.   *$100–$125*

Rabbit in Egg Shell, screw-on closure, rabbit gilded, 5⅜″ height.   *$125–$150*

Rabbit Emerging From Cracked Egg Shell (AE608–S842), 5¼″ height.   *$50–$60*

Rabbit Family, marked, missing closure, 4¾″ height.   *$100–$125*

Rabbit Nibbling Carrot, missing closure, 4½″ height.   *$75–$100*

Rabbit Pushing Baby Chick in Buggy (AE602–S861), 4″ length.   *$250–$275*

Rabbit Pushing Cart, 4″ height.   *$75–$100*

Rabbit Pushing Wheelbarrow (AE601–S838), 4⅛″ height.   *$125–$150*

Rabbit Reclining (AE615–S864), 3½″ length.   *$50–$60*

Rabbit Rectangular Base (AE616–S859), 4 ½ " height.

$25–$35

Rabbit Sitting (AE612), feet and paws extended, 5 ½ " height.

$50–$75

Rabbit Sitting (AE617–S852), 4 ½ " height; *Nibbling Carrot* (AE609–S850), 4 ½ " height; each. $25–$50

Rabbit Sitting on Egg (AE607–S48), 4 ½ " height. $100–$150

Racer With Helmeted Driver (AE641), #4 on front grille, 3 ⅝ " length. $50–$60

Radio With Speaker (AE643–S778), 4 ½ " height. $75–$100

Railroad Lantern (AE447–S674), 5 " height. $15–$25

Rapid-Fire Gun (AE129–S2), 7 ⅜ " length. $175–$200

Reo (AE62–S43), rough under closure, 4 ¼ " length.

$400–$450

Republican Elephant GOP (AE206–S369), C2, 3 ½ " length.

$100–$125

Rocking Horse With Clown Rider (AE652–S502), 4 ⅜ " length.

$200–$250

Rocking Horse With Saddle (AE652–S498), 4 ½ " length.

$100–$125

Rocking Settee (AE653–S514), 2 ½ " height. $75–$100

Running Rabbit on Log (AE603–S863), 4 ¼ " length.

$100–$125

Safety First New Year's Baby Barrel Bank (AE668–S306), 3 ¾ " height. $450–$500

Santa Claus Descending Chimney (AE673–S882), 5 " height.

$75–$100

Santa Claus With Folded Arms (AE671–S891), 4 ½ " height.

$75–$100

Santa Claus With Folded Arms and Stern Face (AE670), green glass, 5 ¼ " height. $100–$150

Santa Claus Standing Next to Brick Chimney (AE672–S889), 3 ⅝ " height. $250–$300

Shelf Clock Bank (AE163–S262), 3⅞" height. $75–$100

Sideboard With Mirror (AE112–S513), 4" height. $75–$100

Signal Lantern (AE398–S622), 5⅛" height; *Lantern* (AE441–S647), 4½" height; each. $50–$75

Signal Lantern (AE404–S633), C1, 5¼" height; *Signal Lantern* (AE405–S634), 5¼" height. $25–$35

Signal Lantern, C2, 5¼" overall; *Signal Lantern* (S623), 6" height; each. $15–$25

Skookum, embossed figure, 3½" height. $75–$100

Skookum Tree Stump Bank (AE681–S310), 3⅝" height.
     $100–$125

Soldier on Monument Base (AE682–S878), 5⅝" height.
     $400–$500

Soldier and Tent (AE688), 3⅜" height. $1,500–$1,700

Souvenir Shelf Clock (AE162–S263), 3¼" height. $100–$150

Spinning Top (AE776–S555), wood winder, 3¾" height.
     $100–$125

Spirit of St. Louis (AE90–S30), pink glass and tin, 4⅜" length.
     $200–$250

SS Colorado (AE102–S207), C2, 6½" length. $325–$350

Stern-faced Santa Claus (AE669–S886), 5⅛" height.
     $100–$150

Stop and Go Traffic Sign (AE706–S1132), 4¼" height.
     $100–$150

Submarine With Periscope (AE101–S208), 5⅛" length.
     $200–$250

Suitcase, tin slide closure, 3⅝" length. $50–$60

Swan Boat With Rabbit and Chick in Egg (AE713), 4¼" length. $550–$600

Telephone (AE731), 1¾" height. $25–$35

Telephone (AE735), 4⅛" height. $50–$75

Telephone (AE736–S917), clear, 4½" height. $25–$50

Telephone (AE742–S901), 6½" height. $200–$250

Telephone (AE753–S918), 5" height. $25–$50

Telephone, Redlich's No. 4, 4⅜" height. $35–$50

Tiny Auto (AE32–S81), 3" length. $15–$20

Toonerville Trolley (AE767–S1262), 3¾" height. $400–$450

Top Hat (AE301–S479), 2⅛" height. $25–$35

Toy Village, five different houses, lithographed tin. $300–$325

Toy Village, six different buildings. $100–$150

Trophy, ruby flashed with gold trim, screw-on base, 3¾"
height. $50–$75

Trunk (AE789–S539), opal glass, 2¾" length. $75–$100

Tubular Lantern (AE426), 6" height. $15–$25

Tubular Lantern (AE427–S638), 6¼" overall. $15–$25

Uncle Sam Barrel Bank (AE801–S300), chip on base, 3⅞"
height. $250–$300

Uncle Sam's Hat Bank (AE303–S475), 2½" height. $50–$60

Upright Piano Bank (AE577–S768), 2⅞" height. $200–$250

Victory Lines Bus (AE115–S1144), 5" length. $50–$75

Victrola and Tin Horn (AE575–S773), missing record, 4¾"
height. $100–$150

Volkswagen (AE58–S84), 6" length. $15–$25

Wagon (AE822–S35), 3⅛" length. $75–$100

Water Wagon Pulled by Mule (AE539–S121), 4½" length.
                                                           $50–$75

West Brothers Co. Limousine, with tin pierced wheels and tin
slide top, 4" length. $35–$50

Westmoreland Specialty Co., limousine with tin pierced wheels,
2½" height. $25–$35

Wheelbarrow (AE832–S1175), 6⅛" length. $50–$75

Windmill (AE840), Pfeiffer's moonface and eagle head, 6"
height. $500–$550

Windmill (AE845), Teddy and flag, 6″ height. $500–$550

Windmill With Performing Bear (AE83–S168), 4½″ height.
    $200–$250

Witch With Broom (AE594–S463), 4⅝″ height. $300–$350

Woody Station Wagon (AE56–S73), 4⅞″ length. $20–$30

Yellow Taxi (AE36–S75), 4¾″ length. $75–$100

Holiday Toys

✳ ✳ ✳

Of all the myriad folk symbols associated with holiday celebrations, Santa Claus is the most universally beloved. Toys in his image head the Christmas list of an ever-widening circle of followers. Once a thin, dour-looking old gentleman, the transformation took place when Thomas Nast characterized Santa as a plump, jolly old elf, based on the Clement Moore poem, *The Night Before Christmas.* Sharing top billing with Santa toys are those depicting reindeer and the Christmas tree, an old German custom which spread worldwide during the 19th century. Christmas-related collectors specialize not only in toys, but seek out early Dresden, paper and figural glass ornaments, papier-mâché and composition candy containers, and jack-in-the-boxes.

Until recently, many of the countless other holiday playthings were ignored. Today, however, holidays such as Easter, Halloween, Valentine's Day, St. Patrick's Day, and even Washington's birthday yield fascinating and highly decorative relics of the past that are highly collectible. Of all the topical categories in the hobby, there is none more fanciful, or created in any wider range of materials, than holiday keepsakes. For further insight into the field, we recommend *Christmas Ornaments, A Festive Study,* and *Holidays Toys and Decorations,* both by Margaret Schiffer.

CHRISTMAS

Buckaroo Santa, Kriger Novelty, 1924 patented, composition and wood, push-pull toy, 7 ½ ″ height. $200–$300

Father Christmas and Reindeer Pull Toy, German, early 1900s, papier-mâché, moss and wood platform with metal wheels, Santa is pulled by four reindeer, 6″ height. $1,000–$2,000

Reindeer, German, 1915, handpainted tin mechanical, 9″ length, rides behind two large (6″ height) wheels. $150–$200

Santa Acrobat on Stick, maker unknown, 1904, painted wood with Christmas tree and voice box. $200–$250

Santa Claus, E. S. Peck, sold by New York Stationery and Envelope Co., 1886, stuffed figure based on Thomas Nast cartoon of Santa, 16½″ height. $350–$450

Santa Claus, German, 1900s, painted chalk, very early solemn-looking version with hands tucked in sleeves, 22″ height.
$4,000–$5,000*

Santa Claus, Strauss, 1920s, lithograph tin mechanism, Santa figure has high pointed hat, drawn by two reindeer which bob up and down when activated, 12″ length. $350–$400

Santa Claus at Chimney, mechanical bank arm drops coin down slot in chimney, 6″ height. $1,000–plus

Santa Claus Sleigh, Hubley, 1921, cast-iron pull toy, pulled by two reindeer (another version shows only one), 13″ length.
$1,000–plus

Santa Claus Wagon, German, circa 1910, wood with fabric-covered composition, horses on wheels, painted stencilled sign in red/yellow, "St. Claus Dealer in Good Things," pull toy, 28″ length. $1,000–$2,000**

Santa Claus Walker, Arthur Hotchkiss patented, Ives, 1882, composition with cloth clockwork, 10″ height.
$6,000–$7,000

Santa With Galloping Reindeer, R. Bliss, circa 1890s, lithograph with wood cutouts, Bliss logo on back panel, Santa in sleigh drawn by two reindeer, 18″ length. $1,000–$1,500

Santa Handcar With Mickey Mouse in Pack, Lionel, 1937, composition and pressed steel. $2,000–plus

---

*Sold for $5,500 at December 1986 Christmas Auction at Rick Opfer's in Timonium, Maryland. It was missing chalk tree.
**Toy minus leather tacking brought $1,400 at Atlanta Toy Auction in October 1986.

Santa Claus, one of the most popular walking toys patented by Arthur Hotchkiss of Cheshire, CT, in 1875, who sold the rights to Ives. The above cut appeared in an 1893 Ives catalog. Note the price of $2.75 which was several days pay for the average laborer in the 1890s. $5,000 plus range.

Santa Jack-in-the-Box, composition and wood, German, 1900s, 5" height.   *$150–$200*

Santa With Pack, 1890s, cast iron with Santa before big safelike rectangle, 5" height, 2½" width.   *$500–$600*

Santa in Roadster, Karl Bubb, early 1920s, lithograph tin mechanism, superb lithography and detail designate this as one of the classic Santas, 11" length × 10" height.

$1,200–$1,500

Santa on Rocking Horse, German, 1915, painted wood and composition, dappled horse rocks and Santa rings bell, 7" height mechanism.   *$600–$700*

Santa Roly-Poly, Schoenhut, 1915, composition, 9″ height.
$500–$600

Santa and Sleigh, possibly Scandinavian, circa 1910, composition and wood, pulled by one reindeer (sleigh looks very Nordic), 3″ height. $750–$850

Santa in Sleigh, Kyser & Rex, 1880s, cast iron, 13″ length.
$1,000–$2,000

Santa Sleigh With Goats, Althof Bergman, 1890s, painted tin clockwork, considered to be rarest and most desirable of all Santa Claus toys, 9″ height × 18″ length. $15,000–$16,000

Santa Standing, still bank, 1890s, cast iron, 5½″ height.
$500–$600

Santa With Tree, still bank, 1890s, cast-iron figure, tree is wood with metal pine needles, 7″ height. $1,000–plus

Santa With Tree, still bank, 1890s, cast iron, 5½″ height, variation of bank but with Christmas tree in one arm.
$1,000–plus

Santa Walker, Japan, 1960s, celluloid and tin wind-up, 6″ height. $100–$200

St. Nicholas Standing Figure, German, 1915, painted tin mechanism, carries branch in one hand, 7½″ height.
$1,000–$2,000

Walking Santa, Chein, 1930s, lithograph tin mechanism, 6″ height. $300–$400

EASTER

There is a wide variety of papier-mâché and composition candy containers featuring Easter rabbits, chickens, eggs, and other Easter items that do not readily identify as toys, but are nonetheless often in specialty collections.

Bunny Express, Marx, 1936, Easter Rabbit Express, scale model train toy, large tin rabbit with glass eyes, engine pulls two hopper cars, originally sold at Easter filled with jelly beans, 18″ length. $800–$900

Chanticleer Card with Rabbit (see "Lehmann Toys" listing).

Peter Rabbit Chickmobile, Lionel, 1935, yellow handcar, steel and tin composition, rabbit is on one end and Easter basket on other, 9½" length.   *$800–$900*

Pumpkin-Head Walker, German, 1910, composition, clock clockwork, 7" height.   *$600–$700*

Rabbit Balance Toy, German, 1910, papier-mâché rabbit with steel and cast-iron balance, figure 3" height.   *$300–$400*

Rabbit Bowling Game, German, 1870s, papier-mâché with glass eyes, 24" length.   *$1,000–$2,000*

Rabbit Driving Car, German, circa 1910, papier-mâché rabbit with moss-covered open roadster, glass eyes, 8" height.
$750–$850

Rabbit in Tin Roadster, French, 1900s, lithograph tin mechanical, composition rabbit with cloth, raises and lowers spectacles as car moves along, 16" length × 16" height.   *$1,000–$2,000*

Spook Bank, maker unknown, contemporary, cast aluminum, pumpkin-headed figure with black cat, 6" height.   *$75–$100*

Witch Riding Goose, Strauss, 1920s, lithograph tin wind-up.
$100–$200

Rabbit in Rabbit Cart, Ideal Toy Co., Detroit, Michigan, 1890s, painted cast iron, 5½" height, $500–$600; Ideal Rabbit Chariot, 1890s, painted cast iron, 9¼" length, also came in gilt, $750–$850.

Lehmann Toys, 1895–1930

✳ ✳ ✳

Originating in Brandenburg, Germany, and later in Nuremburg, Ernest Paul Lehmann continues its toy operation to this day. American collectors generally think of Lehmann's glory years as extending from 1895 to 1929. After 1933, Lehmann exported toys to the United States on a sporadic basis. The unprecedented popularity of Lehmann toys on these shores may be attributed to their attractive lithography and patina, their attention to detail, and the infinite variety of animation and mechanical action in both friction and clockwork. Animals, tricycles, bicycles, motorcycles, and comic and serious human figures all comprise a small cosmos, more than justifying a separate category in this guide. Lehmann toys were sold in the United States through jobbers, i.e., Butler Brothers, Baltimore Bargain House, George Broadway Rouss, H. Wolf, and others. Montgomery Ward was a major mail-order outlet for Lehmann.

Note: The date 1881 is occasionally found on a Lehmann specimen; it has no bearing on its date of manufacture and is simply the date the firm was founded. Lehmann toys were targeted to England, France, the United States, and to their own country. Alternate names varied in accordance with these markets. Lehmann was not one to give up on a good thing. The popular Balky Mule and Climbing Miller were offered in the Lehmann catalog over a span of 25 years. All Lehmann toys were trademarked on both the box and the toy itself, with the exception over a brief period of time of the Climbing Monkey, where the mark appears on the box only. The simulated green velvet jacket immediately identifies it as Lehmann.

Lithographic art on the original boxes of Lehmann toys, although sel-
dom accurately depicting the toy contained therein, is so colorful and
aesthetically appealing as to clearly enhance the value of a toy. Note
that a number of boxes bear patents of as many as four different coun-
tries, with Great Britain and the United States clearly the major markets for these whimsical toys.

Adam, porter, baggage truck, separate trunk of chocolates,
1912–1914. $900–$1,200

African Mail, ostrich pulling two-wheel cart and native driver,
1892–1926 (later issues have "Kamerun," "Zulu," "Afrika"),
5″ height. $800–$900

AHA, closed delivery van, 1911, same body as "Karitas," 1911 (550). $700–$800

AJAX, acrobat, figure with club, 1912, 9½" height (659). $600–$700

ALSO, automobile, red or green variations, friction, same as OHO, 4.1" length (700). $500–$600

AM POL, tricycle, Amundsen, monkey, map, South Pole, very similar to "New Century" cycle, orates Amundsen trip, 1912, 4.9" length (681). $1,000–$2,000

AUTIN, boy drives soapbox delivery wagon, wagon same as cat. 98, The American Boy, 6" length. $400–$500

Autobus, double-decker 5th Avenue bus, red and yellow, 1907–1915, also yellow and brown version, 8" length (590). $900–$1,100

Autohouette, garage with galop, 6" length (771/760). $600–$700

Autohouette, garage with sedan (771/765). $600–$700

Autohouette, garage with galop, sedan (772). $500–$600

Auto-Post, mail van, similar to Royal Mail (575). $600–$700

Baldur, taxi-limo, with Lehmann banner as hood ornament, 1920, 10" length (739). $600–$700

Balky Mule, clown in cloth dress and balking mule, no name on toy, "The Comical Clown," "Stoerrischer Esel," 1902–1926, 8" length. $200–$300

Bear, in man's dress, 1910–1912. $300–$400

Berolina, cabriolet automobile, nonmechanical, 1924 (749). $500–$600

Boxer, four Chinese tossing Chinaman in blanket, "Tossing the Heathen Chinese," "Diligent Chinese." $2,000–$3,000

Brennabor, automobile, two lamps, 1929 (777). $500–$600

Broncho, horse and cowboy, 1907–1924, "Wild West" (625). $500–$600

BV Aral, tank wagon (835). $400–$500

Captain of Kopenick, tin and cloth, 7½" height. $700–$800

Chanticleer Cart, rooster pulls rabbit in Easter egg, 1898–1917, 6½" height, also see DUO. $500–$600

Climbing Mice, tin gravity, 15" height. $200–$300

Climbing Miller, miller climbing pole topped with windmill with flour sack on head, name not on toy, also known as Guston, 18½" height. $200–$300

Coco, Negro climbing coconut tree, same action as climbing miller, 1894–1904. $500–$600

Columbia, Dancing Sailor, "Brandenburg," "Mars," 1910–1912, 7½" height (535). $500–$600

Crawling Beetle, wings unfold, no name on toy, 1914. $200–$300

Crocodile, litho tin mechanical, 9" length (442). $300–$400

Daedalus, British airplane, 1939. $600–$700

Dancing Darky, two-dimensional jointed 8" figure. $200–$300

Dancing Doll, tin, 1914, 9" height. $200–$300

Deutsche Reichpost, mail truck, red and gold with navy interior, 1927–1933, 7¼" length (786). $800–$900

Dowle Garage, "Galop," racer and sedan. $450–$550

DUO, rooster, rabbit in cart, rabbit's ears move up and down when activated, friction and clockwork, 1904 (722). $500–$600

DUO, rooster, rabbit in egg-shaped cart, friction, framed around cart, 1904–1913. $500–$600

Echo, motorcycle and rider, brown clothing, 1923, 4" length (725). $2,000–$3,000

EHE and Co., open or auto dray truck and driver, 1910, 6¾" length (570). $600–$700

Emden, cruiser, Count Von Luckner's raider, 1917 (729). $600–$700

EMGEH, machine gun (735). $200–$250

EPL, I, dirigible, gold with red fins (Los Angeles), 1912, 9¾" length (651). $700–$800

EPL, II, dirigible, 1915, 9¾" length (652). $900–$1,000

Express, white porter pulling two-wheel baggage truck, 1886–1925, 4¾" height. $500–$600

Express, man pulling cart (770). $400–$500

Fatzke, auto two figures, clockwork, "Naughty Boy," "Ruppliger Junge," 1904 (495). $800–$900

Flying Bird, bird flies on string, tin with paper wings, name not on toy, 1895, 11" wing span. $600–$700

Futurus, chime on two wheels, the chime is a munitions part left over from World War I, 1918–1925 (740). $200–$300

Gala, automobile, 1929 (780). $300–$400

Galop, racing car, 1925, 5½" length (760). $500–$600

GNOM, truck, Shell. $150–$200

GNOM, trailer. $100–$150

GNOM, garage with two cars (806/807). $125–$175

GNOM, set of three small cars (807A). $100–$150

GNOM, set of three small racing cars (807B). $100–$150

GNOM, set of three racing cars (808). $100–$150

GNOM, filling station (809). $100–$150

GNOM, racing car (810). $75–$125

GNOM, cabriolet (836). $75–$125

GNOM, heavy truck (837) $100–$125

GNOM, fire engine (815). $125–$150

GNOM, Auto Union racing car (816). $150–$200

GNOM, sports car (811). $150–$250

GNOM, car with clockwork (812). $150–$250

GNOM, truck (813). $150–$200

Going to the Fair, lady in boardwalk-type chair pushed by man, friction toy, name not on toy, lady has moving fan, fan sometimes dated 1889, 1889–1894, 4¾" height × 6¼" length. $2,000–$3,000

A selection of Lehmann toys.

Hail Columbia, spiral sailor, "Jolly Jack Tar," "Patriot Toy,'' "Blitzmatrose," 1892–1926 (440). $600–$700

HALLOH, motorcycle, rider, 1934 (683). $1,000–$2,000

HAUPTMANN, captain (soldier) walking (580). $800–$900

Hawkshaw the Detective, walking man, cane, cloth coat, no name on toy, 1910. $1,000–plus

HE 70, French military plane. $450–$550

HE 70, airplane, 1937 (817). $300–$400

HE 70, German military plane. $300–$400

HE 111, airplane, 1939 (831). $300–$400

HE 111, Shell gasoline truck (830). $300–$400

HE 111, bomber (833). $400–$500

HE 111, bomber (834). $400–$500

HEVELLA, automobile, 1929 (778). $400–$500

ICARUS, airship, World War I-type, 1913 (653). $1,000–plus

ICARUS, airplane (818). $500–$600

IHI, meat van with cloth drop curtains, 1907, 6¾" length.
                                                       $750–$850

ITO, sedan, black and red, 1923, 6¾" length (679).
                                                       $600–$700

Jandorf (LU LU), delivery van, double door in deep green, 1913–1914, 7.3" length (763). $500–$600

KADI, see Peking. $600–$700

Karitas, see AHA, Red Cross ambulance, 1915 (727).
                                                       $700–$800

LA LA, delivery van, 1907 (620). $600–$700

LANA, automobile (776). $600–$700

LILA, hansom cab, four moving figures and dog, also known as auto sisters, 1908 (520). $900–$1,000

LOLO, auto and driver, uniformed driver in open car, same as "Naughty Boy" but friction, 1906 (540). $300–$400

London, police tower (791). $300–$400

Luxus, automobile, 3 lamps, 1927 (785). $500–$600

Magic Ball Dancer, ballerina, gyroscope top, name not on toy, "Die Magisch Kugel Tanzerin." $300–$400

Maikaefer, crawling beetle, same as No. 20, 1930 (823).
                                                                 $200–$300

Mandarin, Chinese in Mandarin costume being carried in covered palanquin chair, 1895 (565). $1,000–$1,500

Mars, man driving three-wheeler, 1910–1912, 4.7″ length.
                                                                 $300–$400

Mars, tank, camouflaged. $200–$300

Mars, tank, gray. $200–$300

Mars, propeller toy, Aerial Flyer, three propellers, has date 1881, "Archimedes," 1905–1924. $800–$900

Masuyama, rickshaw, Japanese lady pulled by coolie, fan, revolving, friction and clockwork, 1910–1927, 5″ height.
                                                                 $1,000–$1,500

Mensa, delivery van, three wheels, self-guiding, 1907 (688).
                                                                 $900–$1,000

Mikado family, rickshaw, Japanese lady with rocking baby, 1895–1906, 7″ length. $1,000–$2,000

Minstrel Man, litho pull toy, flat, 7″ height. $200–$300

Motorkutsche, motor coach and driver, made in two (perhaps three) sizes, 1904–1921, 4.9″ length. $300–$400

Mundus, globe top, German text, 1923, 4″ height (757).
                                                                 $250–$300

NA OB, small cart, mule, driver, 1922, 6″ length (680).
                                                                 $200–$300

Nanni, man on tricycle pulling lady in trailer, lady waves handkerchief, "Frightened Bride," "Anxious Bride," 1903, 8.5″ length (470). $1,000–$1,200

Naughty Boy, auto, boy driver, Buster Brown suit, flywheel-propelled car, no name on toy, orange car, same as "Ruppinger Junge Fatze," 1911, 4.9″ length. $800–$900

A selection of Lehmann toys.

New Century Cycle, three-wheel vehicle, man, umbrella, monkey driver, front rig holds American flag on tin pole, name not on toy, "ONKEL," "AUTO UNCLE," 1910.   *$1,000–$1,200*

Nina, flocked cat and mouse, 1932, 11″ length (790).

$800–$900

Nixtum, man with self-made car, "Mordskerl," three-wheel vehicle, 1927–1934 (775).   *$500–$600*

NU NU, one Chinaman and tea cart, friction and clockwork, 1904–1907 (733).   *$600–$700*

OHO, auto, uniformed driver, clown on three-wheeled vehicle, clockwork, green car, 1911, 4″ length. $500–$600

ONO ORBIS, four-wheel truck, driver, globe top, English text, 1923 (762). $400–$500

PAAK PAAK, duck, cart, ducklings, quack, quack, 1910, 7½″ length (645). $400–$500

Paddy's Dancing Pig, Irishman riding pig, may be same as No. 38, 1912, 7½″ height (500). $600–$700

Panne, touring car, red and silver with silk flag (687).
          $700–$800

Peking, two Chinese carrying sea chest (KADI), friction and clockwork (723). $600–$700

Performing Sea Lion, or performing seal, flippers move, 7½″ length, 1907 (445). $300–$400

Pilotto, airplane roulette. $200–$300

Pretzel Vendor, or Baker, pair fighting on tricycle, 5″ length, 1905 (450). $2,000–plus

Primus, roller skater, 1910–1922 (670). $1,000–$2,000

Quex, motorcyclist, 1934 (800). $1,000–$1,500

RARA AVIS, bird. $200–$300

Red Cycle, man on tricycle, 1903 (471), same tricycle as Cat. 470 (Mars). $600–$700

RIGI, cable car, 1929 (795). $500–$600

ROON, motorcycle and rider, rider wears black clothing, 1923 (726). $1,000–$1,500

ROTA, perpetual mobile with ring (805). $300–$400

St. Vincent, naval cruiser, 1926 (672). $1,000–$1,500

SALUS, automobile (734). $600–$700

Shenandoah, dirigible, also made with name "Los Angeles" (766). $800–$900

SKIRLOF, skiing man, 1929 (781). $1,500–$2,500

SNICK SNACK, man walking pair of dogs (724).
          $1,000–$1,500

A selection of Lehmann toys.

TAKU, naval cruiser (671). $500–$600

TAM TAM, top, 3″ diameter, 1914 (677). $200–$300

TAP TAP, man pushing wheelbarrow, 6½″ length x 5″ height,
1885–1906 (560). $400–$500

Taxi, yellow sedan, 1922 (755). $500–$600

Terra, touring sedan, 9.6″ length, 1913–1928 (720).
                                                                $600–$700

Titania, automobile, two lamps, 1929 (779). $700–$800

Tom, "JOCKO," climbing monkey on string, 1903–1910 (385).
                                                                $200–$250

Truck and Driver, yellow with European postal insignia, 5¼″
length (585). $400–$500

TUT TUT, auto driver in white suit and hat, squeak horn, 6.7″
length, 1904–1926 (490). $650–$750

TYRAS, walking dog, 1905 (432). $600–$700

UHU, amphibian auto with celluloid windscreen, paddles on
wheels, driver swivels, 9.4″ length, 1906–1922 (555).
                                                              $1,000–$2,000

Valleda, touring sedan with folding seats (730). $700–$800

Vinetta, monorail car with gyroscopic mechanism, red, green
with gold trim, 9¾″ length. $900–$1,200

Walking Down Broadway, Mr. and Mrs. Lehmann, couple strolling with dog, 6¼″ length, 1889–1894. $1,000–$1,500

ZICK-ZACK, two figures, one black, one white, on two-wheeled
carnival (Zig Zag) carriage, 4.9″ length, 1907–1914 (640).
                                                                $700–$800

ZIKRA, Mexican cart with driver pulled by zebra, 1913, U.S.
patented, "Dare Devil," NA-NA, variation of "Balky Mule".
                                                                $300–$400

ZULU, ostrich, two-wheel cart, driver, 1926, later version of "African Mail," friction and clockwork, 7″ length (721).
                                                                $500–$600

PERELMAN TOY MUSEUM SALE, 1988

It is difficult to determine from Perelman's Great Grab of '88 inventory list the quality and condition of their Lehmanns. One thing is certain: the prices realized, in *most* instances, are modest indeed, compared to those at recent auctions and shows. At Richard Opfer's Pre-Christmas Auction in 1988, for example, an Echo motorcyclist brought $3,300; Los Angeles zeppelin, at $3,300, and the Duo cart, at $2,530, were both bolstered by original boxes. The Africa ostrich mail cart sold at $660 (as compared to $275 at Perelman). A number of ex-Perelman Lehmanns showed up shortly thereafter at the Allentown Toy Show at substantially enhanced price tags, such as the EPL-II zeppelin at $2,700 and the Uhu amphibian auto at $3,750 (and we thought the Uhu that brought $1,540 at the Atlanta Toy Museum Sale in 1986 was a bit steep!).

Included here are most of the less common Lehmanns in Perelman's sale. Please note that we have also given our own price estimates in the ensuing pages, with more complete descriptions of each toy.

Adam Porter, baggage truck.	$1,250
Aha Delivery Van.	$950
Ajax Acrobat w/Clubs.	$600
Anxious Bride (Nani).	$1,500
Autobus, 5th Ave. double-decker bus.	$1,250
Balky Mule, boxed.	$400
Balloon Luna.	$3,000
Bucking Broncho.	$650
Chimney Sweep/Pretzel Vendor, on tricycle.	$4,000
Duo, rooster/rabbit in cart.	$850
Echo, motorcycle w/rider.	$3,000
Ehe & Co., truck/driver.	$700
EPL-II, dirigible.	$1,200
Flying Bird, paper-winged bird on string.	$750

Going to the Fair (boxed).	$3,500
Kadi, a.k.a. Peking.	$750
Lila, hansom cab.	$1,000
Lolo, friction version of Naughty Boy.	$250
Mandarin, Chinese being carried in palanquin chair.	$1,750
Masuyama, rickshaw.	$1,650
Mensa, delivery van.	$1,250
Mikado Family, rickshaw.	$2,500
Miss Blondin.	$4,500
Naughty Boy, auto/boy driver.	$950
Nu Nu, Chinaman and tea cart.	$600
Paddy's Dancing Pig, Irishman riding pig.	$700
Rigi, cable car.	$650
Sailor, a.k.a. Dancing Sailor.	$600
Tut-Tut, auto/driver.	$800
Tyras, walking dog.	$700
Uhu, amphibian auto.	$1,750
Vinetta, monorail car.	$1,500
Zick-Zack (Zig-Zag), two-wheeled carnival carriage.	$850
Zig-Zag, same as above, but Lehmann's U.S. version.	$3,750

Horse-Drawn Wagon, James Fallows, 24″ length with lithographed paper panel, $5,000–$6,000.

Mechanical Banks. Clown on Globe, J. & E. Stevens, 1890s, $1,500–$2,000. Speaking Dog, Shepherd, 1885, $1,000–$1,500. Eagle and Eaglets, J. & E. Stevens, 1883, $700–$800.

Toys and Notions Cart, Ives, Blakeslee & Williams, 20″ length, $4,000–$6,000.

Horse-Drawn Pumper, tin clockwork, James Fallows, 1880s, orange-red boiler, black tank, $10,000–$12,000.

Three early tin horse-drawn wagons, maker uncertain. Peddler's Wagon in center is possibly Hull & Stafford, 13″ length, all in $1,500 to $2,500 range.

Sand Toys. Dancer, German, 1890s (left). Couple with Baby, French, 1890s (center). Black Musicians, German, 1875 (right); each $1,000–$2,000.

Santa Claus Candy Container, German, circa 1910, $1,000–$1,500. Reindeer with lead antlers, felt over composition, circa 1920; $1,000 the pair. Lamb German Pull Toy, circa 1910, $300–$350. Sleigh is handmade, date uncertain.

Black Rider on Tricycle, Gunthermann, circa 1900s, $500–$700. Dancing Couple, painted tin mechanical, Gunthermann. German, $900–$1,100.

Boy in Hoop Bell Toy, Ives, Blakeslee, circa 1875, $3,000–$4,000. Dog in Hoop, Stevens & Brown, 1872, and Horse in Hoop, also Stevens & Brown, among the more common hoops which range from $1,000–$2,000.

Three-Wheeled Walking Horse, Ives, 1890s, cast iron, 7" length, $3,000–$4,000.

Early tin windup train engines: right to left: "Osceola," Ives, 15" length. Maker unknown, 10" length. "Victory," Ives, 10" length, $3,000–$4,000. Pair on far left are George Brown engines, 7" and 5½" length, $1,000 each.

Express Wagon, James Fallows, 1880s, painted and stencilled tin, 26" length, $6,000–$7,000.

West Point, A Game for the Nation, maker unknown, circa 1910, $200–$250.

George Washington Candy Container, German, early 1900, bisque face, cloth covered, 13″ height, $700–$800.

Two-Horse Pumper, Bliss, litho-on-wood, 1880s, $3,000–$4,000.

Left. *Marx Amos 'n' Andy Walkers, 1930s, $1,000–$1,500.* Right. *Auto-peripatetikos, first U.S. clockwork toy, E. R. Morrison patent, 1862, $2,000 with original box, $1,250 minus box. (Perelman Museum Sale prices realized.)*

Left. *"Automatic Toy Dancers," circa 1874, the basis for a number of Ives platform clockwork toys, $3,000–$4,000.* Center. *Ives "Peek-a-boo" Clockwork Cat in Stein, $2,500–$3,000.* Right. *General Butler Walker, Ives, 1876, $5,000 plus.*

Marbles

Few toys evoke any fonder recollection of childhood days than marbles. Dating back to as early as Roman times, they reached the height of their popularity during the Victorian Age. Mention of "knuckle down to your taw, aim well, shoot away," is included in 18th-century America children's books. Charles Francis, of New York, writing in *The Boy's Own Book* in 1829, graded various marble types. The Dutch marbles of glazed clay received the lowest rating, those of yellow stone with spots of black and brown followed in ascending order, while the taws of red-veined pink marble ranked supreme. Marble manufacturing in the United States centered in Ohio, with Samuel Dyke of South Akron a leading purveyor of clay marbles in the 1880s (marbles had been imported primarily from Europe until the mid-19th century). The National Onyx Marble and the Navarre Glass Marble Co. of Navarre, Ohio, and M.B. Misler of Ravenna were leading makers into the 20th century. Many marbles of brown or blue glazed clay were fashioned at Bennington, Vermont, and in potteries in Ohio, Indiana, and Pennsylvania. Montgomery Ward was one of the leading distributors of marbles in the 1890s.

The most coveted marbles today are the pricey and rare sulfides of clear glass with encased white figures of animals, birds, flowers, political figures, and comic characters. Glass marbles of the Venetian swirl variety, often called "glassies," feature colored glass in a clear glass marble, much akin to paperweights produced by leading glass companies.

Marbles comprise such an esoteric area of specialization, with a language all its own, that we hesitate to describe and price these items. We do know that the sulfides featuring leading personalities and comic characters can range from $200 to $300 and up. Latticino Swirls, each with their own unique design that defies description, ranging in diameter from 1¾″ to 2″, often command prices of $100 on up, and wide-banded core marbles also are highly desirable and on the expensive side.

For further exploration of this subject, we recommend *Collecting Antique Marbles*, by Paul Bauman (see "Bibliography"). More information is also available through the *Marble Collectors Society of America* (see "Collecting Organizations" listing), which publishes a newsletter, *Marble Mania*.

Military Miniatures

In the fourth edition of our *Official Price Guide to Collectible Toys*, we cited the vastly accelerated prices at auction generated by Britains, Courtenay, Stadden, Barclay, and other military hollow cast-lead soldiers. James Opie's *Britains Toy Soldiers, 1893–1932, Britains Toy Soldiers, 1893 to Present*, Peter Johnson's *Toy Armies* (Forbes Museum) and the latest, by Henry I. Kurtz, lead soldier specialist at Phillips, New York, *Art Of The Toy Soldier*, have done much to thrust militariana into a well-deserved place in the spotlight.

The following rather astounding prices realized at auction over the past year clearly reflect the high esteem accorded these delightful miniatures: a 15th century Knights Tournament Scene with 25 figures, primarily Stadden and Lasset, $1,430; a Britains Louw Wepener Regiment, "Armies of the World," $2,860; a Tipco Mercedes Führermobile, early 1940s, $1,320; a Britains United States Military Band issued from 1956–1959 (there was a reissue several years later), $4,180; Hauser Half-Truck Prime Mover and Troop Carrier No. 731, $2,200; Britains "Walking Elephant," ca. 1890, with rider under spinning parasol, $2,530. An unboxed set, #2184, of the Bahama Police sold for the same, while from the prestigious Natalie Hays Hammond Collection on the block at Phillips in June 1987, the Richard Courtenay Fighting Knights, numbering 18 figures, sold for $13,500, an average price of nearly $700 per figure! A mounted replica of Sir John Havering wielding a battleax reached $1,650. Even the more recent lead figures are attracting big money: Gebruder Henrich, a contemporary rival of Heyde, was represented by a boxed set of khaki-clad United States Cavalry troopers—$1,045, or over twice pre-sale estimates.

We are grateful to Henry I. Kurtz, Lead Soldier Specialist for Phillips, New York City, and author of what many consider the definitive book on military miniatures, *The Art of the Toy Soldier* (see Bibliography), who provided us with the following information on various makers specializing in these fascinating replications in scale.

ALYMER

Confederate Artillery Gun Team (60 mm scale), with gunners, officer, flag bearer, cannon, and wooden base. $175–$200

Confederate Cavalry mounted at walk with carbines at the ready and flag bearer with Confederate standard; in original box.
$75–$100

Confederate Horse-Drawn Artillery Gun Team, with six-horse team, three mounted gunners, three seated on limber chest, and 12-pounder Napoleon Gun; in original box. $200–$225

Confederate Infantry (33 mm scale), marching with rifles at shoulder arms, with officer and flag bearer carrying Confederate battle flag; in original box. $75–$100

Union Army Horse-Drawn Artillery Gun Team, with six-horse team, three mounted gunners, three seated on limber, and 12-pounder Napoleon Gun; in original box. $175–$200

Union Cavalry mounted at walk with carbines at the ready and standard bearer with national flag; in original box. $50–$75

Union Infantry (33 mm scale), marching with rifles at shoulder arms, with officer and flag bearer carrying United States flag; in original box. $75–$100

BRITAINS

Early Part Set #1, The Life Guard mounted at the walk in review order (second version: fixed arm, tin strip swords, and aiguillettes, ca. 1900). $100–$125

Set #1, The Life Guards mounted at the walk with figures on Household Cavalry and walking horses and officer on cantering horse; in original illustrated box. $100–$110

Early Set #2, The Royal Horse Guards (The Blues) mounted in review order (single-eared horses, troopers wearing aiguillettes), with later officer on rearing horse (dated 1909). $250–$275

Set #2, Royal Horse Guards mounted at the walk with officer on rearing horse, ca. 1920, set in original early box with illustrated label. $175–$200

Set #3, 5th Dragoon Guards (Princess Charlotte of Wales) mounted at the walk (first version: ca. 1890, Germanic-style horses, tin strip swords), with officer on rearing horse; in original early Printer's box with separate compartments and the name "G. Preston Rhodes, 1896" written in small, neat script on the label. $1,200–$1,300

Set #5F, Farm Wagon, with farm hand and two horses; in original box with illustrated lid. $125–$135

Rare Early Set #7, 7th Royal Fusiliers marching at the slope (first version: ca. 1900, oval bases, valise packs, detached rifle slings), with fixed-arm, bemedaled officer. $550–$575

Early Version Set #8, 4th Queen's Own Hussars, mounted at the gallop with sabers (dated 1901, one-eared horses), with trumpeter on trotting horse (dated 1902, correct for this set); in original Whisstock box. $425–$450

Set #8, 4th Queen's Own Hussars mounted at the gallop with trumpeter. $175–$200

Set #8, 4th Queen's Own Hussars mounted at the gallop with sabers, with trumpeter on trotting horse, ca. 1945; set in original Whisstock box. $125–$135

Rare Early Set #9, Rifle Brigade marching at the slope with officer (dated 1905) (E/G, small holes, casting flaws in left feet of several figures, possible retouching of black leather belts and equipment). $385–$400

Early Set #11, The Black Watch charging in review order (oval bases, dated 1903); in original Whisstock box (G/F, one bayonet missing, chips, scuffing, box G/F, portion of lid side panel missing). $325–$350

Set #12F, Timber Barriage with farm hand, two horses, and logs (extra non-Britains log); in original box with illustrated lid (E/G, box E/G). $140–$150

Early Set #16, The East Kent Regiment standing at the ready, with bugler, drummer, and officer, ca. 1920; set in original Whisstock box. $300–$325

Early Set #17, The Somersetshire Light Infantry (Prince Albert's) standing and kneeling at the ready (half-booted), with officer (dated 1905) and adult bugler (full trousered), ca. 1915; set in original Printer's box with battle honors. $1,000–$1,200

Early Set #19, West India Regiment marching at shoulder arms with British officer, mounted on walking horse, ca. 1910; set with extra enlisted man. $350–$375

Part Set #19, West India regiment marching with rifles at the shoulder and mounted British officer, ca. 1935; set in a Brittannia box. $175–$200

Set #20F, Farmer's Gig with farmer and horse, in original illustrated thin cardboard box (M/E, box E); together with a group of farm figures by Britains, Johillco, Timpo, and Cherilea, including cows, shire horse, men with wheelbarrows, blacksmith with anvil. $135–$150

Early Set #24, 9th Royal Lancers mounted at the halt in review order (first version: cast-lead lances, cross-legged horses, ca. 1900), with officer turned in the saddle. $350–$375

Early Set #24, 9th Queen's Royal Lancers mounted at the halt (second version: dated 1903), with officer turned in the saddle and carrying tin strip sword (correct complement of figures but incorrect horse colorings—three black and one brown instead of two of each). $200–$225

Early Set #26, Boer Infantry marching at the slope (first version: ca. 1897, light khaki uniforms, black hats and valise packs), with bayonets clipped off rifles (see Opie, *Britains Toy Soldiers 1893–1932,* p. 115) and rare officer holding sword in movable left arm. $1,000–$1,200

Early Set #27, Band of the Line marching in review order (half-booted, dated 1911), with oval base, fixed-arm drum major.
$225–$250

Part Set #27, Band of the Line marching with various instruments and drum major, ca. 1920 set, half-booted bass drummer and drum major. $125–$150

Set #27, Band of the Line marching in review order with full instrumentation and drum major; in original box. $200–$225

Set #28, Mountain Gun of the Royal Artillery, with screw gun, mules, ammunition, six gunners, and mounted officer, ca. 1930; set in original Whisstock box. $900–$950

Set #30, Drums and Bugles of the Line, with three buglers, two side drummers, bass drummer, and drum major, ca. 1940; set in original illustrated box. $250–$275

Set #31, 1st Dragoons (The Royals) mounted at the walk in review order with officer on rearing horse; pre–World War II set in original Whisstock box. $425–$450

Display Set #32, *"Zoo Series,"* including camel, lion and lioness, kangaroo, polar bear, zebra, and other animals, together with one coconut and two date palm trees; tied in original box with color label. $250–$275

Set #32, Royal Scots Greys (2nd Dragoons) mounted at the walk in review order with officer on cantering horse; in original box with illustrated label; together with three unboxed Picture Pack Scots Greys officers. $250–$275

Set #33, 16th/5th Lancers mounted at the halt in review order with officer turned in the saddle; in original box. $250–$275

Early Set #34, Grenadier Guards standing firing (second version: half-booted, dated 1901), with drummer boy and officer; in original Whisstock box. $350–$375

Early Set #35, Royal Marine Artillery marching at the slope in review order (third version: half-booted, box packs, detached rifle slings, dated 1905), with officer; in original early Printer's box. $375–$400

Early Set #36, The Royal Sussex Regiment marching at the slope (first version: fixed arm, oval bases, ca. 1895), with mounted officer. $475–$500

Set #36, The Royal Sussex Regiment marching at the slope in review order with mounted officer; in original box.

$225–$250

Early Set #37, Band of the Coldstream Guards marching in review order (full-trousered except for half-booted drum major, bass and side drummers, dated 1911), with nearly complete instrumentation. $300–$350

Set #37, Full Band of the Coldstream Guards marching in review order with full instrumentation and drum major, ca. 1930; set. $500–$550

Early Set #38, Dr. Jameson and the South African Mounted Infantry (first version: fixed arm, ca. 1895) in khaki jackets, gray pants and hats, with Dr. Jameson holding pistol. $600–$650

Set #39, The King's Troop, Royal Horse Artillery in review order at the gallop, with six-horse team, drivers with whips, limber, gun, mounted outriders, and officer; original box. $750–$800

Set #39, King's Troop, Royal Horse Artillery in review order at the gallop, with gun, limber, six-horse team outriders, and mounted officer; original box. $400–$452

Rare Early Display Set #40, 1st (The Royal) Dragoons mounted in review order (second version: dated 1902), with officer on rearing horse with throat plume, and the Somerset Light Infantry kneeling and standing at the ready; (first version: oval bases) with boy bugler and officer (dated 1903); in original "Types of the British Army" box. $2,000–plus

Display Set #41, The Royal Scots Greys mounted at the walk with officer, and the Grenadier Guards standing firing with officer and drummer; tied to original backing card. $100–$125

Early Set #43, 2nd Life guards mounted at the gallop in review order (short carbines, dated 1901), with trumpeter on galloping horse; in original early illustrated box. $500–$550

Set #44, Queen's Bays (2nd Dragoons Guards) mounted at the gallop with lances, with white-plumed trumpeter (see Wallis, *Regiments of All Nations,* p. 31) on trotting horse.

$175–$200

Early Set #45, 3rd Madras Cavalry mounted at the gallop (ca. 1900 set) with lances and trumpeter. $400–$450

Set #45, 3rd Madras Light Cavalry mounted at the gallop in review order with trumpeter; pre–World War II set in original "Soldiers of Greater Britain" illustrated box. $650–$675

Set #46, Hodson's Horse (4th Duke of Cambridge's Own Lancers) mounted at the gallop in review order; pre–World War II set in original "Armies of the World" box. $400–$425

Early Set #47, 1st Bengal Native Cavalry mounted at the gallop with swords, in brown tunics, blue plastrons, red turbans, with trumpeter on dapple gray, ca. 1920; set.   *$500–$550*

Set #47, Skinner's Horse mounted at the gallop in review order with trumpeter; pre–World War II set in original "Armies of the World" box.   *$400–$425*

Early Part Set #48, Egyptian Camel Corps mounted with rifles (wire-tail camels) in review order; together with early Bikanir Camel Corpsmen (wire-tail camels) from Set #123 (G/F, two troopers).   *$450–$475*

Set #48, Egyptian Camel Corps (last version: two troopers, three camels); together with part Set #123, Bikanir Camel Corps.
          $250–$275

Part Set #48, Egyptian Camel Corps mounted with rifles, ca. 1930 set; together with an early version of Egyptian Camel Corpsman with wire-tail camel and detachable rider.
          $300–$325

Early Set #49, South Australian Lancers mounted at the gallop with officer (second version: dated 1901), in khaki service uniforms with red plastrons and spiked foreign service helmets; in original "Our Colonial Army" box.   *$1,000–$1,200*

Display Set #50, The Life Guards mounted at the walk and the 4th Hussars at the gallop, ca. 1940; set in original "Types of the World's Armies" box.   *$325–$350*

Early Set #66, 1st Bombay Lancers mounted at the gallop in apple-green uniforms, blue turbans slashed with white and red, with officer holding sword in place of usual trumpeter, ca. 1900 set.   *$250–$300*

Set #66, 13th Duke of Connaught's Own Lancers mounted at the gallop in review order with trumpeter; pre–World War II set in original "Armies of the World" box with slot-in card and corrugated backing.   *$475–$500*

Rare Early Set #68, 2nd Bombay Native Infantry marching at the trail (oval bases, ca. 1900), in blue uniform jackets and turbans and red trousers, with sapper carrying ax and officer with sword; in original early Printer's box.   *$900–$950*

Set #68, 4th Bombay Grenadiers (formerly 2nd Bombay Native Infantry) marching at the slope in review order (blue tunics faced in red, white turbans, and red trousers), ca. 1930; set tied in a red box.   *$175–$200*

Set #71, Turkish Cavalry mounted at the gallop in review order with officer, ca. 1930; set in original Whisstock box with slot-in card.   *$350–$375*

Early Display Set #73, including Band of the Line (slotted-arm, oval base, except for bass drummer, dated 1908, and two side drummers, one of which is post–World War I and substitutes for missing trombonist), correct instrumentation except as noted above; the 17th Lancers mounted at the troop in Ulundi period, foreign service dress, with trumpeter and quite rare officer turned in saddle; the Gordon Highlanders marching at the slope (dated 1901) with two pipers (oval bases); Royal Horse Artillery at the gallop (first version) with gun, limber, six-horse team, and two seated men for limber and bucket seats (no mounted officer), two seated men; Royal Scots Greys mounted at the walk with officer (dated 1902); Royal Welch Fusiliers marching at the slope with two pioneers carrying axes, flag bearer, officer (all dated 1905), and goat mascot; 2nd Life Guards mounted at the walk with officer on rearing horse (second version); Life Guards figures with aiguillettes, officer dated 1909; general officer; set in original two-tray wooden box with hinged lid and individual cardboard boxes for mounted figures; black-and-gold "Types of the British Army" label.   *$3,400–$3,500*

Set #74, The Royal Welch Fusiliers marching at the slope with officer and goat mascot; in original box.   *$175–$200*

Set #79, Royal Navy Landing Party with gun, limber, crew, and officer with sword (original string missing); in original box (E, box G/F, tears in lid, creases, warping to box).   *$425–$450*

Early Set #81, 17th (Duke of Cambridge's Own) Lancers mounted at the trot with lances (dated 1902), in Ulundi period foreign service dress, with officer turned in the saddle in place of more common trumpeter (see Opie, *Britains Toy Soldiers 1893–1932*).   *$400–$450*

Set #81, 17th Lancers mounted at the trot with bugler, in Battle of Ulundi period, blue foreign service uniforms with white plastrons and pith helmets, ca. 1930; set in original Printer's box with regimental battle honors.   *$600–$650*

Set #82 (Two), Colours and Pioneers of the Scots Guards, with color bearers carrying furled colors. $250–$275

Early Set #91, United States Infantry at the ready (dated 1905) in Spanish-American War period uniforms, with officer firing pistol and holding sword in movable right arm; in original Printer's box. $300–$325

Rare Version Set #94, 21st Lancers (Empress of India's) mounted at the gallop in active service order and steel helmets, with trumpeter, ca. 1930; set in original Printer's box with corrugated backing and cut-out slot-in card. $650–$675

Rare Early Version Set #98, King's Royal Rifle Corps (oval bases, "pigeon chests," ca. 1900) running at the trail with officer, in dark green uniforms, red trim, and home service helmets.
$250–$275

Set #101, Band of the Life Guards mounted at the walk in State Dress with full instrumentation and kettledrummer, ca. 1935; set. $550–$575

Set #103, Band of the Royal Horse Guards (slotted arms, one-eared horses, ca. 1900) mounted in State Dress with bombardon, two trombones, two trumpets, bass tuba, bassoon, kettledrummer, fife, cymbals, and two clarinets. $2,000–$2,100

Set #104, City Imperial Volunteers standing on guard in khaki service uniforms and bush hats, with officer fring pistol and holding sword; pre-World War II set in original box. $650–$675

Early Set #105, The Imperial Yeomanry mounted at the trot in khaki service dress (dated 1900); two light-brown and two dark-brown horses instead of usual two brown and two black, indicating that two sets may have been combined. $300–$325

Rare Set #108, 6th Inniskilling Dragoons mounted at the trot in olive-green khaki uniforms, ca. 1935; set in original Whisstock box. $825–$850

Set #110, The Devonshire Regiment (11th Foot) marching at the trail in khaki service dress with webbing equipment and foreign service helmets with pugarees, ca. 1935; set in original Whisstock box with slot-in strip and corrugated backing. $250–$275

Set #112, The Seaforth Highlanders (Ross-Shire Buffs) marching at the slope in review order, ca. 1920; set in original Whisstock box. $275–$300

Early Set #113, The East Yorkshire Regiment at attention in review order (dated 1901); in original Whisstock box with battle honors.   *$350–$375*

Early Version Set #114, The Queen's Own Cameron Highlanders marching at the slope (second version: dated 1901, box packs, Slade Wallace equipment) in foreign service dress; retied in original Whisstock box.   *$300–$325*

Set #114, The Queen's Own Cameron Highlanders marching at the slope in foreign service dress and pith helmets, ca. 1930; set in original Whisstock box with corrugated backing. *$135–$150*

Set #115, Egyptian Cavalry mounted in review order with lances and officer with sword; in original box.   *$200–$225*

Set #117, Egyptian Infantry at attention; pre–World War II set in original Whisstock box with slot-in card and corrugated backing.   *$450–$475*

Set #120, The Coldstream Guards kneeling firing, with kneeling officer holding binoculars; tied in original window box.
                                                     $75–$100

Set #123, Bikanir Camel Corps mounted with rifles; pre–World War II set in original "Types of the Indian Army" box.
                                                    $525–$550

Early Version Set #124, Irish Guards lying firing (dated 1901), half booted, feet together, green bearskin plumes, with kneeling officer holding binoculars; in original Whisstock box.
                                                    $775–$800

Rare Early Set #125, Royal Horse Artillery Gun Team, "B" Series (45mm), in review order (dated 1901), complete with six-horse team, gun, limber, four outriders, and officer (see L. W. Richards, *Old British Model Soldiers, 1893–1918,* plate 49).
                                                    $400–$425

Set #126, "B" Series (45 mm), Royal Horse Artillery at the gallop in active service order (dated 1904), with six-horse team, limber, gun, four mounted outriders with carbines, and officer with sword; in original Whisstock box.   *$1,100–$1,200*

Early Set #128, 12th Royal Lancers mounted in review order with slung lances (dated 1902) and officer with sword; in original Printer's box with battle honors.   *$450–$475*

Rare Version Set #134, Japanese Infantry charging in dark blue tunics; in original Printer's box. $650–$675

Set #134, Japanese Infantry charging in review order, ca. 1930; set. $250–$275

Rare Version Part Set #135, Japanese Cavalry mounted in review order in dark blue uniforms. $300–$325

Early Set #137, Royal Army Medical Corps Unit (oval bases, dated 1905), with stretcher bearers, stretchers, casualties, wasp-waisted nurses, medical officers, and chief surgeon.

$425–$450

Set #138, French Cuirassiers mounted in review order with officer. $100–$125

Part Set #142, French Zouaves charging, with two mounted officers; along with Part Set #191, French Turcos charging, in original box for Set #142. $125–$150

Rare Early Version Set #144, Royal Field Artillery at the walk in review order, with six-horse team (collar harnesses, twisted wire traces, dated 1906), officer, two gunners seated on the limber, and two on bucket seats mounted on the gun. $750–$775

Early Set #145, Royal Army Medical Corps Ambulance Wagon in review order (collar harnesses, valise packs, dated 1906), with four-horse team, two Royal Army Service Corps drivers (correct for this set), two RAMC orderlies seated on wagon; along with stretcher team and two wounded men from Set #137.

$600–$625

Set #146, Royal Army Service Corps Wagon in review order drawn by two-horse team (strap harness version), driver with whip and two riders on wagon, ca. 1930; set in original box with black-and-gold "Types of the British Army" label. $500–$525

Set #147, Zulus of Africa charging with spears and knobkerries; tied in original box with small catalog sheet included.

$175–$200

Rare Set #149, Painters and Ladder, with two house painters in white smocks carrying a ladder and third holding paintbrush (designed to stand on ladder); in original box. $350–$375

"Racing Colors of Famous Owners" Series, including Sets RD 149, Baron Guy de Rothschild; RC 153, Mr. S. Wooten; and RC 160, Mr. R. James Speer; each set consists of a large-scale (approximately 10 centimeters high) horse and detachable jockey, all in their original boxes. $375–$400

Set #152, North American Indians mounted with rifles and tomahawk (extra figure with rifle in place of second Indian with tomahawk), ca. 1950; set retied in original "Britains Wild West" box with color illustrated label. $225–$250

Early Set #153, Prussian Hussars mounted in review order with lances (double dated 1903/1908) and officer with sword; original "Types of the German Army" Printer's box (five figures).
$425–$450

Set #157, The Gordon Highlanders in tropical service dress firing from three positions, ca. 1940; set in original Whisstock box. $275–$300

Rare Set #161, Boy Scouts with Scoutmaster, including Boy Scouts with staffs and patrol flags and scoutmaster carrying stick, ca. 1920; set in original Whisstock box. $250–$275

Early Set #166, Italian Infantry marching at the slope in review order (dated 1910) with officer; in original Whisstock box (eight figures). $950–$1,000

Same version as above, but ca. 1935. $400–$450

Set #169, Italian Bersaglieri marching with slung arms and officer; in original box. $125–$150

Rare Set #170, Greek Cavalry mounted at the trot with carbines and officer with sword; in original "Types of the Greek Army" Printer's box. $375–$400

Rare Early Set #173, Serbian Infantry charging (oval bases, dated 1904); in original "Types of the Serbian Army" Printer's box. $875–$900

Rare Early Set #174, Montenegrin Infantry marching at the slope with officer (dated 1904); in original "Types of the Montenegrin Army" Printer's box. $550–$575

Set #177, Austrian Infantry of the Line marching at the slope in review order, ca. 1935; set (eight figures). $775–$825

Set #179, North American Cowboys mounted and on foot with lassos, rifle, and pistols; tied in original "Britains Wild West" box. $225–$250

Set #179, North American Cowboys mounted with pistols and lassos, ca. 1935 (five figures). $75–$100

Rare Set #186, Mexican Rurales (Rurales de la Fedaración) marching with slung rifles in brown jackets, gray trousers, and tall-crowned sombreros, with officer in smaller sombrero; along with two extra men. $450–$475

Set #190, Belgian Chasseurs à Cheval mounted at the halt in review order with carbines and officer with sword on cantering horse (five figures). $150–$175

Set #194, British Army Machine Gun Section firing from the prone position, ca. 1940; set in original Whisstock box (no backing card); together with a mixed group of prewar first- and second-grade machine gunners from Sets 194 and 198, in a Whisstock box for Set #194. $150–$175

Early Set #196, Greek Evzones marching at slope in review order; red jackets, white kilts, red caps, ca. 1930; set in original "Types of the Greek Army" box. $200–$225

Set #196, Greek Evzones marching at the slope in review order, ca. 1935; set in original "Armies of the World" box (G/F, noticeable chipping on jackets and kilts of several figures; box G). $200–$225

Set #197, 1st King George's Own Gurkha Rifles (the Malaun Regiment) marching at the trail in review order; pre–World War II. *Price Indeterminate*

Set #225, King's African Rifles marching at the slope in active service dress, ca. 1935; in original "Soldiers of the British Empire" box with an original print by Richard Simkin of "The East Africa Rifles" (eight figures). $225–$250

Set #241, Chinese Infantry advancing with swords, wearing green, red, blue Boxer uniforms, ca. 1920; in original "Types of the World Armies" box with slot-in card and corrugated backing (eight figures). $425–$450

Set #299, West Point Cadets marching at slope in summer dress, in original box; also includes group of cadets in winter dress from Set #432 (fourteen figures). $250–$275

#302A Display Set, The Royal Sussex Regiment marching at the slope with the 1st Dragoons mounted at the walk with officer, ca. 1920; in original "Armies of the World" box (eighteen figures).   *$250–$275*

Set #312, The Grenadier Guards in winter greatcoats marching at slope behind officer; in original box (eight figures).

$125–$150

Set #313, Royal Regiment of Artillery Gunners in service dress and steel helmets (issued in 1940–1941 only); with kneeling and standing gunners, including pair with ramrods; in original Whisstock box (eight figures).   *$700–$725*

Set #318, Royal Horse Artillery Gun Team at the halt in active service dress wearing khaki uniforms and peak caps; includes six-horse team, three drivers with whips, limber, gun, mounted officer, and team of standing and kneeling gunners with standing officer holding binoculars (16-piece version as issued); in original box with "Royal Horse Artillery Review Order" on black-and-gold label, "Active Service" stamped on red box paper (sixteen figures).   *$9,000–$9,200*

Set #320, Doctors and Nurses of the Royal Army Medical Corps with two Medical Corps officers in review order and four nurses, ca. 1930; in original box.   *$525–$550*

Set #334, United States Aviation enlisted men marching in service dress, with peak caps, ca. 1940; in original "Types of the U.S.A. Forces" box with corrugated backing and slot-in strip.

$375–$400

Set #432, German Army Infantry marching at the slope in field uniforms with officer holding sword; in original window box.

$100–$125

Set #434, RAF Monoplane (first version: square-tipped wings), with pilot and air-craftsmen, ca. 1935; set in original hangar box.   *$1,500–$1,600*

Set #1203, Tank of the Royal Tank Corps, Carden Lloyd type, with driver, machine gun, and gunner (original version with rubber treads), ca. 1935; in original box.   *$125–$150*

Set #1250, Royal Tank Regiment marching in active service dress and black berets with officer, minus guns, ca. 1935; in original "Types of the British Army" box with corrugated backing (six figures). $250–$275

Sets #1257 and #1475, group of Yeomen of the Guard, standing and walking in ceremonial dress with pikes (sixteen figures).
$175–$200

Set #1283, Grenadier Guards firing in three positions; tied in original box (eight figures). $125–$135

Set #1288, Band of the Royal Marines marching in review order with corps of drums and double bass horn, ca. 1940; set.
$300–$375

Set #1293, Durban Infantry (Light) marching at slope in khaki service dress and pith helmet. $350–$375

Set #1294, British Infantry in tropical dress, marching at the slope. $225–$250

Set #1301, United States Army Military Band marching in active duty dress with full instrumentation and drum major, ca. 1940; in "Types of the World Armies" box with "Reiss Bros." label on underside of box. $925–$950

Set #1318, British Army Machine Gun Section, with prone and sitting gunners; in original "Famous Regiments of the British Army" box. $110–$125

Set #1330, Royal Engineers General Service Limbered Wagon in review order with driver and two-horse team. $225–$250

Set #1331, Royal Army Service Corps General Service Limbered Wagons in khaki service dress, with two-horse team drawing two small wagons and rider with whip. $400–$425

Set #1335, Six-Wheeled Army Lorry with driver, ca. 1935.
$100–$125

Same as above, post–war version. $75–$100

Set #1339, Royal Horse Artillery mounted at the gallop in khaki service order and peak caps; six-horse team, drivers with whips; limber with ammo chest, gun, four mounted outriders, and officer on galloping horse; in original "Types of the British Army" box. $3,200–$3,300

Set #1342, 3rd Battalion, 7th Rajput Regiment, marching at the slope in review order, in scarlet tunics with yellow facings, dark blue turbans and trousers; ca. 1940; in original "Armies of the World" box with slot-in card and corrugated backing.

$600–$625

Set #1349, Royal Canadian Mounted Police at full gallop in summer uniforms, led by officer, ca. 1945; in original "Soldiers of the British Empire" box. $150–$175

Set #1383, Belgian Infantry in service dress and steel helmets firing in standing, kneeling, and prone positions; in original box. $225–$250

Set #1424, Bodyguard of the Emperor of Abyssinia standing at attention in dress uniforms, barefooted. $250–$275

Set #1433, British Army Covered Tender, caterpillar type, post–World War II, including driver; in original box. $125–$150

Set #1436, Italian Colonial Infantry, Ethiopian Campaign era, marching at the slope in mustard-khaki uniforms; also wearing pith helmets and black shirts. $250–$275

Set #1440, Royal Field Artillery Gun Team mounted at the walk in khaki service dress with peak caps; six-horse team, three drivers with limber, whips, guns; officer with sword on cantering horse; in original "Types of the Army" box.

$3,300–$3,400

Set #1448, British Army Staff Car, with staff officer and driver with upraised right arm, ca. 1935; with rectangular metal frame windscreen. $350–$375

Set #1470, The State Coach of England drawn by eight Windsor Greys, with four positions, and King George VI and Queen as passengers, ca. 1940; in original box with black-and-gold illustrated label. $275–$300

Set #1475, Attendants to the State Coach with Footmen, Outriders, and Yeomen of the Guard in State Dress; from original "Historical Series" box. $225–$250

Set #1510, Royal Navy Sailors in regulation dress marching without rifles, ca. 1940; in original "Types of the Royal Navy" box. $150–$175

Set #1512, Army Ambulance (pre–World War II version) with square radiator and white tires, driver and wounded man on stretcher, ca. 1935; in original box. $300–$325

Set #1513, Volunteer Corps Motor Ambulance, in regulation blue with white Maltese Cross emblem on panels of van, driver in blue uniform, and wounded man on stretcher, in original box. $475–$500

Set #1518, British Infantry, Waterloo Period (1815), standing at attention with rifles at the shoulder; includes two sergeants carrying pikes, plus officer bearing sword. $200–$225

Set #1521, Royal Air Force Biplane with removable pilot; issued in late 1930s only. $5,500–$5,600

Set #1527, Band of the Royal Air Force marching in review with full instrumentation; includes drum major; pre–World War II in original box. $550–$575

Set #1539, Mammoth Circus, featuring ringmaster, lion tamer, man on stilts, boxing clowns; kangaroo, elephants, tigers, prancing steeds, equestrienne, tub, ring, and other figures; in original box. $1,200–$1,300

Set #1542, New Zealand Infantry marching at the slope with officer (small-headed edition), issued in 1937–1940 only; in original box with slot-in card and corrugated backing. $450–$475

Set #1544, Austrailian Infantry marching at the slope in service dress, with officer. $125–$150

Set #1555, Changing of the Guard at Buckingham Palace, with full band of Coldstream Guards, marching auxiliary to the Coldstream Guards; includes officers, Scots Guards at present arms with officers, Coldstream and Scots Guards, color bearers, and sentry boxes; with original box. $1,300–$1,400

Set #1620, The Royal Marine Light Infantry marching at the slope, including officer, issued 1938–1940 only. $350–$375

Set #1621, 12th Frontier Force Regiment ($3/12$ Sikhs) marching at the slope in khaki service dress, pre–World War II, in original "Soldiers of the Empire" box with slot-in card and corrugated backing. $750–$775

Set #1622, Band of the Royal Marine Light Infantry, issued in 1938–1940 only, marching in review; figures wear scarlet tunics, blue trousers, white ball-topped helmets; includes clarinets, tubas, drums, cymbals, trombones, baritone, horns, cornets, fife, bassoon players; also drum major; retied in original "Types of the Royal Navy" box. $5,100–$5,200

Set #1624, United States Army Bomb Throwers in active service dress with helmets and gas masks, ca. 1940; in original box. $100–$125

Set #1631, The Governor General's Horse Guard of Canada mounted in review order with officer astride rearing horse; in original box. $100–$125

Set #1633, Group of Princess Patricia's Canadian Light Infantry, including officer; set incomplete. $50–$75

Set #1634, Governor General's Foot Guards of Canada marching at the slope in review, with officer; ca. 1945; set in original "Soldiers of the British Empire" box. $150–$175

Set #1640, Air Force Searchlight, battery-operated; also Set #44D, small-scale (20 mm) State Coach; set #1HU (Household Utensils), pots and pans; all original boxes. $100–$125

Set #1654, Snow White and the Seven Dwarfs, issued 1938-1941 only. $800–$850

Set #1662, Knights of Agincourt mounted on foot, Knight with banner; Knights with Mace #1659; Knight with Sword #1660; Knight with Lance, #1661; plus four Knights from #1664. $275–$300

Set #1664, Knights of Agincourt in action on foot, bearing lances, mace, sword, and battleax; in original box. $125–$150

Set #1711, French Foreign Legion marching at slope; in original "Foreign Legion" box. $125–$150

Set #1720, Band of the Royal Scots Greys (2nd Dragoons) mounted at the walk with kettledrummer; tied in original box. $500–$525

Set #1722, Pipes and Drums of the Scots Guards, with full complement of pipers, side drummers, bass drummer, drum major; tied in original box. $850–$875

Set #1730, Royal Artillery Team of Gunners with standing and kneeling gunners carrying shells, ca. 1940; in original Whisstock box. $175–$200

Set #1758, R.A.F. Fire Fighters in asbestos suits, issued in 1939–1941 only. $400–$425

Set #1828, British Infantry of the Line standing at ease in battle dress and steel helmets, issued in 1939–1941 only; in original "Armies of the World" box. $2,000–$2,100

Set #1832, Ten-Wheeled Covered Lorry with Two-pounder (40 mm) Light Antiaircraft Gun, pre–World War II (square radiator version); in original box. $200–$225

Set #1856, Polish Infantry marching at the slope in blue and gray uniforms and helmets; includes officer. $100–$125

Set #1858, British Infantry in battle dress marching with slung arms, ca. 1940; in original box with slot-in card and corrugated backing. $375–$400

Set #1876, Bren Gun Carrier, Carden Vickers type with driver, Bren gunner, and second guard; in original box. $100–$110

Set #1892, Indian Army Infantry marching at the trail in service dress with British officer leading, holding swagger stick, ca. 1940; in original "Types of the Colonial Army" box.
$425–$450

Set #1893, Indian Army Service Corps marching at the trail with mule, mule-handler, and British officer with swagger stick, ca. 1940; in original "Types of the Colonial Army" box.
$425–$450

Set #1894, Pilots of the R.A.F. in full flying kit, including Women's Auxiliary Air Force (W.A.A.F.s), issued in 1940–1941 only; in original "Types of the Royal Air Force" box with slot-in strip and corrugated backing. $575–$600

Set #1895, Pilots of the German Luftwaffe in full flying kit, issued in 1940–1941 only, in original "Armies of the World" box with slot-in card and corrugated backing. $950–$1,000

Set #1901, Regiment Louw Wepener marching at the slope in dark-olive tropical service dress with officer; in original box.
$750–$800

Set #1911, Officers and Petty Officers of the Royal Navy in winter blue and summer white uniforms, ca. 1940; in original "Types of the Royal Navy" box. $300–$325

Set #2010, British Airborne Infantry, "The Red Devils," in battle dress marching with slung arms; Bren gunner and officer; in original box. $325–$350

Set #2011, Royal Air Force display set; includes pilots, officers, flight sergeants, W.R.A.F.s, motorcycle dispatch rider, detachment of the Royal Air Force Regiment with Bren gunner and officer. $525–$550

Set #2014, United States Marine Corps Band marching in review; in original box. $800–$850

Set #2025, Cameron Highlanders in tropical service dress firing in standing and prone positions; officer standing, holding binoculars. $125–$150

Set #2027, Red Army Guards Infantry marching in review with officer; also mounted cavalry officer (from set #2028); in original box. $250–$275

Set #2031, Australian Infantry marching at the slope in battle dress with turned-up Aussie bush hats and officer in peaked cap carrying swagger stick; in original box. $225–$250

Set #2035, Svea (Swedish) Life Guard marching at the slope in ceremonial dress, with three extra men and officer. $75–$100

Set #2036, Royal Scots Greys mounted on the walk with officer; Scots Guards marching at the slope with piper and officer; Black Watch charging; in original display box. $325–$350

Set #2043, Rodeo, with cowboys mounted and afoot, including rider on bucking bronco, others with lassos; steer, wild horse, and others; includes wooden fence rails and poles for assembling a corral; in original display box (twelve pieces, plus corral). $1,000–$1,100

Set #2044, United States Air Corps marching with slung rifles, 1949 Pattern Blue Uniforms; in original "Regiments of All Nations" box. $150–$175

Set #2045, Clockwork Van, light-green body, blue cab, with driver in blue suit and peak cap; in original box. $450–$475

Set #2051, Uraguayan Military School Cadets marching at slope in review order (most recent version, ca. 1955); in original box.
$225–$250

Set #2055, Confederate Cavalry mounted at the trot with carbines, officer bearing sword; in original box. $150–$175

Set #2057, Union Artillery Gun with gunners; in original box.
$100–$125

Set #2059, Union Infantry in action, including officer bugler and standard bearer carrying national flag; in original box.
$100–$125

Set #2062, The Seaforth Highlanders charging, minus pipers or mounted officer. $75–$85

Set #2068, Confederate Cavalry and Infantry, including four mounted troopers with carbines and officer with word; infantry in action firing and at the ready, with bugler, standard bearer holding confederate battle flag, while officer fires pistol; in original box. $375–$400

Set #2069, Union Cavalry and Infantry, includes pair of mounted troopers with carbines, trumpeter, and officer with sword; infantry in action, with standard bearer holding national flag, plus bugler, ca. 1960; in original box. $200–$225

Set #2071, Royal Marines at present arms with officer holding sword at salute; in original box. $200–$225

Set #2077, The Kings Troop, Royal Horse Artillery, at the walk in review, with six-horse team, three drivers with whips, limber, and gun. $300–$325

Set #2080, Royal Navy Sailors marching at the slope with officer; in original "Types of the Royal Navy" box. $200–$225

Set #2082, Coldstream Guards at attention, with officer; tied in original box. $225–$250

Set #2084, Colour Party of the Scots Guards with ensigns carrying regimental colors of the King, escort of four sergeants.
$275–$300

Set #2085, Household Cavalry Musical Ride with kettledrummer, four trumpeters in State Dress, nine troopers each of the

Life Guards and Royal House Guards mounted on trotting and walking horses with lances at carry; in original two-tray box.
$800–$850

Set #2093, Band of the Royal Berkshire Regiment marching in Number One Dress, issued in 1954–1959 only, with full instrumentation; includes bandmaster and drum major.
$2,700–$2,800

Set #2095, The French Foreign Legion in action, firing from three positions and charging; machine gunner and kneeling officer holding binoculars.
$175–$200

Set #2096, Drum and Pipe Band of the Irish Guards marching in review order with six pipers, bass and side drummers, cymbalist, and drum major, 1954–1956 edition; in original box.
$500–$525

Set #2098, Venezuelan Military School Cadets marching at the slope in review order with standard bearer carrying Venezuelan national flag; in original box.
$200–$225

Set #2100, Republic of Venezuela Military School Cadets with officer; Infantry in service dress marching at the slope with standard bearer; also sailors marching with officer; tied in original box.
$550–$600

Set #2101, United States Marine Corps Color Guard with two color bearers carrying Stars and Stripes and United States Marine Corps flag (inaccurate blue, rather than red flag; see Wallis, Regiments of All Nations, p. 127).
$475–$500

Set #2108, Drums and Fifes of the Welsh Guards with side, tenor, and bass drummers, plus drum major.
$600–$625

Set #2109, Highland Pipe Band of the Black Watch, including pipers, side and tenor drummers, bass drummer (plastic drums), pipe major, and drum major; tied in original box. $725–$750

Set #2110, United States Military Band marching in yellow and black dress uniforms with complete instrumentation; four trombones, four trumpets, two sousaphones, two French horns, two bass tubas,* three clarinets, two bassoons, fifer, bugler, bass and side drummers (plastic drums), cymbalist, and drum major.
$4,000–$4,100

*In lieu of saxophones more commonly found in these sets.

Set #2111, Colour Party of the Black Watch marching in review order with Sovereign's Standard and regimental color bearers, escort of four sergeants; in original box. $550–$600

Set #2113, Full Band of the Grenadier Guards with full instrumentation (extra tenor horns in lieu of pair of French horns), drum major in State Dress and jockey cap, plus band director; in original box. $950–$1,000

Set #2116, Band of the Royal Air Force marching in review (produced 1956–1959) with plastic drums, the most recent version; full instrumentation, plus drum major; in original box.
$400–$425

Set #2152, Waterloo Artillery Gun with two Royal Artillery gunners. $75–$85

Set #2154, Centurian Tank with revolving turret and gun barrel that moves up and down; sand colored to blend with desert.
$325–$350

Set #2155, United Nations Infantry marching in battle dress and blue helmets (a late 1950s edition), with slung carbines, Bren gunner, and officer with swagger stick; minus "Famous Regiments" box. $300–$325

Set #2177 (later issued under #9154), Group of Ft. Henry Guard Bandsman, including three fifers, five side drummers, four bass drummers, and a drum major; also includes window-front display box. $275–$300

Set #2184, Bahamas Police standing at attention with sergeant and British officer (officer has movable arm). $2,000–$2,100

Set #2186, Band of the Bahamas Police marching in review: one trombonist, one drummer, a French horn player missing from set; includes drum major and British bandmaster.
$1,900–$2,000

Unnumbered and Partial Sets

Rare "A" Series Display Set #302A (partial), containing The Royal Sussex Regiment marching at the slope and the 1st Dragoons mounted at the walk with officer, ca. 1920; set in original "Armies of the World" box (E/G/F, one infantryman has badly dented chest, one cavalry trooper missing; box F, portions of lid side and end panels missing, taped tears). $200–$225

Army Service Supply Column (Boer War period), including two supply wagons, each drawn by a four-horse team with two drivers holding whips, and two seated men, cardboard supply boxes marked "A.S.C." (only four to each wagon instead of normal complement of six), and escort of ten infantrymen marching at the trail (oval bases, dated 1901) in khaki service uniforms, Slade Wallace equipment and turned-up slouch hats, with mounted officer holding sword extended (dated 1902); see Opie, *Britains Toy Soldiers, 1893–1932*, pp. 118, 120–121.   *$250–$300*

Rare Equestrienne Mechanical Toy, consisting of a horse galloping around in a circle, as in a circus ring, and designed so that as the horse passes under a bar, an equestrienne standing on its back leaps over the bar and lands again on the horse, ca. 1900 (G/F, chips, some wear).   *$775–$800*

A Group of Mounted and Foot Arabs of the Desert from Sets 164 and 2064, along with two palm trees.   *$250–$275*

Salvation Army Officers, Band and Colours, including 14-piece band in red uniforms with white frogging, and blue caps and trousers piped with red; bandmaster in blue uniform and white epaulettes playing cornet, male officers in blue uniforms, open coats, and red shirts, female officers carrying copy of the "War Cry," a tambourine and empty-handed, and color bearer with removable tin flag, ca. 1935 figures.   *$6,380**

Extremely Rare "Walking Elephant," ca. 1890 toy, which an early W. Britains & Sons catalog describes as follows: "This is a well-made model of an elephant with a rider on its back. On spinning the parasol, which the rider carries, and placing the elephant on a smooth table, it will walk along, moving its legs in a most natural manner."   *$2,400–$2,500*

"Waltzing Couple," ca. 1900 toy, consisting of a British officer in scarlet mess jacket and yellow-and-blue pillbox cap and his dancing partner in pale-blue dress with hooped skirt; the figures are approximately 3 ½ inches (85 mm) height. See article entitled "The Waltzing Couple" in *Old Toy Soldier Newsletter*, Vol. 5., No. 6 (a copy of which is included in the lot), which

*Price realized at Phillips Auction, May 10, 1986 (estimated: $2,500 to $3,000).

contains the following description: "Made before the populari-
zation of spring-driven toys, this toy is operated in the method
used frequently by Britains on their early toys. A string is wound
round the girl's waist; when pulled, the lower half of the skirt
revolves, causing a vibration which propels the figures around
any smooth surface. There is a spindle inside the center of the
woman on which her skirt revolves." $2,500–$2,600

Part Set #66, 1st Bombay Lancers mounted at the gallop with
trumpeter (one trooper missing), in apple-green uniforms, blue
turbans slashed with white, and red sashes, ca. 1910; set in
wrong Britains box. $375–$400

Early Part Set #104, City Imperial Volunteers standing on guard
in khaki service dress (oval bases, dated 1900), with square-
based officer (dated 1900) firing pistol and holding sword in
movable right hand; in original box with illustrated lid and price
tag from A. W. Gamage Ltd. $425–$450

Rare Early Part Set #104, City Imperial Volunteers standing at
the ready with officer firing pistol with left hand, holding sword
in right (oval bases, ca. 1900). $600–$625

COURTENAY

Archbishop of Sens, Pos. 4, falling wounded, mace dropping
from right hand, signed R. Courtenay. $425–$450

Black Prince, Pos. M-2, mounted with lance in movable right
arm. $200–$225

Cardinal Wolsey and Mary Queen of Scots, plus Yeoman of the
Guard (Beefeater), portrait figures. $300–$325

Castilian of Ampasta, Pos. 4, reeling from blow, battleax dropping from right hand. $475–$500

Count of Noyers, Pos. 7, lunging forward, battleax extended.
  $500–$525

Dauphin of France, Pos. M-2, mounted with lance in movable
right arm. $100–$125

Duke of Bourbon, Pos. 14, advancing with sword in right hand,
shield in left, movable visor. $425–$450

King Henry V on Horseback, Courtenay, ca. 1954, $825 to $850. *(Photo courtesy of Phillips, NY)*

Duke of Brittany, Pos. H-1, mounted with lance in movable right arm. $400–$425

Dunois, Pos. M-3, mounted with lance in movable right arm.
$150–$175

Earl of Nassau, Pos. Z-1, lying mortally wounded on field of Poitiers, 1356. $375–$400

Edward, The Black Prince, Pos. H-6, mounted in full black armor with gold crown, royal arms on jupon, preparing to deliver blow with battleax. $1,000–$1,100

English Bowmen, in bassinet helmets and studded jerkins, firing bows. $375–$400

Erle of Rochechouart, falling wounded, clutching arrow in his right side, sword slipping from right hand. $200–$225

Erle of Sancerie, Pos. X-1, reeling from blow, mace in right hand, helmet falling from head. $300–$325

Erle of Tankerville, Pos. 17, advancing with sword in movable right arm, shield upraised in left. $150–$175

Fallen Knight, Sieur de Rosay, Pos. 13, with arrow in his side.
$800–$825

Jean de Melun, Sieur d' Esprenne, Pos. 11, bareheaded, arrow piercing right shoulder, extending gauntlet in token of surrender.
$250–$275

Joan of Arc, mounted on horseback, partially turned in saddle, holding banner in movable right arm.
$425–$450

John, Count of Saarbrucken, Pos. 10, preparing to deliver blow with sword held across body.
$600–$625

John, Duke of Berry, Order of The Star, standing in full armor with cloak.
$400–$425

John MacDonald, advancing, preparing to deliver blow from long-poled battleax raised overhead.
$350–$375

King of Castile, Pos. 6, standing with sword at ready in right hand.
$300–$350

King Charles I and Charles II of England, also figure of Nell Gwynn, Charles II's mistress, curtsying (three figures).
$325–$350

King Edward III, Pos. 9, battleax in movable right arm, shield in left, together with an Esquire of Edward III advancing with sword in movable right arm (two figures).
$325–$350

King Henry V, in full golden armor and crown, with sword in movable right arm; astride horse with armor and full trappings; complete with original Courtenay identification and signature tag; in original box with "Military Miniatures" shop label.
$825–$850

King Henry VIII of England, and his six wives, including Catherine of Aragon, Anne Boleyn, Jane Seymour, and the rest of his entourage; also includes the royal executioner and headsman's block (nine figures).
$450–$500

King John of France, Pos. 6, sword in right hand, shield in left; marked "Made in England" only under green base.
$250–$275

King Richard I of England, in full armor and surcoat swinging broadsword, pre–World War II figure; black base. $375–$400

King of Scotland, Pos. 3, lunging with sword extended.
$325–$350

Lord de la Warr, Pos. 15, attacking with sword in raised right arm, shield in left, movable visor, ca. 1940 figure; black base.
$650–$675

Louis, King of the Fortunate Isles, Pos. Z-5, bareheaded, poised for blow with sword extended in right arm. $425–$450

Queen Elizabeth I of England, portrait figure, holding royal scepter and orb; also two of Elizabeth's most distinguished courtiers and seafarers, Sir Walter Raleigh, bowing, and Sir Francis Drake (three figures). $325–$350

Queen Phillipa, portrait figure, in royal robes; also medieval lady-in-waiting in steeple hat (two figures). $375–$400

Robert, Lord Scales, Pos. 3, defending with mace in right hand, shield on left arm; movable visor. $325–$350

Robin Hood, personality figure, standing with left hand on long bow; Friar Tuck is advancing with staff in hands; also three early Courtenay-type figures of Robin Hood's "Merrie Men." $900–$925

Sieur de Pontchartrain, Pos. 19, bare-headed, wearing eye patch, swinging broadsword above head. $400–$425

Sir Edward Despencer, Pos. X-1, advancing with mace held aloft in raised right arm; shield on left arm. $400–$425

Sir Edward Despencer, Pos. 3, lunging with sword extended in right hand; movable visor. $325–$350

Sir Eustace Ribeaumont, Pos. 9, bare-headed, battleax in movable right arm, shield in left, ca. 1945; figure unmarked under green base. $250–$275

Sir John Chandos, Pos. 9, battleax in right arm, shield in left, detachable helm, pre–World War II figure; black base.
$175–$200

Sir John Dalton, Pos. H-6, mounted on horse with lance in movable right hand; detachable rider. $1,000–$1,100

Sir John Dalton, Pos. 6, sword in right hand, ca. 1940 figure; black base. $300–$325

Sir John de Hampton, Pos. Z-5, sword in lowered right hand; movable visor. $425–$450

Sir John Londale, astride horse with full tournament trappings; lance in movable right arm and detachable great helm.
$600–$625

Sir Miles Stapleton, K.G., Pos. M-2, mounted with lance in movable right arm.
$325–$350

Sir Pierre Bussière, Pos. 5, attacking with sword in right hand, shield in left.
$425–$450

Sir Richard Talbot, Pos. 17, advancing with battleax in right hand; shield held aloft in left.
$135–$150

Sir Robert Dacre, Pos. 22, poised to advance a blow from his battleax, held in right hand.
$500–$525

Sir Robert Holland, lunging ahead with sword extended in right hand, shield in left.
$450–$475

Sir Robert Umfraville, Pos. 14, advancing with sword in right hand, shield in left.
$275–$300

Sir Sanchet d'Ambreticourt, K.G., mounted on fully caparisoned steed, lance atilt in movable right arm and with detachable helm.
$700–$725

Sir Stephen Cossington, Pos. H-2, mounted on steed with lance in movable right arm, shield in left movable visor.
$350–$375

Sir Thomas Holland, K.G., Pos. 2, advancing with sword in movable right hand; shield on movable left arm.
$375–$400

Sir Thomas Werenhale, attacking with sword in right hand, shield in left; also St. Clair, Earl of Orkney, standing, swinging broadsword, two figures; ca. pre–World War II.
$450–$475

Sir Walter Hoplan, Pos. 14, advancing with sword extended in right hand, shield in left; movable visor.
$450–$475

Sir Warin Bassingberne, Pos. 7, attacking with sword thrusting in right hand.
$450–$475

Sir William de Montegu, French knight, defending his son, Walter, Pos. 8 (two figures).
$425–$450

Sir William Seagrave, Pos. 20, attacking with battleax extended in raised right arm.
$325–$350

Thierry d'Auffay, "le Hardi," Pos. 15, attacking with sword in raised right hand and shield protecting in left; movable visor.
$300–$325

Thomas Kingston, Pos. M-1, astride rearing horse bearing half-trappings; knight holds battleax in movable right arm, shield protected on extended left arm; pre–World War II figure on black base. $775–$800

William de Ermine, Pos. 16, advancing with battleax in right hand; shield on upraised left arm. $400–$425

William, Earl of Wills, K.G., Pos. M-3, astride horse, partially turned in saddle; carries sword in movable right arm and detachable great helm. $500–$525

EDMUND'S TRADITIONAL TOY SOLDIERS

Edmund's Traditional Toy Soldiers are 54 mm replicas of Union and Confederate regiments of 1861–1862. An artist, Edmund Fangonilo, produced the colorful sets of the Civil War volunteers in a limited edition of 100 sets.

Eighty-third Pennsylvania Volunteer Infantry Regiment, marching with rifles at shoulder arms. Wearing French-style Chaseur à Pied uniforms with tasseled forage caps; bugler with plumed shako; also 23rd Pennsylvania Volunteers (Birney's Zouaves) in uniforms marching at shoulder arms; includes sergeant; in original boxes signed by artist. $75–$100

Fifth New York Volunteer Infantry Regiment (Duryea's Zouaves), standing at attention with rifles at order arms, in full Zouave uniform; officer holds sword at carry; also 114th Pennsylvania Volunteer Infantry (Collis' Zouaves) marching with rifles at shoulder arms; officer with sword at carry; both sets in original boxes signed by artist, Fangonilo. $100–$125

First Special Battalion Louisiana Infantry (Wheat's Tigers) marching with slung arms in Zouave-style uniforms, in fezes, some straw hats; also Battalion of Washington Artillery of New Orleans, marching with rifles at trail; officer with sword at carry; both sets in original boxes, signed by artist. $100–$125

First Texas Cavalry (Texas Mounted Rifles), marching dismounted with sabers at the shoulder, including officer; also the Charleston (South Carolina) Zouaves marching with rifles at shoulder, in modified Zouave uniform; sergeant carries sword; both sets in original boxes with artist's signature labels.

$100–$110

First Virginia Cavalry Regiment ("Jeb Stuart's Own"), marching dismounted with officer holding sword at carry; also 23rd Regiment Virginia Infantry (Brooklyn Grays) marching with rifles at shoulder arms; officer with sword; both sets in original boxes, with artist's signature labels.   *$100–$110*

HAFFNER

The following appear in Size 2, 50 mm scale, except where noted.

British Royal Horse Guards, mounted in review order with carbine and trumpeter, ca. 1900 figures.   *$425–$450*

French Cuirassier Figure, mounted at the walk, with detachable rider; horse trappings and movable reins, extra large (100 mm) size.   *$400–$425*

HEYDE

George Heyde of Dresden, Germany, was producing miniatures as early as 1840–1850. The firm specialized in solid and semi-round size #2 military figures, but also produced a number of sets in the 48- to 50-mm size range. Heyde was wiped out in the Dresden fire-bombing in 1945. The miniatures of Gebruder Heinrich of Furth, Germany, are frequently confused with those of Heyde.

American Revolutionary War Artillery Unit, with six-horse team, three riders with whips, limber, cannon, and gun crew, foot as well as mounted officers (made especially for Lord & Taylor's Toy Department); bears special "Lortoy" label on box end panel.   *$225–$250*

American Sailors, marching at the slope, ca. 1900, wearing white uniforms and tropical service hats. $200–$225

Baylor's 3rd Continental Dragoons, charging with raised sabers; trumpeter, officer, standard bearer. $525–$550

British Grenadier Guards Band (65 mm scale), with various brass instruments including French horn, bassoon, bass and bombardon, and side drums; drum major. $275–$300

British Guards Band, standing at attention; includes various brass and reed instrumentalists; drum corps, bandmaster, and standard bearer. $150–$175

British Line Infantry, marching at slope, 1900 (65 mm scale), with two mounted officers. $350–$360

British Line Infantry Band, 1900 (65 mm), various instruments; drum major with mace. $275–$300

Display Set #699, United States Infantry and Cavalry, Spanish-American War era, ca. 1900, with infantry marching at the slope; mounted and foot officers and standard bearer; cavalry-mounted figures bear drawn sabers; in original oversized display box.
          $900–$1,000

LUCOTTE

Lucotte of Paris, France, is one of the earliest toy makers, producing miniatures as far back as the 1780s. Many examples featured the Lucotte logo, "LC," and the Imperial Bee of Napoleon under, or on, the base of each figure. Lucotte was later acquired by Mignot, and many Napoleanic military figures were reissued under the Lucotte-Mignot aegis.

Bavarian Infantry Band, marching in pale blue uniforms faced in buff yellow and white-plumed shakos, with full range of instruments including serpentine, triangle, and glockenspiel; bandmaster, drum majors, and a Negro in Turkish costume carrying a "Jingling Johnny." $2,200–$2,300

Bulgarian Infantry, attacking, World War I period uniforms, green jackets, gray trousers and peak caps, two buglers, flag bearer, and officer with upraised sword. $600–$650

French Imperial Guard Grenadiers, 1810, marching at the slope in winter uniforms, with fifer, horn player, and officer, along with two sappers and a standard bearer from other sets.

$600–$650

French Line Infantry Fusiliers, 1808, marching at the slope in blue and white uniforms, shakos, and full packs, with mounted and foot officers, drummer, fifer, and standard bearer.

$700–$725

French Marines of the Imperial Guard, marching at the slope in blue uniforms laced and trimmed in scarlet and scarlet-plumed shakos, with regimental and imperial standards; foot and mounted officers.

$1,100–$1,200

French Napoleonic Infantry Band, marching with full instrumentation, including serpentines, early horns, and glockenspeil, with bandmaster and drum major.

$1,300–$1,400

French Napoleonic Light Infantry, marching in white uniforms faced with green and orange-plumed shakos, with drummer and standard bearer.

$600–$625

A Group of Assorted French Napoleonic Cavalry Figures, including Gendarmes d'Elite, Guards of Honor, Polish Lancers, and others, ca. 1920 figures.

$350–$375

A Group of Cavalry Figures, including French Napoleonic cuirassiers and carabinier, two mounted National Republican Guardsmen, 1910–1914, and others.

$250–$275

A Group of World War I United States Infantry, in campaign hats and steel helmets, including several firing from the prone position, a steel-helmeted officer with binoculars, and two artillerymen, one carrying a shell, the other kneeling.

$100–$125

A Lot of World War I Figures, including Turkish Infantry at the salute with officer holding Turkish flag and a group of German Infantry marching at the slope.

$125–$150

Mounted Band of the 5th French Hussars, in yellow and pale-blue uniforms, white pelisses and white-plumed back busbies; with horn players, trombonist, triangle player, cymbalist, and bandmaster.

$900–$950

Napoleon and His General Staff, including Napoleon in his green Chasseur uniform coat and various general officers and aides-de-camp.   *$350–$375*

Napoleon's Guard of Honor, mounted at the walk in green and red uniforms with pelisses and plumed shakos; with officer, standard bearer, and trumpeter.   *$600–$625*

Lucotte-Mignot

The following figures were made from original Lucotte molds and issued by C. B. G. Mignot in a limited edition of 100 sets.

French Napoleonic Field Forge, 1812, drawn by four-horse team with two drivers (gloss paint); tied in original box.   *$150–$175*

French Napoleonic Pontoon Wagon, with four-horse team, two drivers with whips, wagon, pontoon boat, and bridge planking; tied in original box.   *$200–$225*

Mounted Kettledrummer (Timbalier), of the Grenadiers of the Guard in elaborate Hussar-style uniform mounted on dapple-gray horse with detachable saddle trappings and kettledrums and movable reins; together with a mounted kettledrummer of Cuirassiers in Turkish-style Mameluke uniform; both in original boxes.   *$225–$250*

Napoleon's Berline Coach, drawn by four-horse team with two liveried mounted drivers holding whips; the coach is made of wood, with a removable roof, and the undercarriage is made of metal; tied in original box.   *$375–$400*

MIGNOT

C. B. G. Mignot, a long-established name in military miniatures, traces its beginning to the venerable Lucotte firm founded in the French Revolution era. Mignot, with its three principals, Cuperly, Blondel, and Gerbeau (the initials of their surnames being C. B. G.), acquired Lucotte in 1825; the name was changed to C. B. G. Mignot in 1900, when Henri Mignot became a partner. A number of miniatures have been produced in limited editions of 100 sets, using the old Lucotte molds and bearing the name Lucotte-Mignot.

Algerian Spahis, mounted at the trot with rifles, in red and blue uniforms, white turbans and cloaks (gloss paint), with trumpeter and standard bearer; in original box. *$125–$150*

Ancient Assyrian Infantry, marching in light armor with spears, bows, and shields; tied in original box. *$175–$200*

Ancient Egyptian Light Infantry, marching with spears, bows, and other weapons; also standard bearer, tied in original box.
$125–$150

Austrian Cuirassiers, 1812, mounted at the trot with sabers, in white uniforms trimmed in red, black cuirasses and plumed helmets, with trumpeter, and with officer and standard bearer on rearing horses; tied in original box. *$150–$175*

Austrian Infantry, 1805, standing at attention with rifles at the carry (special issue), in white uniforms trimmed in black and light infantry caps, with officer, drummer, and flag bearer; tied in original box. *$125–$150*

Baltazar Cavalry Regiment of Louis XIV, 1670, mounted with sabers in blue uniform coats faced with red-and-white trim, red pants, high boots, and black hats, with officer and standard bearer; tied in original box. *$250–$275*

Band of the Alpine Chasseurs, marching in summer white uniforms and blue berets, with full complement of drums, horns, and bandmaster holding baton, ca. 1950; set. *$300–$325*

Band of the Paris Guard, 1910, marching in dress uniforms with full instrumentation and bandmaster holding baton; tied in original box. *$200–$225*

Band of the Polish Legion of the North, 1806, marching with full instrumentation including serpentine and "Jingling Johnny," in red-and-blue uniforms with plumed shapskas, and bandmaster holding baton; tied in original box. *$200–$225*

Band of the 17th Regiment Chasseurs (Light Infantry), 1809, with full instrumentation, including serpentine, triangle, and "Jingling Johnny," in yellow uniform coats faced in red, light-blue trousers trimmed in white and green-and-white plumed shapskas; tied in original box. *$325–$350*

British Life Guards, Waterloo period, mounted at the trot with trumpeter, officer, and standard bearer; tied in original box.
$125–$150

Confederate Infantry, assaulting with fixed bayonets, with standard bearer carrying Confederate battle flag and officer with sword (one enlisted man missing), ca. 1950; set in original box.
$175–$200

Dahomien Warriors, Rare, firing rifles with chief brandishing bloody knife in one hand and holding severed head in the other, ca. 1940; set tied in original box.
$125–$150

Demi-Round 54 mm French Line Infantry, 1890–1910, marching at the slope in review order with officer, ca. 1930; figures in wrong Mignot box.
$125–$150

Special Diorama "Defense of the Flag" (Defense du Drapeau), 1810, with French Napoleonic Fusiliers in action firing rifles and charging with fixed bayonets, with sapper wielding ax, drummer, flag bearer, officer with telescope, fascines, portions of burnt-out building, and stone wall; in original diorama box with scenic backdrop.
$350–$375

Special Diorama Display Set, ca. 1920, depicting French Colonial Infantry and Zouaves (40 mm scale, semi-round figures) attacking a Moroccan fort, including machine gunners, mule-drawn artillery, medical corps aid station, mounted and foot officers, fort and defenders, and an assortment of palm trees and shrubbery; tied in original diorama box with fold-down front.
$300–$350

Dutch Lancers of the Imperial Guard ("The Red Lancers"), 1812, mounted at the halt on standing horse (special issue), in red uniforms and shapskas and blue plastrons, with officer, trumpeter, and standard bearer; tied in original box.
$300–$325

Dutch Light Infantry, 1806, marching at the slope in green uniforms faced with yellow and green-plumed shakos, with officer, drummer, and flag bearer; tied in original box.
$125–$150

Egyptian Infantry, marching at the slope with officer, bugler, and standard bearer, ca. 1960; set.
$125–$150

Eighth Bavarian Infantry Regiment, 1810, standing at atten-

tion with rifles at the carry (special issue), in blue uniforms faced
with yellow and trimmed in red, and caterpillar-plumed light
infantry caps, with officer, drummer, and standard bearer; tied
in original box. $125–$150

Ethiopian Infantry, Rare Part Set assaulting, period of the Italian invasion of Ethiopia (apparently produced only 1936–1937),
with officer and flag bearer. $125–$150

Fifth Battalion of the Pupilles (Orphans) of the Imperial Guard,
1812, at attention with rifles at the carry (limited issue), in white
uniforms faced with green and purple-plumed shakos, with officer, drummer, and special issue standard bearer at attention;
tied in original box. $250–$275

Fifth Belgian Light Dragoons, 1815, mounted at the trot with
sabers, in light-green uniform coats faced in yellow, gray trousers trimmed in green, and green-and-yellow plumed shakos,
with trumpeter and officer holding standard; tied in original
box. $175–$200

First Regiment Isenburg Grenadiers, 808, marching at the slope
in medium-blue uniforms faced with yellow and white-and-red-
plumed bearskin hats; tied in original box. $135–$150

First Regiment Polish Light Horse (Vistula Lancers), 1808,
mounted at the trot with slung lances in dark-blue uniforms with
yellow plastrons and trim and plumed shapskas, with trumpeter
and standard bearer on rearing horse; tied in original box.
$150–$175

Foot Guard of Amsterdam, 1810, marching at the slope in green
uniforms faced with lavender, buff trousers and red-plumed
shakos, with drummer, officer, and flag bearer; tied in original
box. $150–$175

Fourth Regiment French Hussars, 1808, mounted at the trot
with sabers in medium blue uniforms frogged in yellow, red-
and-black pelisses and red-plumed shakos, with trumpeter and
officer with regimental flag; tied in original box. $150-$175

Fourth Regiment Swiss Infantry, 1810, standing at attention
with rifles at the carry (limited issue), in red uniforms faced with
blue and plumed shakos, with drummer, officer, and standard
bearer; tied in original box. $125–$150

French Army Flag Bearers of the Napoleonic Wars, Two, the standard bearer of the 3rd Voltigeur Regiment of the Young Guard and the regimental flag bearer of the 13th Voltigeur Regiment; each with separate wooden base and in their original boxes.   *$350–$375*

French Army Light Coach, Review at Longchamp, 1900 (special issue), with calèche (open coach) drawn by four-horse team, military driver in line infantry uniform, general officer in full dress with cocked hat and aide-de-camp in line infantry officer's uniform; tied in original box.   *$700–$725*

French Carabiniers (Heavy Cavalry), 1812, mounted at the trot in white uniforms trimmed in blue, gold cuirasses and red-plumed helmets, with trumpeter and standard bearer on rearing horses; tied in original box.   *$135–$150*

French Chasseurs à Cheval (Light Cavalry), mounted at the trot with sabers, in dark green uniforms trimmed in red and plumed shakos, with trumpeter and standard bearer; tied in original box.   *$135–$150*

French Chasseurs d'Afrique, mounted, in blue and red uniforms with red képis and white havelocks (gloss paint), with standard bearer and trumpeter; in original box.   *$100–$125*

French Colonial Infantry, marching at the slope in blue tunics, white trousers, and pith helmets, with officer, bugler, and standard bearer, ca. 1950; set tied in original box.   *$275–$300*

French Cuirassiers, 1914, marching dismounted in dress uniforms, sabers at the shoulder (gloss paint), with officer, trumpeter, and standard bearer; in original box.   *$125–$150*

French Dragoons of the Imperial Guard, 1810, mounted at the trot with sabers, in green-and-white uniforms trimmed in red and plumed helmets, with trumpeter and standard bearer on rearing horse; tied in original box.   *$135–$150*

French Foreign Legion, marching at the slope, 1930 green-khaki service uniforms (gloss paint), with white képis and havelocks, with officer, bugler, and standard bearer; in original box.
                                                      $135–$150

French Foreign Legion Camel Corps, 1900–1910, mounted on trotting camels (special issue), with blue-and-white-uniformed

Legionnaires holding rifles or carrying slung rifles, with trumpeter, standard bearer, and officer; tied original boxes.

$400–$425

French Grenadiers of the Line, 1809, standing at attention with rifles at the carry (limited issue), in blue and white uniforms and plumed shakos, with drummer, officer, and standard bearer; tied in original box. $150–$175

French Light Infantry, 1810, marching at the slope in dark blue uniforms trimmed in yellow and plumed shakos, with officer, drummer, and flag bearer, ca. 1950; set tied in original box.

$175–$200

French Line Infantry Fusiliers, 1914, in horizon-blue uniforms and Adrian helmets, assaulting, with officer, bugler, and standard bearer, ca. 1930; set in original box (G/F, chips, slight paint fading, bugler, coloring mismatched). $150–$175

French Marines of the Guard, 1812, marching at the slope in blue uniforms trimmed and faced in orange, and black shakos with tall red plumes (gloss paint), with officer and drummer; tied in original box. $100–$125

French Military Aviation Reconnaissance Monoplane (Avion de Reconnaissance), 1914, with tinplate monoplane, pilot, mechanic, and officer with map in horizon-blue uniform (limited issue); tied in original box. $650–$675

French Napoleonic Chasseurs, Group, marching at the slope, with officer, ca. 1920 figures. $85–$100

French Napoleonic Cuirassiers, 1809, mounted on standing horses (special issue), in blue and white uniforms, cuirasses, and plumed helmets, with officer, trumpeter, and standard bearers; tied in original box. $350–$357

French Napoleonic Guards of Honor, 1813, mounted at the halt (special issue), in green uniform jackets and pelisses trimmed in white and plumed shakos, holding musketoons at the carry, with officer, trumpeter, and standard bearer; in original box.

$350–$375

French Napoleonic Gun Team, 1812, with four-horse team, two drivers with whips, limber, and cannon; tied in original box.

$150–$175

French Navy Matelots (Marins Blancs), marching at the slope in summer white uniforms with officer, bugler, and standard bearer, ca. 1950; set tied in original box. $250–$275

French Navy Work Party, 1910, in summer uniforms, with sailors swabbing the deck, carrying mess tins, coils of rope, and other implements; tied in original box. $175–$200

French North African Goumiers, mounted on camels, with officer and standard bearer (limited issue); in original boxes.
                                                        $325–$350

French North African Spahis, 1890–1910, mounted with sabers on charging horses (special issue), wearing red and blue uniforms, white turbans and cloaks, with officer, tumpeter, and standard bearer; tied in original boxes. $350–$375

French Revolutionary Volunteers, 1795, marching at the slope in blue-and-white uniforms and tricolor trousers, with officer, drummer, and standard bearer, tied in original box.
                                                        $135–$150

French Royal Guard, period of Louis XV, marching at the slope in blue uniforms with red facings and turnbacks, with officer, drummer, and standard bearer; ca. 1950; set in original box.
                                                        $200–$225

French Sailors, 1914, marching at the slope in summer white uniforms (gloss paint), with officer and bugler; in a Mignot box.
                                                        $200–$225

Génie de La Garde (Engineers of the Guard), at attention with muskets at the carry (special issue), in blue-and-white uniforms trimmed in red and crested helmets, with officer, drummer, and special issue standard bearer at attention; tied in original box.
                                                        $175–$200

Grenadiers of the Clèves-Berg Regiment, 1810, marching at the slope in white uniforms faced with pale blue and red-plumed bearskin hats, with drummer, officer, and flag bearer; tied in original box. $135–$150

Grenadiers of the First British Foot Guards Regiment, 1813, marching at the slope in scarlet and white uniforms and bearskin hats, with officer, drummer, and flag bearer; tied in original box. $135–$150

Japanese Infantry, period of the Russo-Japanese War, march-ing at the slope in blue uniforms trimmed in red, peak caps and gaiters, with officer, bugler, and flag bearer, ca. 1950; set.

$275–$300

Kleber's French Dragoon Regiment, 1799, mounted at the trot with sabers, in red and white uniforms and plumed helmets, with trumpeter on dapple gray and officer and standard bearer on rearing horses; tied in original box. $250–$275

Marine Fusiliers, 1910–1914, marching at the slope in horizon-blue overcoats, caps with red pompons and full packs (gloss paint), with officer, bugler, and standard bearer; in original box. $125–$135

Medieval Archers, attacking with long bows, crossbows, swords, and pikes; in original box. $175–$200

Special Display Set of a "Modern Fortification" (Fort Moderne), ca. 1930, with French troops (40 mm scale, semi-round) assault-ing, firing rifles and machine guns, manning cannon, fort with ramparts, heavy cannon, earthworks, swivel gun in turret and various trees; shrubs, and bushes; tied in original fold-out dio-rama box with appropriate scenic backdrop. $1,600–$1,700

Napoleon's General Staff, mounted on rearing and trotting horses, with Napoleon in his chasseur uniform with greatcoat, mounted on his white horse Marengo (gloss paint); tied in orig-inal box. $150–$175

Paris Guard, 1910, marching at the slope in blue dress uniforms with plumed shakos and aiguillettes (gloss paint), with officer, bugler, and standard bearer; in original box. $125–$150

Polish Legion of the Vistula, 1808, at attention with muskets at the carry (special issue), in blue uniforms faced with yellow and red-plumed shakos, with officer, standard bearer, and drummer; tied in original box. $200–$250

Prussian Hussars, 1813, mounted at the trot with sabers, in black uniform coats and pelisses trimmed in white, gray trou-sers trimmed in red and short-plumed shakos, with officer and standard bearer; tied in original box. $175–$200

Prussian Infantry, 1806, marching at the slope in blue and gray uniforms and grenadier caps, with officer, drummer, and flag bearer, ca. 1950; set in original box. $175–$200

Prussian 13th Regiment of the Line, marching at the slope in blue, white, and gray uniforms with cocked hats, with officer, drummer, and standard bearer; tied in original box (M/E, scuff marks on trouser legs of one infantryman).   *$175–$200*

Rumanian Infantry, 1910–1914, marching at the slope in blue uniforms trimmed in red and caps with feather plumes, with officer, bugler, and standard bearer, ca. 1950; set.   *$150–$175*

Russian Grenadiers of the Guard, 1812, standing at attention with rifles at the carry (special issue), in green uniforms with orange facings, white crossbelts and trousers, and brassplated mitre caps, with drummer, officer, and standard bearer; tied in original box.   *$150–$175*

Sakalaves, Rare, marching at the slope and with slung arms, in blue uniforms, white trousers, yellow gaiters, and red fezes, ca. 1930 figures; together with another ca. 1950 group standing, firing.   *$200–$225*

Second Regiment Chevaux Légers (Light Cavalry), 1812, mounted at the trot with slung lances, in green uniforms faced with orange and plumed helmets, with trumpeter, and standard bearer on rearing horse; tied in original box.   *$135–$150*

Second Regiment French Foreign Legion, 1863, period of the Mexican Campaign and the Battle of Camerone (issued 1981 as a special set to commemorate the 150th anniversary of the Foreign Legion), with Legionnaires marching at the slope in white képis, blue tunics, and red trousers; bugler, officer, and standard bearer; tied in original box.   *$175–$200*

Siamese Royal Guard, marching at the slope in scarlet tunics, olive-green trousers, and white peak caps, with officer, bugler, and standard bearer, ca. 1940; set in original box. *$200–$225*

Spanish Cavalry, 1808, mounted at the trot with sabers, in pale-green uniforms with white frogging and red trim and plumed shakos, with officer, trumpeter, and standard bearer; tied in original box.   *$150–$175*

Spanish Hussars, 1808, mounted at the trot with sabers, in pale-green uniforms trimmed in white and red and plumed shakos, with officer, trumpeter, and standard bearer; original box.
     $200–$225

Swiss Battalion of Neufchatel (Battalion de Neufchatel), 1803, marching at the slope in orange uniforms faced with red and plumed black shakos, with officer, drummer, and standard bearer; tied in original box. $225–$250

Three-tier Diorama Box of 30 mm flats depicting French Napoleonic troops including Hussars and Lancers; Line Infantry marching past Napoleon seated in front of his field tent, surrounded by staff officers; and a field kitchen with staff from Napoleon's field train preparing dinner for the Emperor; original box with appropriate scenic backdrop. $225–$250

Three-tier Diorama Box of 30 mm flat figures depicting Napoleon's Egyptian Campaign of 1798, with French Chasseurs à Cheval, Line Infantry, and Camel Corpsmen in action against Egyptian troops and on parade; in original box with scenic backdrop. $225–$250

Tonkinese Infantry standing and kneeling, firing, in blue uniforms and white straw hats, ca. 1925; set. $150–$175

Two-tier Boy Scout Display Set with French Boy Scouts marching with staffs, including bugler, flag bearer, and scoutmaster on upper tier; also Boy Scout encampment, tent, and Boy Scouts cooking over open fire, various trees, shrubs, and other scenic props, ca. 1935; set tied in original display box with scenic backdrop. $1,000–$1,100

Union Army Horse-Drawn Ambulance Wagon, with two-horse team, ambulance, driver with whip, and stretcher team with wounded soldier, ca. 1950; set in original plain cardboard Mignot box. $150–$175

Union Infantry, assaulting with fixed bayonets, with officer wearing Hardee hat and standard bearer carrying national flag, ca. 1950; set in original box. $200–$225

Voltigeurs d'Infanterie Légère (Light Infantry Skirmishers), 1809, attacking with fixed bayonets, in medium-blue uniforms faced with scarlet and white and scarlet-plumed shakos, with officer, drummer, and standard bearer; tied in original box.
                                                       $300–$325

Voltigeurs of the 33rd Regiment of the Line, 1806, standing at attention with rifles at the carry (special issue), in white uniforms faced with purple and plumed shakos, with officer, drummer, and flag bearer; tied in original box. $125–$150

West Point Cadets, marching at the slope in winter dress uniforms with cadet officer and standard bearer with Corps of Cadets flag; tied in original box. $125–$135

West Point Cadet Color Guard (Garde du Drapeau), marching in summer dress with cadet officers carrying National Standard and Corps of Cadets flag and escort of two riflemen, ca. 1950; set tied in original box. $225–$250

S.A.E.

S.A.E. is an offshoot of American Authenticast, a Long Island, New York, firm founded after World War II. A Swede named Ericsson resumed casting these miniatures after Authenticast went out of business and the figures were imported from South Africa by distributors Curt Wennberg and Fred Winkler, beginning in 1952 and extending through the 1960s. S.A.E. initials signify South African Engineers. The miniatures listed below were cast in 30 mm scale.

Set #1306, British Grenadier Guards, advancing and firing, with officers; in original box. $45–$55

Set #1216, British Royal Artillery, 1776 (American Revolutionary War), with pair of cannons, two gun crews, and sections of stockade; in original box. $55–$65

Set #1062, Confederate Infantry, marching at the slope, with marching band, standard bearer, and officer, in original box; also with Confederate Cavalry figures. $50–$60

Set #1815, Dutch Grenadiers of the Imperial Guard, in action, with standard bearer and officer; in original box. $75–$100

Set #6414, French Field Artillery Gun Team, 1815, with six-horse team, gun, limber. $65–$75

Set #6414, French Napoleanic Field Artillery Gun Team, 1812, with six-horse team and three drivers, limber wagon, and cannon; in original box. $65–$75

Set #1405, Hessian Fusiliers, 1776, standing, firing, with officer

and standard bearer, in original box; also British Cavalry, 1776, attacking with pistols and sabers, with officer, in original box.
$125–$150

Set #3203, Indian Army Cavalry, 1910, mounted at the walk in review order, including troopers of the Skinner's horse, 10th Bengal Lancers; in original box.
$50–$60

Set unmarked, Life Guards, mounted at the halt in review order with trumpeter and officer; in original box.
$75–$100

Set #6422, Royal Engineers Pontoon Team, 1815, with pontoon wagon, boat, and bridge planking drawn by six-horse team with three drivers; in original box.
$45–$55

Set Unmarked, Skinner's Horse, mounted at the halt in review order; in original box.
$75–$85

Set #1401, Troops of the 30-Years War, advancing with muskets and pikes, mounted and foot soldiers, in original box; also with Set #1402, marching, including mounted and foot soldiers.
$100–$125

Set #1053, Union Cavalry (Rush's Lancers), mounted at the walk with officer and standard bearer, with national flag; in original box.
$45–$55

SELWYN

An Englishman, Roy Selwyn-Smith, produced a line of intricately painted hollowcast medieval knights, over a period of less than a year, in 1951. Lacking support due to the untimely death of his financial backer, Otto Gottstein, Smith sold the molds to Britains Ltd., which reissued the figures in 1954, under the name "Knights of Agincourt." The following examples are original Roy Selwyn-Smith editions.

Bishop of Winchester, mounted with lance on rearing horse.
$375–$385

Selwyn Miniatures

Black Prince, mounted in full armor, with mace raised to strike.
$325–$335

Count of Anjou, holding banner, mounted on standing steed.
$335–$350

Harry Hotspur, mounted at the charge, with mace raised overhead.
$300–$325

Sir Eumery de Lucy, mounted with lance.
$275–$300

STADDEN

Diorama, comprised of 54 mm Figures of British Line Infantrymen, 1812–1815 War, in defensive formation against cavalry; kneeling and standing soldiers firing and at ready, drummer falling wounded, sergeant with espontoon; wooden base and landscaping.
$325–$350

Group of British Line Infantrymen (War of 1812), and a drummer of a Line Infantry Regiment, ca. 1760; a piper of the Black Watch; a Swiss Infantryman, 1806; a British Grenadier, 1700; a Hesse-Kassel Infantryman, 1770; and a figure of Lord Somerset, aide-de-camp to the Duke of Wellington; bearing Stadden imprint.
$525–$550

Mixed Group includes Grenadier Officer of the 28th Foot, Gloucestershire Regiment, 1740; Grenadier of 2nd Foot Guards, 1750; American Continental Soldier, Pennsylvania Line, 1779; French Chasseur of Imperial Guard, 1808; Seaforth Highlander Officer, 1779; Black Watch Highlander, 1815; plus 85 mm figure of Coldstream Guards Private, 1815.
$850–$875

STAR SOLDIERS

Sets 5, 6, and 7. Fife and Drum Band of the Grenadier Guards (limited edition of 70 sets cast and painted by Frank and Jan Scroby), 1900, includes five drummer boys, four boy fifers, five adult fifers, bass drummer, triangle player, cymbalist, and drum major; in original box.
$350–$375

Sets 12, 13, and 13A. Pipe Band of the 42nd Royal Highland Regiment, the Black Watch, in khaki foreign service dress (part of above limited edition), 1900, includes ten pipers, four side drummers, two tenor drummers, bass drummer, and drum major; in original boxes.
$275–$300

Star Collectibles

This firm originated with a midwesterner, Michael Curley, and his wife, Star (hence the name), who imported the miniatures from Marlborough, a small toy firm in Wales which features military miniatures cast by Frank and Jan Scroby. Following Michael Curley's death, his wife continued to import a limited edition under the Star name of 50 and later 100 sets.

PHILLIPS AUCTIONS, 1988

The following auction prices are from Phillips' New York City sale on June 11, 1988, and their Christmas Collectibles sale of December 10, 1988. They do *not* reflect the 10% buyer's premium. The June sale consignments were from the collection of David P. O'Neill of Cleveland, Ohio, as well as other collectors. The Christmas sale reflects a number of consignors.

The Britains sets are listed sequentially by set number. The term "Early" is used in certain lots as a determination (in the opinion of Phillips) that the sets date from the 1893–1918 period.

Condition classifications are as follows:

M—mint   F—fair
E—excellent   P—poor
G—good

The number of figures in each set is shown in parentheses. If a set is incomplete, it will be so noted.

Britains

Britains Special Production, steel-helmeted version of Colour Party of Scots Guards, ca. 1940; three Sergeants marching at slope; pair of officers with King's Colour and regimental standard (tin flags), pair of officers w/swords, in original "Types of the World's Armies" box; E, box G/F.   *$11,110*

Early Set #7, 7th Royal Fusiliers (City of London), ca. 1900; marching at the slope (1st version, smaller heads); valise packs; detached rifle slings; bemedaled officer in early illustrated box; G, box G/F.   *$1,000*

Early Set #13, 3rd King's Hussars, 1903; mounted with short carbines on cantering horses; officer on prancing horse with throat plume; E/G, box F (5). $1,000

Early Set #24, Mountain Gun of the Royal Artillery, ca. 1900 (1st version, round bases); guns, gunners, mules, and mounted officer in original Whisstock box; G (three figures mismatched from later set), box F (12). $750

Early Set #27, set dates from period 1893–1918, band of the line marching in review order with drum major, intermediate version ca. 1910; slotted arm, oval base bandsmen, and square-based side and bass drummer; in original box; E/G, box G/F (12). $1,500

Set #28, Mountain Gun of the Royal Artillery; screw gun, ammunition, gunners, mules, and mounted officer; E, box G/F. $350

Set #38, South African Mounted Infantry, ca. 1920; four fixed-arm mounted riflemen; fixed-arm officer with pistol; in original Printer's box; E/G (some retouching to horses), box G/F (5). $900

Early Set #45, 3rd Madras Light Cavalry mounted at gallop in review order with trumpeter, ca. 1910; in Soldiers of Great Britain box; E/G, box E/G (5). $750

Set #63, 10th Bengal Lancers (double row box); eight lancers, trumpeter, officer at gallop in review order; in original Sons of the Empire—Our Indian Army display box; E, box E/G (10). $1,900

Early Set #79, British Naval Landing Party, ca. 1900; sailors pulling gun and limber, with ammunition, and petty officer (first version, oval bases), original Whisstock box; E/G, box G/F (11). $1,800

Early Set #94, 21st Empress of India's Lancers mounted at gallop, 1901; in active service dress with lances and trumpeter (2nd version, one-eared horses); in original Printer's box; G, box G (5). $1,700

Early Set #106, 6th Dragoon Guards mounted at gallop (2nd version, one-eared horses), 1901; long carbines; fixed-arm officer; original Whisstock box; E, box E/G (5). $1,300

Early Set #116, Sudanese Infantry marching at the trail in review order (1st version, oval bases), 1901; in original Soldiers of the British Empire box; E/G, box G (8). $1,100

Set #118, American Soldier Company Military Game, "Zulus," 1906; six Britains Zulu warriors, collapsible tent; original box with Beiser tray; G, box G. $1,200

Early Set #134, Japanese Infantry charging (1st version, original paper labels under oval bases bearing date of 1st issue), 1904; in original Printer's box; E/G (8). $800

Set #172, Bulgarian Infantry marching at trail in review order with officer, ca. 1935; in original Types of the Bulgarian Army box; E, box E (8). $900

Set #175, Austrian Lancers mounted in review order with sabers, 1902; with officer, trumpeter; in original; Types of the Austro-Hungarian Army box; G, box E/G (5). $1,300

Set #186, Mexican Infantry marching with slung arms in brown and gray uniforms, ca. 1930; tan sombreros, with officer; original Whisstock box; G, box E/G (8). $800

Set #203A, Royal Engineers Pontoon Section in khaki service dress, peaked caps, ca. 1930; four-horse team; two drivers w/ whips; pontoon wagon; pontoon w/bridge planking; in original Whisstock box; E/G, box G (9). $2,000

Set #219, Argentine Military Cadets marching at the slope in review order, ca. 1935; Types of the Argentine Army box; E/G, box E/G (8). $1,500

Set #1440, Royal Field Artillery Gun Team mounted at the walk in khaki service dress and peaked caps; six-horse team; three drivers with whips, limber, gun, and officer with sword on cantering horse in original Types of the British Army box; E/G, box F (9). $1,400

Set #1555, Changing of the Guard at Buckingham Palace; full band of Coldstream Guards, Scots Guards at present arms; Coldstream Guards marching at the slope; officers, standard-bearers, and sentry boxes in original illustrated display two-tray box; E/G, box G. $1,300

Set #1720, Mounted Band of the Royal Scots Greys; full instrumentation and kettledrummer; (7). $550

Set #1901, Regiment Louw Wepener marching at the slope in dark blue-green tropical service dress with officer in wrong Britains box; some color fading and one figure missing bayonet; E/G (8).   *$1,100*

Set #2109, Highland Pipe Band of the Black Watch with pipers, side and tenor drummers; pipe major and drum major; tied in original box; M, box E (20).   *$1,200*

Set #2110, U.S. Military Band marching in yellow and black dress uniforms with complete instrumentation: four trombones, four trumpets, two sousaphones, two French horns, two bass tubas (in place of saxophones usually found in set), three clarinets, bassoons, fifer, bugler, bass and side drummers, cymbalist, and drum major; in original box; E, box G (25).   *$4,500*

Set #2115, Drums and Bugles of the Royal Marines (issued only in 1956); five buglers, three side drummers, one tenor drummer, 1 bass drummer, cymbalist, and drum major; tied in original box; M/E, box E (12).   *$2,400*

Set#2184, Bahamas Police at attention with Sergeant and British officer; E/G (8).   *$700*

Set #2185, Bahamas Police Band; 15-piece version; drum major, three side drummers, bass drummer, cymbalist, fifer, cornetist, tenor horn, euphonium, and tuba players, one clarinet player; one clarinetist and drummer missing; G/F (13).   *$1,100*

Courtenay

Earl of Angus, position 2; advancing with battleax in movable right arm; ca. 1940; E.   *$550*

Earl of Glouster, 13th-century knight, Edward I era; standing, holding banner with arms of Clare in right hand; shield at rest in left; signed R. Courtenay, Courtenay's signature faded but legible; E.   *$800*

Earl of Nassau, position Z-1; lying mortally wounded on Poitiers field, 1356; lying next to him is a battleax. Courtenay signature (originally from the Natalie Hays Hammond collection); E.
                                                                                    $475

John de Sarnesfield, Squire of Black Prince, position H-3; mounted with lance in right arm; shield in left, movable visor; signed R. Courtenay; E/G. $750

John Fineux (double figure), defending his Lord Sir Nicholas Keriel, position 8; signed R. Courtenay; E/G. $700

John, Lord Beaumont, K.G., mounted on horse with full ornamental trappings (hollowcast version); lance in movable right arm; detachable helm crested with gold lion; E. $750

John Viscount de Melun, Order of the Star, standing in full armor and cloak; Courtenay signature (also from Natalie Hays Hammond collection); G. $300

King Jean II, astride Joan of Arc horse (conversion) with sword in right arm, extended to rear; detachable helm; G. $650

Mounted Knights of Agincourt, including sets #1659, Knight with mace; #1660, Knight with sword; #1661, Knight with lance, charging; all in original boxes; M/E (3). $400

Personality Figures, King Charles I and Charles II, both signed R. Courtenay; E (2). $450

Personality Figures, King George V and Queen Mary, in royal robes; signed Courtenay; E (2). $475

Personality Figures, King George VI, royal robes holding scepter and orb; Queen Elizabeth in royal robes; signed Courtenay; E (2). $475

Sir Bartholemew Burghursh, astride horse with full tournament trappings; detachable helmet; original identification tag with Courtenay signature; E/G. $850

Sir Bartholomew Burghursh, K.G., position H-1; mounted with lance in movable right arm, with movable visor; R. Courtenay signed; E/G. $700

Sir John, Lord Beaumont, position H-1; mounted with lance in movable right arm; movable visor; R. Courtenay signed, E.
Price Indeterminate

Sir John Mallory, position 17, advancing with sword; paired with Sir John Bertram, position 17, advancing with sword; ca. 1940; black bases; E (2). $700

Sir Thomas Holland, K. G., M-2 position; mounted with lance in movable right arm; detachable helm; ca. 1940; black base; E/G. $850

Sir William Segrave, position 17; advancing with sword; paired with Sir Bernard Brocas, position 17, advancing with sword; ca. 1940; black bases; E (2). $600

Thierry D'Auffay Le Hardi, position 14; advancing bare-headed with sword and shield; detachable helm; signed R. Courtenay; E. $550

Thomas, Earl of Warwick, K.G. (special conversion by Courtenay); long, flowing surcoat and mantle of pressed tin; elaborate quartered coat-of-arms, sword in upraised arm; movable visor, black base; E/G. $900

Thomas, Lord Braose, astride cruciform horse (an adaptation of a Holger Eriksson model); battleax in movable right arm; black case; E/G. $850

Two English Archers, wearing livery of Earl of Salisbury, firing long bows; ca. 1940; E (2). $400

William, Lord Latimer, position H-3; mounted with lance in movable right arm; shield in left movable visor, lambrequin flowing from helmet crested with black feathers; R. Courtenay signature; black base; E/G. $850

Miscellaneous

Heyde: Polar Exploration Display Set, members of Admiral Byrd expedition; canvas-topped dog sled with driver; radio operator, radio; man in kayak; another raising signal flags to top of flagpole; polar bears, walrus; various scenic props; in original box; G/F, box G (29). $800

Potsdamer Zinnsoldaten: Special Presentation Set, Royal Marines Chastize Midwest Brigands, depicting Royal Marines Landing Party, ca. 1900, under cover of British warships, attacking Arab warriors armed with scimitars, spears, and jezails; exploding shell and other scenic props; tied in original display box; M, box E (27). $550

Warren: Set #42, U.S. Staff Car (Officer's Car in Warren's cat-

alog), steel-helmeted driver; two seated soldiers with folded
arms; U.S. regimental standard, troop guidon; in original box;
E/G, box G (6).   *$1,200*

GUERNSEY'S AUCTION, 1989,
BURTT EHRLICH COLLECTION

Phillips Auctions in New York City and London have been identified as specialists in military miniature sales over the past few
years, and indeed they have held any number of significant toy
soldier conclaves recently. The prize, however, for orchestrating
the most ballyhooed toy soldier extravaganza of all went to
Guernsey's on February 18, 1989, with the Burtt Ehrlich Collection. The eminent collection had been handsomely show-
cased in *The Art of the Toy Soldier,** with 300 full-color
photographs. Although the 679 lot sale topped estimates at
$309,782, prices for some of the "high ticket" individual lots
proved to be not as "earthshaking" as anticipated. The following examples include hammer price, as well as the 10% buyer's
premium.

Aga Khan, Britains, British Racing Colours of Famous Owners
Series; jockey and racehorse.   *$522*

Arabs on Charging Horses, Heyde; large-scale (90 mm)
figures.   *$1,540*

Band of the Life Guards, Britains Set #101; with original box
and catalog.   *$770*

British General Staff, Heyde; complete set with original two-tier
box; provenance of having been purchased at London's Ham-
ley's toy store by Queen Mary for youngest son, Prince John;
horse-mounted Hussars; G, Box F.   *$14,300*

City of London and Royal Welsh Fusiliers, Britains; some missing bayonet tips; G (27).   *$302.50*

Civil War U.S. Army Set, Mignot; (6).   *$275*

*Coauthored by Ehrlich and Phillips' consultant, Henry L. Kurtz; Ab-
beville Press, New York, 1987 (see Bibliography).

Indian Camp, Heyde; Indians on foot, fishing in canoes, hunting buffalo, in war dance costumes; (52).   *$1,320*

Mechanical Horse Race Game, Britains; four jockeys astride racehorses on wires that pivot on central pole.   *$1,760**

Middle Ages Diorama, Mignot; castle besieged by archers and cavalry; painted background; original box.   *$1,210*

Moroccans, Mignot; in original box; purchased by an agent for Malcolm Forbes, proving that he doesn't *always* set auction highs; (12).   *$137.50*

Noah's Ark, Britain Set #1550; 1940; Noah, wife, animals; (44).   *$6,600*

Royal Fusiliers, Royal Sussex Regiment and Seaforth Highlanders, Britains Set #1323.   *$275*

U.S. Pilots, Britains #332; figures F, original box F.   *$385*

Victorian Family, Britains; seated mother, father, son, daughter, baby (some damage and chipped paint, but reputed to be only example in the U.S.).   *$6,600*

*Well under estimated $3,000–$3,500.

Nautical Toys

As was the case with aviation toys, the topical category of boats and ships is clearly monopolized by European makers. Obvious exceptions would include Messrs. Ives, Fallows, Reid, and Bliss with their classic early painted and lithographed tin, paper-on-wood, and cardboard fleet of colorful sidewheelers and Noah's Arks. Then too, there are the highly uncommon Ives oarsmen in painted tin and the cast-iron sculls by Ives and Wilkins, which attract topical sports collectors as well. "Ruling the waves" in nautical playthings are the German makers Maerklin, Bing, Planck, Carette, Schoenner, and Radiguet, whose golden era extended form the early 1900s to World War I. Superbly enameled tinplate pacquette boats and warships with clockwork mechanisms produced in this span have recently brought outrageous prices at auction. The record-breaking price of $28,600 for a beautifully scaled replica of the liner *Lusitania* by Maerklin, believed to be unique, was achieved at a Sotheby Collector's Carousel in 1983 and may stand up for some time to come.

PAINTED AND LITHOGRAPHED
TIN AND WOOD

Adirondack Sidewheeler, Dent Hardware, 1920s, approximately 10″ length. $500–$600

American Clipper Ships, W.S. Reed, 1877, 42″ length.
$1,000–$2,000

Atlanta Steam Yacht, Ives, 1893, with or without whistle, three cast-iron wheels, 19″ and 23″ length sizes.   *$5,000–plus*

Brooklyn Torpedo Boat, German, circa 1905, 30″ length, painted tinplate.   *$5,000–plus*

City of New York, Wilkins, 1900, cast iron, 15½″ length.
        $600–$700

Columbia Sidewheeler, W.S. Reed, 1800s, lithographed wood, 24″ length.   *$1,200–$2,200*

Crescent, George W. Brown, 1870, painted tin, 14½″ length.
        $3,000–plus

Dime Boat, maker unknown, 1800s, lithographed wood, tugboat, 6″ length.   *$1,000–$1,500*

Diving Submarine, A.C. Gilbert, 1920s, tin clockwork, 12″ length.   *$300–$400*

Gem of the Ocean, R. Reed, 1880s, lithographed wood, sidewheeler, 24″ length.   *$3,000–$4,000*

General Taylor, maker unknown, circa 1880, handpainted tin.
        $3,000–plus

Gunboat, Earnst Planck (German), circa 1900, painted sheet metal, 16⅝″ length.   *$1,600–$1,700*

Gunboat, German, 1910, 7″ length, red and white body, black and green stripes.   *$300–$400*

Gunboat With Airplanes, Carette, circa 1914, painted tinplate clockwork, 17″ length.   *$3,000–$4,000*

H. M. S. Blake, R. Bliss, British war cruiser, bright blue, 19″ length.   *$1,000–$2,000*

Indiana Battleship, Morton Converse, patented in 1900, lithographed tinplate, wood, 32″ length.   *$1,000–$2,000*

Leviathan Ocean Liner, Bing, circa 1925, painted tinplate, clockwork, 39″ length.   *$5,000–plus*

Live Steam Launch, Weeden, 1915, painted tin, 20″ length.
        $600–$700

Merchant Marine Ship, Ives, 1920s, painted tin mechanical, 11″ length.   *$600–$700*

Battleship, Ideal, Detroit, Michigan, lithograph paper on wood pull toy, 20″ length, $1,200–$1,400. "Gem of the Ocean" attributed to R. Bliss, early 1900s, lithograph paper on wood, 27″ length, $1,800–$2,000.

Missouri Battleship, German, circa 1913, painted tinplate clockwork, 28″ length.   *$5,000–plus*

New Mexico Battleship, S. Orkin, 1920, painted tinplate, 25″ length.   *$1,000–$2,000*

Ocean Liner, Arnold, lithographed tin mechanical, 1920s, 11½″ length.   *$500–$600*

Ocean Liner, Kingsbury, circa 1920s, painted steel, red, white, and buff, gilt rails, clockwork mechanical, adjustable rudder.
$500–$600

Ocean Liner, Marx, 1929, lithographed tin, 11½″ length.
$400–$500

Ocean Passenger Liner, Greppert & Kelch, 1920, lithographed tin clockwork, 12″ length.   *$500–$600*

Orobar Ocean Liner, German, 1920s, painted tinplate, battery-operated lights, 12″ length.   *$1,000–$1,200*

Pacquet Boat, Maerklin, 1914, painted tinplate, clockwork, winding mechanism on second stack, 8″ and 10″ length sizes.
$3,000–$4,000

Paddlewheeler, Carette, 1910, painted tin mechanical.
$1,000–$2,000

Providence, W. S. Reed, 1880s, lithographed wood.
$2,000–$2,500

Schwaben Gunboat, German, circa 1910, painted tinplate, 16″ length.   *$3,000–$4,000*

Sirene, Meltete at Parent, France, 1890s, paddlesteamer clockwork, 29½″ length.   *$1,200–$2,200*

Speedboat, Hess, 1920s, lithographed tin friction, 12″ length.
$300–$400

Speedboat, Lionel, 1930s, lithographed tin mechanical, two passengers, 18″ length.   *$300–$400*

Steamboat, maker unknown, 1892, cabin with awning, 20″ length.   *$1,000–$2,000*

Steamboat, Mathias Hess (German), 1908, painted tin, three-wheeler floor toy, 10½″ length.   *$1,000–$2,000*

Four Sidewheel Steamer toys. *Top left:* "St. Johns," $5,000 plus; *Top right:* "Pacific," $2,000 plus; *Center:* "Water Witch," $2,000 plus. Top two toys attributed to George W. Brown, third, maker unknown.

Steam Launch, Weeden, 1920s, tinplate, 15 ½ " length.
$300–$400

Submarine, Ives, 1900s, painted tinplate, gray with red trim, 10 ½ " length.
$500–$600

Submarine, maker unknown, 1936, steel, clockwork, actually dives and rises, 10 " and 13 " length sizes.
$350–$400

Two-Masted Sailing Ship, W.S. Reed, 1877, lithographed wood clockwork, 38 " length.
$1,000–$2,000

Union, R. Bliss, 1880s, lithographed wood, sidewheeler, 24 " length.
$2,000–$3,000

Union Ferry Boat, Bing, circa 1917, painted tinplate clockwork, 21 " length.
$5,000–plus

Three-Masted Sailing Vessel With Figurehead, possibly Bliss, 1880s, litho-on-wood, $1,000–$2,000.

Vixen Racing Yacht, Ives, 1920s, painted tin mechanical, 13″ length.　　　　　　　　　　　　　　　　*$500–$600*

Volunteer IXL, Fallows, late 1890s, painted, stained, and stenciled tin clockwork, 16″ length.　　　　*$5,000–$6000*

Warship, Dayton, tin pressed-steel friction toy, 15½″ length.
　　　　　　　　　　　　　　　　　　　　$900–$1,000

Warship, maker unknown, tin mechanical friction wheeled toy, 15½″ length.　　　　　　　　　　　　　*$400–$500*

CAST-IRON BOATS

Chris Craft, Hubley, 1920s, painted cast-iron cabin cruiser, with anchor, *Chris-Craft* embossed on bow, 11″ length. *$600–$700*

City of New York Sidewheeler, Harris, 1900s, painted cast iron, name embossed along side of paddlewheel.　　　*$650–$750*

Puritan Sidewheeler, Harris, circa 1903, cast iron, white with red trim, gray roof, black stack, 10¾″ length.　　*$400–$500*

A catalog page from a premier toy boat maker, Gebruder Maerklin, c. 1915. These handsomely enameled tinplate toys featured long-running clockwork mechanisms and copied the original down to the last-minute detail. Unfortunately, the prices on Maerklin toy boats have escalated to a range of what you might expect to pay for a real yacht.

Puritan Sidewheeler, Wilkins, 1895, painted cast iron, white with red trim, orange roof, black stack, 10⅜″ length.

$500–$600

Showboat, Arcade, 1928, painted cast iron with *Showboat* painted across side, 11″ length. $800–$900

Sidewheeler, Dent, 1910, painted sidewheeler, unidentified, 11″ length. $500–$600

A popular spinoff among nautical toys, and actually a collecting specialty in itself, is the Noah's Ark. Lithograph paper on wood and tin
with wooden figures. American, maker unknown, 1890s, $650–$750.
Lithograph paper on wood, Noah's Ark, German, 1880s, $1,200–
$1,400.

Static Speed Boat, Hubley, 1920s, with driver, painted cast iron,
three wheels, 10″ length.   *$600–$700*

PERELMAN TOY MUSEUM SALE

Cast-Iron Nautical Toys

Adirondack Sidewheeler, Dent Hardware, 12½" length.

                                                   $1,000

City of New York Sidewheeler, Harris Toy Co., wheeled cast-iron pull toy, 15½" length.   *$1,250*

Kearsarge Gunboat, Wilkins Toy Co., 1912, cast iron.   *$1,500*

Puritan Sidewheeler, Harris Toy Co., 1903, cast iron:
   Medium.   *$850*
   Small.   *$375*
   Tiny.   *$275*

Riverboat, Dent Hardware, 1890s, oversize.   *$2,500*

Showboat, Arcade Mfg. Co., 1929, cast iron, 11¼" length.

                                                   $1,250

Penny Toys

Penny toys originated in late Victorian and Edwardian England, receiving their name because they sold for a bargain price of a penny, a ha'penny, or a tuppenny. Because they brought to even the poorest child's home the wonders of leverage, flywheels, friction, springs, and crankshafts, they soon found popularity in America and France as well.

The major manufacturing centers from 1890 to World War I were Kienberger & Co., Johann Philipp Meier, Johann Distler, and Walter Stock in Nuremberg for tin and lead models and Sonnenberg for wood. Penny toys were also manufactured in Japan, France, and the United States, plus a limited number in the United Kingdom. A between-the-wars phase of celluloid versions proved short-lived because of the fragility and inflammability of that material.

In recent years, penny toys have been fervently pursued by miniaturists and Victorian doll house collectors, as well as toy enthusiasts. These once paltry geegaws, to quote Leslie Daiken, founder of the British Toy Museum, are vivid embodiments of fashion and custom, travel and pleasure, trade and child's play.

Aeronautical, German, lithographed tin, 7″ height.

$100–$125

Alligator, German, 5″ length. $75–$100

Armored Car, German, 1910, camouflaged lithographed tin, 2⅞″ length. $75–$100

Auto, Gesch, German, 1910, earliest auto penny toy, stained tin. $150–$200

Baby Carriage, German, 1900s, lithographed tin, with baby, 2 ½" height. $100–$150

Battleship, J. Ph. Meier, 1900–1914, three-deck ship bears name "Thunderer," triple stack belches smoke with crosscut using sawhorse on platform, 3 ½" length. $150–$200

Beetle, German, 1900s, 3" length. $50–$75

Billiard Player, Kienberger & Co. (German), circa 1920s, lithographed tin, spring-loaded wire rod pool mechanism, 4" length. $200–$300

Bird Cage on Stand, German, 1900s, lithographed tin with bellows, 8" height. $100–$150

Boattail Race Car, GF, German, 1910, lithographed tin. $100–$125

Boxers, Ferman, CKO, 1900, squeeze toy. $50–$75

Boy on Sleigh, Johann Philipp Meier, 1920s, two pairs disk wheels, lithographed tin pull toy, 2 ¾" height. $300–$400

Brown Horse on Wheeled Platform, Sonneberg, Germany, 1900s, pull toy, brown with red and yellow trim, 5" height. $150–$200

Butcher's Cart, German, lithographed tin. $100–$150

Child in Highchair, German, 1890s, lithographed tin, 2 ½" height. $200–$250

Chinaman With Umbrella, German, 1900s, Chinaman rides on small wagon, 3" length. $150–$200

City of London Police Ambulance, German, 1900s, flywheel mechanical, lithographed tin, 4" length. $250–$300

Clown in Barrel, Stock, German, 1910, lithographed tin, 3" length. $350–$400

Clown Prodding Donkey, German, 1920s, lithographed tin leverage toy, clown tries to persuade donkey to budge with stick, 4" length. $150–$200

Dancing Man, German, 1900s, 4" height. $50–$75

Dancing Minstrel, Johann Distler (German), late 1920s, lithographed tin, jointed tin black figure dances on platform, crank mechanical (miniaturized version of Tombo, Dapper Dan, et al.), 3 ½ " height. $125–$175

Delivery Van, German, 1920, lithographed tin. $100–$125

Dirigible, German, early 1920s, lithographed tin, string toy, four-bladed propellor spins, 3 " length. $200–$300

Doll's Baby Carriage, German, 1910, painted molded lead, 3 " length. $200–$300

Electric Omnibus, German, 1900s, lithographed tin, passengers ride in open air on roof as well as inside omnibus, hollow tin driver is seated in open cab, flywheel mechanical, 4 ½ " length.
$300–$400

Elephant Clicker, German, 1900s, lithographed tin. $50–$75

Express Boy, German, 1920s, bellhop sits on trunk. $25–$50

Express Parcel Delivery Truck, German, 1920s. $100–$200

Fire Engine, C. K. O., lithographed tin, 5 ½ " height.
$50–$100

Fire Truck With Firemen, German, 1890s, lithographed and nickeled tin mechanical, 4 ½ length. $200–$300

Fleecy Lamb, German, circa 1870, wood with real wool, 2 ½ " length. $300–$400

Garage, German, 1900s, lithographed tin with gas pump, 4 " length. $75–$100

Garage With Two Cars, German, 1900s, 2 ½ " height.
$50–$100

Girl Feeding Rooster, German, 1920s, wheeled platform.
$250–$300

Girl on Swing, German, 1900s, lithographed tin. $200–$300

Grand Hotel Wagon, German, 1930s, lithographed tin, horse-drawn carriage, bright red and yellow, gilded spoke wheels, 5 ¼ " length. $300–$400

Hansom Cab With Driver, German, 1915, lithographed tin, pulled by dappled horse. $200–$250

Hay Wagon, German, 1920s, horse-drawn, lithographed tin.
$100–$200

Hens and Chicks on Nest, German, 1915, lithographed tin.
$200–$300

Hook and Ladder Truck, German, 1900s, two helmeted passengers seated back to back, overhead ladder in open truck, fire bell, flywheel mechanical, lithographed tin, 4½″ length.
$300–$325

Horse and Cart, German, painted tin, ¾″ length. $50–$75

Horse and Cart, German, 1910, lithographed tin. $75–$100

Horse-Drawn Hanson Cab, German, 1900s, lithographed tin.
$100–$150

Horse on Platform, J. M., German, 1900, 3″ height. $50–$75

Hot Air Balloon, German, early 1920s, lithographed tin, two-pulley string mechanical, single revolving propellor above air bag plus tiny anchor, 2½″ height. $200–$250

Jack-in-the-Stove, English, circa 1910, spring-operated lithographed tin, man's head pops out of top of parlor stove, 4″ height. $300–$400

Knight on Horseback, German, 1900s, lithographed tin, 4″ height. $100–$150

Landau Roadster, German, lithographed tin. $100–$125

Limousine, German, 1900s, lithographed tin, 2½″ length.
$50–$75

Locomotive, German, 1900s, stained tin, earliest locomotive penny toy, friction drive. $125–$150

Locomotive, KiCo, German, 3¾″ length. $50–$75

Man and Twirler, German, 1920s, lithographed tin, 7″ height.
$50–$100

Merry-Go-Round, German, lithographed tin mechanical, 4½″ height. $150–$200

Monkey Climbing Ladder, German, 1920s, 6¾″ length.
$75–$100

Monoplane, German, circa 1915, lithographed tin mechanical, large propeller, oversized pilot sits in open cockpit, 5″ length.
$300–$400

Mother Pushing Girl in Sleigh, German, 1890, lithographed tin.
$300–$400

Mule Cart, German, 1910, lithographed tin, 6″ length.
$200–$225

Nodding Goose, 1920s, lithographed tin, platform toy.
$100–$150

Oarsman, German, 1900s, 2 men in scull on wheels, lithographed tin, 6½″ length.
$250–$300

Ocean Liner, German, 1910, lithographed tin wheeled pull toy.
$200–$300

Open Touring Car, German, 1900s, lithographed tin, 4½″ length.
$100–$200

Pool Player, German, 1910, 4″ length.
$100–$125

Pug Dog, English, 1900s, hollow tin, painted, 2″ length.
$100–$200

Pumper Fire Engine, pale blue, 4″ length.
$200–$225

Quarter Moon, German, 1915, lithographed tin.
$200–$250

Race Car With Driver, German, 1920s, lithographed tin, 2½″ length.
$100–$125

Racing Car, CFO, German, lithographed tin.
$100–$125

Roosters, German, CKO, 1990, squeeze toy.
$75–$100

Rotating Ferris Wheel, English, 1900s, lithographed tin with cars covered with tin awnings, 4″ height.
$200–$250

Scale, German, 1900s, 3″ length.
$100–$125

Sedan, German, 1890s, lithographed tin, 4½″ length.
$100–$125

Sewing Machine, German, lithographed tin with drawer, 3″ height.
$100–$125

Skier, German, 1920s, lithographed tin, wheeled toy.
$200–$250

Squirrel on Treadmill, French, 1910, lithographed tin mechanical. $100–$125

Submarine, German, 1930s. $50–$75

Sulky, German, 1920s, lithographed tin. $250–$300

Swordsmen, German, Kellerman, 1900s, squeeze toy. $35–$50

Tank Truck, German, 1920s, lithographed tin. $75–$100

Taxi, German, circa 1910–1915, driver seated in front, open section, lithographed tin with nickeled wheels, friction mechanical. $150–$175

Tin-Top Jitney Bus, glass chassis, tin wheels, approximately 3 ½ ″ length. $250–$300

Toonerville Trolley, German (Cracker Jack). $300–$400

Torpedo Touring Car, German, 1920s, lithographed tin. $50–$75

Touring Car, J. M., German, 1900s, lithographed tin, 3 ¼ ″ length. $75–$100

Town Car, Johann Philip Meier, German, 1920s, open limousine with brightly lithographed details including headlamps, spoked wheels, tin, 3 ⅜ ″ length. $200–$250

Toy Airplanes on Pole, German, 1900s, spring action, 6 ″ height. $100–$200

Train, Japan, lithographed tin $50–$75

Train Car, German, 1900s, lithographed tin, 2 ½ ″ length. $100–$125

Trolley, French, lithographed tin, 3 ″ length. $75–$100

Truck, J. Distler, German, 1910, lithographed tin friction. $100–$200

Two Ducks, German, 1915, lithographed tin. $75–$100

Political and Patriotic Toys

❉ ❉ ❉

POLITICAL AND PATRIOTIC TOYS
INNER CIRCLE

The following is a selection of the most elite toys in the political-patriotic category:

Abraham Lincoln or Gideon Wells, Gerrard Calgani, 1860s, automated sand toy.

Benjamin Harrison, maker unknown, 1888, Grover Cleveland bisque scale toy.

General Butler Walker, Ives, 1880s, clockwork, or Tilden the Statesman, Ives, 1880, clockwork.

General Grant Smoking Cigar, Ives, circa 1876, clockwork.

Moody-Sanky, maker unknown, 1880s, still bank, cast iron.

Rocking American Eagle Bell Ringer, maker unknown, 1890s.

Uncle Sam and the Don, Gong Bell, 1903, bell ringer cast metal.

Uncle Sam on Velocipede, Ives, 1890s, clockwork.

U.S. Capitol, W.S. Reed, 1884, lithographed wood histograph.

William H. Taft "Egg" Still Bank, cast iron, 1908.

Woman Suffragette, Automatic Toy Works, 1875, wood clockwork, or Political Stump Speaker, Ives, 1882, wood clockwork.

HONORABLE MENTION: Theodore Roosevelt Teddy and the Bear, and Teddy and the Lion mechanical banks, J. & E. Stevens, early 1900s; Magic General Grant and General Butler, A. A. Davis, 1880s, glass novelty jigglers; Teddy Roosevelt Nodder, maker unknown, 1900s, composition; Uncle Sam and John

Bull, Gong Bell, 1900s, bell ringer; Uncle Sam's Chariot, Kenton, 1929, cast-iron pull toy; Uncle Sam Mechanical Bank, Shephard, 1886; Windfield Shay Bottling Up Cervera, mechanical banks, 1898.

POLITICAL TOYS

Sulfide marbles are known to have appeared with presidents' images for the following candidates: William McKinley, Theodore Roosevelt, Alton Parker, and William Howard Taft. They are highly prized by both political and marble collectors alike, and they often command prices ranging from several hundred dollars and up.

John F. Kennedy inspired two board games, the P. T. 109 and JFK's New Frontier, both by Parker Bros. and valued at $10–$12 and $15–$20, respectively. Parker Bros. also produced a Presidential Election Board Game in 1892, which the company has periodically updated. The early version is $25–$50.

Presidents, as well as presidential candidates, are listed alphabetically.

William Jennings Bryan

William Jennings Bryan Puzzle, maker unknown, 1908; lithograph and tin dexterity puzzle with metal balls; object is to place balls within center of shallow cups that serve as eyes; T. Roosevelt mate.   *$500–$600*

William Jennings Bryan Still Bank, Uncle Sam hat in milk glass with lithograph on tin disk bust portrait of Bryan across coin slot at top; 2" height; red, white, blue hat; black and white photograph; Taft mate (from 1908 race); these novelties were actually candy containers.   *$75–$85*

Benjamin F. Butler

Benjamin F. Butler Jiggler Toy, A.A. Davis, Nashua, NH, ca. 1870s; 2" height, lithographed paper figure of Butler on tiny spring in 3" diameter glass-topped wooden bowl. Bowl is painted blue or olive green. (Gen. Butler, like his fellow Union leaders, McLellan and Grant, also entered politics following the Civil War. Butler was a Greenback Party nominee for Governor in 1878 and for President in 1884.)   *$600–$700*

General Butler Still Bank, J. & E. Stevens, $1,200–$1,500.

Benjamin Franklin Butler Still Bank, J. & E. Stevens, patented, 1878; cast-iron figural bank in shape of frog, 6¼″ height (often called the "Butler Frog Bank"); green, yellow, black, white paint; Butler/frog holds paper currency in one hand; slogans "For the Masses" and "Yachts For Me" are embossed on arms.

$1,200–$1,400

Gen. Butler Walker, Chas. Hotchkiss patent, for E.R. Ives, 1876; tin figure in clothing with rollers on feet; clockwork mechanism, 10″ height; black, brown, flesh tones; blue, white clothing.

$3,000–plus

Grover Cleveland

Grover Cleveland Political Euchre Card Game, maker unknown, 1880s (Hake 3043); caricatures of Cleveland, Harrison, and other hopefuls appear in lieu of Kings, Queens, Jacks.

$100–$150

Calvin Coolidge

Calvin Coolidge Ceramic Still Bank, maker unknown, 1924; slogan on base, "Do As Coolidge Does . . . Save"; 4″ height; brown or terra-cotta color.

$100–$200

Thomas E. Dewey

Thomas E. Dewey Standing Figure, maker unknown, painted cast metal, 4″ height; name embossed on base (Hake 2004); black and white. $25–$50

Dwight D. Eisenhower

Dwight D. Eisenhower Still Bank, maker unknown, cast metal, 4 ½″ height; bronze finish; these banks often bore the inscription of local savings banks and were commemorative rather than campaign oriented. $15–$25

Dwight Eisenhower Elephant Gravity Toy, maker unknown, 1950s; plastic; "I Like Ike" elephant moves up and down inclines; 2 ½″ length; gray, white. $25–$30

Dwight Eisenhower "I Like Ike" Walking Elephant Wind-up, Linemar, 1952; felt over tin; battery operated; elephant waves "I Like Ike" banner in trunk as it walks; 6″ length; gray, white. $150–$200

U.S. Grant

U.S. Grant Jiggler Toy, A.A. Davis, Nashua, NH, ca. 1870s; lithographed paper figure of Grant on tiny spring in 3″ diameter glass-topped bowl; bowl is painted blue, olive, or brown; a mate to the Butler Jiggler. $600–$700

U.S. Grant Smoking Cigar Clockwork Toy, E.R. Ives, ca. 1876; painted tin figure with clothing sitting on wood platform; 14″ height; when activated, Grant puts cigar in mouth and puffs out smoke (special smoke pellets are used). $15,000–plus

U.S. Grant Still Bank, maker unknown; cast-iron bust, 5 ½″ height; bronze finish. $50–$75

Warren G. Harding

Warren G. Harding Still Bank, maker unknown; 1920s; cast metal in bronze finish; 4 ½″ height (another giveaway bank issued by local money lenders). $35–$50

Benjamin Harrison

Benjamin Harrison vs. Blaine "Blocks of Five Administration Puzzle," © *New York Herald,* 1884; wood tiles within wood frame, 4″ × 4″; James Blaine from Maine was Harrison's Secretary of State and also aspired to the nomination for the presidency (Hake 3011). $65–$75

Benjamin Harrison vs. Grover Cleveland Arm-Wrestler Figures, maker unknown, 1888; wood and composition figures on string; 6″ height; black and white paint. $500–$600

Benjamin Harrison vs. Grover Cleveland Balance Scale, maker unknown, ca. 1888; bisque figures of pair swathed in American flag, slings hang from opposite ends of wood and tin balance (with scales seemingly tipped in Cleveland's favor); figures are 2½″ height; balance is 5½″ length; figures painted black, white; flags in red, white, blue (Hake 3149). $650–$750

Benjamin Harrison and Uncle Sam Marionettes, maker unknown, 1890s; wood, papier-mâché, cotton figures guided by strings; Uncle Sam is 12″ height; Harrison is 2¼″ height; red, white, blue, black. $700–$800

Harrison-Cleveland White House Game, maker unknown, 1888; slanted lithograph of White House in box under glass; wooden marbles with portraits of candidates; trick is to balance one ball in house, the other outside fence. $400–$500

Rutherford B. Hayes

Rutherford B. Hayes Mechanical Bank, J. & E. Stevens, 1876; cast iron, 8″ height; black, white, green paint (may have been a prototype, as only one example is known).

                                Price Indeterminate

Herbert Hoover

Herbert Hoover Elephant Still Bank, probably Kenton, 1932; cast iron; 4¾″ height, 7″ length; white with "Hoover & Curtis" embossed in black trim (Hake 2127). $100–$200

"Herbert Hoover Wins, Prove It!" Puzzle, Cahoes Novelty Co., Cahoes, NY, 1928; 5½″ square cardboard with wood tiles; Smith mate. $65–$75

"Hoo But Hoover" Ceramic Owl Figure, maker unknown, 1932; 4″ height; painted black.   *$75–$100*

Hubert H. Humphrey

Hubert H. Humphrey Donkey Still Bank, maker unknown, 1968; 4″ height; cast iron; natural finish.   *$25–$50*

Lyndon Johnson

Lyndon Johnson and Barry Goldwater Nodders, Remco Industries, 1964; 5½″ height; vinyl dashboard figures with lithographed "Barry" and "L.B.J." pinbacks on lapels; black, tan, red, gray; red, white, blue pinbacks (Hake 2257 and 2290) in special presentation box.   *$15–$20*

Alfred Landon

Alfred Landon Elephant Still Bank; probably Kenton, 1936; cast iron, 5″ height; gray with red blanket and gold lettering, "Land On Roosevelt, 1936" (Hake 2121).   *$125–$150*

Alfred Landon Elephant Wooden Pull Toy, maker unknown; die-cut wood figure on wheeled platform 5″ height; 8¾″ width; green, black, white, Roosevelt donkey mate from '36 race.
$60–$75

Abraham Lincoln

Abraham Lincoln Animated Sand Toy, Gerrard Calgani, 1860s (possibly unique); counter-clockwise movement of box sets sand wheels in motion; Lincoln cranks hurdy-gurdy, while monkey (with face of Gideon Wells, Lincoln's Secretary of the Navy) saws away on violin; lithographed cardboard figures, wood box with glass.   *$3,000–plus*

Abraham Lincoln Whirligig Toy, handcarved by Janna Jenner, New York City, 1986; 12½″ height; polychromed wood.
$125–$135

William McKinley

William McKinley Figural Cap Bomb, maker unknown, ca. 1896; pewter, 2″ height bust; natural.   *$85–$100*

William McKinley Spinning Top, Gibbs Mfg. Co., Canton, OH, 1896; wood and metal with gold paper band picturing McKinley and running mate, Garret Hobart; slogan: "On Top, Protection, Sound Money, Prosperity"; 2″ height (Hake 3034). *$150–$200*

William McKinley Tile Cribbage Board, maker unknown, 1890s; portrait of McKinley at both ends of board; 8½″ length; multicolored.   *$150–$200*

William McKinley "Without New York: 16 to 1, Campaign Puzzle of 1900," maker unknown; wooden sliding block puzzle; object is to win presidency without New York; octangular lithographed box with cameo portraits of McKinley/Teddy Roosevelt vs. Bryan/Stevenson; 4″; red, blue, black, white.
$150–$175

Richard Nixon

Nixon Jigsaw Puzzle, © 1970, The Puzzle Factory, New York City; double-sided puzzle measures 21¾″ × 14¾″; one side shows Nixon as George Washington; reverse is of Spiro Agnew as Superman; red, white, blue, black.   *$12–$15*

Richard Nixon/Spiro Agnew Bubble Blowing Pipes, maker unknown, 1968; ceramic caricatures, 7″ length, each. *$20–$25*

Richard M. Nixon/Spiro Agnew Elephant Still Bank, maker unknown, 1968; 4″ height, cast iron in natural finish. *$25–$35*

Richard Nixon/Spiro Agnew Hand Puppets, maker unknown; rubber-headed caricatures with cloth bodies, each. *$40–$50*

Ronald Reagan

Ronald Reagan Cardboard Mechanical Toys (two versions), "Bible Into Action Year . . . Blessed are you who hunger" and "Make My Day: Grenada, Lebanon"; first figure dressed as preacher, second dressed as cowboy; dated 1984, each.
$10–$12

Ronald Reagan Jellybean White House Ceramic Still Bank, 4⅝″ height × 5½″ width; white.   *$15–$20*

"Ronald Reagan Strikes Out on Foreign Policy" Whirligig Toy, by cartoonist Edward Larson, ca. 1980; four figures in poly-

chromed wood and tin—pitcher, catcher, batter, and umpire; Reagan as batter; umpire calls Reagan out as he swings.

$2,000–plus

Franklin D. Roosevelt

FDR Doll, maker unknown, 1930s, molded and painted cloth body with oilcloth shirt and shoes, floppy hat, pair of canes.

$200–$300*

"New Deal" Safe FDR Still Bank, Kenton, 1936, cast iron, 5" height.   *$100–$150*

Roosevelt (FDR) "Happy Days" Barrel Still Bank, Chein, 1936, tin with slot in top, 4" height.   *$15–$25*

Theodore Roosevelt

Roosevelt Bear on Bicycle, maker unknown, 1900s, lithographed tin (flat) on steel sheet bicycle, with iron weight.

$250–$300

Standing Teddy Roosevelt Nodder, German, 1910, composition.   *$300–$400*

Teddy Bear Still Bank, maker unknown, 1900s, cast iron, "Teddy" appears on side, 2½" height.   *$150–$200*

Teddy Dexterity Puzzle, German, 1900s, lithographed tin and glass, small white marbles, object is to place balls in indentations for Teddy's prominent teeth, 3" diameter.   *$250–$300*

Teddy Puzzle, maker unknown, 1908, lithographed tin and cardboard and metal balls, object is to place metal balls within center of shallow tin cups that serve as eyeglasses.

$500–$600

Teddy Roosevelt "Knock Him Out" Novelty Toy, Scientific Toy Co., Hartford, Connecticut, patented 1893, wood mechanical, lithograph paper-on-wood figure of Teddy pops up via spring mechanism, paper label (black on red) reads "For Parker Nit-Knock Him Out; We Want Roosevelt."   *$450–$500*

*Brought $500 at Atlanta Toy Museum Auction, October 1986.

Teddy Roosevelt Rough Rider Papier-Mâché Figure; maker unknown, late 1890s, tan, brown, black, gray, $125 to $150.

Teddy Roosevelt Rough Rider, German, 1900s, painted tin wind-up, 7″ width, 7″ height.   *$500–$600*

Teddy Roosevelt Rough Rider, maker unknown, 1900s, cast-iron still bank, gold with silver and black trim, 5″ height.
                                          $100–$150

Teddy Roosevelt Rough Rider, Gong Bell, 1903, cast-iron pull toy.   *$500–$600*

Teddy Roosevelt Rough Rider Papier-Mâché Standing Figure, Teddy in uniform, 5″ height; painted multicolor.
                                          $125–$150

   Note: See also "Banks, Still."

Teddy Roosevelt Rough Rider Still Bank, bust figure, maker unknown; cast iron, 5″ height; gold with silver-and-black trim.
                                          $100–$150

Teddy Roosevelt Rough Rider Bust Still Bank; maker unknown, 1900; 2" width × 3" height, $150 to $200.

Teddy's Teeth Tin Whistle, Teddy's Teeth Co., Chicago, Illinois, lithograph tin, made shrill blast, "more noise than a horn," the ultimate in political kitsch, 3" length.   *$35–$50*

African Safari Items

Teddy Roosevelt Safari Figure, Schoenhut, ca. 1910; wood-jointed, 6" height with cloth outfit, khaki clothes, painted figure (part of T.R.'s "Adventures In Africa" consisting of 12 figures, plus tents, tables, rifles, other accessories, and a folding diorama).*   *$700–$800*

"Teddy and the Lion Vanish" Puzzle, maker unknown; 1900s; 3" width × 4" height (Vanish puzzles comprised a geometric paradox; figures are dissected and rearranged so that a portion or all of the original appears to have vanished).   *$75–$100*

---

*A complete set, with original box, sold for $12,000 at the October 1986 Atlanta Toy Museum Auction.

William Howard Taft

"Billy Possum" Still Bank, maker unknown, 1908, cast iron, silver on black base, slogan reads "Billy Possum" and "Possum and Taters" on opposite sides of base. $250–$300

Peaceful Bill/Smiling Jim Still Bank, maker unknown, 1908, cast iron, bust masks of successful running mates William Taft and James Sherman apear back to back, bronze finish, 4″ height. $250–$300

Taft "Bill the Beamer" Roly-Poly, Bill the Beamer Co., New York, circa 1909, white composition, figure holds baseball in right hand, 4½″ height, 3″ diameter (Taft was the first President to officially throw out the first baseball at a World Series). $150–$200

Taft "Billy Possum" Prosperity Still Bank, maker unknown, 1908, ceramic, caricature of Taft's head on possum's body, 5″ height (Hake 3021). $150–$200

Taft "The Egg" Still Bank, J. & E. Stevens, 1908, cast iron, egg-shaped caricature with top hat on figure, very common bank, 3½″ height. $900–$1,000

Taft "Happy Billy Possum's Prosperity Puzzle," National Novelty Co., Worcester, Massachusetts, 1908, lithographed cardboard game with marbles, object is to send marbles through dimensional image of William Howard Taft and into White House gate, 6″ square. $150–$200

Taft Roly-Poly, maker unknown, 1900s, celluloid, stained black, green, and tan, 1½″ height. $150–$200

William Howard Taft Dexterity Puzzle, maker unknown, 1908, lithographed tin background and frame, glass fronted, object is to place metal balls in center of shallow tin cups that are Taft's eyes. $700–$800

William Howard Taft Roly-Poly, maker unknown, 1900s, papier-mâché, 5¼″ height. $200–$250

Woodrow Wilson

Woodrow Wilson/Thomas Marshall Coin Bank, maker unknown, 1916, oval celluloid, slogan appears: "Our Country. Our Flag. Our President. Help Re-Elect Woodrow Wilson," with cameo portraits of Wilson and Marshall, red, white, and blue colors, 3″ length. $300–$350

PATRIOTIC TOYS

Freedom Bell Ringer, Gong Bell, 1880, tin and cast-iron pull toy, kneeling black figure in tin with bell and American Flag, 6″ length.   *$900–$1,000*

Independence 1776–1876, Gong Bell, 1876, nickel-plated steel pull toy with cloth flag, features bronze eagle perched on Liberty Bell, 9½″ length.   *$800–$900*

John Bull and Uncle Sam, Watrous Mfg. Co., 1905, cast iron and steel, 7″ length.   *$450–$550*

Rocking Eagle Bell Toy, maker unknown, circa 1890, cast iron, eagle on rockers holds large Liberty Bell in beak, 4¾″ length.   *$650–$750*

Uncle Sam Accordion Toy, German, 1920s, papier-mâché with firecrackers that come out of head, cloth and paper-covered wood box.   *$250–$300*

Uncle Sam and the Don Bell Toy, Gong Bell, 1903, Uncle Sam and Spanish Don engage in sword duel with bells at end of swords, 7½″ length.   *$1,000–$1,200*

Uncle Sam Going to the Fair Velocipede, Ives, 1875, tin and wood, clockwork three-wheeler, 9″ length (other Ives variations featured little girl, both black and white, monkey, and clown).   *$5,000–plus*

Uncle Sam Mechanical Bank, C. G. Shepherd, 1886, cast iron, Uncle Sam puts coin in his satchel, beard moves up and down, 8½″ height.   *$650–$750*

Uncle Sam Three-Coin Register Bank, Durable Toy and Novelty Co., 1900s, tin, a popular bank with youngsters over the years but not necessarily with collectors.   *$25–$50*

Uncle Sam Waving Hat, maker unknown, 1916, lithograph wood and cloth, he flips hat from one hand to the other, 10½″ height.   *$100–$150*

Uncle Sam's Chariot, Kenton, 1929, cast-iron pull toy, Uncle Sam rides in eagle-shaped chariot drawn by two horses, 12″ length.   *$750–$850*

Uncle Sam's Hat Bank, Chein, 1930s, lithograph tin, 5″ height.   *$25–$50*

Soft Toys

It is often possible to estimate a soft toy's vintage by its pile. Rayon pile, for example, was used during the 1920s; synthetic pile came to the fore in the late 1940s. Steiff toys carried an identifying mark, the hexagonal metal button in the ear, from 1905 to date. Often the ear tags are missing but check the left ear for a hole that might have been left by the tag. The most prized teddy bears are those from Steiff and Ideal Novelty and Toy Co., especially those covered with mohair. Straw, kapok, and excelsior were the more common stuffings in older teddy bears.

IDEAL, STEIFF, AND MISCELLANEOUS SOFT TOYS

Ideal Novelty and Toy Co., Brooklyn, NY

Teddy Bear, 1903–1906, yarn nose and mouth, felt-padded paws, diagonal stitching from ear to nose, light cinnamon color mohair, 13″ height. $400–$500

Steiff

Antelope, 1950s, 8 ½″ height. $50–$75

Baby Chick, 1950s, mohair, 4″ height. $20–$35

"Bambi" Deer, circa 1960s, velvet, 5″ height. $35–$50

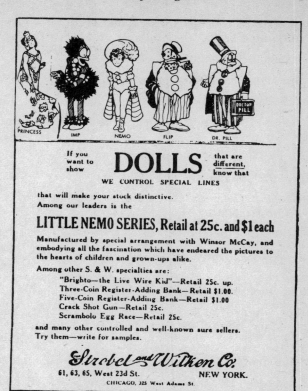

Comic enthusiasts bemoan the lack of toys inspired by that most imaginative of early comic strips, "Little Nemo in Slumberland." Created by Winsor A. McCay, it was as if he discovered the nightmare as an art form. Dolls featuring characters from the strip advertised by Strobel and Wilken can command prices in the $500 range.

Black Shirt Cadet, 1900s, black hat with fringe, swivel neck, gray pants, black shirt, 8 ¼″ height.   *$800–$1,000*

"Boy" Cowboy, 1950s, rubber head, felt body and limbs, 8″ height.   *$150–$200*

Bulldog, circa 1960s, mohair, 6″ height.   *$25–$35*

Camel, 1950s, mohair, with ear tag.   *$15–$20*

Chef Doll, 1900s, swivel neck with center seam, blue glass eyes, chef's hat, jointed body, 10" height. $800–$1,000

Chimp, 1950s, 9 ½" height. $50–$60

Cocker Spaniel, circa 1960s, mohair, 6" height. $25–$35

Donkey, 1950s, plush and mohair, 5 ½" height. $50–$75

Donkey, circa 1960s, plush, glass eyes and ear buttons, 8" height. $25–$50

Duckling, 1950s, mohair, 4" height. $15–$25

Elephant, 1950s, straw stuffing, 6 ½" height. $25–$50

Elf Boy, 1910, swivel neck, center seam, brown glass eyes, green outfit with brown leather shoes, 8" height. $900–$1,100

Fawn, 1950s, 7 ½" height. $50–$75

"Flossy" Goldfish, 1950s, straw stuffing, 4¾" height. $25–$50

Fox, 1950s, mohair, 6" length. $25–$50

French Legionnaire, 1900s, swivel neck, jointed body, long blue coat, red pants, blue glass eyes, mustache, ribbon on sleeve, 10¾" height. $1,200–$1,500

Frog, 1950s, mohair, 4" height. $25–$50

Gendarme, early 1900s, velvet hands and feet, felt body and limbs, 14" height (a center seam in their faces and prominent noses are telltale features of turn-of-the century Steiff soft toys). $300–$400

German Foot Soldier, circa 1915, plush mohair and felt, 13 ½" height. $75–$100

Giraffe, 1950s, 11 ½" height. $50–$75

Goat, 1950s, mohair, 8" length. $25–$50

Green Tiger, mohair, with ear tag. $25–$50

"Grissy" Donkey, 1950s, straw stuffing, 7 ½" height. $25–$50

Ground Hog, 1950s, mohair, 5" height. $25–$50

Halloween Cat, 1950s, 7" height. $25–$35

"Hucky" Crow, 1950s, mohair, 4″ length. $25–$50

Indian Doll, 1900s, swivel neck with center seam, beaded eyes, black mohair wig, brown fringed "Buckskins," orange vest, 16″ height. $1,200–$1,500

Kitten, 1950s, 7″ height. $25–$50

Koala Bear, circa 1960s, mohair, glass eyes and ear buttons, 8″ height. $50–$75

Lamb on Wheels, 1925, pull toy, woolly coat, felt ears, muzzle and legs, glass eyes, metal platform with wooden wheels, ear button, 13″ length. $400–$500

Llama, circa 1960s, mohair, 6¾″ height. $50–$75

Man in Tuxedo, 1900s, swivel head with center seam, beaded eyes, black knee britches, red coat with tails, black leather shoes, 16″ height. $1,000–$2,000

"Mat Sailor," 1950s, rubber head, felt body and limbs, sailor plays accordion, 8″ height. $200–$250

"Maxi" Mole, 1950s, mohair, no tag or button, 4¾″ height. $35–$50

"Michi" and "Michmu" Porcupines, 1930s, wearing costumes, 20½″ height. $300–$400

Okapi, 1950s, mohair, 8″ length. $25–$50

Orangutan, 1950s, 5″ height. $25–$50

Pair Peasant Boy and Girl, circa 1910, swivel necks, boy has blue glass eyes, blue shirt, brown pants, 13″ height, girl has center facial seam, bead eyes, white mohair wig, jointed felt body, 12½″ height. $900–$1,100

Peasant Girl, 1900s, swivel neck with center seam, blond mohair wig, red skirt and weskit, 15½″ height. $1,000–$1,500

"Peggy" Penguin, 1950s, 8½″ height. $50–$75

Penguin, 1950s, mohair, no tag or button, 6½″ height. $25–$50

"Perry" Squirrel, circa 1960s, mohair, 5″ height. $25–$50

"Pieps" Mouse, 1950s, mohair, 3″ height. $25–$50

Piglet, 1950s, mohair, 6″ length. $25–$50

"Pinky" Pekinese, circa 1960s, mohair, 6″ length. $25–$50

Pony With Saddle, 1950s, straw stuffing, 4¾″ height.
$25–$50

Poodle on Wheels, circa 1910, fine plush, glass eyes, on four cast-iron wheels, 13″ length. $600–$700

Rabbit Puppet, circa 1960s, mohair, 12″ height. $25–$50

Rabbit on Wheels, 1950s, plush and mohair, 3½″ height.
$50–$75

Reclining Poodle, circa 1960, 8″ height. $50–$100

Reindeer, 1950s, 9½″ height. $50–$75

"Robby" Small Seal, circa 1960s, mohair, 4½″. $50–$75

Rooster, 1950s, mohair, 6″ height. $25–$50

Seated Puppy, circa 1960s, mohair, 6″ height. $25–$50

Sheep, 1910, mohair and velour, glass eyes, 37″ length.
$600–$700

"Slo" Turtle, 1950s, mohair, no tag or button, 7″ length.
$25–$50

Small Owl, circa 1960s, mohair, 4½″ height. $35–$50

"Snobby" Poodle, circa 1960s, mohair, 6″ height. $25–$50

Spotted Pony,. circa 1960s, mohair, cream and brown, 8″ height. $50–$75

Squirrel, circa 1960s, mohair, 5″ height. $50–$75

Sunny Jim, attributed to Steiff, circa 1910, cloth head stitched in two sections, beaded eyes, felt orange jacket, yellow vest, top hat, 11¾″ height (a good example where lack of positive Steiff identification drastically affects price). $300–$400

Teddy Bear, 1903–1910, paws with felt padding, rounder face than Ideal version, light cinnamon color mohair, 13″ height.
$500–$600

Teddy Bear, circa 1906, black shoe-button eyes, hump, 16″ height, light golden color. $800–$1,000*

*Sold for $1,100 at Skinner Auction, December 1985.

Teddy Bear, 1906, golden mohair, black shoe-button eyes, hump, felt pads, 15 ½ ″ height. $900–$1,000

Turkey, 1950s, plush and mohair, 6 ″ height. $50–$75

Miscellaneous

Bear, German, 1950s, unjointed, velveteen lower body, 22 ″ height. $100–$125

Calico Cat, maker unknown, 1890s, patent printed. $25–$50

Cobbler Doll, Lenci, 1900s, swivel head, jointed body with brown pants, checkered shirt, black cap with tassel, green neckerchief, 17 ″ height. $500–$600

Dog on Wheels, German, 1950s, St. Bernard type with glass eyes, mohair fur, steel frame, and rubber wheels, 21 ″ length.
$50–$100

Oriental Silk Tiger Cat Pin Cushion, maker unknown, 1890s.
$25–$50

Rabbit Squeak Toy, German, 1890s, glass eyes, pink bow, ears wiggle when bellows are squeezed, mohair, 7 ″ height.
$200–$300

Seated Dog, German, 1900s, yellow fur with cinnamon chest and head, glass eyes, 11 ½ ″ height. $100–$125

Stuffed Dog, maker unknown, United States, 1910–1920, pearl button eyes, rounded face, straw stuffed, after 1920 this type of toy was stuffed with cotton, 4 ″ height. $25–$30

Teddy Bear, English, 1930s, brushed wool flannel, 16 ″ height.
$300–$350

Teddy Bear, German, 1910, black, shoe-button eyes, hump, cinnamon plush, 14 ¼ ″ height. $500–$600

Teddy Bear, German, early 1920s, long snout, small hump, mohair fur, 20 ″ height. $200–$300

Teddy Bear, German, maker unknown, circa 1930, mohair, "Winnie The Pooh" type, 12 ″ height. $100–$200

Teddy Bear, Shuco, circa 1930, mohair, 10 ″ height.
$150–$200

Teddy "Crowler" Bear, Germany, circa 1920, straw stuffed, 16½" height. $500–$600

Velvet Rabbit, maker unknown, 1890s, black and rust color. $100–$125

COMIC AND CHARACTER SOFT TOYS

Billiken Doll, E. I. Horsman & Co., New York City, 1909–1911, composition head, plush body, The Billiken Co., 11" height (originally created by Florence Pretz of Kansas City, Missouri). $100–$200

Charlie Chaplin, Louis Amberg & Son, New York City, 1915, cloth body with composition head and hands, by special arrangement with Essanay Film Co., cloth label features Indian Chief emblem of Amberg, 14" height. $400–$500

Donald Duck, Knickerbocker Toy Co., 1938–1940, wears felt red tunic and furry black hat of drum major or band leader, 16" height. $300–$400

Dopey, England, Chad Valley, circa 1939, all cloth body, velvet slippers, 6" height. $100–$150

Dopey, Knickerbocker Toy Co., 1939, velvet stuffed body with composition face, approximately 8" height. $250–$300

Ferdinand the Bull, Knickerbocker Toy Co., 1940s, plush figure, felt flower in mouth, 10" height. $200–$250

Fred Flintstone, T. M., Japan, circa 1960s, licensed under "Hanna Barbera Productions 1962," vinyl and cloth, 10½" height. $25–$50

Grumpy, Knickerbocker Toy Co., 1939, velvet stuffed body with composition face, approximately 8" height. $250–$300

Ignatz Mouse, Knickerbocker Toy Co., New York City, 1931, Ignatz seems to be spitting image of Mickey Mouse, including the saucer-pie eyes, big shoes on feet, round ears, and pointed snout, 12" height. $300–$400

Krazy Kat, Averill Mfg. Co., New York City, 1916, Krazy has long carrot-shaped nose, high, almost sticklike upright ears, big bow ribbon around neck, fabric shoes, 20" height.
$600–$700

Krazy Kat, Knickerbocker Toy Co., New York City, 1931, 12″ height. $500–$600

Little Pixie People, Victoria Toy Works, England, circa 1940, cotton heads, velvet and felt bodies, tag reads "I'm one of Norah Wellings' Little Pixie People," tag hangs around neck, marked similarity to Palmer Cox Brownies, 9¼″ height, each.
                                                                    $50–$100

Mickey Mouse, Ann Wilkinson Designs, England, 1980, cotton stuffed, designed and made in England for Bloomingdale's Department Store, New York City, 9″ height. $50–$100

Mickey Mouse, Charlotte Clark design for Walt Disney Enterprises, 1930, the FIRST stuffed Mickey doll, bright red pants, 12″ height. $600–$700

Mickey Mouse, Dean's Rag Book Co., London, 1932–1935, cotton and velvet plush, standing, toothy grin, pointed snout, floppy ears, round painted eyeballs encased in clear plastic with floating pupils, 9″ height. $200–$300

Mickey Mouse, Margarete Steiff & Co., New York City, 1931, 4¼″ height, felt; 6½″, 8¼″, 10½″, 12½″, and 16¾″ height sizes, velvet (price range depending on size). $1,500–$8,000

Mickey Mouse, Margarete Steiff & Co., 1931, purple pants, yellow gloves, and bright orange shoes, distributed by George Borgfeldt Corp., New York City, 19″ height. $3,000–$5,000

Mickey Mouse Tricycle, Steiff, circa early 1930s, stuffed, jointed Mickey, velvet fabric, long whiskers on Mickey's snout, seated on bellows squeaker, tricycle (actually it's a four-wheeler) of wood with steel wire, pull toy, 8½″ height. $3,000–$5,000

Mickey the Cowboy, Knickerbocker Toy Co., 1936, designed by Charlotte Clark, 10″ height. $600–$700

Minnie Mouse, Ann Wilkinson Designs, England, 1980, cotton stuffed, designed and made in England for Bloomingdale's Department Store, New York City, 9″ height. $75–$100

Minnie Mouse, Knickerbocker Toy Co., mid-1930s, stuffed velvet, Minnie wears lace pantaloons under red polka dot skirt, bright orange shoes, 14″ height. $500–$600

The surreal comic strip "Krazy Kat" by George Herriman predated Walt
Disney's Mickey Mouse by over a decade, but an Ignatz Mouse doll by
Knickerbocker featured in this 1930s advertisement bears a remark-
able resemblance to the Disney creation, clearly flirting dangerously
with copyright infringement. All this does is further enhance the doll's
value among crossover collectors in today's market. Ignatz/Mickey,
$500–$1,000; Krazy Kat, $350–$700.

Minnie Mouse, Margarete Steiff & Co., New York City, 1931,
4 ¼ " height, felt; 6 ½ ", 8 ¼ ", 10 ½ ", 12 ½ ", and 16 ¾ " height
sizes, velvet (price range depending on size).   *$1,000–$2,000*

Pinocchio, Knickerbocker Toy Co., 1939–1940, mostly composition, jointed with felt outfit and hat, 14" height. **$300–$400**

Pinocchio Hand Puppet, Crown Toy, early 1940s, "Walt Disney Ent." incised on neck, composition head, mohair body, 9" height. **$75–$100**

Popeye, maker unknown, circa 1930–1950, cloth head and body, smokes corncob pipe, large plastic buttons on blue tunic, 16" height. **$200–$300**

Raggedy Ann, Georgene Novelties, New York City, 1930–1950, designed by John Gruelle, original creator of these classic rag dolls, cloth-stuffed doll with reddish brown yarn hair, black button eyes, triangular red painted-on nose, 20" height.

$200–$250

Snow White, Knickerbocker Toy Co., 1940s, composition face and limbs, cloth body, 12" height. **$600–$800**

Two-Gun Mickey, Knickerbocker Toy Co., 1936, designed by Charlotte Clark, 12" height. **$700–$1,000**

CELEBRITY DOLLS

The Brownies, Arnold Print Works, North Adams, Massachusetts, 1892, cotton sheet, figures of soldier, Irishman, and Indian, which were to be cut out and stuffed with cotton, straw, etc., designed by originator of The Brownies, Palmer Cox, also featured Uncle Sam, Dude, John Bull, Highlander, and others, 12 figures in all appeared in each yard of fabric, 8" height.

$400–$500

The Captain and Katzenjammer Kids (set of three), Knickerbocker Toy Co., circa 1925, cloth dolls with painted and applied features, bulbous noses, cloth costumes, Hans: 14" height, Fritz: 16" height, The Captain: 18" height, each. **$600–$700**

Fritz (Katzenjammer), Saalfield Publishing Co., 1914, printed cloth-stuffed doll. **$400–$500**

Gunga Din Nodder, maker unknown, 1939, composition and cloth stuffed, all white native uniform, inspired by the movie, although this doll in no way resembles Sam Jaffe who played the waterboy, Gunga Din, 18" height. **$125–$200**

Jerry Mahoney, maker unknown, 1950s, ventriloquist doll, composition face, cloth body, TV kiddie star of the 1950s, 25″ height.   *$150–$200*

Katzenjammer Kids (each), Samstag & Hilder Bros., 1908, cloth dolls, Hans and Fritz.   *$350–$500*

Mammy Doll, George Borgfeldt & Co., New York City, 1930s, designed by Tony Sarg, cloth body with composition head and limbs, red print bandanna on head, big white apron, black mohair wig, one of the most desirable of scores of Mammy dolls that have appeared in a variety of material since 1850, 20″ height, white baby, 8″ height.   *$350–$400*

Nancy and Sluggo (each), Georgene Novelties, 1940s, licensed by Ernie Bushmiller, United Artists Synd., Sluggo: 14½″ height, Nancy: 14″ height (the comic strip "Nancy" by Ernie Bushmiller originated in the early 1920s).   *$200–$300*

Topsy-Turvy Doll, maker unknown, 1880, linen and cotton, originated in post–Civil War South, called topsy-turvy or double-enders because doll could be flipped from black to white as long black skirt revealed desired side, 14″ height. *$300–$350*

W. C. Fields, Effanbee (Fleischaker & Baum), New York City, circa 1930, cloth body with composition head, shoes, limbs, "An Effanbee product" inscribed on back of shoulder, wears felt coat, white beaver top hat, white felt spats over black shoes, mouth moves as per ventriloquist's dummy, string from back of neck works jaw when pulled, 18″ height (the W. C. Fields Effanbee doll has gone as high as $500 at auction within the past year).

                                            $300–$400

Space Toys

✳ ✳ ✳

MECHANICAL SPACE TOYS AND ROBOTS

Many of the listings on the following pages will show only one set of figures rather than a price range. Those with one price reflect hammer prices at the Christmas Collectibles Auction at Phillips, New York City, December 10, 1988, in which a major consignor of mechanical space toys and robots was G. Van Dexter, a long-time collector. Of the 79 consigned lots, we have chosen to present a representative sampling. Where price ranges *do* appear, they correspond closely to those given for similar toys listed by dealers and collectors in the pages of *Antique Toy World* and *Antique Trader*, plus in various mail listings. Please bear in mind that this is one of the most volatile of toy collecting categories, and we have seen vast discrepancies in price.

Phillips' Van Dexter Collection Sale

Apollo Astronaut Robot, Plus Two Other Small Robots, two are S.Y.; third is by Shudo; 5½" to 7" heights; lot of three; no boxes.   *$250*

Apollo X Moon Challenger, by T.N.; *Fire Rocket X-007,* by Y; X moon runs, stops, raises up, opens fins with flashing lights; X-007 runs, hits wall, ejects pilot; tin; friction-powered; 15½" and 14½" heights; lot of two.   *$120*

Astro Dog, by Y; black and white dog with bubble dome helmet holds briefcase and U.S. flag; walks, wags tail, and barks; 10½" height.   *$120*

Astronaut With Space Gun, by A.N.; 1960s; man in space suit with oxygen tank on back; arms swing as he walks; 7 1/2 " height.   *$1,100*

Atom Rocket Space Ship, by M.T.; non-fall action, flashing light; moving antennae; beep-beep sound; tin; battery-operated; 9 1/2 " length.   *$100*

Attacking Martian Robot, by S.H.; 1960s; tin, battery-operated; two guns emerge firing as door opens in robot's chest; lights flash and robot walks again; 11 " height.   *$300*

Col. Hap Hazard, Japan, 1960s; with original box; astronaut in space suit.   *$1,100–$1,200*

Combattler and *Getta-1,* tin wind-up Super Heroes; Japan, manufacturer unknown; 9 " height.   *$190*

Cragston Mr. Robot, by Yonezawa; bump-and-go; revolving lights inside clear plastic dome; no box; 11 " height.   *$400*

Cragston Robot, battery-operated robot with clear plastic dome-covered head; flashing light; noise; tin; missing antennae; with box (box has some damage); also a NASA station; 10 1/2 " height.   *$650*

Danguard and *Aztecaser,* Japan, manufacturer unknown; tin walkers with plastic heads; Super Heroes; lot of two; 9 " height.   *$225*

Earth Sphere With Orbiting Sputnik Satellites, tin, West German; #3 Rocket Jet Racer, Small Flying Saucer, Space Rocket Car (last three are friction-powered and lack boxes); lot of five; 5 1/2 " to 7 1/2 " lengths.   *$300*

Flashy Jim or *R7 Robot,* by Ace; lighted eyes; remote control; tin; 7 " height.   *$170*

Flying Saucers (group of four): Airport Saucer, UFO-XO5, X-7-A, and King Flying Saucer; all with flashing lights, bump-and-go action; plastic; battery-operated; three by M.T.; one by K.O.; 7 " and 8 " diameters.   *$120*

Frankenstein Monster, Marx, 1950s; remote control toy; 12 1/2 " height; failed to meet reserves: estimated.   *$1,200–$1,500*

Gaiking and *Grandaezer,* Japan, manufacturer unknown; tin wind-up walkers with plastic heads; 9 " height.   *$130*

Getkokamen, Japan; 1960s; litho tin wind-up; masked alien in cape. $150–$200

Ground Zero and *Great Mazinger,* Japan, manufacturer unknown; lot of two Super Hero walking figures; tin, with plastic heads; 9″ heights. $170

Highwheel Robot, by K.O.; gears turn in chest and sparks fly; tin, plastic; wind-up; 9″ height. $150

Laughing Robot, by Waco; lights flash; mouth opens, showing huge teeth; laughs hysterically; plastic; battery-operated; 13″ height. $250

Mach Baron, Horutesie #5, and *Mazinga,* tin wind-up Super Heroes, with plastic heads; Japan, manufacturer unknown; 9″ height. $300

Marvelous Mike Tractor, by Saunders; robot-driven tractor; keeps reversing direction; tin; no box; 13″ length. $150

Mercury Capsule, by S.H., Japan; 1960s; friction toy; makes sparks and beep-beep noise; 9½″. $125–$200

Mercury Explorer, space tank by T.P.S.; with bump-and-go action; rotor blades revolve on top. $100–$200

Missile Robot, Mighty Robot; Laser Robot; Capt. Astro; Astronaut; Mechanical Robot; tin and plastic; crank-wind and wind-up; by Mego, N.T.P.S., Ahi, and Daiya; lot of six; 5″ to 6½″ heights. $650

Mr. Mercury, Japan, 1960s; remote control-operated robot; mechanism revealed in visor over eyes and in robot's stomach. $200–$250

Mr. Robot, The Mechanical Brain, by Alps; walks with flashing lights in each hand; some rust; 8″ height. $475

Mobile Space T.V. Unit, by T.N.; space tank with trailer; astronaut atop tank operates T.V. camera; lights up and shows lunar landscape; tin, battery-operated; 10½″ length. $2,300

Moon Explorer Robot, by K.O.; walker with spinners rotating atop plastic helmet; tin; crank-operated; 7″ height. $1,200

NASA Astronaut, by Marx; figure is in space suit; rotating blades spin atop head; plastic; battery-operated; 12″ height. $400

New Space Explorer Robot, by S.H.; walks, stops; doors open in chest and T.V. screen shows Apollo flight; tin, battery-operated; 11″ height.   *$100*

Peace Corps Man, tin wind-up by S.Y.; keeps changing directions as bell rings; Apollo Moon Rocket, tin wind-up, by M.T.; lot of two; 5 ½″ to 7″.   *$275*

Pioneer Rocket Launcher, by Kraemer; spring release operation, tin; Space Tank, by Cragston; spinning cockpit, tin, friction power; Luna Hovercraft, by T.P.S.; flashing lights, tin, remote control; lot of three; 6″ to 8″ lengths.   *$150*

Planet Explorer, Japan, early 1950s; litho tin wind-up; plastic nose section; large honing device on roof; 10″ length.
                                                          $200–$300

Planet Robot, by K.O.; "Robbie" type, walks and sparks fly in chest, tin; 9″ height.   *$130*

Planet Robot, Sparky; Japan, 1960s; key-wind motor; wrench hands; flashing dome atop head.   *$200–$300*

Radar Robot, by T.N.; walks with blinking light in antennae; eyes light up; remote control; 8″ height.   *$3,250*

Ratchet Robot, by T.N.; mechanic type; holds wrench in hand; walks with sparks flying from chest; tin wind-up; no box; 8″ height.   *$275*

Robby the Robot, by Nomura; walks with moving pistons in clear dome on top of head; tin, remote control; 8 ½″ height.   *$850*

Robo Tank Z, half robot, half tank; bump-and-go; flashing dome; stops, fires gun; battery-operated; 10 ½″ height.   *$400*

Robot, by Cragston; head is covered by clear plastic dome; walks and raises and lowers gun with flashing light and noise; tin, battery-operated; missing antennae; 10 ½″ height.   *$425*

Robot, by Cragston; 1950s; skirt-type bump-and-go action; tin, with plastic head; battery-operated; 11 ½″ height.   *$3,200*

Robot ST-1 (German Sparky), German; 1960s; litho tin wind-up.   *$600–$650*

Roto Robot, by S.H.; walks with flashing light in chest; constantly rotates upper body; Attacking Martians (two), by S.H.; all three are battery-operated; 8 ½″ to 9″ heights.   *$110*

R-7 Robot or *Flashy Jim*, manufacturer unknown; walking robot with flashing eyes; remote control; no box; excellent condition. **$600**

Space Capsules (lot of three), by S.H.; United States w/Orbiting Astronauts, tin, battery-operated; two Capsule Mercurys, one with "Friendship 7" on side, pilots inside that turn around, tin, friction-powered. **$160**

Space Dog, by K.O.; runs, wiggling his ears, moving mouth and eyes; no box; 6″ length. **$375**

Space Dog, by K.O.; same as above, but with red and black ears and battery-operated; no box. **$250**

Space Explorer Robot, by Yonezawa; starts as box; legs appear as it rises; arms pop out; screen opens in chest showing an "operating astronaut"; lights flash in visor and it walks like Frankenstein; battery-operated; 10″ height. **$750**

Space Explorer Robot, by S.H.; walks, shows flight of Apollo on T.V. screen in chest; tin, battery-operated; 11″ height. **$130**

Space Man Astronaut, Cragston; 1960s; man carries space gun; wears helmet, oxygen mask; light in helmet and left hand; 9″ height. **$1,600**

Space Man Robot, by S.H.; walks with swinging arms; blinking light in helmet; tin, battery-operated; no box; 11″ height. **$300**

Space Patrol Tank, by Y.; runs with flashing light; cockpit opens and closes; tin, battery-operated; 8½″ length. **$170**

Space Shuttle, by Mitli; Spaceship XY07, by Nemito; Spaceship XP-07, tin, friction-powered; all with revolving blades; lot of three; 6½″ to 7½″ lengths. **$70**

Space Tank, by S.H.; two guns move back and forth, with ack-ack sound effects; friction-powered; tin; 8½″ length. **$450**

Space Tank, by S.H.; changes direction when hitting an object; forward and reverse not functioning; missing antennae; tin, battery-operated. **$140**

Sparky Robot, by K.O., walks; sparks in face; tin wind-up; 6½″ height. **$120**

Spector Man Spaceship, Japan, 1970; robot with peaked hat riding in spaceship; chimp's picture appears on dorsal fin.
$100–$150

SP-1 Space Car, by Linemar; Robot Torpedo, crank-wind; Sparkling Rocket, string-operated, by San; lot of three; 6 ½ " to 10" lengths.   *$750*

Super Astronaut Robot, manufacturer unknown; "face-in-visor" type; walks, stops, and pivots torso; chest opens and guns blaze away; near-mint and boxed; 11 ½ " height.   *$120*

Super Explorer Robot, by S.H.; walks, stops, screen lights up in chest to show flight in space; battery-operated; tin and plastic; boxed; 11" height.   *$90*

Super Giant Robots (two), by S.H.; they walk, stop, fire guns, rotate torsos; tin; only one box; 16" height.   *$275*

Swinging Baby Robot, by Yonezowa; baby rocks to and fro on swing; opening and closing mouth; tin wind-up; 6 ½ " height.
                                                               $200

Two Robots (lot of two), by Y.; early-type walkers with clawlike hands; one a wind-up; the other is remote control; 6" heights.
                                                             $1,600

Urutora Man, Japan, 1960s; litho tin wind-up; alien creature with crested head.   *$200–$250*

Urutora Seven, Japan, 1960s; litho tin wind-up; grinning alien with crested head.   *$150–$200*

U.S.A. NASA Apollo Space Ship, by M.T.; late 1960s; bump-and-go action; astronaut circles outside space ship; battery-operated.   *$90*

Winner 23, Star Jet, No. 1 Jet, No. 5 Jet, jet racers, by Ashitoy, San, and K.D.D.; battery, friction, and wind-up; tin; two with boxes; 5" to 7" lengths.   *$350*

X-9 Space Robot Car, Japan, 1960s; litho tin/plastic, battery-operated w/original box; car manned by square-headed robot; tall dome on hood.   *$1,100–$1,200*

Zabitan and Jet Mouse, Japan, manufacturer unknown; Super Heroes; tin walkers with plastic heads; 9" height.   *$325*

Zoomer the Robot, Japan, manufacturer unknown, early 1950s; stiff walking motion; tin canlike ears; wind-up; 5" height.
                                                             $1,800

Sports and Recreation

One popular and topical collecting category that requires little stimulation from crossover specialists in toy banks, games, and clockwork tins is that of Sports and Recreation. Virtually every athletic endeavor, from gymnastics to bowling, has been recreated in some highly animated toy form. Probably the pinnacle of perfection in this field is the coveted Calamity (or Football) mechanical bank, in which one can almost feel the impact of colliding players as the coin is inserted. Probably the most fiercely contested subcategory among sports toy enthusiasts is that of bicycling, with billiards, of all things, represented in infinite variety by any number of manufacturers, including Lilliputian-sized Cracker Jack giveaways.

BASEBALL

All Stars Car, T.K., Japan, early 1960s, lithographed tin, friction. $25–$35

All Stars Mr. Baseball Junior w/Automatic Batting Machine, Japan, early 1960s, tin, battery-operated, names of major league teams and lithographed illustrations are pictured on sides of batting platform. $400–$500

Baseball Batter Still Bank, A. C. Williams, early 1909, 5¾″ height. $300–$400

"Batsman," Gong Bell, 1913, $1,200–$1,400; "Touchdown," Gong Bell, 1913, $1,000–$1,200. Football- and baseball-related toys are increasingly in demand from specialty collectors.

Baseball Truck, Banner Plastics, 1950s (from Carnival Caravan set), diamond layout and large spinner on truck bed. *$25–$35*

Batsman, Gong Bell, 1913, bell-pull toy, bat strikes bell as toy rolls along.   *$1,000–$1,500*

Crossed Bats and Ball Still Bank, early 1900s, 5″ height.
                    $400–$500

Danny McLain's Horsehide Hauler, A.M.T., late 1960s, scale plastic model kit. *$40–$50*

Home Run King, Strauss, 1924, lithographed tin mechanical, 6½" height. *$350–$400*

Nice Catch, Japan, late 1940s, celluloid wind-up, painted, Bill Dickey (in Yankee uniform) goes after pop-up, 5½" height. *$50–$100*

BICYCLING

Bicycle Race, French, 1900s, painted tinplate clockwork on wooden base, three riders compete via steel shafts attached to hub, possibly a gambling game, 9.6" width. *$1,500–$2,000*

Bicycle Race, Muller and Kadeder, 1880s, painted tin clockwork, two riders on steel rods race around central hub, 6" height. *$1,000–$1,500**

Bicyclist, German, early 1900s, painted tin blown figure, 11" length. *$1,200–$1,500*

Bicyclists, manufacturer unknown, 1930s, five aluminum figures, 12" length. *$100–$125*

Four Cyclists on Tandem Bike, Ives, 1890, cast-iron pull toy. *$8,000–$10,000*

Steam Tricycle, French, 1900s, soldered tin, steam powered, 7.9" length. *$900–$1,000*

Tricyclist, German, 1910, lacquered tinplate, push toy, 4.7" height. *$500–$600*

Tricyclist on Highwheeler, French, 1900s, painted tin, clockwork, 4.7" length. *$1,000–$1,100*

Tricyclists, French, early 1900s, painted tin, clockwork, pair of riders in bright uniforms, bell rings each time wheel turns full cycle, 11" length. *$2,000–$3,000*

*Sold for $1,300 at Ralston Auction in 1981.

BILLIARDS

Great Billiard Champ, KiCo, 1895, painted tin mechanical, 6⅜″ length. $500–$600

Pool Player, German, 1910, lithographed tin mechanical, 14½″ length. $400–$500

Pool Player, Gunthermann, lithographed tin mechanical, mustachioed player, 7½″ length. $600–$700

> *Note:* There are scores of variations on the Pool Player toy, mostly German, from the 1920s.

BOATING AND SAILING

Cat Boat Sailing Bank, cast-iron still bank, 13″ height.
$300–$400

Oarsmen, Ives, 1882, painted and stenciled tin clockwork, blue and red trim, 12″ length. $8,000–$10,000

Racing Scull, U.S. Hardware, 1890s, cast iron, four oarsmen and coxswain, 9″ length. $5,000–$6,000

Racing Scull, U.S. Hardware, 1910, cast iron, eight oarsmen and coxswain, 14½″ length. $5,000–$6,000

Racing Scull, Wilkins, 1890s, cast iron, four oarsmen and coxswain, 10½″ length. $1,000–$2,000

Rowing Scull, German, late 1890s, clockwork tinplate boat with composition men (four) rowing and coxswain, wooden oars propel craft, 39″ length. $3,000–$4,000

Skiff Trainer, Fernand Martin, 1910, painted tin mechanical, 7″ length. $600–$700

FISHING

Boy Fishing, New Hampshire Hill Brass Co., 1905, cast iron, bell pull toy, boy reeling in fish, 6½″ length × 5½″ height.
$1,000–$2,000

Fisherman, mechanical bank, manufacturer unknown, contemporary, cast iron, 12″ length. $300–$350

FOOTBALL

Football Player, still bank, cast iron, player kneeling with large football on shoulders, 5¾″ height. $600–$700

Football Player, still bank, manufacturer unknown, cast iron, gold finish, player holds football under one arm, 5¾″ height.
$300–$400

Football Players, Secor, 1923, lithographed tin, cloth, 8″ width × 2″ height. $600–$700

Harvard Football Player, German, 1904, tin figure with celluloid ball, mechanical, 9″ height. $1,000–$2,000

Sandy Andy Fullback, Strauss, 1920s, lithographed tin mechanical, 6½″ length. $300–$400

Touchdown, Gong Bell, 1913, cast-iron pull toy, two boys kick ball to each other through posts with bell in middle, 6″ length.
$2,000–$3,000

GOLF

Golfer, Strauss, 1924, lithographed tin mechanical with chute for balls, 6¾″ height. $300–$400

Hole in One, Japan, 1960s, lithographed battery-operated mechanical bank, small lever sends penny into 18th hole, 6½″ height. $200–$250

Play Golf, Strauss, 1930s, lithographed tin mechanical, 11½″ length. $300–$400

Set of Golfers, Schoenhut, 1920s, painted wood figures on metal shafts, balls, boundary markers, bunkers, sandtraps, greens, felt, figures on shafts are 36″ length. $600–$700*

*Sold for $1,210 at Atlanta Toy Museum Auction in October 1986.

GYMNASTICS

Acrobats, Ives, 1893, composition clockwork.

Price Indeterminate

Acrobats Bell Toy, Gong Bell, 1903, cast-iron pull toy, 6¾″ length. $1,000–$2,000

Balance Swing, Gibbs, 1910, painted tin and steel, 14½″ height. $200–$250

Gymnast on Trapeze, Wyandotte, 1940s, lithograph tin mechanical, 9″ height. $100–$200

Little Acrobat, Fernand Martin, 1910, painted tin mechanical.

$500–$600

Tic Tac, Marx, 1930s, lithographed tin mechanical acrobat, 12″ height. $200–$250

Triple Acrobats, Marx, 1935, nickeled finish wind-up, 19″ height. $300–$350

HORSE RACING AND HORSEBACK RIDING

Horse and Driver, Watrous, 1905, bell pull toy, cast iron, 7″ length. $650–$750

Horse and Jockey, German, 1910, painted tin, on wheeled platform, 4″ height. $400–$500

Horseback Riders, Fallows, 1895, painted tin. $2,000–$3,000

Horses and Jockey Ring Toy, German, 1910, painted tin, 6½″ diameter. $400–$500

Jockey and Horse, German, 1904, painted tin, 6½″ height.

$500–$600

Jockey and Horse, manufacturer unknown, 1920s, tin lithographed and cast-iron balance toy, 9″ height. $300–$400

Jockey Riding Horse, German, 1900s, lithographed tin penny toy, 2½″ width. $100–$150

Rider and Sulky, German, manufacturer unknown, 1920, cast iron, 8¾" height. $300–$400

ICE SKATING

Skating Mechanical Bank, Kyser & Rex, 1880s, cast iron, four skaters (two fallen on ice), when coin is inserted two figures move around to a figure in rear who awards a girl skater a wreath, 4½" height. $6,000–$7,000

MISCELLANEOUS

Bowler, manufacturer unknown, mechanical bank, contemporary, cast iron, 11" length. $300–$350

Boy Flying Kite, German, 1910, painted tin mechanical, 13½" height. $350–$400

Boy Juggling Balls, German, 1910, painted tin mechanical with celluloid balls, wears light blue sailor suit. $350–$400

Boy on Stilts, German, 1904, painted tin mechanical, 9" height. $500–$600

Hunter, German, 1915, painted tin mechanical, man with big hat and gun, 9" height. $200–$300

Hunter, New Hampshire Hill Brass Co., 1905, bell ringer, cast iron, hunter aims gun at rabbit, 6" length × 5" height. $1,000–$2,000

Matador and Bull, German, 1904, matador rides bull, tin lithograph. $400–$500

Matador and Bull, German, 1920s, lithographed tin mechanical, the pair face each other across long steel shaft which undulates as toy is activated (similar to Maggie and Jiggs toy by Nifty), 7" length. $300–$400

Soccer Player, German, 1920s, tin, spring cocking mechanism, kicker, 7" height. $300–$400

Tennis Player, mechanical bank, manufacturer unknown, contemporary, cast iron, 10 5/8 " wide   *$250–$300*

PRIZE FIGHTING

Knockout Prize Fighter, Strauss, 1920s, lithographed tin wind-up, 6 1/2 " height.   *$500–$600*

ROLLER SKATING

Boy on Roller Skates, German, 1914, tin mechanical with hair wig, boy skates on one foot.   *$500–$600*

SKIING

Skier, Chein, 1930s, lithographed tin mechanical, 6 " height.   *$300–$350*

Ski Jumper, Schoenhut, 1920, wood, ski track with skier coming down steep ramp to vault over goal post, 26 1/2 " length.   *$500–$600*

SLEDDING

Double Ripper Sled, New Hampshire Hill Brass Co., 1905, bell pull toy, cast iron, four figures on bobsled, 9 " length, 4 " height.   *$1,000–$1,500*

Gyro Coaster, 1924, 9 " length.   *$200–$250*

Sled Rider, Dayton, 1914, pressed-steel tin friction toy, 9 " length.   *$300–$350*

SWIMMING

Beach Patrol, Hubley, 1932, cast-iron pull toy, advertising Jantzen swimsuits, male figure on surfboard, 8 " height.   *$1,000–$2,000*

Surf Girl, Hubley, 1932, cast-iron pull toy, girl on surfboard advertising Jantzen swimsuits, companion to Beach Patrol toy, 8″ height.   *$1,000–$2,000*

Swimmer, Tinkertoy, Evanston, Illinois, circa 1930s, animated pull toy in which swimmer does crawl when toy is pulled, wood, metal.   *$50–$60*

Tin Toys

✳ ✳ ✳

There are any number of purists among tin toy collectors who prefer to remain frozen in time in the glory days of the late 19th century. This marked the era when Ives, George Brown, William Fallows, Hall & Stratford, and Althof Bergmann excelled with delicately sculptured hoop toys, animals, and human figures acting out little tableaus on wheeled platforms. Without question, 19th-century classic tins bring out the very best among American toy makers in terms of patina, superb craftsmanship, and an unerring eye for detail in recapturing a glorious "coming of age" for this nation of ours. Never before have so few toys been desired by so many.

Early Tin Horse and Carriage, possibly George Brown, 1880s, $300–$400. (Opfer Auctions photo.)

Early American Painted Tin Kitchen, 19″ length, $300–$400. (Opfer Auctions photo.)

Elephant with removable canopy, tin with cast-iron wheels, 1870s, $2,200. (Price realized at Opfer Christmas sale, 1988; Opfer Auctions photo.)

Early American Tin Toys: Horse With Cart, possibly George Brown, $412.50. (Price realized at Opfer Christmas sale, 1988; Opfer Auctions photo.)

ROLLING HOOP AND PLATFORM TOYS

The classic and elegant hoop toys of the 1870–1890 era were small, usually not exceeding 6″ or 7″ diameter, and encircled various human as well as familiar animal figures. They were part of the standard repertoire of Althof Bergmann, as well as James Fallows, George Brown, and Merriam Mfg.

Boy With Hoop, Stevens and Brown (speculative), 1870s, bell chime is attached at hub of hoop, wire rods connect chime with handle of two-wheel cart on which running boy figure is attached. $2,000–plus

Boy Riding Dog, Althof Bergmann, 1874, boy waves and holds dog's collar with other hand, 4¾″ length. $1,000–$2,000

Boy With St. Bernard, Althof Bergmann, 1874, boy with dog on leash, dog carries bucket in jaws, 4¾″ and 6½″ length.
                                                       $2,000–plus

Dog in Hoop, Stevens and Brown, 1872, pointer-type running with high curled tail, 6″ diameter. $1,500–$2,000

Hoop With Boy or Girl, Althof Bergmann, 1874, 6½″ and 8″ diameter. $900–$1,100

Hoop With Elephant, Althof Bergmann, 1874, 6¼″ and 8″ diameter. $900–$1,100

An array of toys that can readily be viewed as sculptural art. Although the jobber made no mention of maker by name, these painted and stenciled tin platform and hoop toys are possibly George Brown, Althof Bergmann, or Hull and Stafford, c. 1880s, and would rate in the $1,000–$2,000 and up stratosphere.

Rabbit in Hoop, Merriam, 1870s, blown-tin white rabbit, one of the most uncommon of all rolling hoops. *$2,000–plus*

Shepherd and Flock Platform Toy, Althof Bergmann, 1890s, shepherd with crook, dog, goat, and four sheep, 13 ⅓″ length. *$1,500–$1,600*

Two Musicians and Menagerie Platform Toy, Althof Bergmann, 1890, drummer and fifer lead parade of two lions, two bears, and elephant, 11 ½″ length (variations included horse with monkey rider, elephant, and dog, 9″ length; also 7″-length version of three sheep and a goat). *$5,000–plus*

White Horse in Hoop, attributed to George Brown, 1870s, hoop of corrugated tin, 8″ diameter.   *$5,000–plus*

PERELMAN TOY MUSEUM SALE, 19TH-CENTURY TIN AND WOOD CLOCKWORK TOYS

Acrobat Clockwork Toy (The Acrobat), Henry Brower, New York City, 1873, bisque-headed figure revolves on high bar.   *$4,500*

Automated Tea Drinker, maker unknown, circa 1890, Mandarin raises teacup to lips, then returns to original position, with original box.   *$8,500*

Banjo Player, Jerome Secor, late 1870s, clockwork; painted tin.   *$15,000*

Black Boxers, Automated Toy Boxers, patented 1876, Automatic Toy Works, distributed by Ives.   *$12,500*

Black Washerwoman, attributed to Ives, Blakeslee & Williams, 1880s, clockwork platform toy, 10″ height.   *$15,000*

> *Note:* A White Washerwoman (German, maker unknown, 1880s, parian-headed clothed figure) also sold at Perelman at $15,000.

Boy Riding Perambulator, a.k.a. Champion Velocipede, Stevens & Brown, 1870, 5½″ height.   -   *$12,500*

Broadway and 5th Avenue Omnibus, George W. Brown, circa 1874, clockwork tinplate, painted and stenciled two white horses, yellow with red floral and eagle/shield stenciling, 13″ length.   *$36,300**

Brudder Bones, Jerome Secor, late 1870s, end man on minstrel shakes bones between fingers and sways, clockwork.   *$12,000*

Carousel, Althof Bergmann, 1870s, painted tinplate.   *$22,500*

Carousel, Bi-Plane, Muller & Kadeder, 1909, with four airplane gondolas, painted tin, 14½″ height.   *$5,500*

Carousel, Clown-Operated, Ernst Plank, early 1900s.   *$4,500*

Circus Rider, Althof Bergmann, 1870s, lady bareback rider on white horse, painted tin.   *$35,000*

---

*This Omnibus was *not* sold at Perelman, but at Sotheby's Auction in New York City, November 1988.

Crawling Baby, a.k.a. Creeping Doll, Ives (actually manufactured by Automatic Toy Works and distributed by Ives), patented 1871 by R.J. Clay, 11″ length.   *$1,750*

Dancing Darky, Ives, 1873, clockwork platform toy.   *$9,000*

Fighting Frogs Pull Toy, Fallows, circa 1880, pair of green and yellow lead frogs face each other on wheeled platform, kick each other when toy is pulled, lead and tin, 7½″ length.   *$5,800*

General Grant Smoking Cigar Platform Toy, Ives, 1877, patented by A. H. Dean.   *$15,000*

Girl Cyclist, Althof Bergmann, 1880s.   *$30,000*

Girl Riding Perambulator, Ives, 1875, 9″ height.   *$12,500*

Grandmother Rocking Cradle, Automatic Toy Works, patented 1878 by Lewis Pattberg & Bros., one arm fans baby while other rocks cradle, clockwork platform toy.   *$25,000*

Kitten in Stein Clockwork, a.k.a. Peek-a-Boo, Ives, 1890s.
$3,500

Lady Seated at Sewing Machine (Sewing Machine Girl), R.J. Clay, patented 1875, jointed bisque dressed doll, foot begins to move on treadle and sewing machine sews when activated.
$25,000

Nineteenth-Century Clockwork Walkers

Ives Clockwork Walkers were patented by Arthur Hotchkiss in 1875 and 1876. Figures move on heavy roller feet of cast iron. Heads are of molded metal and the figures wear cloth on wood outfits. They are 10″ high.

Chinaman	*$6,500*
General Butler	*$4,000*
Old Black Joe	*$3,750*
Sailor Boy	*$8,500*
Santa Claus	*$6,000*

Also included in the Hotchkiss series are: The Jackass, $4,000–$4,500; The Turk, $4,000–$4,500; Tilden the Statesman, indeterminate (only one is known); and Zouve, $4,000–$4,500.

Hotchkiss Walkers, Ives, 1875–1876, at Perelman Museum Sale—
Chinaman: $6,500; General Butler: $4,000; Old Black Joe: $3,750;
General Grant Cigar Smoker, 1877 patent by A. Dean: $15,000.

McGinty Dancer (skeleton), Ives, 1890s, platform toy, clockwork.   *$4,000**

Mechanical Alligator, Ives, Pilkington, 1875 patent, 22″
length.   *$13,500*

Mechanical Bear, Ives, patented 1872, R.J. Clay.
   Black version w/box.   *$1,200*
   White version w/box.   *$2,000*

Mechanical Piano Player, Jerome Secor (Bridgeport Toy Co.),
circa 1880, bisque doll, wood piano, cast iron, 10¾″ height ×
10½″ width.   *$10,000*

Missing Link or *Great What Is It?*, J. M. Cromwell, 1865, monkey in scarlet tunic dances on stage beneath canopy, rings miniature bells as it jiggles, 9½″ height.   *$7,500*

Monkey Churner, Ives, Albert H. Dean patent, late 1870s, clockwork platform toy.   *$6,500*

*Another example sold at Opfer's 1988 Christmas Auction for $11,000.

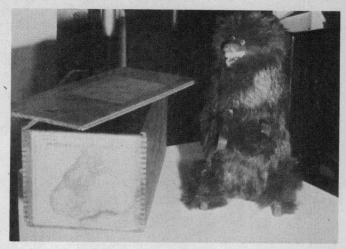

Mechanical Bear, Ives, patented 1872, with original box, $1,200–$1,500.

Monkey Prancing, Ives, Charles Hotchkiss patent, 1887, monkey performs on all fours, platform toy.   *$3,500*

Monkey Riding Perambulator, Ives, 1875, 9″ height.   *$25,000*

Niagara Sidewheeler,* George Brown, 1870, handpainted, stenciled tin clockwork.   *$40,000*

Oarsman, Ives, Blakeslee & Co., 1869, patented to Nathan S. Warner (listed as No. 2 toy in Ives' listing), painted tin clockwork.   *$9,500*

Old Woman and Boy Peddler's Wagon, Ives, Blakeslee & Co., patented 1874, horse-drawn, woman and boy have papier-mâché faces, horse and rig are tin, 17″ length.   *$38,500*

Old Woman in a Shoe, Ives, 1893, tinplate shoe with four wheels, drawn by two horses.   *$6,500*

Omnibus Carriage, Francis Field & Francis (also attributed to Hull & Stafford), 1860s, tin, painted green and red with stenciled floral design and leaf and shell trim.   *$38,000*

*Other Sidewheelers included Electra, at $6,500, and Union, at $7,500.

Our New Clergyman, * Ives, circa 1880–mid–1890s, black clergyman in flowing robes leans forward in pulpit and gestures with open Bible, 11″ height. $4,500

Pair of Equestrian Riders, Hull & Stafford, 1870s, 8¾″ tin platform pull toy. $7,500

Political Stump Speaker, Ives, 1882, wood platform, clockwork. $12,500

Preacher at the Pulpit, Ives, 1890s, smiling black figure leans over pulpit with Bible in hand, clockwork wood platform toy. $4,500

Protector Pumper, James Fallows, 1880s, tin. $18,500

Rigs, Clockwork Tin

The following is a small, representative sampling of early tin rigs at Perelman.

Confectionary Wagon, maker undetermined, U.S., circa 1850–1900, blue, 14½″ length. $12,500
   Smaller size, in red. $7,500

Cuzner Trotter, Ives, patented by J. Cuzner, 1871 (carried by Ives as late as 1893), single horse, there is also a double-horse version), 12″ length. $4,500

Double Galloper, Ives, patented by Edward Ives, 1874, man in rig moves arm up and down with whip in hand when activated, large size. $27,500

G.A. Schwarz Toys, Fancy Goods Peddling Van, maker undetermined, circa 1880, painted & stenciled, olive green, gold stenciling, 21″ length. $33,000

Philadelphia Chestnuts, Fancy Goods Wagon, maker undetermined, painted tin, stenciled. $22,000

---

*This platform toy, along with Political Stump Speaker, Preacher at the Pulpit, and Woman's Rights Advocate, was designed by R.J. Clay and is very similar in action to the other three.

A Modern Style
Buggy, with Two
Galloping Horses
and Dressed
Whipping Driver.

The Driver
holds the reins in
one hand while
with the other he
applies the whip
vigorously while
the Horses trot.

No. 14-2 ¦ Patented, 12 inches long, Per Dozen, $24.00 With patent whipping (Dressed) driver.

MECHANICAL HORSE AND BUGGY, WHIPPING DRIVER.

A
Pretty Toy,
Strong and
Attractive.

The Horse
Gallops and
the Driver
Whips the
Horse.

No. 15-1 Patented, Galloping Horse, 17 in. long, Dressed Whipping Driver, Price per doz., **$30.00**

MECHANICAL HORSE WITH OLD LADY DRIVER, AND BOY HOOK BEHIND.

A Large and
a very Comi-
cal Toy. The
Small Boy
"Hooking
Behind"
makes this a
Novel Toy.

The motion
of the old
Lady Driver
is very per-
fect. She
moves her
entire body
back and
forth very
naturally.

No. 15-3   Patented Galloping Horse, 17 inches long.... Price per dozen, **$33.00**

Ives Catalog Page of Horse-Drawn Rigs, circa 1890, clockwork, all prices
are in the four-figure range. "Old Lady Driver and Boy Hook Behind"
sold at $40,000 at Acevedo Sale of Bernard Barenholtz Collection in
1989.

Single Galloper, Ives, 1870s, $3,000–$4,000.

Santa in Sleigh, attributed to Althof Bergmann, late 1890s, tin clockwork with metal bells, cloth Santa outfit, sleigh pulled by pair of goats on double wheels; the classic Christmas toy.

$32,000

Teeter-Totter (The Seesaw), Ives, Albert H. Dean, 1873, boy and girl dressed figures with wooden heads and bodies, painted tin face masks, metal seesaw, metal-jointed legs, arms, clicking sound as figures move up and down. $15,000

Toy Acrobats, Ives, patented by C.A. Hotchkiss, 1892, bisque figures make full or half turns, backward and forward turns on horizontal bar. $22,500

Toy Gymnast, a.k.a. Jubilee Trapezist, Automatic Toy Works, patented 1875 by William Hubbell. $4,500

Trotting Horse, Ives, 1890s. $10,000

Walking Horse on Platform, Ives, Blakesly, circa 1893, horse walks on wheeled platform when toy is pulled. $2,750
    A second example w/box. $5,000

Walking Horse With Dog Cart, Ives, Blakesly, circa 1890s.

$7,500

Whistler Train, Ives, Blakeslee & Williams, 1880s, painted and stenciled. $18,500

Woman's Rights Advocate, Automatic Toy Works, platform clockwork, 1875. $12,500

Tin Toys

12 **Ives, Blakeslee & Williams Co., 294 Broadway, New York. Factory, Bridgeport, Conn.**

399

Mechanical Circus Dancer.

Mechanical Skeleton Dancer.

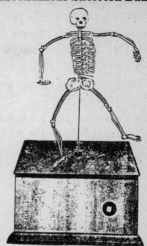

No. 22-9. Patented. 15 inches high.
Price per dozen, **$33.00.**
When wound up the Horse will gallop and the figure will dance in a very lively manner.

No. 22-13.

" McGinty " Dancer. 10½ inches high.
Price per dozen..........................**$24.00**
A Mechanical Skeleton that is full of motion.

The Famous Dancing Darkies.

Dancing Monkies

These cuts show our Single Dancers only; do not fail to see our Double Dancers, they are very attractive.

		PER DOZEN.
No. 22-1.	Single Dancers	**$21.00**
" **22-2.**	Double Dancers	**$24.00**

WHITE DANCERS.

No. 22-3.	Single Dancers	**$21.00**
" **22-4.**	Double Dancers	**$24.00**

Each in box. 10 inches high.

		PER DOZEN.
No. 22-6.	Single Dancers	**$21.00**
No. 22-7.	Double Dancers	**$24.00**

10 inches high.

Ives Catalog Page of Platform Toys, 1890s, clockwork. Skeleton Dancer
(top right) sold at $11,000 at Opfer's 1988 Christmas Sale.

Woman With Child and Horse Hoop Toy, Merriam Mfg., 1870s, clockwork, painted tin.   **$37,500***

Woman Churning Butter, Ives, patented 1874, clockwork platform toy, wooden head with sheet brass face, cotton gown, apron, and dust cap.   **$4,000**

Woman Dancing, Ives, patented 1886, cast-metal head and hands, wood jointed.   **$5,000**

Woman on Swing, Ives, patented 1872 by N.S. Warner; clockwork platform toy (also man version).   **$6,000**

Woman Rocking Cradle, Ives, patented by R.J. Clay, late 1870s.   **$25,000**

---

*A record price for a 19th-century hoop toy. A Dressed Boy Hoop Toy by George Brown sold at $5,000.

Transportation Toys

* * *

AIRCRAFT

Any number of toy makers capitalized on the inaugural flight of the Wright brothers in 1903 by introducing very fanciful replications of the primitive kitelike flying machine. Unfortunately, there were prolonged lapses extending through World War I and the late 1920s when the marvelous early flyers were never immortalized in tin, wood, or cast iron. (Obvious exceptions were the dirigibles or zeppelins, including the famed Los Angeles and the Graf Zeppelin.) The reasons for this lack of imagination or marketing acumen are obscure. Perhaps it was due to the early incursion of scale model aircraft kits, an entity in itself whereby the great aircraft of the world were recreated to a "T." Lindbergh's solo trans-Atlantic flight finally awakened U.S. toy makers, as did the pioneering flights of Rear Admiral Richard Byrd, Amelia Earhart, Wiley Post, Billy Mitchell, and others. Lindbergh's "Spirit of St. Louis" was copied to a fare-thee-well. What is generally available from U.S. makers are cast-iron or tin mutations that appear to be so clumsy as to be incapable of actual flight. By far, the most imaginative and whimsical aircraft toys emanate from continental Europe, where Maerklin, Bing, Carette, Jepp, and others produced truly representative, handsomely enameled, clockwork-powered flying machines.

Cast Iron

Air Express, Dent, 1920s tri-Motor, bright colors with red and gilt trim, nickel-plated props and gear, this model also available in cast aluminum. $400–$500

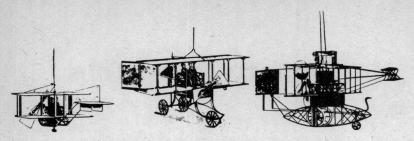

Few captured the glory of the early days of aviation than did the German firm of Gebruder Maerklin. These superbly enameled clockwork toys, c. 1915–20, all rank in the rare echelons of toy collecting.

"Air Force," maker unknown, 1930, red, blue, and aluminum colors, 6¼" length.   *$150–$200*

Air Force UX 166, maker unknown, 1930, red, blue, and aluminum, 6¼" length.   *$200–$250*

Air Ford, maker unknown, 1929, green with gilt trim, nickeled prop and wheels, 4" length.   *$400–$500*

"Air Line," Dent, circa 1920, cast iron, also in bright colors with nickeled trim, two sizes: 10¾" and 12½" wingspan.

$350–$450

Airship, maker unknown, 1922, tin mechanical covered with light canvas, bi-wing, pilot in open cockpit.   *$75–$100*

"America," maker unknown, 1930, cast iron, triple engines, balloon rubber tires, two passengers, ratchet attachment, wire spring drive, pull cord, "America" appears on wing, 14" length.   *$300–$400*

Army Plane, Champion, circa 1930, nickel-plated fuselage, red, blue, or silver wings, air-cushion rubber tires.   *$200–$250*

"Bremen," Hubley, 1933, floor runner, prop moves when wheels move, imitation exhaust, 10⅛" length.   *$500–$600*

"Bremen," maker unknown, 1929, green with gilt trim, nickel accessories, three aluminum-finish passengers, "Bremen" appears on fuselage, 7¼" length.   *$300–$350*

Cabin Monoplane, Arcade, 1932, black body with orange wheels, nickel wheels, prop and running gear, 7½" length.

$400–$500

Ciro-Plane, Hubley, 1936, assorted colors, 4½" length.

$200–$250

"Dornier" or DOX Plane, Hubley, 1936, painted aluminum with red wings, four sizes: 3¾", 4¾", 6", and 7¾" length.

$200–$300

Ford Cabin Plane, Dent, 1920s, corrugated wing and body, triple nickel-plated engines and polished steel props, two sizes: 9⅝" and 12" length.

$400–$450

Ford Tri-motor, Dent, 1920s, corrugated cast-iron finish, silver painted, "Ford" embossed on tail section rudder, approx, 9½" length.

$400–$500

"Friendship," maker unknown, 1930, amphibian, triple engines, ratchets, spring steel drive, "Friendship" on wings, 11¼" length.

$500–$600

"Lindy," Hubley, 1928, 11¼" length, also with slight variations in 9½" size.

$500–$600

"Lindy," maker unknown, 1929, cast aluminum, red trim, nickel accessories, 4½" length.

$150–$200

"Lindy" Glider, Hubley, 1933, pull toy, rider detaches, ratchet motor, 10" length.

$250–$300

Lockheed Sirius, Hubley, 1933, two passengers in open cockpit, rubber tires, 8½" length.

$250–$300

Ford Tri-Motor, Dent, 1920s. Corrugated cast iron, rubber wheels, $400–$500.

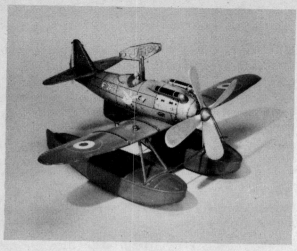

Tin clockwork seaplane "F-260," by Jep, French, c. 1935; with pilot, twin engines, propeller and two pontoons, 19" wingspan, $2,000 plus. (Photo courtesy of Sotheby's, New York.)

"*Lone Eagle,*" American Flyer, lithographed tin mechanical, brass fittings, adjustable rudder, 21½" length.   *$250–$300*

"*Lucky Boy,*" Dent, 1920s, high-wing monoplane, bright colors, available in five sizes, also in cast aluminum as well as cast iron.   *$200–$250*

Mail Plane, Keystone, 1929, pressed steel, green and red fuselage, rubber tires, cabin door opens, leather mail bags, pull toy.   *$800–$900*

Monocoupe, Arcade, 1928, cast iron, four sizes: 4", 5", 6", and 7" lengths.   *$300–$400*

R.A.F. Monoplane, Britains, 1940s, lithographed tin, 8" length.   *$1,000–$1,200*

Single-Engine Closed Cockpit, Hubley, 1938, assorted colors with nickel-plated wings, 3½" and 4½" lengths.   *$200–$250*

Single-Engine Monoplane, Kilgore, 1930, 4¼" length.
                                                   $200–$250

Tri-Motor, Arcade, 1932, cast iron with nickeled wheels and props, assorted colors, 3¾" length.   *$200–$300*

Tri-Motor T.A.T., maker unknown, two-tone red, blue, ivory, orange, and lavender, 11" length. $250–$300

Twin-Engine Cabin Model, Hubley, 1938, assorted colors, 4½" length. $200–$250

United Boeing, Arcade, 1937, green finish, 3⅝" length. $250–$300

Fixed Wing

Air Devil, F. Strauss, 1927, blunt-nosed lithographed tin mechanical, stands on nose, spins, then rights self, 8¼" length. $200–$300

Airplane and Hangar, Cardini, 1915, lithographed tin bi-plane mounted on support rods flying atop hangar with lead-weight world globe as counterbalance, bi-wing, 8½" length. $1,200–$2,000

Amphibian Plane, Chein, 1930s, lithographed tin mechanical, 7¾" length. $100–$150

Around the World Spinning Airplane, U.S., maker unknown, 1920s, tin wind-up, $300–$400. (Mid-Hudson Gallery photo.)

Army Bomber, Boycraft, 1929, bi-wing, pressed steel, 24 ½ " length.   *$600–$700*

Army Bomber Tri-Motor, Marx, 1935, lithographed tin with ratchet noise maker, 25 ½ " length.   *$300–$400*

Bi-plane, Kingsbury, 1920s, sheet-steel mechanical, rubber tires, yellow fuselage with red wings, pilot is cast iron, called "The Taxiplane," 16" length.   *$500–$600*

Bi-plane, maker unknown, patented 1921, sheet steel, hand-painted friction toy, 16" length.   *$300–$400*

Bi-wing, Girard Mfg., 1920s, lithographed tin mechanical, Air Force insignia on wings, 9 ½ " length.   *$400–$500*

Bleiriot Monoplane, Gunthermann, 1910, lithographed tin clockwork, 10" length, 9" wingspan.   *$1,000–$2,000*

Boeing Strato Cruiser, Japan, 1960s, lithographed tin, friction, 16" length.   *$200–$300*

Cabin Plane, maker unknown, 1920s, lithographed tin, 18" length.   *$350–$450*

China Clipper, Wyandotte, 1940s, painted pressed steel.
                                                  $250–$300

C-R-S Monoplane, maker unknown, 1920s, has French tri-color on tail section, 15 ½ " length.   *$500–$600*

Dare-Devil Flyer, Marx, 1930, lithographed tin monoplane and dirigible at opposite ends of rod spin atop Empire State Building.   *$500–$600*

Empire Express Monoplane, maker unknown, pressed-steel friction, 19" length.   *$300–$400*

Fighter Plane, Marx, 1940s, lithographed tin mechanical, pair of machine guns shoot sparks from each wing, 7" length.
                                                  $150–$200

Four-Engine Bomber, Marx, 1940s, lithographed tin mechani-cal, 13" length.   *$200–$300*

French Monoplane #250, Jepp, France, 1920s, lithographed tin mechanical, two passengers in open cockpit, 7⅝" length.
                                                  $600–$700

High-Wing Monoplane, Boycraft, 1929, pressed steel, motor noise ratchet, 21½″ and 23½″ lengths. $500–$600

High-Wing Monoplane, Keystone, 1929, 8-cylinder motor ratchet attachment, red and olive drab finish, rubber tires, 25″ length, 24″ wingspan. $350–$450

International Airline Tri-Motor, Marx, 1931, lithographed tin, 17½″ wingspan. $300–$400

Loopover Monoplane, Marx, 1947, lithographed tin, 6″ wingspan. $200–$300

Monoplane, French, 1910, lithographed tin mechanical, pilot in open cockpit, high landing gear, 6″ length. $600–$700

Monoplane, Kingsbury, 1925, lithographed mechanical, 12″ length. $700–$800

Parachute Plane, maker unknown, 1929, lithographed mechanical, 15¾″ length. $200–$300

Rollover Monoplane, Air Force, Marx, 1930s, 6″ wingspan. $200–$300

Single-Engine Monoplane, Tipp and Co., circa 1936, bears No. 1416, dark blue, purple, and yellow with black stripes and red prop, 12½″ wingspan. $500–$600

Sky Bird Flyer, Marx, 1930s, lithographed tin, variation of Dare-Devil Flyer except that it spins atop lighthouse, 8½″ height. $500–$600

"Spirit of America," American Flyer, 1928, lithographed tin pull toy, friction, 20″ length. $500–$600

"Spirit of Columbia," American Flyer, 1928, lithographed tin, friction, 18½″ length. $500–$600

Transport, Boycraft, 1932, tri-motor, all three props spin, rubber tires, 23½″ length. $600–$700

Tri-Motor, Boycraft, 1931, nickel-plated steel, three props, one stable, two spinning, cabin door opens, 21″ and 23″ lengths. $600–$700

Tri-Motor, Steelcraft, 1930s, painted pressed steel, 18" length.
$800–$900

Tri-Motor, Keystone, 1933, pistons in engines move up and down making clicking noise, leather mail bags, swinging doors on each side, 25" length. $700–$800

Tri-Motor Monoplane, Kingsbury, circa 1920s, 15" length.
$800–$900

TWA, Twin Engine Transport, Marx, 1940s, lithographed tin mechanical double tail, 13" length. $300–$400

TWA 727, Japanese, 1960s, lithographed tin, friction, 17½" length. $200–$300

U.S. Air Force Voodoo, Japanese, 1970s, lithographed tin, friction. $200–$300

U.S. Mail Plane, Steelcraft, 1930s, painted pressed steel, battery-operated lights, 21" length. $400–$500

U.S. Marines Monoplane, #59, Marx, 1935, ratchet noise maker, lithographed tin, 25½" length. $300–$400

Wright Bros. Aircraft, Muller & Kadeder, 1909, painted tin with three props, string toy, flies in circles:
   6" length. $700–$800
   8¾" length. $800–$1,000

Zeppelins and Hot Air Balloons

Airship, German, 1910, painted tin, double-blade celluloid propellers, two passenger baskets, string wind-up, 10½" length.
$250–$300

Akron, maker unknown, lithographed tin, all white.
$300–$400

Akron Zeppelin, Champion, circa 1930, balloon rubber tires, lithographed tin. $300–$350

Dirigible With Umbrella Parachute, maker unknown, 1910, painted tin, side propellers, openwork basket, string toy; when balloon rises to top of string, parachute is released by automatic lever, 10" length. $400–$500

Floor Zeppelin, Marx, 1930, lithographed tin mechanical, aluminum finish, flies in circles when suspended in air, 9½" length. $250–$300

Flying Zeppelin, F. Strauss, 1929, aluminum and brass.

$300–$400

Glass Zeppelin, maker unknown, 1920s, crocheted stocking over glass tube, hanging basket, 24″ length. $400–$500

Graf Zeppelin, maker unknown, 1920, lithographed tin, 8″ length. $250–$300

Graf Zeppelin, maker unknown, 1932, lithographed tin mechanical. $250–$300

Graf Zeppelin, maker unknown, 1935, lithographed tin mechanical, dull silver finish, double-disc wheels, 30½″ length

$150–$200

Hot Air Balloon, German, early 1900s, handpainted tin string toy, 8″ height. $500–$600

Lehmann Zeppelin (see "Lehmann Toys" listing).

Los Angeles Zeppelin, Dent Hardware, 1920s, cast iron with nickel-plated wheels, 12⅝″, 10¾″, and 8¾″ lengths in various colors, Dent also produced these sizes in cast aluminum.

$300–$400

Metalcraft Zeppelin Construction Kit, Metalcraft, 1920s, sheet steel. $400–$500

Monoplane, Girard Mfg., 1920s, painted tin mechanical, 12½″ length. $500–$600

New York Zeppelin, F. Strauss, 1920s, lithographed tin with celluloid propellers, 9″ length. $300–$400

Trans Atlantic, F. Strauss, 1920s, lithographed tin, 9″ length.

$300–$400

Zeppelin, Muller & Kadeder, 1909, painted tin with two gondolas, side and front props, replica of first zeppelin, 9¼″ length, also available in 12½″ and 5½″ lengths. $500–$600

Zeppelin, Boycraft, 1929, lithographed steel with spinning propellers, 28″ length. $300–$400

Zeppelin, Boycraft, 1931, "Graf Zeppelin," pressed steel, aluminum finish, 27¼″ length, also available in 30″ length.

$250–$300

Zeppelin Kit, A.C. Gilb, 1929, erector set builds zeppelin and other models, 53″ length assembled (Erector Set #8).

$300–$400

Zeppelin-Tipp, German, 1920s, "Graf Zeppelin," lithographed mechanical, 24″ length.

$900–$1,000

ANIMAL-DRAWN VEHICLES

Clearly dominating the early cast-iron toys of the 19th century were the animal-drawn rigs produced by such leading makers as Ives, Pratt & Letchworth, Carpenter, and Wilkins. From the dawning of the 20th century to the 1950s, horse-drawn phaetons, hansom cabs, drays, and fire pumpers coexisted side by side with the increasingly popular motor toys, with Dent Hardware, Hubley, Arcade, and Kenton the major forces in the field. The combination of power, speed, and grace embodied in these horse-drawn toys makes them the favorites of interior decorators as well as the legion of equine fanciers who collect topically. Major competition also comes from inveterate fire-fighting toy collectors.

The following is a representative selection of the rarest and most beautiful ever cast:

Depot Wagon, Carpenter, circa 1880, painted cast iron, pair of galloping horses, six removable standing passengers.

$2,000–plus

Double-Horse Carriage, Pratt & Letchworth, 1890s, cast iron, $1,000–$1,200.

Four classic Carpenter cast-iron rigs. *Top:* Pony Phaeton, $1,200–$1,400; *second row:* Double Truck, around $1,000; *third row:* Contractor Wagon, $800–$900; *bottom row:* Tally-Ho, $10,000 plus (an example sold at $25,000 at the Acevedo Sale of Bernard Barenholtz Collection in 1989). Cuts are from 1892 Carpenter Catalog.

Flying Artillery, Ives, 1890s, $4,400 at Opfer's 1988 Christmas Auction.

English Trap, Kenton, 1890s, painted cast iron, four passengers, driver, coachman, Victorian lady with small boy, horse and trap plated in bronze, 15″ length (Trap: from "trappings," symbolizing elegance). $1,000–$2,000

Hansom Cab, Pratt & Letchworth, late 1890s, painted cast iron, prancing steed, yellow cab, yellow coachman, 12″ length.
$700–$800

Horse-Drawn Caisson, Ives, 1890s, painted cast iron, brass cannon, 23″ length. $2,000–plus

Horse-Drawn Surrey, Pratt & Letchworth, 1890s, painted cast iron, 16″ length.   - $1,000–$2,000

Horse-Drawn Tally-Ho Coach, Carpenter, 1890s, painted cast iron, two pair rearing horses, seven passengers, 26½″ length.
$10,000–plus

Oxford Trap, Dent Hardware Co., circa 1910, painted cast-iron coachman and woman passenger, single white horse.
$800–$900

Horse Cart With Driver, Wilkins, 1890s, $300–$400.

Spider Phaeton Carriage, Hubley, circa 1910, $1,540 at Opfer's 1988 Christmas Auction.

Derby Hatted Driver and Four-Wheel Horse Cart, maker unknown, 1890s, $300–$400. (Opfer Auctions photo.)

Horse Drawn Pumper, litho on wood, Bliss, 1877, $3,000–$4,000.

Spider Phaeton, Hubley Mfg. Co., circa 1906, painted cast iron, pair horses, woman driver, groom in rear.   *$1,000–$2,000*

Three-Seated Brake, Hubley, 1890, painted cast iron, pair of horses, six passengers, 18″ length.   *$4,000–$5,000*

Two-Seated Brake, Hubley, circa 1900, painted cast iron, three passengers and driver, only a few of this rare specimen are known to exist.   *$5,000–$6,000*

Cast Iron

Buckboard, Kenton, 1929, two horses, lines, 12½″ length.
$250–$300

Cairo Express, Kenton, 1924, elephant pulling cart with native driver, 10″ length.   *$600–$700*

City Transfer, Kenton, 1929, covered rig, 30″ length.
$1,500–$2,000

Coal Cart, Kenton, 1929, small mule and cart, 10″ length, other sizes.   *$200–$300*

Coal Wagon, Kenton, 1929, one horse, painted and decorated, with lines, 16¼″ length, other sizes.   *$500–$600*

Concrete Mixer, Kenton, 1941, 13⅝″ length.   *$700–$800*

Contractor's Dumping Wagon, Kenton, 1929, pull lever and three boxes will dump, hack driver, 16″ length.   *$400–$500*

Covered Wagon, Hubley, 1928, two horses, 15″ length.
$350–$500

Covered Wagon, Kenton, 1952, removable cover on wagon, 15⅜″ height.   *$500–$600*

Depot Wagon, Carpenter, 1880, six removable figures, galloping horses.   *$2,000–plus*

Dray, Kenton, 1929, four large horses, traces and lines, with barrels and boxes, 33″ length.   *$1,200–$1,400*

Dray, Kenton, 1929, painted, six blocks and six barrels, 23½″ length.   *$600–$700*

Dray, Kenton, 1929, three horses, lines and traces, with barrels, 16½″ length.   *$400–$500*

Dray, Kenton, 1929, two large horses, painted lines and traces with six barrels, 16½″ length, other sizes   *$400–$500*

All of the Horses, Tongues, Shafts and Platforms used in my Toys are guaranteed to be made of MALLEABLE IRON.

No. 7.—GALLOPING HORSE, which is removable from Platform.

Patented Nov. 16th, 1880; May 10th, '81; July 19th '81; and March 20th, '83.

Packed Three dozen in a Case. - - - - - - - Price per dozen

No. 8.—SMALL HORSE & CART, with removable Figure and galloping Horse.

Patented May 25th, 1880; reissued March 14th, '82; patented Nov. 16th, '80; May 10th '81; July 19th '81; Dec. 20th, '81; Nov. 21st, 81; March 20th, '83; Oct. 23rd, '83; May 13th, '84.

Packed Three dozen in a Case. - - - - - - - Price per dozen

No. 9.—PONY CART, with removable Figures and galloping Horses.

Patented May 25th, 1880; reissued March 14th, '82; patented Nov. 16th '80; May 10th '81; July 19th, '81; Nov. 21st, '82; March 20th '83; October, 23rd, '83; May 13th, 84.

Packed Three dozen in a Case. - - - - - - - Price per dozen

Catalog from 1880s by Francis W. Carpenter, Harrison, Westchester, New York, one of the premier cast-iron and malleable-iron toy makers. Although Carpenter discontinued numbering his toys in consecutive order at some unspecified time, his first dozen toys are well-documented. His very first was a cast-iron freight train with two gondolas, a tender and locomotive. (Secor shared the first patent, on June 8, 1880, of a cast locomotive toy.) The rigs shown here are valued between $1,500 and well beyond the $2,000 range.

Patrol Wagon, three-horse team, 21½", $600–$700.

Express Wagon, Kenton, 1929, two horses, lines and traces, 16½" length, also 12½" length.   *$400–$500*

Farm Wagon, Kenton, 1929, painted:
    14" length.   *$400–$500*
    10¼" length.   *$500–$600*

Fire Chief, Kenton, 1929, painted:
    14" length.   *$400–$500*
    9¼" length.   *$500–$600*

Fire Patrol, 1904, two galloping horses, driver and five firemen in blue suits and helmet hats, 13" length.   *$1,000–$2,000*

Fire Patrol, Kenton, 1929, three horses, three firemen and driver, painted:
    13" length.   *$1,000–$2,000*
    14½" length.   *$2,000–$3,000*

Fire Patrol, Kenton, 1929, two horses, driver, three firemen, gong, painted:
    19" length.   *$700–$800*
    18" length with three horses.   *$650–$700*
    18" length with two horses.   *$600–$650*

Galloping Horse, Carpenter, 1880, removable from platform.
                                                   $500–$600

Ice Wagon, Hubley, 1920, one horse, painted, 9½" length, other sizes.   *$200–$300*

Ice Wagon, Kenton, 1929, two horses, painted, 16½" length.
                                                   $200–$300

Log Wagon, Kenton, 1929, Negro driver, painted, 16″ length.
$700–$800

Milk Wagon, Kenton, 1952, removable driver, 12¾″ length.
$350–$500

Mule and Coal Cart, Kenton, 1929, Negro driver, painted, 14″ length. $500–$600

One-Horse Coal Tipping Cart, Carpenter, 1880.
$1,000–$2,000

One-Horse Dray, Gong Bell, 1903, painted, 11½″ length.
$600–$700

One-Horse Dump Cart, Carpenter, 1880, removable figures, galloping horse and tipping cart. $800–$900

Ox Cart, Kenton, 1929, Negro driver, ox, 7″ length:
painted. $200–$300
silver finish. $200–$300

Police Patrol, Kenton, 1929, gong, lines, and traces, one driver, two policemen, and one prisoner, painted, 19″ length.
$1,200–$2,000

Pony Cart, Carpenter, 1880, removable figures and galloping horses. $1,000–$1,500

Pony Express Wagon, 1893, 14″ length. $800–$900

Road Phaeton, Kenton, 1929, painted, 10½″ length.
$300–$400

Sand and Gravel Wagon, Kenton, 1952, two horses, 15″ length, also 10″ and 10½″ lengths. $300–$350

Small Horse and Cart, Carpenter, 1880. $800–$900

Stake Wagon, Kenton, 1952, two horses, 10½″ length, also 11″ size with single horse. $300–$400

Sulky, Kenton, 1929, 9¼″ length, also other sizes.
$150–$200

Sulky, Kenton, 1952, 7¼″ length. $50–$75

Surrey, Kenton, 1929, 12″ length. $300–$400

Surrey, Kenton, 1929, 14″ length. $400–$450

Transfer Wagon, Kenton, 1929, two horses, 19″ length.
$500–$600

Two-Horse Dump Cart, Carpenter, 1880, removable figures, galloping horses and tipping cart.
$800–$900

Two-Horse Express Wagon, Carpenter, 1880, removable figure, galloping horses.
$1,000–$1,500

Painted Tin

Bow Cart, Althof Bergmann, 1874, high-wheeled cart drawn by white horse, 8″ length and 11½″ length sizes.
$800–$900

Boy Soldier With Gun, Althof Bergmann, 1874, running figure on four-wheeled platform carries gun over left shoulder, 3½″ and 7″ height sizes.
$1,000–$2,000

Boy Soldier on Wheels, Althof Bergmann, 1874, grim looking young man on four-wheeled platform wields saber in left hand, 3½″ and 7″ height sizes.
$1,000–$1,500

Boy on Wheels, Althof Bergmann, 1874, running boy on four-wheel platform blowing bugle, 3½″ height.
$1,000–$2,000

Bread, Cakes, Pies, Bakery Wagon, Althof Bergmann, 1874, 10″ and 14″ length sizes.
$2,000–$3,000

Cab, Althof Bergmann, 1874, tin with cast-iron wheels, drawn by one white horse, 8″ and 10½″ length sizes.
$800–$900

Cab With Girl, Sheep-Drawn, Althof Bergmann, 1874, another bit of whimsey, with girl on small-wheeled platform tending sheep as it draws cab, 8″ and 10½″ length sizes.
$900–$1,100

City Car, Althof Bergmann, 1874, four wheeler, pair of horses, "City Car" stencilled on side, several variations, one features only a single wheel under car, another reads "City R. R. Cars," 12″ to 19″ length sizes.
$2,000–$3,000

Dog Cart, Althof Bergmann, 1874, open two-wheel dray, white dog prances in style, 4½″ length (several variations by A. Bergmann, including pulling cab and several elaborate carriages, all drawn by identical dog, St. Bernard type).
$700–$800

Express Wagon, Althof Bergmann, 1874, Bergmann produced over a dozen variations, from single horse to as many as a team of four cantering steeds, sizes ranged from 6″ to 47″ lengths, the larger rigs fall into the "well nigh unattainable" category.

$2,000–$3,000

Gig With Boy, Althof Bergmann, 1874, single horse, 10½″ length, boy runs alongside of horse on small-wheeled platform, approximately 3″ length, also an 8″ length size.

$1,000–$1,500

Girl on Wheels, Althof Bergmann, 1874, girl skipping rope, 3½″ height. *$1,000–$2,000*

Goat Drawn by Bow Cart, Althof Bergmann, 1874, billy goat pulls two-wheeled open cart, 8″ and 10″ length sizes.

$800–$900

Hard-Soft Coal Two-Wheeled Cart With Driver, Althof Bergmann, 1874, "Coal, Kindling, Wood" stencilled in arc above cast-iron wheels, driver seated low in front of cart with feet dangling just behind horse, 17″ length. *$2,000–$3,000*

Horse-Drawn Dump Cart, Althof Bergmann, 1874, cart on two wheels tilts backward to unload, 13″ length, several versions, including example with driver. *$800–$900*

Julian Carriage, Althof Bergmann, 1874, drawn by two horses, four-wheeled open carriage, horses with single wheel under each, 21″ length. *$1,000–$2,000*

Milk Wagon, Althof Bergmann, 1874, pair white horses, four milk cans in front of elaborate open wagon, driver sits primly in rear, painted tin with cast-iron wheels. *$3,000–$4,000*

Milk Wagon With Driver, Althof Bergmann, 1874, single horse, milk cans in front, "Pure Milk" stencilled on side of wagon, 8¾″, 13½″, 14″ length sizes. *$4,000–$5,000*

Omnibus, Althof Bergmann, 1874, driver and pair of horses, "People's Line" appears atop side of four-wheel rig, 9½″, 11½″, 17″, and 21″ length sizes, a variation by Bergmann in 14″ and 21″ sizes featured stencilled words "U.S. Mail Wagon." *$5,000–plus*

Open-Sided Cab, Althof Bergmann, 1874, two-wheeled cab is no wider than its cast-iron wheels, features passenger, 8″ length.
$1,000–$1,500

Patent Racer, Althof Bergmann, 1874, boy sits high up on cart drawn by single horse, also available with adult driver.
$1,200–$2,000

Pony Cart With Boy, Althof Bergmann, 1874, boy again on wheeled platform carries small whip, pony on same platform as boy, 8″ and 10½″ length sizes.   *$1,000–$2,000*

Railroad Omnibus, Althof Bergmann, 1874, four horses, lad driving, long casketlike shape of omnibus, 40″ length.
$3,000–$4,000

Rockaway, Althof Bergmann, 1874, single horse-drawn four-wheel wagon with canopy, 13″ length, also 10″ length.
$1,000–$1,500

Rockaway, Althof Bergmann, pair of horses with driver, tin with cast-iron wheels, 22″ and 15½″ length sizes.   *$1,500–$2,000*

Sulky, Althof Bergmann, 1874, horse drawn, man driver, one of the classic Bergmann examples with intricate web of wire and tin comprising the rig itself.   *$2,000–$3,000*

Two-Horse Buggy and Driver, Althof Bergmann, 1870–1890, gold pair horses, red saddles, red cart with gold stencilling, green wheels and trim, clockwork mechanical, 17″ length.
$2,000–$3,000*

Water Cart, Althof Bergmann, 1874, horse-drawn flat cart with large barrel on brackets, driver perched atop barrel (water tank), 11½″, 13″, 17″ length sizes.   *$2,500–$3,500*

Perelman Toy Museum, Cast-Iron Miscellaneous

Alphabet Man, mfg. unknown, 1880s, cast-iron educational toy, as lever is pressed, alphabet leters come into view on collar.
$20,000**

Barouche, Horse-Drawn Carriage, Pratt & Letchworth, late 1890s, cast iron.   *$6,000*

---

*Sold for $2,470 at Skinner Auction, Bolton, Massachusetts, December 1985.
**Reportedly, a record for an educational toy.

Beer Cart, Kenton hardware, 1912, cast iron. $750

Butcher's Cart, Welker & Crosby, 1890s, cast iron. $950

Caterpiller, Arcade, 1912. $2,200

Circus Wagon, animated, Kyser & Rex, cast iron. $6,500

City Delivery Wagon, Harris, 1890s. $3,800

Conestoga Wagon, Francis W. Carpenter, 1880s, cast iron.
$850

Depot Wagon, Francis W. Carpenter, 1880s, cast iron. $1,500

Double Bicyclists, Wilkins Toy Co., early 1900s, pair of messenger boys riding side by side, 6″ length. $22,500

"Eagle" Milkwagon, Hubley. $650

Elevated Railway, Hubley, pat. 1893, clockwork, malleable iron and steel, single track. $10,000

Fast Mail Cart/Walking Horse, Ives Blakesly, 1880s, cast iron.
$2,250

Four Bicycle Riders on Tandem Cycle, Ives, circa 1890, cast iron, steel, toy moves on long chain. $28,000

Four-Seater Brake, Wilkins Toy Co., 1890s, cast iron. $32,000

Hay Rake, Wilkins, 1890s, cast iron. $2,500

Horse-Drawn Cement Mixer, Kenton Hardware, 1916, cast iron. $1,200

Hubley Royal Circus Cast-Iron Pull Toys. Hubley produced its Royal Circus from 1919 to 1926. The following examples sold at the Perelman Museum Great Grab of 1988:

Band Wagon, large, 30″.	$8,000
Band Wagon, small, 22½″.	$3,500
Cage Wagon, blue, 9¼″.	$400
Cage Wagon, green, 9¼″.	$400
Cage Wagon, gray, 9¼″.	$650
Cage Wagon, monkey trapeze, medium.	$1,750
Cage Wagon, red.	$600
Cage Wagon, white.	$650
Calliope, 16″ length.	$2,500
Clown Trapeze, 16″ length.	$3,500
Giraffe Wagon, 16½″ length.	$3,500

Horse on Platform. $750
Hubley Farmer's Van. $4,000
Hubley Revolving Monkey Cage, 21½" length, four horses.
                                                          $30,000

Landau, Wilkins Toy Co., Keene, N.H., early 1900s, cast iron.
                                                           $5,500

Monkey on Tricycle, Hubley, 1932, cast iron w/rubber tires,
6½" height. $5,000

Oarsmen, U.S. Hardware Co., New Haven, Connecticut, pat.
1898, cast-iron racing shell, 9" length, a.k.a. Four Oar Marine
Crew. $2,500

Oarsmen, Varsity, U.S. Hardware, pat. 1898:
  Medium. $3,750
  Small. $1,500

"Pikes Peak" Covered Wagon, Ives, 1890s, cast iron.
                                                           $1,250

"Polar" Ice Wagon, Kenton, 1912. $1,250

"Pure Lake Ice Wagon," Harris Toy Co., cast iron. $3,750

Reindeer Sleigh (Oversized), Hubley Mfg., early 1900s. $37,500

Santa Claus Sleigh, Kyser & Rex, 1890s, pair of reindeer, Santa
under blanket piled with toys, 13" length. $3,500

Street Cleaner, Wilkins, 1890s, cast iron. $5,500

Spider Phaeton, Hubley Mfg., 1900s. $3,750

Sprinkler Wagon, Wilkins Toy Co.; 1895, cast iron and tin, 17"
length. $7,500

Tally-Ho, Carpenter Mfg. Co., New York City, patented 1880
(produced over 12-year span), four galloping horses, six passengers and driver, the ultimate cast-iron transportation toy known
as Coach #555, 26" length. $15,000

Two-Seated Brake, Hubley Mfg., 1900s (an example sold at
$8,000 at the Acevedo Sale of Bernard Barenholtz Collection in
1989). $6,000

Victoria Phaeton, Kenton Hardware, 1900s cast iron. $4,000

MOTOR TOYS

One of the largest categories in overall popular appeal among toy collectors is the vast assembly line of miniature motor toys produced in the United States or imported from Europe or Japan from 1894 to 1942, the generally acknowledged cut-off date for most purists. So sizable, so diversified, and so complex is the field, with its substrata of pleasure cars, trucks, taxis, buses, racers, tractors, cranes, and bulldozers—plus miniatures of the same—that each deserves a special guide all its own and, in fact, does often appear in published form. The ultimate in tunnel vision books is the recent opus on *Miniature Emergency Vehicles*. Arcade, Dent, Hubley, Kenton, Kilgore, and Wilkins all produced authentically detailed (down to the last hubcap and hood ornament) fleets of motor toys.

Advertising Motor Toys

Many of the more fascinating toys in the twentieth century could not be purchased in stores or through catalogs. They were advertising premium toys. Some were giveaways, while others required a coupon or set of box tops, along with a nominal payment. Jobbers often presented these toys to their dealers for special promotions and product introductions. Magazines and newspapers offered them as inducements to subscribe to their particular publication. Apparently produced in relatively limited quantities, they are eagerly sought by advertising collectors as well as motor toy specialists. Among major U.S. suppliers: Marx, NYC, New York, as well as Metalcraft of St. Louis, Missouri, with at least 30 different models in their "Business Leaders" series. Leading U.S. makers in cast-iron advertising vehicles were Arcade and Dent Hardware. Among European examples, those by Nuremberg makers' Tipp & Eberl, Hess, Bing, and Fischer are prized for their careful attention to detail, with nicely lithographed tin wind-ups of double buses and delivery vans.

Commercial Advertising Motor Toys

Advertising Trucks, Lindstrom, early 1930s, litho tin, cab: 3″ length, trailer: 3½″ length. Examples were known featuring large logos on trailer panel of Uneeda Biscuit, National Biscuit

Co., Palmolive Soap, Pep-O-Mint Lifesavers, Land O Lakes Sweet Cream Butter.   *$150–$200 each*

Advertising Limousine, Fischer, Germany, circa 1913, litho tin wind-up, sparkler mechanism in rear to simulate "backfire." Names of local mercantile stores were printed on roof, 8½" length.   *$300–$400*

Advertising Machinery Carrier With Baby Ruth Candies-Gum Steam Shovel, metalcraft, 1930–1931, pressed steel, carrier: 14½" length, steam shovel: 7" length, red, green, and black.
                                                      $750–$850

Bamberger's Delivery Truck, Eberl, Germany, circa 1910, litho tin wind-up, open-front truck with driver, "Bamberger's, Newark, N.J." on side panel, 7½" length, black, gold.   *$800–$900*

"Blue Diamond" (Road Contractors) Dump Truck No. 809, Smith-Miller Toy Co., Los Angeles, California, 1950s, pressed steel, with hydraulic lift and self-operating tailgate. *$400–$500*

Breyer's Ice Cream Panel Truck, Dent Hardware, 1930, cast brass, shows refrigerator doors at side, 8½" length, red, gold trim.   *$500–$600*

Bunte Candies Truck, Metalcraft, 1933, pressed steel, 12½" length.   *$400–$500*

Carr's Biscuits London Transport Bus, Chad Valley, circa 1950, double decker, litho tin, detachable top reveals supply of biscuits, 10½" length, red with yellow and black trim, white windows.   *$200–$300*

Citröen Pickup Truck, Citröen, France, circa, 1929 (based on Citröen C6 chassis, contained load of cloth sacks with Chevron logo, 17", yellow, black.   *$800–$900*

Coca Cola Delivery Truck, Metalcraft, 1928, pressed steel with rack for mini Coke bottles, 11" length, red, blue, white, redeemable via 6-pack Coke coupons, also came in two other sizes.
                                                      $600–$700

Crumpsall Cream Crackers Delivery Van, Chad Valley, Great Britain, circa 1948, litho tin novelty container, wind-up, 8¼", red, black, yellow, white tires.   *$200–$300*

Del Monte Quality Canned Fruits Double Decker Bus, German, mid–1930s, litho tin wind-up, 10½" length, black roof, red and yellow, "No. 2126" on radiator hood. $500–$600

Dewar's White Label Double Decker Bus, Lesney, Great Britain, die-cast miniature, 2¼" length, red, yellow. $100–$200

"Elsie's Dairy (Bordon) Van, Fisher-Price, 1948–1949, Beau-Re-gard, the driver, plays bell, 9¾" length, Elsie on side logo, clear milk bottles, wood, plastic. $50–$100

Esso Articulated Gasoline Tanker, Great Britain, mfg. un-known, (possibly Mettoy), 1940, litho tin wind-up, 8" length, yellow w/red trim. $300–$400

F.L. Cailler's Chocolates Double Decker Bus, Gunthermann, circa 1930, British style double decker with open cab, 9¼" length, red, blue, tan. $500–$600

Freeman's Dairy Truck, Dent Hardware, circa 1930, red, painted, cast iron (in addition to this Pennsylvania dairy, other company names appeared for use as premium, 5¾" length.
          $300–$400

Greyhound Scenicruiser, Japanese, 1960s, litho tin wind-up, 14½" length. $60–$70

Goodrich Silvertown Tires, Wrecker Metalcraft, 1931–1932, pressed steel, 12" length. $400–$500

Heinz 57 Varieties Delivery Truck, Metalcraft, 1933, pressed steel, 12" length, black, white, green, rubber tires. $500–$600

"Hessmobil" Limousine, J.L. Hess, late 1920s, friction, litho-graphed tin, 9" length, dark blue body, black roof and fenders, yellow trim. $900–$1,000

Hochchild, Kohn & Co. Delivery Van, Eberl, Germany, circa 1907, litho tin wind-up, Logo and "Baltimore's Best Store" slo-gan on side panel, 7" length, goldenrod and black w/silver wheels. $900–$1,000

Huntley & Palmer Six-Wheeled Bus, Great Britain, circa 1929, top lifts to reveal cookies, litho tin wind-up, double-decker with open cab, detail of passengers, 9½", red, blue, yellow.
          $300–$400

Junior Supply Co. Caged Truck With Driver, Dent Hardware, circa 1930, cast-iron caged body, opening rear doors, 15½" length, red w/gilt label, litho tin autovan, promoting a Boston firm, cut windows on either side of cab, barrel and spring mechanism.   *$650**

Kroger Truck, Metalcraft, 1929, pressed steel, 11⅛" length (redeemable through store coupons for each 25¢ spent at Krogers.)   *$600–$700*

Lincoln Transfer and Storage Co. Moving Van, Marx, 1928, litho tin wind-up with driver, 13" length.   *$400–$500*

London "News of the World" E-Class Tramcar, Lesney, Great Britain, die-cast metal miniature, 1956, 3" length, red, white top, yellow legend.   *$70–$100*

Moxie "Moxiemobile," maker unknown, 1917, built on a Dort automobile chassis, Moxie salesman astride horse (flat tin) straddles front and rear seats.   *$400–$500*

No. 92 E.A. Runnels Co. Delivery Van, Ferdinand Strauss, circa 1920.   *$350–$400*

"Philadelphia/New York Express" Truck, Dent, circa 1923, cast iron, 16" length, red.   *$3,000–$4,000*

Reading Novelty Co. (Reading, PA) Delivery Van, Strauss, circa 1913, litho sheet tin, 9¼" length.   *$550–$600*

Roi-Tan Cigars, "An Auto A Day Is Given Away," maker unknown (Chevrolet model), 1939, pressed steel, two-door sedan with logo on roof, side panel promotes Sophie Tucker Radio Show.   *$300–$400*

"Say It With Flowers," United States (possibly Arcade), 1920s, cast-iron motorcycle with side car, original box.   *$12,000***

Sentinel Rigid Steamwagons, six-wheeler steam lorry, Tipp & Co., Germany, 1930, litho tin wind-up, tipping body with hinged tailgate, 20" length, yellow, brown.   *$500–$600*

*Perelman Sale price realized.
**Price realized at Perelman Sale.

Shell, BP, and Pratts Gas Pump and Oil Cabinet Set, Tipp & Co., circa 1920, litho tin, battery-lit glass globes, 9½" length.
$450–$500

Shell Gasoline Tanker, probably Mettoy, Great Britain, 1940s, litho tin, 8", red, yellow.
$300–$400

Shell Oil Truck, Metalcraft, 1933, pressed steel, stake truck with small tin containers of Shell Oil, available through Shell jobbers, 12½" length, red cab, yellow truck body.
$500–$600

Shell Gasoline Tanker, Rossignol, 1920s, France, "Essence for Automobiles," tin wind-up, 8¼", red, black, yellow.
$500–$600

"Star Brand Shoes Are Better" Racer, maker unknown, 1930s. "The Winner" appears on rear assembly, free giveaway, which arrived folded flat in envelope, flat tin.
$75–$100

Strawbridge & Clothier Delivery Truck, Tipp & Eberl, Germany, circa 1905, litho tin wind-up, 7½" length, open cab.
$3,500*

Sunshine Biscuits Delivery Truck, Loose–Wiles Biscuit Company, 1933, 12½" length, red, yellow, black.
$400–$500

Victory Gums & Lozenges Bus, Hercules, tin litho, 18" length.
$200–$300

Virol Health Strength Double Decker Bus, Johann Distler, Germany, circa 1929, litho tin wind-up, top deck is open, marketed as "Fares Please" model; it features pressed tin, figure of conductor collecting fares.
$600–$700

White Motor Co., Cleveland, Metalcraft, 1928, "Towing & Repairs" embossed on top of radiator, sheet steel, 11½" length.
$550–$650

Wright's Coal Tar Soap "General" Double Decker Bus, Gebruder Bing, mid–1920s, litho tin wind-up, 7¼" length, red, yellow.
$600–$700

*Price realized at Perelman Sale.

Perelman Toy Museum

Advertising Specialty Toys

Jantzen "Beach Patrol Boy" and "Surf Girl," Hubley, 1932, cast-iron pull toys, 8″ height.   *$7,500 (the pair)*

"Old Dutch Cleanser" Pull Toy, Hubley, 1932, cast iron, embossed "Chases Dirt," 9″ height.   *$5,500*

Automobiles (1887–1950)

Cabrio Super (Convertible Coupe) Kellermann, Germany, 1914, blue, 9″ length.   *$100–$200*

Christmas Car, Tipp & Co., Germany, 1920s, litho tin wind-up, Father Christmas driver, detailed illustration of Christmas toys, illuminated (by battery) Christmas tree projects from rear trunk lid, multicolored, 12.2″.   *$1,500–$2,000*

Coupe, Kingsbury, 1929, tin mechanical, tan with red, brown trim, white rubber tires, 9″ length.   *$3,200**

De Dion Open Tourer, Gebruder Bing, 1912, mauve with orange detail, 9½″ length.   *$1,000–$1,500*

Delivery Van, Arcade, 1931, cast iron, rubber tires, red, 8½″ length.   *$700–$800*

Limousine, George Carette, circa 1911, lithographed tin, clockwork, headlamps, rubber tires, beveled glass windows, driver, three passengers, red with gold trim, 12″ length.

          $3,000–$4,000

Limousine, Karl Bub, circa 1918–1922, lithographed tin wind-up, opening doors, driver, open compartment for chauffeur, black and maroon, 13½″ length.   *$2,000–$2,500*

*Price realized at Perelman Sale, 1988.

Christmas Car, Tipp & Co., Germany, 1920s, $1,500–$2,000.

Live Steam Open Car, Weeden, circa 1910, handpainted tin, lead wheels, red body, black seat, stencilled flag, 9″ length.
$3,000–$4,000

Mercedes 220 Deluxe Saloon, #112, Tipp & Co., late 1920s, salmon red with cream roof, 13″ length. $2,000–$3,000

Model T Ford, Orober, 1920s, lithographed tin mechanical, soft top, black, 7 ½″ length. $400–$500

Open Front Sedan, Karl Bub, 1914, painted tin mechanical, red body, black top and spoked tires, 8″ length. $1,500–$2,000

Open Passenger Car, Fallows, patented 1887, spring mechanism, red w/black trim, 7″ length. $1,200–$1,500

Open Touring Auto, Gebruder Bing, circa 1904, lithographed tin, steel and brass clockwork, black with gilt and silver trim, 9″ length. $1,000–$2,000

Open Touring Auto, Jouets de Paris, circa 1920, clockwork with gearshift, lithographed tin, blue, black folding hood and fenders, gray tires, 14″ length. $1,500–$2,000

Open Touring Car With Two Seated Passengers, Carette, circa 1906, white with red and black trim, red lantern, 10½″ length. $5,000–$6,000

Panhard Levassor Sedan, Jep (France), circa 1929, key-wind mechanism, spotlight, horn, license plates, brown, black w/red piping, 13″ length. $1,500–$2,000

Phaeton Automobile With Woman Driver, Wilkins Toy Co., circa 1905, tin wind-up, cast-iron driver, blue with gilt trim, 9¼″ length. $1,000–$1,500

Roadster With Driver, Ives Blakeslee, circa 1898, painted cast iron with banistered seat, clockwork. $3,000–$4,000

Rolls Royce Coupe, Wells, England, circa 1935, lithographed tin mechanical, off-white w/black trim, silver grid and windshield, 9″ length. $1,500–$2,000

Sedan, Gebruder Bing, circa 1904, lithographed tin clockwork, blue, 9″ length. $1,000–$1,500

Sedan, Kingsbury, 1929, painted sheet-steel mechanical, rubber tires, black with pale blue hubcaps, white tires, 10½″ length. $3,200*

Stutz Bearcat, Structo, Freeport, Illinois, circa 1920, steel body, cast-iron steering wheel, clockwork, black, red, white, 15″ length. $600–$700

Superflex Limousine, Ingap, Italy, circa 1925, lithographed steel clockwork, lit headlamps, yellow w/red fenders, roof, gilt grille, insignia map of Italy appears on tires and grille, 11¼″ length. $2,000–$3,000

Touring Auto (Open) With Passengers, S. Gunthermann, circa 1903, painted tin clockwork, white with gilt and black trim, 8″ length. $6,500**

Touring Car, Bing, 1920s, lithographed tin clockwork, hand-brake, two-tone red and maroon body, gray top, yellow, aqua-

*Price realized at Perelman Sale.
**Price realized at Perelman Sale.

marine trim, 9 ½ ″ length.   *$600–$700*

Touring Car, Republic Tool Products Co., Dayton, Ohio, circa 1920, friction, with driver, pressed steel, pale blue, gilt trim, 12 ½ ″ length.   *$600–$700*

Automobiles, Tinplate, Post–World War II (1950–1980)

Dale Kelley's *Collecting the Tin Toy Car, 1950–1980*, clearly underscores the almost universal fascination with toy automobiles, particularly those scale model replicas of real-life road runners. The leading manufacturers in the post-war era, unquestionably, were the Japanese and European; the sleek, handsomely detailed motor toys already have achieved classic status.

Air Express, KIS, Chevrolet Van, lithographed tin, friction, 8″ length.   *$50–$75*

Airport Limo Bus, China, lithographed tin, friction, makes popping sound when activated, 15″ length.   *$50–$75*

Allied Van Lines, Linemar, lithographed tin, friction, 13½″ length.   *$50–$75*

Antique Deluxe Tourer, 1925, SSS, lithographed tin, friction, 10½″ length.   *$75–$100*

Armored Car, Savings Bank Van, SB, locking rear door, lithographed tin, 10″ length.   *$50–$75*

Arnold Convertible, BMW grille on convertible, painted tin windup, 10″ length.   *$200–$250*

Arnold Convertible, Cadillac grille on convertible, lithographed and painted tin, mechanical, 10″ length, composition passengers.   *$100–$150*

Arnold Convertible, Ford grille, painted tin, plastic windshield, 10″ length.   *$150–$200*

Arnold Convertible, Germany, Packard grille, painted tin windup, 10″ length.   *$200–$250*

Arnold Convertible, Primax, Packard grille, Germany, painted tin, remote control mechanical action, composition passengers, 10″ length. $150–$200

Benz Taxicab, Bandai, lithographed tin, battery operated, 10¼″ length. $100–$150

Buick, Japan, lithographed tin, friction, 11¼″ length.
                                                            $150–$200

Buick Alps, lithographed tin, friction, 10¼″ length.
                                                            $350–$400

Buick Century, Irco, lithographed tin, battery operated, friction, remote control. $75–$100

Buick, Ichiko, lithographed tin, friction, tin passenger figures, 11″ length, gold and chrome trim. $75–$100

Buick Orion, TN and Showa, Electromobile, painted tin, battery operated, 8¼″ length. $50–$75

Buick Riviera, Haji, lithographed tin, friction, removable roof, doors that open, plastic windows roll up and down, movable back seats, 11½″ length. $75–$100

Buick Riviera Highway Patrol, Bandai, lithographed tin, plastic, battery operated, antenna, 10¾″ length. $50–$75

Buick, TM-Y, lithographed tin, friction, 12″ length.
                                                            $300–$350

Buick, TN, lithographed tin, friction, with mechanical wipers, gold and chrome trim, 16″ length. $75–$100

Cadillac, Bandai, lithographed tin and plastic, battery operated, steering wheel actually steers, 13½″ length. $75–$100

Cadillac, Bandai, lithographed tin, friction, 11½″ length.
                                                            $100–$125

Cadillac Electricmobile, TN, lithographed tin, friction, battery-operated headlights, horn, and steering, gold and chrome trim, 13½″ length. $500–$550

Cadillac, Gama, Germany, lithographed tin, friction, 12½″ length. $400–$450

Cadillac, Ichiko, lithographed tin, friction, 19½″ length, gold and chrome trim. $150–$200

Cadillac Kingsize, Iwaya (Korea), lithographed tin, battery-operated lights, honking horn, 13 ½ " length.   *$50–$100*

Cadillac Playthings, Japan, lithographed tin, battery operated, copper and chrome trim, 9 ¾ " length.   *$50–$75*

Cadillac, San-Y, lithographed tin, friction, 11 ½ " length.
     $150–$175

Cadillac Special Convertible, Bandai, lithographed tin, die cast and flocked interior, friction, 17 ½ " length.   *$700–$800*

Cadillac, SSS, Tokyo, lithographed tin, friction, 17 ½ " length, two-tone green, red plastic taillights, opening hood.
     $100–$125

Camaro, Taiyo, lithographed tin, battery operated, 10 ½ " length, racing colors.   *$50–$75*

Chaparrel 2F, Alps, lithographed tin and plastic, battery operated, 11 ½ " length racing colors.   *$50–$75*

Chevrolet Bakery Delivery Van, Japan, lithographed tin, friction, 99 " length.   *$50–$75*

Chevrolet Bel Aire Station Wagon, Santa Brand ATC, lithographed tin, friction, 10 " length.   *$300–$350*

Chevrolet Corvair, HS, lithographed tin, friction, 9 ½ " length.
     $50–$75

Chevrolet Corvair, Y, lithographed tin and plastic, friction, 9 " length.   *$50–$75*

Chevrolet Corvette Highway Patrol, Taiyo, lithographed tin, battery operated, 10 " length.   *$50–$75*

Chevrolet Highway Patrol, Japan, lithographed tin, battery operated, 14 " length.   *$50–$75*

Chevrolet Impala, Bandai, lithographed tin, friction, 11 " length.   *$200–$250*

Chevrolet, Japan, lithographed tin, friction, 12 ½ " length.
     $50–$75

Chevrolet, Linemar, lithographed tin, friction, 11 ½ " length.
     $500–$600

Chevrolet, ST, lithographed tin, friction, 11 ½ " length.
     $100–$150

Chevrolet, TN, lithographed tin, friction, 10½" length.
$75–$100

Chrysler, Ichiko, lithographed tin, plastic drivers, 12" length.
$50–$75

Chrysler, TM, lithographed tin, friction, windows that open, 11½" length, gold and chrome trim. $500–$550

Continental Super Special, Cragston, lithographed tin, friction, mechanical wipers, jet exhaust system, 14" length.
$200–$250

Corvette, Yonezawa, Japan, 1958, orange and silver.
$600–$700

Ferrari, China, lithographed tin, friction, 9¾" length.
$50–$75

Firebird, Bandai, lithographed tin, friction, 10" length.
$50–$75

Firebird, Cragston, lithographed tin, plastic headlights, inflatable tires, 15" length. $50–$75

First 600, Bandai, lithographed tin, friction, with chrome trim, 7" length. $50–$75

Ford Airport Service—TWA, K, lithographed tin, friction, 13½" length. $75–$100

Ford Ambulance, ATC, lithographed tin, friction, 14" length.
$75–$100

Ford, Bandai, lithographed tin, battery operated, opening hood and rear deck, motor, 10¼" length. $50–$75

Ford, Bandai, lithographed tin, friction, folding front seats, 12" length. $200–$250

Ford Capri, Aoshin (for Kresge), lithographed tin, friction, with sound effects, 11" length, racing colors. $50–$75

Ford Convertible, THC, lithographed tin, friction, 12" length.
$100–$125

Ford Delivery Van, Bandai, advertising flowers, lithographed tin, friction, 12" length. $200–$250

Ford Edsel, Haji, lithographed tin, friction, 11″ length.
$650–$700

Ford English Yellow Cab Taxi, lithographed tin, friction, 10¼″ length. $75–$100

Ford Fairlane 500, THC (Japan), lithographed tin, friction, 11½″ length. $200–$250

Ford Fairlane Retractable, ATC, lithographed tin, friction, 14″ length. $125–$150

Ford GT 40 Swinger, Alps, lithographed tin, battery operated, 10″ length, racing colors. $50–$75

Ford Joustra, France, lithographed tin, friction, operating trunk lid and front seat backs, 12″ length. $250–$300

Ford Model T, Hot Rod, Japan, lithographed tin and plastic, battery operated. $50–$75

Ford Model T, Sunrise, lithographed tin and plastic, battery operated, 10¼″ length. $35–$45

Ford Mustang, racing colors, lithographed tin, battery operated, 10″ length. $50–$75

Ford Mustang Fastback, Bandai, lithographed tin and plastic, battery operated, 10″ length. $75–$100

Ford Mustang Fastback, Japan, lithographed tin, friction, 9½″ length, racing colors. $50–$75

Ford Mustang Fastback, Taiyo, lithographed tin, friction, 10″ length. $50–$75

Ford Mustang Fastback, TN, lithographed tin, friction, 15½″ length, racing colors. $75–$100

Ford Mustang Rusher Mach 1, Taiyo, lithographed tin, battery operated, 10″ length, racing colors. $50–$75

Ford San-Ly, lithographed tin, friction, gold and chrome trim, 11½″ length. $50–$75

Ford Secret Agent Car, TN, lithographed tin, battery operated, laser gun under hood, 9½″ length. $50–$75

Ford Standard Coffee Delivery Van, Bandai, lithographed tin, friction, 12″ length. $200–$300

Ford Station Wagon, TN, lithographed tin, friction, operable rear gate, 10¾" length. $250–$300

Ford T-Bird, Bandai, lithographed tin, friction, 11¼" length. $75–$100

Ford T-Bird Convertible, Germany, lithographed tin, friction, mechanical wipers, composition driver and dog, 13½" length. $200–$250

Ford T-Bird, Ichiko, lithographed tin, friction, 10¾" length. $50–$75

Ford, Y, lithographed tin, friction, includes special hubcaps, antenna, windshield, 12½" length. $250–$275

1915 Ford, Bandai, lithographed tin and plastic, friction, 7½" length. $50–$75

1917 Ford, Japan, lithographed tin and plastic, friction, 9" length. $50–$75

Jaguar, Arnold, Germany, painted tin, friction, remote control, 8½" length. $100–$200

Jaguar, Bandai, lithographed tin, friction, 9½" length. $250–$300

Jaguar E, lithographed tin, friction, 11½" length. $150–$200

Jaguar E, Thunder Chief Race Car, ASC. $75–$100

Jaguar GTX 753, lithographed tin, battery operated, 11" length. $75–$100

Jaguar Racing Car, China, lithographed tin, friction, racing sound when activated, 12" length. $50–$75

Jaguar Sports Car, TM, lithographed tin, friction, 7½" length. $100–$150

Jaguar, Sweden, lithographed and die cast, plastic, friction, 10½" length. $75–$100

Kar Kit, Toy Founders (Detroit, MI), die cast and plastic, makes four separate body styles, 11" length. $275–$300

Karma Ghia, China, lithographed tin, friction, 9½" length. $75–$100

Mazda Cosmo, TN, lithographed tin, friction, 14½" length. $50–$75

Mercedes Benz Dream Car, Japan, lithographed tin, friction, 8″ length, green plastic see-through roof.   *$75–$100*

Note: The following models are listed in numerical order:

Mercedes Benz 190SL, painted and lithographed tin, 9¼″ length.   *$75–$100*

Mercedes Benz 230 SL, ATC, lithographed tin, friction, 11″ length.   *$75–$100*

Mercedes Benz 250S, Daiya, lithographed tin, friction, 14″ length.   *$200–$300*

Mercedes Benz 250SE, Ichiko, lithographed tin, battery operated, 13½″ length.   *$100–$125*

Mercedes Benz 250SL, Bandai, lithographed tin, friction, 10″ length.   *$250–$300*

Mercedes Benz 280S, Polizei, Huki, Germany, lithographed tin, battery operated, remote control, 10½″ length.   *$400–$450*

Mercedes Benz 300 Sedan, JNF, Germany, lithographed tin, battery operated, die-cast door handle, hood ornament, electric lights, 9½″ length.   *$500–$600*

Mercedes Benz 300SL, Japan, lithographed tin, friction, 9½″ length.   *$50–$75*

Mercedes Benz 380SL, Gama, removable roof, opening hood, movable back seats, plastic, friction, 12½″ length.

$100–$125

Mercedes Benz 450SE, Hong Kong, plastic, battery operated, 10¼″ length.   *$50–$75*

Mercedes Benz Police Car, Easton, Taiwan, lithographed tin, battery operated, 10″ length.   *$50–$75*

Mercedes Benz Police Car, Gama, Germany, lithographed tin, molded plastic, battery operated, 9″ length.   *$50–$75*

Mercedes Benz Race Car #5, SH, lithographed tin, friction, 10½″ length.   *$325–$350*

Mercedes Benz Race Car #7, Marusan, lithographed tin, battery operated, 10″ length.   *$50–$75*

Mercedes Benz Race Car #8, San, lithographed tin, friction, 10″ length. $300–$350

Mercedes Benz Retractable Convertible, TT, lithographed tin, friction, 9½″ length. $50–$75

Mercedes Benz Sportswagon, Old Timer, SSK, Gama, Germany, plastic, friction, 8″ length. $50–$75

Mercury Convertible, Huki, lithographed tin, friction, movable headlamps, 14″ length. $275–$300

Mercury Cougar, Bandi, lithographed tin, battery operated, 10″ length. $50–$75

MGA 1600, ATC, lithographed tin, friction, with flocked seating compartment, 9½″ length. $110–$125

Nash Rambler, Bandai, lithographed tin, friction, 11″ length.
$50–$75

Nash Rambler, NK, Korea, lithographed tin, friction, 11″ length. $50–$75

Oldsmobile, Japan, patent information on rear license plate, lithographed tin, battery operated, 14″ length. $200–$250

Oldsmobile, Spain, lithographed tin and plastic, battery-operated remote control, 13″ length. $50–$75

Oldsmobile 80, TN, lithographed tin, friction, makes chugging sound, 7″ length. $50–$75

Oldsmobile 88, Japan, lithographed tin, friction, 13″ length, gold and chrome trim. $125–$150

Oldsmobile Highway Patrol, Ichiko, lithographed tin, battery operated, 13″ length, gold and chrome trim. $75–$100

Oldsmobile Station Wagon, KKK, Rosko, lithographed tin, friction, 9″ length. $50–$75

Oldsmobile Toronado, Bandai, lithographed tin, battery operated, 11″ length. $50–$75

Oldsmobile Toronado, Taiyo, lithographed tin, battery operated, 10″ length. $50–$75

Packard, Caribbean Convertible, "Gigant," Germany, 1952, lithographed tin, friction, 11½″ length, teal blue, rubber tires, turning wheels, battery-operated headlights. $125–$150

Packard, Conway, U.S., 1949, convertible, metal chassis and grille, hard plastic body and windshield, 11 ½ " length, yellow (as well as other colors) with red plaid seats.　　*$150–$200*

Packard Convertible (also came in several sedan body styles), Marusan (SAN), Japan, 1951, 1952, 16 ½ " length (considered to be one of the most desirable of all post-war automotive toys).　　*$1,500–$2,000*

Packard Convertible, Schuco, Germany, 1957, a maverick Studebacker with a Packard grille, painted tin, turning wheels, wind-up motor, 9 ¼ " length.　　*$350–$400*

Volkswagen Beetle, Germany, lithographed tin, friction, 16" length.　　*$300–$325*

Volkswagen Beetle, Taiyo, lithographed tin, battery operated, 9 ½ " length.　　*$50–$75*

Volkswagen Bus, Germany, lithographed tin, friction, opening side and rear doors, slide-back roof, 9 ½ " length.　　*$125–$150*

Volkswagen 53, Taiyo, lithographed tin, battery operated, 9 ½ " length, racing colors.　　*$50–$75*

Volkswagen Kingsize, Bandai, battery operated, lithographed tin and plastic, rear door, see-through engine, sliding sun roof, 14 ½ " length.　　*$150–$200*

Volkswagen Polizei Car, Taiyo, lithographed tin, battery operated, 9 ½ " length.　　*$50–$75*

Volkswagen, Two-tone, Taiyo, lithographed tin, battery operated, 9 ½ " length.　　*$50–$75*

Buses, Cast Iron

American Car and Foundry Bus, 1925, ACF logo, 11 ½ " length.　　*$500–$600*

Auto Bus, Kenton, 1929, painted in assorted colors and trim, 6 ½ " length:
  No passengers on top.　　*$400–$500*
  With passengers (8 ½ " length).　　*$500–$600*

Century of Progress Buses, 1933, cast iron, Greyhound logos on side, 6", 7 ⅝ ", 10 ½ " models, all cast as one piece.　　*$300–$400*

17-Passenger cross-country bus, Kingsbury, pressed steel, $550–$650.

City Bus, Kenton, 1927, assorted colors, 10″ length.
$600–$700

Coast-to-Coast Bus, Hubley, 1928, 13″ length, other sizes.
$650–$750

Double-Decker Bus, 1932, cast iron, red, green, blue with gold trim, nickeled tires, rubber tires optional extra, 11 ¼″ length.
$600–$700

Double-Decker Bus, 1936, cast iron, Chicago Motor Coach logo on top deck, may have been marketed exclusively in Midwest, 8 ¼″ length. $650–$750

Double-Decker Bus, 1938, cast iron, cab over engine model, includes three nickeled passengers, removable, 8″ length.
$750–$800

Double-Decker Yellow Coach Bus, 1926, cast iron, yellow, logo appears on top deck panel, 13 ⅓″ length. $350–$400

Feagol Safety Coach, 1925, cast iron, 12″ length. $200–$250

Great Lakes Expo Bus, 1936, cast iron, blue, white, silver, Greyhound logo stenciled on top, 11 ¼″ length. $600–$700

Inter-City Bus Coach, 1927, Kenton, painted and trimmed in assorted colors, 11″ length. $350–$450

Inter-Urban Bus, Dent, 1920, bright assorted colors, bronze trim, black enameled top, nickel-plated disc wheels with red centers, 10 ¾″ length, other sizes (also made in cast aluminum).
$400–$500

Interstate Double-Decker Bus, Strauss, late 1920s, $250–$300.

New York-Chicago Twin Motor Coach, Dent, 1920, finished in bright enameled colors, bronze trim, top is black enamel, nickel-plated disc wheels, red centers, 10″ length. $500–$600

New York World's Fair Sightseeing Bus, 1939, orange, 10½″ length, also featured several smaller sizes, 7″, 8″, 8½″ length sizes. $500–$600

New York World's Fair Sightseeing Bus, Tractor Version, pulled trailers, blue body, canopy is blue and orange stripes, orange seats, 4½″ length trailer, 3¾″ length tractor. $500–$550

Public Service Bus, Dent, 1920, assorted enamel color finish, gilt trim, black top, nickel-plated disc wheels, red centers, dual-type spare wheel attached to rear, 14¼″ length. $700–$800

Victory Gums and Lozenges Bus, Hercules, 1930s, 18″ length, $200–$300.

Pullman Railplane, mid-1930s, cast iron, 5″ length.
$300–$350

Short Line Bus, 1936, cast iron, local-type Pennsylvania Bus Co., 7¾″ length. $300–$400

Travel Coach, Hubley, 1932, 4¼″ length. $300–$400

White Bus, 1932, cast iron, green, red, blue, nickeled tires, 13¼″ length. $500–$600

Yellow Parlor Coach Bus, 1925, cast iron, Pennsylvania Rapid Transit logo (PRT), iron wheels, 13″ length. $600–$700

Emergency Motor Vehicles, Cast Iron and Pressed Steel

Aerial Ladder Truck, Kingsbury, 1930, ladder raises, 45″ height, 34″ length. $1,400–$2,000

Ambulance, Keystone, 1933, white flag with green cross is attached to radiator, 27½″ length. $500–$550

Auto Chemical Truck, Hubley, 1928:
   15″ length. $700–$800
   12¼″ length. $500–$600

Auto Hook and Ladder, Hubley, 1933, gong, 22″ length.
$400–$500

Auto Hook and Ladder, Hubley, 1934, red with gold striping, rubber tires, gong and two ladders, electric headlights, 11¾″ length. $250–$350

Auto Hook and Ladder, Kenton, 1929, three ladders and gong, 17″ length. $500–$600

Auto Hook and Ladder, Kenton, 1929, 8½″ length, other sizes. $150–$200

Auto Hose Wagon, Kenton, 1929, assorted colors with hose:
   7″ length. $150–$200
   9″ length. $175–$200

Chemical Truck, Kingsbury, 1930, 14″ length. $400–$500

City Ambulance, 1932, cast iron, white, also available in blue, 8″ and 6″ length sizes (smaller version appears in packaged fire toy set, circa 1935). $250–$300

Cast-iron fire rig toys. *Top row:* Hose Cart, Hubley, 1906, $800–$1,000; *second row:* Patrol Wagon, Hubley, 1906, $900–$1,100; *third row:* Ladder Wagon, Hubley, 1906, $900–$1,100; *bottom row:* Fire Station, Carpenter, $1,600–$1,800.

City Fire Dept., Steelcraft, 1933, red double-disc wheels, 29″ length. $350–$400

Fire Engine, Buddy "L," 1933, equipped with pressure pump and separate hose, 23½″ length. $600–$700

Fire Engine, 1928, cast iron, red, spoked wheels, 8″ length. $400–$450

Fire Engine, 1928, cast iron, red with gold trim, rubber disc wheels, driver, 9″ length. $350–$400

Fire Engine, En-Es, 1932, red and gold with rubber balloon tires, 23⅞″ length. $400–$500

Fire Engine, Kingsbury, 1930, 14″ length. $350–$400

Fire Engine, maker unknown, 1904, clockwork motor runs in circle or straight, with driver. $250–$300

Fire Engine, Schieble, 1932, red and gold hose reel, bell, rubber tires, and friction mechanical, 20″ length. $350–$450

Fire Ladder Truck, 1928, cast iron, red with gold trim, removable yellow ladders, rubber disc wheels, 12½″ length. $300–$350

Fire Pumper, 1920, red with gold and aluminum trim, nickel-plated bumper, gong, 13″ length, other sizes. $300–$325

Fire Pumper, Turner, 1926, red with gold trim, 22″ length. $400–$500

Fire Truck, Marx, 1949, siren, tower ladder, two 8″ ladders on side of truck, spring motor, tin, 14″ length. $100–$125

Friendship Pumper, 1890s, double hose plunger action, 15″ length, $700–$800.

Three horse-drawn fire-fighting rigs from Ideal Toy Catalog, early 1900s. Hook and Ladder, $550–$650; Hose Carriage, $650–$750; Fire Engine, $750–$850.

Ford Wrecker, Arcade, 1928, red truck with green crane, nickel-plated wheels, crane actually works, 6 1/8″ length and 5 1/4″ length sizes. $300–$400

"Heavy Transport," Fernand Martin, circa 1910, covered bed.
                                                         $400–$500

Hook and Ladder, Dent, 1920, bright red with ladders attached, nickeled wheels, 7″ and 5 1/2″ length sizes. $200–$300

Hook and Ladder, Dent, 1920, red with bronze trim, three 1 1/2″ wooden ladders painted yellow on red painted racks, 18 1/4″ length. $600–$700

Hook and Ladder, Dent, 1920 red with nickeled wheels, ladders attached, 6 7/8″ and 7 1/8″ length sizes. $250–$350

Hook and Ladder, Hubley, 1906, with three horses and driver, 14″ length. $1,000–$2,000

Hook and Ladder, Hubley, 1906, with two horses, driver:
   9 ½″ length. $900–$1,000
   13″ length. $1,000–$1,500

Hook and Ladder, Hubley, 1920, 17 ½″ length, three horses without gong, also 22″, 23″, 27 ½″, 28″, 29″, 35″ length sizes, each. $1,200–$1,400

Hook and Ladder, Turner, 1926, red with gold trim:
   27″ length. $500–$600
   16″ length. $400–$500

Hook and Ladder, Hubley, 1928, came with and without gong, 9 ¼″ length, other sizes. $200–$300

Hook and Ladder, Hubley, 1936, red with nickel chassis, radiator and ladders, 13″ length, other sizes. $250–$300

Hook and Ladder, Kenton, 1928, gong and ladders, 17″ length, other sizes. $500–$600

Hook and Ladder, Kenton, 1929, three galloping horses, with gong, nickel-plated body, 29″ length. $1,200–$1,500

Hook and Ladder, Kenton, 1929, three galloping horses, with gong, 32 ½″ length. $1,200–$1,500

Hook and Ladder, 1910, yellow, red stripes, driver and steersman, two 8″ ladders painted blue, 15″ length. $500–$600

Hook and Ladder, Steelcraft, 1933, red with solid rubber tires, reel, hose, nozzle, brass bell, and pull cord, 27 ¼″ length.
                                   $600–$700

Hook and Ladder, Structo, 1933, two 15″ extension ladders, bell, red and green headlights, 22″ length. $600–$700

Hook and Ladder Truck, Boycraft, 1931, red with gilt trim, two ladders, 18″ length. $400–$500

Hook and Ladder Truck, Kenton, 1927, gong and 4 ladders, 19 ½″ and 22″ length sizes. $600–$700

Hook and Ladder Truck, Republic, 1932, red trimmed in green striped with gold, 18″ length. $600–$700

Hose Cart, Hubley, 1906, cast iron, $1,000–$2,000.

Hose Cart, double-wheeled, Hubley, 1906, cast iron, $1,000–$1,200. (Opfer Auctions photo.)

Hose Cart, Kenton, 1929, cast iron, $500–$600. (Opfer Auctions photo.)

Hook and Ladder Truck, Wilkins, 1911, with gong, detachable horses, driver and steersman, 34″ length.   *$2,000–plus*

Hook and Ladder Truck, with gong, horses with galloping motion, driver and steersman, 34″ length.   *$1,000–$2,000*

Hose and Ladder Truck, Kenton, 1927, assorted colors, 6¼″ length.   *$300–$400*

Hose Cart, Kenton, 1929, three horses, with hose, 13″ length.   *$500–$600*

Hose Reel, Kenton, 1929, one horse, painted with hose, 14″ length.   *$600–$700*

Hose Truck, Kenton, 1927, assorted colors:
   6¼″ length.   *$200–$300*
   8¼″ length.   *$300–$350*

Hose Truck, Turner, 1935, hose reel, rubber hose and bell, green, red, and gold, 16″ length.   *$300–$350*

Hose Wagon, Kenton, 1929, two horses, painted, with gong, man and hose, 17″ length.   *$600–$700*

Ladder Truck, Dayton, 1932, red and gold, 30″ length.   *$500–$600*

Ladder Truck, Dent, 1920, red with gilt trim, nickeled wheels, two 10″ yellow wood ladders on blue racks, with gong bell, 14¼″ length.   *$600–$700*

Ladder Truck, Hubley, 1933, has gong, 13″ length.   *$300–$350*

Ladder Truck, Kingsbury, 1930, 11″ length.   *$350–$400*

Ladder Wagon, En-Es, 1932, red with gold trim, rubber balloon tires, 16¾″ length.   *$300–$400*

Mack Fire Apparatus Truck, 1928, red with gold ladders, firebell, driver, artificial hose, 21″ length.   *$600–$700*

Mack Motor Fire Truck, Dent, 1920, red with gilt trim, nickeled wheels with red centers, dual wheels in rear, two 10″ wood ladders, hose reel, nozzle, and two suction rubber pipes, 15″ length.   *$700–$800*

Mack Wrecker, Champion, circa 1930, red with rubber tires, 8½″ length, also 7″ length.   *$300–$400*

Packard Fire Engine, Turner, 1926, red and gold, rubber tires, 26 ¼ ″ length.   *$400–$500*

Pontiac Wrecker, Arcade, 1937, green, with nickel radiator, bumper, white rubber tires, red hubs, 4 ¼ ″ length.

$300–$400

Pumper, Dayton, 1932, red and gold, 22 ″ length.   *$500–$600*

Pumper, Dayton, 1932, red, green, and gold, 14 ½ ″ length.

$300–$400

Pumper, Hubley, 1928, 8 ″ length.   *$200–$300*

Pumper, Hubley, 1928, two horses, gong, 14 ″ length.

$300–$400

Pumper, Kenton, 1929, three horses, gong, gallop, lines, traces, and suction hose, painted with gold trim, 22 ″ length.

$1,200–$2,000

Pumper, 1937, cast iron, 4 ½ ″ length.   *$350–$400*

Pumper, Turner, 1935, red, green, and gold equipped with hose reel, two lengths of hose, and bell, 31 ″ length.   *$500–$600*

Pumping Fire Engine, Structo, 1933, large water tank with hose, brass nozzle, two ladders, bell, electric swivel spotlight is movable, red and green headlights with polished brass finish reflector, 22 ″ length.   *$550–$650*

Red Baby Wrecker, Arcade, No. 216, 1932, red body, nickeled supports, chain, hook man and crank, red disc wheels, green crane trimmed in gold, gold bronze headlights, nickeled tires or real rubber tires, two-wheeled jack, 12 ″ length.   *$600–$700*

Red Cross Ambulance, Kenton, 1929, nickel plated (also came painted in various colors), 16 ″ length.   *$1,000–$2,000*

Service Car, Hubley, 1932, 5 ″ length.   *$200–$300*

Turner Fire Department, 1926, house with red engines, 21 ″ length.   *$200–$300*

Turner Garage Set, 1926, 21 ″ length.   *$100–$150*

Water Tower, Hubley, 1920, over a dozen sizes, rarest is 26 ″ length, two horses and gong, or 29 ″ length, two horses, each.

$2,000–plus

Pumper, Hubley, 1906, cast iron, $1,000–$2,000. (Opfer Auctions photo.)

Wrecker, Dent, circa 1920, bright red with gilt trim, black enameled top, yellow wrecking gear mechanically operated, nickeled disc wheels with red centers, 10¼" length.

$400–$500

Wrecker, Hubley, 1933, two-color detachable body, rubber-tired wheels, red hubs, 6¼" length, also 5¼" length. $200–$300

Wrecker, Hubley, 1934, black chassis with light blue, red, or orange body, nickel radiator, 6" length. $200–$300

Wrecker, Hubley, 1934, two-color detachable body, rubber-tired wheels with red hubs and two spare tires, 6¼" length, also 5¼" length. $300–$400

One of the largest of Wilkins' horse-drawn ladder rigs, on exhibit at "Built to Last—The Toys of Kingsbury," at the New Hampshire Historical Society over Christmas, 1986. $700–$800.

Wrecker, Kenton, 1929, crank and cable with hook attached will raise "wrecked" toys to be towed, ratchet will hold "wreck" at any position desired, 10 ¼ " length. $400–$500

Perelman Toy Museum Sale, Police and Fire Patrol Toys

Ben Franklin Model Pumper, 1880s, painted tin. $8,500

Brownie Hose Reel, Wilkins, late 1890s, cast iron. $900

Brownie Pumper, Wilkins, late 1890s, cast iron. $2,000

Burning Building, Francis W. Carpenter, patented 1892, cast iron, firemen rescue occupants of burning house. $30,000

Chemical and Hose Patrol, Hubley, 1912, cast iron. $8,500

Chemical Wagon, Wilkins, circa 1900, chemical tank suspended in middle of rig, three horses. $2,000

Chief Cart, Wilkins, 1890s, cast iron. $3,800

Fire Engine House, maker unknown, 1870s, painted tin. $12,000

Fire House, Ives, 1893, mechanical, bell strikes ten times and doors fly open, engine emerges, cast iron. $5,000

Fire Patrol, Kenton, 1911, cast iron. $2,750

Fire Station and Pump, Kingsbury, cast iron. $1,500

Hook and Ladder, Welker & Crosby, 1890s, cast iron. $12,500

Hose Cart, Kenton, 1911, cast iron. $4,200

Hose Reel, Dent, 1910, cast iron. $3,000

Hose Reel, Wilkins, cast iron. $2,500

Hose Reel, Welker & Crosby, 1890s, cast iron. $12,500

Hose Reel, George Brown, 1870s, oversized, painted and stencilled tin. $32,500

Ladder Wagon, Pratt & Letchworth, 1890s, white horses (mint). $6,000

Ladder Wagon #126, Hubley, 1906, cast iron. $2,200

2nd Regiment Red Cross Ambulance, bell toy, Kenton, $1,000–$2,000. ($2,100 at Perelman Sale; Opfer Auctions photo.)

Live Steam Pumper, Weeden, 1890s, tin and brass.   *$11,500*

Phoenix Pumper, Ives, 1880s, painted tin clockwork.   *$1,250*

Police Patrol, Kenton, 1911, cast iron.   *$2,200*

Pumper, Pratt & Letchworth, 1890s, cast iron.   *$1,000*

Pumper, Dent, 1890s, tandem, oversized, cast iron.   *$4,000*

Pumper, Wilkins, 1890s, oversized, cast iron.   *$3,750*

Pumper #53, Carpenter, 1880s, cast iron.   *$2,500*

Red Cross Ambulance, 2nd Regiment, Kenton, 1929, drawn by two white horses, cast iron.   *$2,200*

Red Cross Ambulance, 7th Regiment, Kenton, 1929, cast iron.
$1,750

Water Tower, Wilkins, circa 1900, double horses, oversized, cast iron.   *$5,000*

Farm and Construction Vehicles

Auto Dump Wagon, 1920, cast iron, number 675 embossed on driver's side, red and gold, later models green and red (toy was a big seller into the 1930s), sand shovel included, 7″ length.
$400–$500

Avery Tractor, 1929, name embossed below engine, green and red, 4½″ length.   *$250–$300*

Caterpiller Tractor, 1928, cast iron with operator, pull toy, "Ten" embossed on side of radiator denotes 10 HP, 7½" length. $300–$400

Contractor's Dump Wagon, 1915, features logo of Ellis Tiger Co., Gladstone, New Jersey, 14½" length. $400–$500

Farmall Tractor, 1928, cast iron, green, red, nickeled farmer, lug wheels, 6" length. $250–$300

Farmall Tractor, 1932, cast iron, gray with gold, red wheels, 6" length. $200–$250

Ford Dump Truck, 1928, red cast iron, green disc wheels or rubber wheels:
  6" length. $200–$250
  7½" length. $250–$300

Ford Dump Truck, 1941, 6½" length (this and the International Pick-Up were the last cast-iron toys produced by Arcade). $400–$500

Fordson Tractor, 1924, cast iron, red and gray, cleated rear wheels, nickeled steering wheel, and removable driver, 4¾", 5", or 6" length. $200–$250

Fordson Tractor, 1928, cast iron, smooth wheels, 6" length. $150–$200

Hay Rack, 1930, cast iron, red and green, removable rack, 15" length. $200–$300

Industrial Caterpillar Derrick, 1932, cast iron, two models, one with four wheels, one with treads, 4½" length × 11" height. $1,000–$2,000

International Dump Truck, 1930, cast iron, dual wheels, 10¾" length. $300–$400

International Harvester "K" Line Dump Truck, 1941, cast iron, dual rear wheels and heavy duty coil spring, 11" length. $300–$350

John Deere Combine, 1930, cast iron, silver trimmed green with gold lettering, yellow wheels, many revolving parts, operator, 16" length. $400–$450

John Deere Gas Engine, 1930, green with gilt lettering, flywheel silver, front wheels pivot, 5½" length. $150–$200

John Deere Manure Spreader, 1930, cast iron, red with gold trim and lettering, yellow wheels, green beaters, hooking tongue for rear attachment to tractor, 16 1/4 " length. $400–$500

John Deere Tractor, 1930, cast iron, green with gold lettering, yellow wheels, nickeled flywheel, pulley and driver, silver steering wheel, 6 1/2 " length. $300–$400

John Deere Utility Wagon, 1930, cast iron, red, green with gold trim, removable wagon box, 15 " length. $250–$300

Mack Dump Truck, 1925–1930s, cast iron (the best selling Mack that Arcade produced), disc wheels, painted wheels, or at extra charge rubber tires, Mack emblem embossed on door panel, 12 " length. $600–$700

Mack High Dump Truck, 1930s, cast iron, thumb lever opens truck bed gates, nickeled wheels, "Coal" often appears stenciled on truck bed, 8 1/2 " length. $500–$600

Mack Hoist Truck, 1928, green and red, revolving cab, solid rubber disc wheels, nickeled chain, crane and driver, 13 " length. $700–$800

Mack Side Dump Truck, 1928, red-yellow, nickeled driver, solid rubber or disc wheels, cast iron, 9 " length. $300–$400

McCormick Deering Plow, 1925–1930, cast iron, red and yellow, silver moldboard, shares, and coulters, 7 3/4 " length.
                                                        $100–$150

McCormick Deering Thresher, 1928, cast iron, gray with red trim, cream-colored wheels, 12 " length, 18 " length with stacker and feeder extended. $300–$400

McCormick Deering Thresher, Arcade, 1929, cast iron, 13 1/2 " length. $400–$500

McCormick Deering Thresher, 1929, cast iron, red, green, or blue, gold trim and logo, movable grain spout and stacker, nickeled wheels, 9 1/2 " length. $300–$400

McCormick Deering Thresher, 1930, cast iron, aluminum trimmed, green and gold lettering, yellow wheels, nickeled pulley and flywheel, many parts removable, 20 1/2 " length.
                                                        $500–$600

McCormick Deering Tractor, Arcade, 1925, cast iron, plows, rakes, etc., can be attached, gray, gold trimmed, red wheels, 7 ¼" length. $300–$400

McCormick Deering Weber-Wagon, Arcade, 1925–1930, horse drawn, cast iron, Deering logo embossed in both wagon thresher and tractor. $300–$400

Oliver Plow, 1928, cast iron, attaches to Fordson tractor, 5 ¾" length. $100–$125

"Red Baby" Dump Body Truck, 1928, cast iron, red, 10 ¾" length. $300–$400

Road Construction Set, 1930s, 7" × 11" box contains 12 components, including tractor and cart, truck, wheelbarrow, road signs, picks, shovels. $400–$500*

Road Roller and Scraper, Arcade, 1932, cast iron, 16" length. $600–$700

Road Scraper, 1932, cast iron, green with red wheels, swing-over dump box, 8 ¼" length. $400–$500

Sandloader, mid-1920s, cast iron and pressed steel, 8 ½" length. $500–$600

Sand Loading Shovel, 1928, cast iron and pressed steel, rubber disc wheels, nickeled chain and levers, 12 ½" length. $900–$1,000

Side Dump Trailer, 1932, red chassis, cast iron, green dumper, nickeled wheels, dumps either side, 7" length. $300–$400

Steam Roller, 1929, green, red with gilt trim, cast iron, nickeled wheels and roller, plus operator, 7 ¾" length. $700–$800

Tractor, 1937, Arcade, cast iron, green with red hubs, rubber tires. $350–$400

Tractor and Trailer, 1928, cast iron, lug back wheels, 12 ½" length. $250–$300

Truck Trailer, 1928, cast iron, removable sides. $100–$200

White Dump Truck, 1929, cast iron, green, red, or blue, nickel-plated wheels, rubber tire wheels extra, 11 ½" length. $300–$400

*Set with original box sold for $425 at Lloyd Ralston Auction in 1981.

"*Yellow Baby*" *Dump Truck*, mid-1930s, cast iron, "Yellow Baby" appears on cab door, "International Harvester" on truck bed, possibly a promotional piece, "The Red Baby" re-christened, yellow, 10¾" length. $300–$400

Motorcycles

Harley, Hubley, 1933, assorted colors, 5¼" length.
                                                      $250–$300

Harley-Davidson Cycle, Hubley, 1928, with two men, 9" length. $500–$600

Harley-Davidson Hill Climber, Hubley, 1932, olive, blue, or orange demountable rider, 8½" length. $700–$800

Harley-Davidson Motorcycle and Side Car, Hubley, 1936, cycle painted red, side car light blue with white rubber tires, 5¼" length, also 6½" length. $300–$400

Harley-Davidson Side Car Motorcycle, Hubley, 1932, painted olive green, 5¼" length, also 6½" length. $300–$400

Harley-Davidson Solo Motorcycle, Hubley, 1932, olive, blue, or orange, rubber tires, demountable rider, motor exhaust, came with either spot rider or cop, 9" length, also 4½" length.
                                                      $700–$800

Indian Armored Car, Hubley, 1932, painted red, rubber tires, exhaust sound, two demountable cops and removable armor plate, 8½" length. $700–$800

Indian Crash Car, Hubley, 1932, painted green cycle with red body, came with hose and reel and gasoline cans, 10" length.
                                                      $800–$900

Indian Delivery, 1933, "Say It With Flowers," painted in light blue with black top, rubber tires, separate rider, motor exhaust, rear door, 10¼" length. $2,000–plus

Indian Side Car Motorcycle, Hubley, 1932, red rubber tires, two demountable riders, imitation exhaust sound, 9" length.
                                                      $600–$700
    With sports figures instead of cops, 9" length. $700–$750

Indian Solo Motorcycle, Hubley, 1932, painted red, yellow, or green, rubber tires, demountable rider, motor exhaust, came with cop or sport rider, 9" length. $500–$600

Indian Traffic Car, Hubley, 1932, painted red and blue, 12″ length. $600–$650

Indian Traffic Car, Hubley, 1933, assorted colors, 6¼″ length, also 3⅜″ length. $300–$400

Motorcycle, Champion, 1930, enameled blue with gold trim, rubber tires, 4¼″ length, other sizes. $150–$200

Motorycle, Hubley, 1933, painted red with rubber tires, exhaust sound and demountable cop, featured electric headlight, 8½″ length. $300–$325

Motorcycle, Hubley, 1934, painted red, dark blue, or orange, electric headlight, 6½″ length. $250–$300

Motorcycle Cop, Hubley, 1928, with two men, 9″ length, other sizes. $400–$500

Motorcycle Cop With Side Car, Champion, 1930, motorcycle and officers enameled blue, side car enameled red, air-cushion rubber tires, 6½″ length, also 5″ length. $250–$350

Motorcycle With Side Car, Hubley, 1928, 4″ length.

$200–$250

Parcel Post Harley-Davidson, Hubley, 1928, 10″ length.

$600–$700

Side Car Motorcycle, Hubley, 1933, red with gold striping, rubber tires, exhaust sound and demountable cop, electric headlight, 8½″ length. $500–$550

"Speed" Cycle, Hubley, 1933, came in various colors, 3¼″ length, other sizes. $100–$150

Tandem Cycle, Hubley, 1936, painted assorted colors, 4⅛″ length. $200–$250

Pleasure Cars

Arcade

Buick Sedan, 1938, aluminum bronze headlights, Buick logo embossed on radiator, 8½″ length. $1,200–$1,400

Chevrolet Coupe, 1925–1928, also provided a companion sedan, cowl parking lights, disc wheels, 8¼″ length.

$900–$1,000

Chevrolet Coupe, 1928, yellow, blue, red, gray, approximately 12″ length.   *$1,000–$1,200*

DeSoto Sedan, 1937–1938, blue with white bumpers, 4″ length (part of Arcade's Miniature series).   *$250–$300*

Ford Coupe, 1932, red, green, blue, spoked wheels, 5″ length.
                                                                $250–$300

Ford Coupe, 1932, red, green, blue, spoked wheels, 5½″ length.   *$300–$350*

Model A, 1928, red, green, blue, yellow, featured rumble seat, 6¾″ length.   *$700–$800*

Model A Sedan, 1928, Tudor model, orange, 6¾″ length.
                                                                $700–$800

Model A Sedan, 1928, 4-door model, red.   *$700–$900*

Model T Ford Four-door Sedan, 1924, spoke wheels, dubbed the "Tin Lizzie," black, 6½″ length:
  Small size.   *$400–$450*
  Large size.   *$600–$700*

Pontiac Sedan, 1937–1938, miniature, 4½″ length.
                                                                $350–$400

Pontiac Sedan, 1937–1938, 6½″ length.   *$450–$500*

Runabout Auto, 1908–1910, wood, pressed steel, cast iron, with nickeled driver, 8¾″ length (possibly first auto off Arcade's assembly line).   *$400–$450*

Champion

Auto Coupe, 1930, red, green, or blue, air cushion-type rubber tires, rear spare tire, 4¼″ length.   *$250–$300*

Coupe, 1930, red, green, or blue enamel, air cushion-type rubber tires, rumble seat and spare tire, 7½″ length.   *$300–$350*

Sedan, 1930, red, green, or blue enameled finish with air cushion-type rubber tires, spare tire at rear of car, 4½″ length.
                                                                $100–$200

Dent

Coupe, 1920, finished in bright colors with nickeled disc wheels, 5⅜″ length (car also came in cast aluminum).   *$200–$250*

Coupe, 1920, 6¼" length × 3¾" height. $250–$300

Roadster, 1920, bright assorted colors, nickel-plated disc wheels, 4⅞" length. $100–$150

Sedan, 1920, bright colors, black enamel top, nickel wheels with red centers and spare wheel, 7½" length, other sizes (4½" size also came in cast aluminum). $300–$350

Sedan, 1920, finished in bright colors, gilt trim, black enameled top with nickel wheels, 6½" length (also made in cast aluminum). $250–$300

Harris

Roadster, 1903, cast iron mechanical, 7½" length. $1,000–$1,500

Hubley

Airflow DeSoto, 1934, assorted colors, nickel-plated radiator, bumper and windshield, with electric headlights, 3¼" length. $400–$500

Chrysler, 1936, 6¼" length. $200–$300

Chrysler Airflow, 1936, painted various colors, nickel-plated radiator, bumpers and windshield, came with electric headlights, 8¼" length, also 6¼" length size. $400–$500

Chrysler Roadster, 1936, assorted colors with electric headlights, 7½" length. $200–$300

Chrysler Sedan, 1936, assorted colors, electric headlights, aluminum radiator, bumpers, running board, spare tire, 6½" length. $300–$400

Chrysler Sedan, 1936, assorted colors, electric headlights, 7¼" length. $400–$450

Chrysler Town Car, 1936, assorted colors, electric headlights, 7½" length. $400–$450

Coupe, 1933, two-color detachable body, rubber-tired wheels with red hubs, 6¼" length. $200–$300

Coupe, 1934, black chassis, light blue, red, or yellow body, contrasting color top, 6" length. $200–$300

Traffic Jam of Miniature Airflow Autos. Key: (1) 1934 Chrysler, Arcade; (2) Chrysler, Japan, 1934 tinplate; (3) Sedan w/wooden wheels, Marx; (4) Chrysler 1934–1935 slush; (5) DeSoto sedan, Sun Rubber, 1934; (6) 1934 Chrysler sedan; (7) Japanese copy of GNOM; (8) Chrysler, Hubley, 1934; (9) Champion sedan (eight windows); (10) DeSoto sedan, Barclay, 1935; (11) Tinplate 1934 Chrysler; (12) Lehmann GNOM, 1934 Chrysler; (13) Tinplate 1934 Chrysler, Japan; (14) Lehmann GNOM; (15) Glass candy container; (16) Tinplate bus w/passenger, unmarked; (17) Champion sedan, six windows; (18) Chrysler, Williams, 1935; (19) Chrysler coupe, Hubley, 1934; (20) Chrysler, Japan, 1934; (21) Town & Country sedan, Chein; (22) Streamline sports convertible, Minic; (23) Chrysler sedan, clockwork, Chein, 1935; (24) Hard rubber 1935 Chrysler coupe; (25) Coupe, Hubley; Hard rubber 1934 Chrysler Coupe; (26)

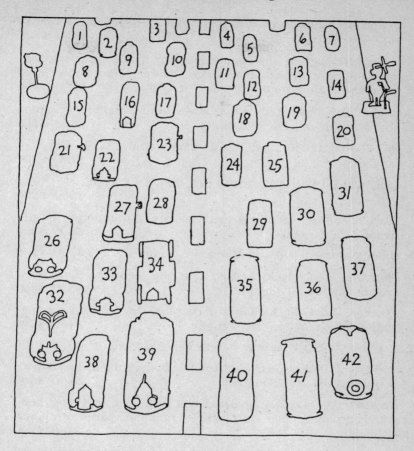

Coupe, Hubley; (27) Chrysler sedan, Japan, 1934; (28) Hard rubber 1934 DeSoto sedan; (29) Streamline sedan, Minic; (30) Coupe, Hubley; (31) 1935 coupe, Williams (repaint); (32) Roadster, cast iron, Hubley; (33) DeSoto sedan, Arcade, 1934; (34) Fenderless tinplate sedan, Japan; (35) Chrysler coupe, Dent, 1934; (36) Sedan, Marx; (37) Chrysler sedan, National Prod., 1934; (38) Chrysler sedan, Dent, 1934; (39) Chrysler sedan, Hubley, 1934; (40) Chrysler sedan, Williams, 1934, 7″ length; (41) Chrysler roadster, Dent, 1934; (42) Chrysler sedan, Hubley, 1934. (Photo by Joel Weissman; sketch by John West; copyright *Antique Toy World*, May 1989.)

Coupe, 1934, black chassis, light blue, red, yellow, or orange body, 3¾" length.   *$100–$200*

Coupe, 1934, green chassis, orange body with contrasting color top, aluminum finish on radiator and bumper, black rubber-tired wheels with aluminum hubs, 6½" length.   *$200–$250*

Coupe, 1936, assorted colors, silver bronze radiator, running boards, bumpers, 4¼" length.   *$100–$150*

Hill Climber, 1936, light blue and black trim, 6¼" length.
$150–$200

Limousine, 1920, gray-striped cast iron, 8¼" length.
$300–$350

Lincoln Zephyr, 1936, assorted colors with aluminum bronze radiator, 6" length.   *$300–$400*

Open Roadster, 1938, cast iron, 4½" length.   *$100–$200*

Phaeton, 1934, black chassis, light blue, red, or yellow body, contrasting top, 6" length.   *$350–$400*

Phaeton, 1934, black chassis, light blue, red, yellow, or orange body, nickel radiator, 3¼" length.   *$150–$200*

Roadster, 1920, cast iron with driver, 8½" length. *$300–$400*

Roadster, 1933, two-color detachable body, rubber-tired wheels with red hubs, 6¼" length.   *$200–$300*

Roadster, 1934, black chassis, light blue, red, or yellow body with contrasting color seat, nickeled radiator, spare tire on rear, 6" length.   *$150–$200*

Roadster, 1934, painted light blue, light green or red with aluminum radiator and bumper, six black rubber-tired wheels with aluminum hubs, detachable body, 6½" length.   *$200–$250*

Roadster, 1936, assorted colors with aluminum bronze radiator, running boards and bumpers, 6⅝" length, other sizes.
$150–$200

Sedan, 1933, two-color detachable body, rubber-tired wheels, red hubs, 5" length, other sizes.   *$150–$200*

Sedan, 1934, black chassis, light blue, red, or yellow body, contrasting color top, nickel radiator, 6" length.   *$250–$300*

Straight-eight Packard sedan, Hubley, $2,000 plus. (Photo courtesy of Phillips Auctions.)

Sedan, 1934, black chassis, light blue, red, yellow, or orange body, nickel radiator, 3 1/4" length. $125–$150

Sports Roadster, 1932, 4 3/4" length. $150–$200

Station Wagon, 1933, two-color detachable body, rubber-tired wheels, red hubs, 6 1/4" length. $350–$400

Studebaker Sedan, 1936, painted various colors, with aluminum bronze radiator, running boards and bumpers, spare tire on rear of car, 5" length. $250–$350

Town Car, 1936, assorted colors, aluminum bronze radiator, running boards and bumpers, 6 5/8" length, other sizes
$350–$400

Kenton

Auto Cab, 1929, 8" length, other sizes. $700–$800

Auto Roadster, 1929, 7 1/2" length, other sizes. $250–$300

Auto Touring Car, 1929, painted and trimmed in various colors, 9 1/4" length. $800–$900

Auto Touring Car, 1929, painted in assorted colors and trim, 9 1/4" length. $800–$900

Coupe, 1929, 8 1/2" length. $400–$500

New Model Coupe, 1929, detachable wheel, 10″ length.
$600–$700

Roadster, 1929, painted and trimmed in assorted colors, 8 ½″ length.
$700–$800

Sedan, 1929, assorted colors with extra detachable wheel, 10″ length, other sizes.
$650–$700

Sedan, 1929, various colors with extra tire and red and green lights showing in rear of car, 3 ¼″ length, other sizes.
$400–$450

Yellow Taxi, 1929, 6 ½″ length, other sizes. $400–$500

Kilgore

Open Ford Roadster, 1929, 3 ½″ length. $200–$250

Williams

Coupe, 1934, red, blue, green, and tan with rubber tires, nickeled rumble seat, 5 ¼″ length. $150–$200

Makers Unknown

Packard, 1930, hood and front doors open, rubber balloon tires, driver, 11″ length. $1,200–$1,500

Roadster, 1929, blue, imitation spare tire, nickeled driver and wheels, 9 ⅛″ length. $300–$350

Sedan, 1910, red striped with gold and silver, 8″ length.
$400–$500

Sedan, 1924, red and black with chauffeur, 12″ length.
$250–$300

Racers

A. C. Williams Co.

Racer, 1932, cast iron, yellow with red hubs and rubber tires, two passengers, built long and low to the ground, 8 ½″ length.
$300–$400

AO (France)

Racer, circa 1900s, painted tin clockwork, red with gold trim, this ingenious car speeds along, then completely falls apart, 7.9″ length (Blondinat [France] made a similar version).

$1,000–$1,200

Arcade Manufacturing Co.

Bullet Racer, 1928, cast iron, blue, red, green rubber disc wheels, 7⅝″ length. $350–$400

Bullet Racer, 1932, cast iron, red, green, yellow, with or without rubber tires, nickeled wheels, 8½″ length. $300–$350

Racer, 1932, cast iron, red, green, blue, 3¼″ length.

$200–$250

Racer, 1935–1936, cast iron, red, silver, blue, two drivers, known as the #1440, 8″ length. $400–$450

Champion Hardware Co.

Racer, 1930, cast iron, front bumper and tail fin, rubber tires, red car with blue driver, 8½″ length. $300–$350

Dayton Toy and Specialty Co.

Racer, 1932, cast iron, red body with gold trim, 11″ length.

$300–$400

Georges Carette

Racing Car #3, 1920s, lithographed tin clockwork, 12½″ length (rare classic). $2,000–$3,000

Greppert Kelch (GK), Germany

Racing Car, 1910s, painted tin, red, 5½″ length. $700–$800

Hubley Manufacturing Co.

Golden Arrow Racer, 1929, tail fin, nickeled wheels (popular for over 7 years), 6¾″ length, made in several other sizes.

$300–$400

Racer No. 1, 1932, cast iron, assorted colors, 8″ length.
$300–$400

Racer, 1933, cast iron, tail fin in 6¾″ length and 8¼″ length.
$250–$300

Racer, 1933, cast iron, without tail fin, 6¾″ length.
$200–$250

Racer, 1934, cast iron, pale blue, red, or orange, electric headlights, without tail fin, 6½″ length. $250–$300

Racer, 1934, orange or red with silver radiator, tail fin, rubber tires. $200–$300

Racer, 1934, assorted colors, with electric headlights, raised hood feature to replace battery, rubber tires. $300–$350

Racer, 1934, silver with red trim, 5¼″ length. $150–$200

Kenton Hardware Co. (Jones and Bixler)

Racer, 1929, silver finish, 5½″, 6½″, and 7½″ length.
$300–$400

Sport Racer, 1925–1927, cast iron, assorted colors, sizes, 7″, 9″, 10¼″ length. $250–$300

Track Racer, No. 8, 1927, cast iron, sizes 7″, 9″, 10¼″ length, assorted colors, more compact, higher off wheels version with doors and step. $300–$400

Kingsbury Manufacturing Co.

Auto Racer, Kingsbury, circa 1919, clockwork aluminum with bell, silver and gilt with orange and green stripes, 9½″ length.
$1,000–$1,500

Bluebird Racer, 1930, pressed steel, disc wheels, rubber tires and bumper, clockwork, 8″ length. $600–$700

Golden Arrow Racer, 1929, pressed steel, bright gold (also red versions), spring motor, rubber tires, 21″ length (exact replica of racer driven by Major Seagrave, world's fastest driver in 1929). $700–$800

Mystery Sunbeam Racer, 1929, pressed steel, bright red finish, tag that originally came with toy indicates Major H. O. Seagrave is at wheel, 19″ length (based on model of actual racing car which set world's land speed record in 1927, futuristic even by today's standards). $600–$700

Napier Campbell Bluebird II, Kingsbury, 1930, tin, clockwork, land speed record racer, driver, rubber tires, light blue, silver, 18½″ length. $1,000–$1,500

Louis Marx

Giant King, 1929, lithographed tin wind-up, has No. "11" on radiator, "7–11" on driver's door panel, available in three colors, 12½″ length. $250–$300

Racer, 1930, lithographed tin wind-up, has "61" on door panel, 5½″ length. $75–$100

Sparks Auto Racer, 1929, lithographed tin wind-up, multicolor, shoots sparks from rear, runs straight or in circles, 8½″ length. $200–$300

Speed King Racer, 1929, lithographed tin wind-up, yellow with red trim, rocket-like contour, "Speed King" appears in bold black letters in engine cowling, 16″ length. $300–$350

Stutz Racer, 1929, lithographed tin wind-up, available in three colors, 16″ length. $300–$400

Pinard (France)

Delage Racer, 1900s, painted tin, 12.2″ length. $700–$800

Racer, 1900s, painted tin, blue, battery-powered spot lamp, 11″ length. $400–$500

Racer, 1900s, painted tin, deep green with gold trim, 15.7″ length. $500–$600

Racer, 1900s, painted tin, light blue, 8.6″ length. $400–$425

Racer No. 4, 1900s, painted tin, yellow, electric headlamp, 13″ length. $600–$700

Note: All the Pinard racers above are long-running clockwork models.

Rossignol

Racing Car, late 1930s, lithographed tin wind-up, modeled on a Peugeot, 15" length. $500–$600

S. G. Gunthermann (Germany)

Gordon Bennett Racing Car, 1920s, lithographed tin clockwork, tan with gold trim, silver headlamps, rubber-rimmed spoke wheels, small squeeze horn, many deem this the gem of all racing toys, 11.8" length (this race car also came in 5.9", 6.3", 7.1" and 8.5" sizes; the 6.3" blue version is rated the most uncommon of all). $2,000–$3,000

Race Car No. 5, 1920s, lithographed tin, clockwork runabout, "No. 5" appears on radiator, 8.7" length. $1,000–$1,500

Structo Manufacturing Co.

Auto Builder No. 8, 1915, pressed steel, green with red spoked wheels, 12 ½" length. $600–$700

Bearcat Racer, 1920s, pressed steel and cast iron, clockwork, 12 ¼" length. $700–$800

Tipp (Germany)

#32 Race Car, Tipp, Germany, 1920s, lithographed tin wind-up with driver. $900–$1,100

Vindix (National Sewing Machine Co.)

Racer, 1928, cast iron, red, yellow wheel hubs, "2" embossed on side, 11" length. $600–$700

Wilkins Toy Co.

Racer, 1911, cast iron and pressed steel, silver finish with red striping, clockwork motor, driver in yellow, rubber tires, 10" length (the classic among early race cars). $1,000–$1,500

Racer, 1912, pressed steel, 9 ¼" length (what looked like a casket on wheels sold successfully over five years in the Wilkins line). $700–$800

Miscellaneous

Hiller Comet Racing Car, 1930s, gas engine, sheet metal, blue body, original decals with "4" and HC logo, 18" length.
$500–$600

Oh Boy Racer, 1929, pressed steel, red with silver windshield, radiator and hood, No. "110" appears at rear, 19¾" length.
$300–$400

Racer, 1924, tin mechanical, orange car with red and black disc wheels, gray driver, rubber tires, 6⅜" length (probably European).
$200–$250

Racer, 1947, tin mechanical, key wind, 13" length.
$300–$400

Rex Racer, 1924, tin mechanical, red with black trim, has spare tire, mud guard, and running board, blue driver, 8" length.
$350–$450

Rocket Racer, 1930, strong spring motor, has rubber bumper, tail fins, 16" length.
$500–$550

Taxi Cabs

Note: See also the "Still Banks" listings for Arcade Yellow Cab examples.

Checker Cab, 1925, cast iron, green checker design across chassis, gray wheel hubs, 8" length.
$400–$500

Ford Yellow Cab, 1933, cast iron, four-door sedan, special Chicago World's Fair edition: "Century of Progress" stenciled on roof, 6⅞" length.
$600–$700

Limousine Yellow Cab, 1930, cast iron, license #3300, 8½" length.
$500–$600

Red Top Cab, 1924, cast iron, red top, white bottom, gray wheel hubs, Red Top logo on rear door panel, 8" length. $500–$600

Yellow Cab, 1925, cast iron, 9" length (1927 model is 5¼" length).
$400–$500

Yellow Cab, 1932, cast iron, black top and trim, Goodrich rubber tires, nickeled radiator, cast iron sign over windshield, embossed "Checker" logo, 9¼" length. $500–$600

Yellow Cab, Arcade, 1925, $500–$600.

Yellow Cab, 1932, cast iron, with black top, 8 ⅛″ length.
$600–$700

Yellow Cab, 1933, cast iron, bronze bumpers, 9 ¼″ length.
$700–$800

Tootsie Toys (Pre–1941)

The following numbers are taken from the Dowst Catalog.

23, Racer, 1927–33, 74 mm. length. $35–$45

170, Interchangeable Truck, 1925–31, 82 mm. length.
$25–$35

185, Fire Department, 1927–31, 91 mm. length. $35–$40

190, Auto Transport Truck, 1931–33, 215 mm. length.
$25–$35

190x, 4-Car Transport, 1933–36, 272 mm. length. $35–$50

4258, Limousine, 1911–28, 47 mm. length. $30–$35

4570, Model T Ford, 1914–26, 77 mm. length. $40–$50

4610, Truck-Ford, 1916–32, 77 mm. length. $30–$35

4629, Sedan-Yellow Cab, 1923–33, 72 mm. length. $35–$40

4630, Delivery Van, 1924–33, 75 mm. length. $35–$40

4636, *Coupe*, 1924–33, 76 mm. length.   *$30–$35*

4638, *Mack Stake Truck*, 1925–33, 82 mm. length.   *$35–$50*

4639, *Mack Coal Truck*, 1925–33, 82 mm. length.   *$35–$50*

4640, *Mack Tank Truck*, 1925–33, 82 mm. length.   *$30–$40*

4641, *Touring Car*, 1925–33, 78 mm. length.   *$30–$40*

4642, *Long Range Cannon*, 1931–41, 95 mm. length.
    $25–$30

4643, *Anti-Aircraft Gun*, 1931–41, 70 mm. length.   *$25–$30*

4644, *Searchlight*, 1931–41, 70 mm. length.   *$25–$30*

4645, *New Mail Truck—Mack*, 1931–33, 76 mm. length.
    $35–$50

4646, *Caterpillar Tractor*, 1931–39, 77 mm. length.   *$35–$50*

4647, *Army Tank*, 1931–41, 79 mm. length.   *$25–$35*

4648, *Steam Roller*, 1931–34, 73 mm. length.   *$25–$35*

4651, *Fagcol Safety Coach*, 1927–33, 90 mm. length.
    $50–$60

4652, *Hook and Ladder*, 1927–33, 105 mm. length.   *$50–$75*

4653, *Water Tower*, 1927–33, 91 mm. length.   *$35–$40*

4654, *Tractor*, 1927–32, 76 mm. length.   *$45–$55*

4655, *Model A Ford Coupe*, 1928–33, 65 mm. length.
    $40–$50

4656, *Buick Coupe in Tin Garage*, 1931–32, 58 mm. length.
    $25–$35

4657, *Sedan in Garage*, 1931–32, 58 mm. length.   *$25–$35*

4658, *Insurance Patrol in Garage*, 1931–32, 58 mm. length.
    $30–$40

4666, *Racer—Bluebird Daytons*, 1932–41, 95 mm. length.
    $35–$45

4670, *Trailer Truck*, 1929–32, 100 mm. length.   *$25–$35*

4680, *Overland Bus With Separate Grille*, 1929–33, 95 mm. length.   *$25–$35*

General Motors Series

6001, *Buick Roadster*, 1927–33, 79 mm. length. $45–$55

6002, *Buick Coupe*, 1927–33, 77 mm. length. $45–$55

6003, *Buick Brougham*, 1927–33, 79 mm. length. $55–$60

6004, *Buick Sedan*, 1927–33, 79 mm. length. $45–$55

6005, *Buick Touring Car*, 1927–33, 79 mm. length. $45–$55

6006, *Buick Delivery Truck*, 1927–33, 82 mm. length.
$45–$55

6101, *Cadillac Roadster*, 1927–33, 79 mm. length. $45–$55

6102, *Cadillac Coupe*, 1927–33, 77 mm. length. $55–$65

6103, *Cadillac Brougham*, 1927–33, 79 mm. length. $55–$65

6104, *Cadillac Sedan*, 1927–33, 79 mm. length. $45–$55

6105, *Cadillac Closed Touring Car*, 1927–33, 79 mm. length.
$45–$55

6106, *Cadillac Delivery Truck*, 1927–33, 82 mm. length.
$50–$60

6201, *Chevrolet Roadster*, 1927–33, 79 mm. length. $35–$45

6202, *Chevrolet Coupe*, 1927–33, 77 mm. length. $35–$45

6203, *Chevrolet Brougham*, 1927–33, 79 mm. length.
$45–$55

6204, *Chevrolet Sedan*, 1927–33, 79 mm. length. $35–$45

6205, *Chevrolet Touring Car*, 1927–33, 79 mm. length.
$35–$45

6206, *Chevrolet Delivery Truck*, 1927–33, 82 mm. length.
$50–$60

6301, *Oldsmobile Roadster*, 1927–33, 79 mm. length.
$50–$60

6302, *Oldsmobile Coupe*, 1927–33, 79 mm. length. $50–$60

6303, *Oldsmobile Brougham*, 1927–33, 79 mm. length.
$55–$65

6304, *Oldsmobile Sedan*, 1927–33, 79 mm. length. $50–$60

6305, Oldsmobile Touring Car, 1927–33, 79 mm. length.

$50–$60

6306, Oldsmobile Panel Delivery Truck, 1927–33, 82 mm. length.

$50–$60

6665, Ford Sedan, 1929–33, 68 mm. length. $35–$40

Miniature Series

101, Coupe, 1931–34, 58 mm. length. $45–$55

102, Roadster, 1932–34, 58 mm. length. $40–$50

103, Sedan, 1931–34, 58 mm. length. $40–$50

104, Insurance Patrol, 1931–34, 59 mm. length. $40–$50

105, Tank Truck—Mack, 1932–34, 59 mm. length. $40–$50

108, Caterpillar Tractor, 1932–34, 52 mm. length. $40–$50

109, Ford Stake Truck, 1932–34, 57 mm. length. $40–$50

110, Racer, 1932–34, 68 mm. length. $55–$65

Large Mack and Graham Commercials

191, Contractor Set, 1933–41, 311 mm. length. $75–$100

192, Milk Truck Trailers, 1933–41, 337 mm. length.

$75–$100

198, Auto Transport, 1935–41, 277 mm. length. $75–$100

801, Mack Stake Trailer, 1933–41, 137 mm. length.

$75–$100

802, Mack Oil Trailer, 1933–39, 138 mm. length. $75–$100

803, Mack Van Trailer, 1933–36, 139 mm. length. $75–$100

804, Mack Coal Truck, 1933–38, 100 mm. length. $75–$100

805, Mack Milk Trailer, 1933–39, 145 mm. length. $75–$100

806, Wrecking Car, 1933–39, 105 mm. length. $75–$100

807, Delivery Cycle, 1933–39, 76 mm. length. $75–$100

808, Milk Delivery Car, 1933–39, 98 mm. length. $75–$100

809, Ambulance, 1935–41, 98 mm. length. $75–$100

810, Wrigley American Railway Express Truck, 1935–41, 103 mm. length. $100–$125

Graham Series (RM refers to rear-mount spare tire, SM to side-mount spare tire)

511, Graham RM Roadster, 5-wheel, 1933–35, 102 mm. length. $60–$70

512, Graham RM Coupe, 1933–35, 102 mm. length. $60–$70

513, Graham RM Sedan, 1933–35, 102 mm. length. $60–$70

514, Graham RM Convertible Coupe, 1933–35, 102 mm. length. $60–$70

515, Graham RM Convertible Sedan, 1933–35, 102 mm. length. $60–$70

516, Graham RM Town Car, 1933–35, 102 mm. length.
                                                  $60–$70

611, Graham SM Roadster, 1933–35, 98 mm. length.
                                                  $60–$70

612, Graham SM Coupe, 1933–35, 98 mm. length. $60–$70

613, Graham SM Sedan, 1933–35, 98 mm. length. $60–$70

614, Graham SM Convertible Coupe, 1933–35, 98 mm. length. $60–$70

615, Graham SM Convertible Sedan, 1933–35, 98 mm. length. $60–$70

616, Graham SM Town Car, 1933–35, 98 mm. length.
                                                  $60–$70

712, La Salle Coupe, 1935–39, 108 mm. length. $100–$125

713, La Salle Sedan, 1935–39, 108 mm. length. $100–$125

714, La Salle Convertible Coupe, 1935–36, 108 mm. length.
                                                  $100–$125

715, La Salle Convertible Sedan, 1935–36, 108 mm. length.
                                                  $100–$125

716, Doodlebug, 1935–37, 102 mm. length. $65–$75

6015, Lincoln Zephyr, 1937–39, 104 mm. length. $100–$125

1934–1935 Ford Series

111, *Ford Sedan,* 1935–41, 76 mm. length.   *$60–$75*

112, *Ford Coupe,* 1935–41, 76 mm. length.   *$60–$75*

113, *Ford V-8 Wrecker,* 1935–41, 81 mm. length.   *$75–$85*

114, *Ford Convertible Coupe,* 1935–36, 76 mm. length.
$75–$85

115, *Ford Convertible Sedan,* 1935–36, 76 mm. length.
$75–$85

116, *Ford Roadster,* 1935–39, 78 mm. length.   *$75–$85*

117, *Zephyr Railcar,* 1935–36, 97 mm. length.   *$75–$85*

118, *Airflow DeSoto,* 1935–39, 76 mm. length.   *$75–$85*

120, *Oil Tank Truck,* 1936–39, 77 mm. length.   *$75–$85*

121, *Ford Pick-Up Truck,* 1936–39, 73 mm. length.   *$75–$85*

123, *Ford "Special Delivery,"* 1937–39, 77 mm. length.
$75–$85

180, *Roamer (Car and Trailer),* 1938–39, 215 mm. length.
$75–$85

187, *Auto Carrier,* 1939–41, 216 mm. length.   *$75–$85*

1006, *Standard Oil Truck,* 1939–41, 149 mm. length.
$75–$85

1007, *Sinclair Oil Truck,* 1939–41, 149 mm. length.   *$75–$85*

1008, *Texaco Oil Truck,* 1939–41, 149 mm. length.   *$75–$85*

1009, *Shell Oil Truck,* 1939–41, 149 mm. length.   *$75–$85*

1040, *Hook and Ladder,* 1937–41, 139 mm. length.   *$60–$70*

1041, *Hose Car,* 1937–41, 116 mm. length.   *$60–$70*

1042, *Insurance Patrol,* 1937–41, 111 mm. length.   *$50–$60*

1043, *Camping Trailer,* 1937–41, 139 mm. length.   *$45–$55*

1044, *Trailer,* 1937–39, 120 mm. length.   *$45–$50*

1045, *Greyhound Deluxe Bus,* 1937–41, 150 mm. length.
$50–$60

1046, *Station Wagon,* 1940–41, 113 mm. length.   *$45–$50*

4634, *Supply Truck*, 1939–41, 111 mm. length.	$65–$75
4635, *Armored Car*, 1938–41, 100 mm. length.	$65–$75

"230" Series (all are small one-piece castings with front fender skirts)

230, *Sedan*, 1940–41, 85 mm. length.	$25–$35
231, *Coupe*, 1940–41, 80 mm. length.	$20–$25
232, *Touring Car*, 1940–41, 76 mm. length.	$20–$25
233, *Roadster*, 1940–41, 81 mm. length.	$20–$25
234, *Box Truck*, 1940–41, 79 mm. length.	$20–$25
235, *Oil Truck*, 1940–41, 79 mm. length.	$20–$25
236, *Hook and Ladder*, 1940–41, 77 mm. length.	$20–$25
237, *Insurance Patrol*, 1940–41, 77 mm. length.	$20–$25
238, *Hose Car*, 1940–41, 79 mm. length.	$20–$25
239, *Station Wagon*, 1940–41, 77 mm. length.	$20–$25
260, *Yellow Cab*, 1940–41, 185 mm. length.	$20–$25
261, *Checker Cab*, 1940–41, 185 mm. length.	$20–$25
262, *Fire Engine*, 1940–41, 185 mm. length.	$20–$25
263, *Hook and Ladder*, 1940–41, 185 mm. length.	$20–$25

Trucks

Army Truck, maker unknown, 1929, canvas tarpaulin can be rolled back, 13 ½ " length. $300–$400

Army Truck, Steelcraft, 1935, body is beige, wheels red, double steel disc wheels, rubber tires, 23 ¼ " length. $500–$600

Army Truck, Structo, 1933, removable canvas tarpaulin, tailgate, headlights, army green finish, 17 " length. $400–$500

Army Truck, Structo, 1933, has three lights, removable canvas tarpaulin, 21 ½ " length. $500–$600

Baggage Truck, Buddy "L," 1931, steel running skid, two-wheel hand truck, three service tanks, 16 " length. $800–$900

Baggage Truck, Buddy "L," 1932, 26 1/4" length. *$900–$1,000*

Beer Truck, maker unknown, 1933, wooden beer kegs, 15 1/2" length. *$700–$800*

"Big Load Van Company" Truck, Marx, 1929, spring motor, rear doors open, 13" length. *$200–$225*

Delivery Truck, Buddy "L," 1932, canopy top, drop-end gate, curved bottom body, 14 1/2" length. *$400–$500*

Delivery Truck, Dayton, 1932, gray and red, 14 1/2" length. *$300–$400*

Dump Truck, maker unknown, 1929, Mack-type truck dumps load, 13 1/8" length. *$400–$450*

Express Truck, Buddy "L," 1932, black enameled body, drop-end gate, silver wheels enameled red, 24" length. *$700–$800*

Express Truck, Buddy "L," 1932, open flare board body with cab, stake pockets, end gate, 14 1/2" length. *$600–$700*

Express Truck, Oh Boy, 1932, black chassis, dark green body, red disc wheels, 22" length. *$400–$450*

Grocery Truck, Kingsbury, 1932, olive green with red wheels, rubber tires, 8" length. *$400–$450*

Insurance Patrol, Buddy "L," 1932, bright red with brass hand-rails and bell, aluminum wheels, 27" length. *$900–$1,000*

Mack Tanker, maker unknown, circa 1927, 9" length. *$300–$400*

Mail Truck, Buddy "L," 1932, screen side panel body, closed cab, double-hinged rear doors and end gate, black with red wheels, 14 1/2" length. *$400–$500*

Model T Flivver Truck, maker unknown, 1925, spring motor, 8 1/2" length. *$200–$250*

Railway Express, Buddy "L," 1931, removable top converts to ordinary truck, rear door with Corbin brass lock, 24 1/4" length. *$700–$800*

Tip Top Dump Truck, Strauss, 1927, body lifts when crank at side of truck is turned, 10 1/4" length. *$200–$250*

Toyland Milk Truck, Marx, 1931, has milk case containing 12 wooden milk bottles, each about 2″ tall.   *$250–$300*

Utility Trucks, Cast Iron

ARCADE

Austin Delivery Truck, 1932, cast iron, blue, green, red, 3¾″ length.   *$450–$500*

Borden's Milk Bottle Truck With Dodge Chassis, 1936, all white with classic milk bottle shape, deep patterned tread tires, 6½″ length.   *$500–$600*

Brinks Express Truck, 1932, cast iron, red with gold and black trim, rear doors open, 11¾″ length.   *$3,000–$3,500*

Chevrolet Delivery Truck, 1937, cast iron, 10¼″ length.
$1,000–$1,200

Chevrolet Utility Express Truck, 1923, cast iron with driver, 9¼″ length.   *$300–$350*

Ford Anthony Dump Truck, 1926, cast iron, gray cab, Anthony logo appears on tailgate, operable hand lever, 8½″ length.
$350–$400

Ford Express Truck, 1932, cast iron, red, green, blue, wire wheels, 5″, 5⅞″, and 7½″ length sizes.   *$450–$500*

International Delivery Truck, 1937, cast iron, bronze bumpers, rear door opens, green with gold trim, driver in blue uniform.
$450–$500

International Dump Truck, 1935, cast iron, green with red rear chassis, 10½″ length.   *$300–$400*

International Stake Truck, 1935, cast iron, green, nickeled radiator, I.H. decal on door panel, 12″ length.   *$300–$400*

Mack Dump Truck, 1932, cast iron, blue cab, yellow dumper.
$400–$450

Mack Dump Truck, 1937, cast iron, red or green, 6½″ length.
$300–$400

Mack Gasoline Truck, 1925, cast iron, nickel driver, 13¼″ length.   *$500–$600*

Mack Lubrite Tank Truck, 1925, cast iron, 13¼" length.
$500–$600

White Co. Ice Truck, 1941, cast iron, White logo on door panel, 6¾" length.
$350–$450

White Dump Truck, 1932, cast iron, red, blue, green, nickeled driver, dual rear wheels, 13½" length.
$650–$750

MISCELLANEOUS

Car-Carrier, 1928, cast iron, green and red, rubber disc wheels, carries Austin green coupe, Austin red delivery truck, Austin blue stake truck, 14¼" length.
$650–$700

Car-Carrier, 1932, cast iron and sheet steel, red with green trailer, four cars: one red coupe, one blue coupe, one red Tudor, one green Tudor, 24½" length.
$2,000–$3,000*

Carry-Car Trailer, 1933, cast iron, green cab, red trailer, holds two green stake trucks, blue Tudor, red coupe, 20" length.
$1,500–$2,000

Carry-Car Truck Trailer, 1928–1931, cast iron, cab is cast iron, trailer-welded steel, nickeled wheels, 24½" length. $300–$350

Car Transport, 1938, cast iron, double decker, semi-trailer, with four sedans resembling '38 Chevys, but not as authentically detailed, 18½" length (atypical of Arcade). $350–$400

Delivery Truck, 1928, cast iron, yellow paneled. $350–$400

Ford Weaver (Ton Truck) Wrecker, 1928, cast iron, featured realistic ratchet to two other toy vehicles, 13" length. $500–$600

International Delivery Truck, 1936, cast iron, red, International decal on door panel, nickeled radiator and headlights, white rubber tires, 9½" length.
$300–$400

Mack Tank Truck, 1929, cast iron, tin tank for gas, 12¾" length.
$400–$500

Milk Truck, 1928, cast iron, word "Milk" embossed on panel, 12" length.
$300–$400

Pontiac Stake Truck, 1930, cast iron, red, green, blue, white, rubber wheels, 6¼" length.
$200–$250

*About 50% less without cars.

White Dump Truck, 1929, cast iron, red, green, blue, wheels nickel plated or optional rubber, 11 ½ " length.   *$300–$400*

White Moving Van, 1928, cast iron, comes with four Model A coupes and sedans or three Model A cars, 13 ½ " length.

$500–$600

Wrecker and Service Car, 1929, cast iron, with walker hoist chain, 12 ½ " length.   *$300–$400*

War Vehicles

Armored Tank, Hubley, 1928, 4 ½ " length.   *$200–$225*

Army Tank With Gun, 1940, cast iron, featured boxed set of cast iron soldiers, fires steel balls via spring-activated crank, 8 " length (scarce toy as it was pulled from market because it proved to be dangerous as a child's plaything).   *$1,000–$2,000*

Midget Tank, maker unknown, 1932, steel, 5 ½ " length.

$100–$125

Pull Tank, Structo, 1933, steel wheels, revolving turret with machine gun, no swivel spotlight, brass reflector, 12 ½ " length.   *$400–$500*

Wooden Toys

✳ ✳ ✳

The earliest wooden toys can be traced back to the 1840s, when woodcarvers from the German forest region of Erzegeberge created fanciful versions. In the United States, the Tower Guild of South Hingham, Massachusetts, and Joel Ellis of Springfield, Vermont, produced wood toys and trains in the mid–19th century. Stencilling was introduced before 1950; lithographing colorful paper glued on wood in the 1870s. Leading practitioners in the late 19th century included Charles W. Crandall, Montrose, Pennsylvania; Milton Bradley Co., Springfield, Massachusetts; W.S. Reed, Leominster, Massachusetts; and Rufus Bliss, Pawtucket, Rhode Island. Interest in wooden toys waned at the beginning of the 20th century, although Gibbs Mfg., Canton, Ohio, and Fisher-Price of East Aurora, New York, continue to produce whimsical, fascinating examples up to contemporary times.

PERELMAN TOY MUSEUM SALE

Painted and Lithograph Paper-on-Wood Toys

American Twin Animal Ark, R. Bliss, 1890, includes painted animals, 17″ length (also came in 13″ and 24″ size). $500

Three Black Musicians Sand Toy, patented 1875 by Henry Mencke, $1,000–$1,500.

Black Musicians, patented 1875 by Henry Mencke, trio includes banjo player, fiddler, and dancer, lithograph paper on wood, paper, glass sand toy. $1,500

Coast Defense Monitor, "Terror," R. Bliss, circa 1910, litho-wood, 22″ length. $850

Crandall's Happy Family, Charles Crandall, 1870–1880, 15 wild animals in circus cage wagon, painted wood pull toy. $2,000

General Sand Toy, German, mid-19th century, animated figure wields saber. $400

Hercules Atlantic and Pacific Wooden Train, Milton Bradley, 1880, includes engine, coal car, litho-wood. $1,500

Hook and Ladder, W.S. Reed, 1877, double horses, two firemen, litho-wood. $3,500

Jackson Park Trolley, R. Bliss, 1892, 18″ length. $2,750

Lime Kiln Club Theater, W.S. Reed, 1870s, four litho-on-wood minstrel players. $7,100*

Monitor Ironclad, W.S. Reed, 1870s, litho-wood replica of historic Civil War vessel. $3,000

New Cathedral Construction Toy, W.S. Reed, patented 1877, case serves as base for various parts, including books and blocks inscribed with scriptural references. $2,500

Noah's Ark with Figurehead, maker unknown, 1910, litho-wood. $1,500

Panorama and History of America, Milton Bradley, 1868, historiscope, views of Columbus landing in New World, up through Civil War era. $500

Panorama of Visit of Santa Claus to the Happy Children, Milton Bradley, 1900, litho paper-and-wood historiscope. $750

Pansy, R. Bliss, 1870s, litho-wood stagecoach, four horses, name appears above door, 29″ length. $3,000

Pumper, Horse-Drawn, W.S. Reed, circa 1877, single horse, detachable steamstack and posts, 15″ length. $3,500
  Smaller pumper. $2,000

Ten Pins, Dog Cart w/Canine Bowling Pins, maker unknown, German, 1880s, papier-mâché fox terrier on wheels, contains eight "Schoolboys," various dog breeds on wooden drums, serving as bowling pins, accompanied by a hound "teacher," 21″ length × 12½″ height. $8,500
  Similar version, but with rooster and chickens $7,500
  Similar version, but with peacock. $5,000

Trolley Car, W.S. Reed, 1878, litho-wood, "Central Park" appears on top panel. $5,500

Ye Hero of '76, Charles M. Crandall, 1876, figure sets into groove in wooden stand, often identified as George Washington.
                                                             $2,000

*Price realized at Opfer's Christmas Auction, 1988.

Young Boy Living Picture, A. Schoenhut, 1890s, two-dimensional animated figures in frame behind glass, activated by clockwork mechanism, wood, brass.   *$750*

Schoenhut

Circus/Safari Animals and Figures

Note that it's often easier to purchase these wild animals and performers separately, rather than buying a Humpty Dumpty Circus complete.

Alligator, painted eyes.	*$350*
Bacterian Camel, painted.	*$175*
Bareback Rider, bisque head.	*$350*
Black Hobo Clown, painted.	*$275*
Buffalo, glass eyes.	*$250*
Clowns (pair), painted eyes.	*$125*
Donkey, painted eyes.	*$100*
Ducks (pair), painted eyes.	*$250*
Elephant, painted eyes.	*$150*
Goat, glass eyes.	*$350*
Gorilla	*$1,000–$1,200*
Horse, painted eyes.	*$175*
Lion, glass eyes.	*$300*
Lion Tamer, bisque head.	*$400*
Poodle, painted eyes.	*$250*
Ringmaster, painted eyes.	*$150*
Seal, glass eyes.	*$300*
Theodore Roosevelt Big Game Hunter, painted eyes.	*$750*
Zebra, painted eyes.	*$250*
Zebu, painted eyes.	*$650*
Zebu, glass eyes.	*$850*

Schoenhut Humpty Dumpty Circus Animals: lion, painted eyes, 8″, $100–$200; camel, glass eyes, 9½″, $200–$300; buffalo, painted eyes, 7″, $200–$300.

Schoenhut Humpty Dumpty Circus Starter Set, with original box, 1920–1930, $250–$300. (Deluxe versions may sell for ten times this amount.)

Comic/Character Toys

Barney Google and Sparkplug, late 1920s, wooden figures with cloth blanket for Sparkplug and cloth outfit for Barney. $850

Boob McNut, mid-1920s, cloth outfit. $1,250

Felix, wooden figure, 1932, 4″ height. $125

Happy Hooligan, with cloth outfit. $750

Maggie and Jiggs, with cloth outfits, Maggie has rolling pin, Jigs has bucket of corn beef. $900

Max and Moritz, cloth outfits, real hair. $2,600

Wynn (Ed Wynn, The Firechief) Fire Station, with horse-drawn rig, 9½″ length. $412.50*

Miscellaneous Toys

African Safari (Teddy Roosevelt's Adventures in Africa Series), circa 1910, 25 wooden figures including Teddy Roosevelt, cameraman, beaters, wild animals. $11,000**

Band Wagon, Circus, 1910, four horses, eight bandsmen, one driver, 40″ length. $14,300**

Cage Wagon, Horse-Drawn, 1910, driver, two dappled horses, leopard, 29″ length. $4,400**

Chinaman Acrobat. $700

Farmer and Cow, wooden figures. $1,500

Golfer, figure on long handle. $500

H.P. Hood Grade "A" Milk Dairy Wagon, with driver and attached dappled horse on wheels. $2,970**

Jolly Jiggers, papier-mâché, wood, cloth outfits, Dutch couple suspended on hooks dance on double platform, figures dance on board when it's compressed, 21″ length × 16″ height.
                                                         $3,800**

Koko. $3,800

*Atlanta Toy Museum Sale, 1986.
**Prices realized at Atlanta Toy Museum Sale, 1986.

Livewire Acrobats (platform squeeze toy). $500

Mary Had a Little Lamb. $1,200

Rubber Ball Shooting Gallery, rabbit, tiger, clown, monkey, clay pipes as targets, 15″ length. $577.50*

**Price realized at Atlanta Toy Museum Sale, 1986.

World's Exposition Toys

Topical collectors soon discover that the major World's Expositions—from the London Crystal Palace in 1851 to World Expo '88 in Brisbane, Australia—inspire a vast miniature cosmos of ingenious playthings that commemorate those events.

Especially noteworthy are the elegantly lithographed paper and paper-on-wood toys. These include foldout peep viewers, sand toys, miniature theaters, and foldout panoramas. Also highly esteemed are the classic Uncle Sam Going to the Fair Velocipede (tin and wood clockwork toys) by Ives, from the U.S. Centennial Exposition, 1876, the Columbus Landing cast-iron bell ringer from the World's Columbian in Chicago, 1893, and the fleet of Arcade cast-iron Greyhound buses from the 1939 New York World's Fair.

In this chapter, please note that items are grouped chronologically by Expo date, beginning with the U.S. Centennial in 1876 and ending with Montreal's Expo '67.

U.S. CENTENNIAL, 1876

Game of '76 (a.k.a. Lion and Eagle) Card Game, Noyes & Snow, box illustrates Capitol Building with eagle attacking lion, multicolor, 5⅞" height × 4¼" width.   *$80–$90*

Globe Bank, Enterprise Mfg. Co., 1875, cast-iron still bank, red with gilt eagle atop globe, 5¾" height.   *$250–$275*

Hero of '76, Charles M. Crandall, circa 1876, tongue-in-groove toy in treated and painted wood, soldier and flag on oblong base, red, blue, black, white, 9½″ height × 6⅜″ length.

$1,000–plus

Independence 1776–1886, Gong Bell Mfg. Co., nickel-plated steel pull toy with cloth flag, bronze eagle perched on Liberty Bell, 9½″ length. $1,000–plus.

Memorial Money Bank (Liberty Bell), Enterprise Mfg. Co., 1876, cast-iron mechanical bank, coin activates lever that slides back and rings bell. $550–$575

Musical Bank, A. Feigl, designer, 1876, cast-iron still bank, bronze finish with verdigris, embossed eagle with Centennial lettering, bank is replica of Liberty Bell, 5¹¹⁄₁₆″ height.

$1,500–$1,600

Rocking Eagle Bell Toy, maker unknown, mid-1880s, cast iron, eagle on rockers holds large Liberty Bell in beak, eagle-gold top, white bottom, blue rocker, 4½″ length. $700–$800

PARIS INTERNATIONAL EXPOSITION, 1889

Boxed Set, Picture Blocks, France, 1889, images form number of combinations, including Arche de Triumphe, Eiffel Tower, and numerous Exposition scenes, painted wood. $250–$275

WORLD'S COLUMBIAN, 1893

Administration Building, Magic International Production Co., 1893, silver finish still bank, 5″ height × 5¼″ width × 1⅝″ depth. $825–$850

Administration Building Mechanical Bank, Magic International Production Co., shelf swings open and closes when coin is inserted and disappears.
    With advertising. $250–$300
    Without advertising. $200–$225

Columbian Expo Silver Puzzle Egg, maker unknown. $30–$35

Columbian Wheel, Hubley Mfg., 1893, six-pointed star wheel of stamped steel is painted vermilion, cast-iron circle, columns, base and figures are black, hanging gondolas are yellow, clockwork mechanism, listed in Hubley's catalog as Model #6, 18" height. $2,000–plus

Columbia Still Bank, Kenton, 1893–1913, gilt finish, 8 3/4" length × 7" width × 7" depth. $750–$775

Columbus—A Puzzle, 1492–1892, Milton Bradley, patented 1891, nine wooden jig-saw pieces, lithographed box pictures Columbus bust in circle with fleet of ships below, multicolored, 5 3/4" height × 5 1/4" width. $35–$40

Columbus Baby Rattle, French, celluloid w/wood handle, bust of Columbus and view of Administration Building, multicolor, 3" diameter. $100–$110

Ei des Columbus (Egg of Columbus), by Richeter (Anchor Blocks) Rudolstadt, Germany, 1893, Anchor stone puzzle made of kaolin clay from Bavaria, brick red-shaped pieces form egg. $45–$50

Ferris Wheel Dexterity Puzzle, maker unknown, Germany, 1893, tin with wooden frame, glass covered, light blue, yellow, red, black, object is to put tiny white balls into the gondolas of the ferris wheel, 4" square. $100–$125

Ferris Wheel Mechanical Bank, maker unknown, tin wind-up toy converted to semi-mechanical bank with cast-iron base, green base, red wheel, yellow seats and passengers, 22" height. $1,100–$1,200

Going to the Fair, Ernest Lehmann, tin friction toy, lady in boardwalk-type carriage or chair pushed by man, lady flutters red fan as carriage is pushed, painted tin, multicolor, 4 3/4" height × 6 1/4" length × 2 1/2" width. $600–$700

Hail Columbia (Jolly Jack Tar), Ernest Lehmann, patented 1892, tin gravity toy, painted tin, multicolor, 4 3/4" height. $550–$600

Landing of Columbus, Gong Bell Mfg., 1892, cast-iron flagship *Santa Maria,* Columbus at prow holding flag, also four bearded oarsmen, gilt finish, chrome bell in stern rings when toy is pulled, 5 1/2" height × 7 1/2" length. $700–$750

Lincoln Park Railroad Train Set, R. Bliss, lithograph paper on

World's Fair (Columbian Exposition, 1893) Bank, J. & E. Stevens, 1893, $900–$1,200.

wood, engine plus two passenger cars, cars contained set of flat blocks and two picture puzzles, multicolor, 18″ length.
$650–$700

Marble Roll Toy, Christopher Columbus, attributed to R. Bliss, lithographed paper on wood with coiled metal spiral springs, alphabet blocks, and silhouetted one-dimensional figure of Columbus with flag in hand on top platform, marble enters at top and shoots through coils to land in targeted partitions at base, multicolored, at 58″ height, rates as the tallest lithograph toy of its kind. $750–$800*

World's Columbian Exposition Horse-Drawn Trolley, R. Bliss, lithograph paper-on-wood trolley drawn by two horses, World's Columbian destination appears on front top tier of trolley, with listings of all Chicago streets en route to Jackson Park fair site via Grand Blvd., multicolored, 25″ length × 10″ height × 7″ width. $1,000–plus**

World's Fair Bank, patented 1893, Charles A. Bailey for J. & E. Stevens Co., comes with and without "World's Fair Bank" raised lettering, gilt-finish mechanical bank, coin-activated lever se-

*Brought $1,800 at Atlanta Toy Museum Auction in 1986, despite missing flag.
**Sold for $2,600 at Atlanta Toy Museum Sale, despite photocopied replacements of side curtains and seat supports.

cures deposit as Indian chief bearing peace pipe emerges from concealment in log, 8³/₁₆″ base length.   *$900–$1,200*
Same as above, but multicolored (handpainted by Bailey).
$3,000–plus

World's Fair Masonic Temple and Fort Dearborn, maker unknown, 1892, brass finish still bank, 6⅛″ height × 6″ width × 2¾″ depth.   *$450–$475*

World's Fair '93, jobbed by Ives, 1893, pottery globe-shaped still bank, white with blue lettering, "My Expenses to Chicago World's Fair," and illustration of train, 5¼″ height.
$350–$375

World's Fair Spinning Top, pull-string-type/whistling, maker unknown, 1893, lithographed tin, views of Columbus' fleet, Exposition buildings, multicolor, 3½″ diameter.   *$90–$100*

World's Fair St. Railroad Trolley No. 372, Wilkins Toy Co., circa 1892, cast iron, name and trolley no. embossed on sides, white horse on single wheel, drivers, red trolley, red, black, white drivers, 13½″ length.   *$1,000–plus**

PARIS EXPO, 1900

Ferris Wheel, brass, sheet metal on wooded base, gilt, 6″ height.   *$190–$200*

PAN AMERICAN, 1901

Buffalo Lying Down, maker unknown, 1901, still bank, pottery, "Expo 1901," two-tone brown, 3⅛″ height × 6½″ length.
$225–$250

Frying Pan Bank, maker unknown, 1901, still bank, tin die-cut shape, black, 11¾″ length × 6″ width.   *$225–$250*

LOUISIANA PURCHASE, 1904

Donkey, "I Made St. Louis Famous," possibly Arcade, 1904, still bank, brown, 4¹¹/₁₆″ height × 5″ length.   *$750–$800*

*Brought $1,300 at Atlanta Toy Museum Sale in 1986.

Game of Elections, McLoughlin Bros., 1904, originated at LPIE to circumvent religious group's objections to card games, litho cardboard box, multicolored. $35–$40

PANAMA-PACIFIC, 1915

Through the Locks to the Golden Gate, circa 1915 board game, Milton Bradley, two round, colored wooden pieces and spinner, multicolored lithograph board, box cover shows young man and woman with vignettes of Panama Canal locks and Expo Administration Building, instruction on face of board, 15″ height × 9″ width. $70–$80

SESQUICENTENNIAL, 1926

Liberty Belle, silk-screened cloth doll, Annin & Co., 1926, kapok-stuffed, skirt in shape of Liberty Bell, "150 Years of American Independence/1776–1926 Sesquicentennial," multicolor, 13¾″ height. $70–$75

Tiny Toy Furniture Set, Souvenir of Sesq . . . June–Sept. 1926, cardboard box 3″ × 3″ × 6″ contains block of wood cut in shape of four toy tables and six chairs, largest table—6″ length × 3″ height, all fit neatly together, natural finish. $30–$35

CHICAGO WORLD'S FAIR (CENTURY OF PROGRESS), 1933–1934

A Century of Progress Puzzle, Scrambled Eggs, Scrambled Eggs Inc., three-dimensional wooden puzzle, dark blue with gold and light blue "A Century of Progress" decal, multicolored Art Deco box, 2½″ length. $30–$35

Century of Progress Greyhound Buses, Arcade,* Greyhound logos on each side, GMC identification and ACPIE logo on top, one-piece casting w/blue trim, 6″ length. $75–85
Same as above in 7⅝″ length, two-piece casting. $95–$100

*Smallest bus doesn't appear in Arcade's catalog and was probably an advertising giveaway. Sale of CPIE buses helped pull Arcade out of economic slump during Depression.

Same as above in 10½" length, two-piece casting. *$100–$110*
Same as above in 12" length, two-piece casting.   *$140–$150*

Century of Progress Puzzler, sliding block type, wood blocks have name designations (i.e. airplanes, automobiles, world wonders, etc.), based on the famed Dad's Puzzler, lithograph box with Fair scenes and "The Best Souvenir at Chicago. Take One Home and Try to Solve It," black on white, 5" height × 5½" width.   *$25–$30*

Century of Progress Still Bank, Arcade, "Century of Progress" in raised letters on obverse, "Chicago—1934" on the other, Administration Building, cast iron, cream-colored with blue roof, 4½" height × 7" width × 2" depth.   *$100–$110*

Ft. Dearborn Lincoln Logs, colorful lithographed box with illustration of Ft. Dearborn and official CWF logo, multicolor, 10½" height × 14" width.   *$75–$85*

Jig-Saw 1933 World's Fair Puzzle Pinball Machine, Rock-Ola Mfg. Co., 1933, ball is shot into a bottom hole to set up a corresponding puzzle piece or land in a top hole and line up entire column, multicolor, dimensions unavailable.   *$450–$475*

Lone Star Ranger Game, lithographed cardboard box w/leather holster inscribed "Tower of Water—Chicago World's Fair," outline of tower with Fair logo in black, "Tiger" cast-iron cap pistol in dark green metallic finish, leather belt with wooden bullets, box: orange and black, 12" length × 5" width.   *$30–$35*

World's Fair Picture Puzzle, Chicago 1933, Rand McNally & Co., 1932, 300 cardboard pieces with full-color box depicting aerial view of the Fair, which is also puzzle picture inside, by artist H. J. Pettit, multicolored, 11½" height × 17½" width.
$35–$50

GOLDEN GATE INTERNATIONAL, 1939

Fair Faces Puzzle, faces are printed on four cardboard sections, litho on cardboard, multicolored, four pieces in combination make 256 separate cartoon faces, 6" height × 5" width.
$25–$30

Pan American China Clipper,* Wyandotte Toy Co., pressed steel, red wing, white body, Golden Gate International decals, 9½" length, 13" wingspan. $140–$150

NEW YORK WORLD'S FAIR, 1939

New York World's Fair Bus, Arcade, cast iron, NYWF and Greyhound logos on sides of bus, blue trim on orange, nickel-plate rear, 10½" length. $110–$120
  7" length. $95–$100
  8½" length. $100–$110

New York World's Fair Sightseeing Bus-Tractor, Arcade, canopied trailer hooks on, nickeled driver, blue-and-orange-striped canopy, body blue with orange seats, also available with extra trailers, rubber tires, tractor 3¾" length, trailer 4¼" length. $150–$160

Remington Typewriter Advertising Still Bank, "See the New Remington Portable Typewriter. Souvenir to the Fair," National Products Corp., gold finish, white metal, 1⅜" height × 2⅞" width. $30–$35

Underwood Typewriter Advertising Still Bank, National Products Corp., bronze finish, white metal, 1⅜" height × 2¼" width. $25–$30

World's Fair Building Still Bank, maker unknown, brass finish, white metal, 2¼" height × 2⅝" width. $35–$40

NEW YORK WORLD'S FAIR, 1964–1965

Greyhound Tour Bus, Greyhound Mfg., two-piece metal replica with driver's cab and open-air trailer bus, cast metal, black rubber tires, cab is a friction toy, front grille has Greyhound symbol, "Go Greyhound and Leave Driving to Us" on side of cab, NYWF Unisphere symbols appear on cab, orange and blue, 9" length × 2½" height. $85–$90

Nodder Toy, maker unknown, plastic figure with globe-shaped head, multicolored, 6½" height. $20–$25

*The China Clipper was a major attraction at GGIE.

Unisphere Dime Register Mechanical Bank, U.S. Steel, multi-colored, press-down trap, 2⅝" square with round corners.

$10–$15

Unisphere Mechanical Bank, maker unknown, 1964, white metal, silver finish, 5" height. $10–$12

Unisphere/Rocket Ship Mechanical Bank, chrome finish, rocket ship shoots coin into Unisphere, 11" height. $25–$30

EXPO '67 MONTREAL

Translucent Globe Still Bank, maker unknown, blue translucent plastic, with black and white map outlines, 4½" height, 4" diameter. $15–$20

RESOURCES

Shows and Exhibits

The ideal place to see a large variety of the best the hobby has to offer is at an antique toy show. Following is a list of the most prominent.

All American Collector's Show, held at the Glendale, California, Civic Auditorium; held on January 23–24 and August 19–20 in 1989, but dates could vary. For information: Tauni Brustin, All American Collector's Show, 1325 W. Washington Blvd., Venice, CA 90291; (213) 392–6676.

Allentown Toy Show, held annually at the Allentown, Pennsylvania, Fairgrounds on the first Saturday in November. For information: David Bausch, 252 N. 7th St., Allentown, PA 18102; (215) 432–3355.

Antique Toy Circus Maximus, County Fairgrounds, Kalamazoo, Michigan, Saturday, May 20 (the 9th annual event was held on May 20 in 1989). For information: Bruce Beimers, 1735 Lamberton Lake, Grand Rapids, MI 49505; (606) 361–9987 (after 3:30 PM).

Chicago Toy Show (the largest doll and toy show in the world), April 16, June 25, and October 22 (in 1989) at Kane County Fairgrounds, St. Charles, Illinois (dates may vary from year to year). For information: Jack Regan, 29718 N. Virginia Lane, Wauconda, IL 60084; (312) 526–1645.

Detroit Antique Toy Show and Sale, Holiday Inn, Livonia-West, Livonia, Michigan. 17th annual show was held on May 7 in 1989. For information: John Carlisle, 409 Bewley Bldg., Lockport, NY 14094; (716) 434-2470.

Eastern National Gaithersburg Antique Dolls, Toys, and Games Show and Sale, Fairgrounds, Gaithersburg, Maryland; held on June 3 & 4 in 1989. For information: Bellman Production, 11959 Philadelphia Rd., Bradshaw, MD 21021-1899; (301) 329-2188.

International Antique Toy Convention, normally held in June, September, and January at such sites as Newark International and Philadelphia International airports. For information: Bob Bostoff, 331 Cochran Place, Valley Stream, NY 11581.

For information on other shows, see *Antique Toy World's* monthly listings.

Auctioneers

✳ ✳ ✳

Noel Barrett Auctions &
  Appraisals
Carversville, PA 18913
(215) 297–5109

Butterfield & Butterfield
220 San Bruno Avenue
San Francisco, CA 94103
(or) 7601 Sunset Boulevard
Los Angeles, CA 90046

Christie's East
219 East 67th Street
New York, NY 10021
(212) 570–4141

Garth's Auctions Inc.
2690 Stratford Road
Delaware, OH 43015

Hake's Americana &
  Collectibles
P.O. Box 1444
York, PA 17405
(717) 848–1333
Mail auctions

Stephen Leonard
P.O. Box 127
Albertson, NY 11507
(516) 742–0979
Mail auctions

Ted Maurer
1931 N. Charlotte Street
Pottstown, PA 19464
(215) 323–1573

Mid-Hudson Auction Galleries
One Idlewild Avenue
Cornwall-on-Hudson, NY
  12520
(914) 534–7828
Toy Specialist: Joanne C. Grant

New England Auction Gallery
Box 682
Methuen, MA 01844
(617) 683–6354
Mail auctions

Richard Opfer Auctioneering,
  Inc.
1919 Greenspring Drive
Timonium, MD 21093
(301) 252–5035

Phillips Auctioning &
  Appraising Phillips Ltd.
406 East 79th Street
New York, NY 10021
(212) 570-4830
Contacts: Harry I. Kurtz or
  Eric Alberta
Toy Consultant: Jack Herbert

Lloyd W. Ralston Auctions
447 Stratfield Road
Fairfield, CT 06432
(203) 366-3399

Robert W. Skinner, Inc.
Route 117
Bolton, MA 01740
(617) 779-5528
Auctions general line of antiques, but normally has
  several major toy auctions
  each year. Skinner also has
  a Boston gallery.

Sotheby's
1334 York Avenue at 72nd
  Street
New York, NY 10021
(212) 606-7000
Collectibles Contact: Dana
  Hawkes, (212) 606-7424

Rex Stark
49 Wethersfield Road
Bellingham, MA 02019
(617) 966-0994
Mail auctions

Theriault's
P.O. Box 151
Annapolis, MD 21404
(301) 269-0680

Richard W. Withington, Inc.
Auctions & Appraiser
Hillsboro, NH 03244
(603) 464-3232
Holds periodic toy and game
  auctions but specialty is
  dolls.

Toy Collector Publications

✳ ✳ ✳

The following publications regularly cover the subject of toy collecting:

Antiques & Collecting Hobbies
1006 South Michigan Avenue
Chicago, Illinois, 60605
Monthly

Antiques & The Arts Weekly
(Newtown Bee)
Newtown, Connecticut 06470
Weekly

Antique Toy World
P.O. Box 34509
Chicago, Illinois 60634
Monthly

Antique Trader Weekly
P.O. Box 1050
Dubuque, Iowa 52001
Weekly

Automobile Miniature
9, rue de Saussure, 75017
Paris, France
11 issues per year

Collector's Gazette
17 Adbolton Lodge, Whimsey
  Park
Carlton, Nottingham, England
Bi-monthly

Collectors' Showcase
P.O. Box 27948
San Diego, California 92128
Bi-monthly

The Doll Reader
Hobby House Press
Riverdale, Maryland 20840

Doll Talk
Kimport Dolls
P.O. Box 495
Independence, Missouri 64051

The Doll and Toy Collector
International Collectors Publications
The Old Exchange, Pier Street,
  Swansea SA1 1RY,
United Kingdom

Guide to Buyers, Sellers, and
    Traders of Black Collect-
    ibles
CGL, Box 158472
Nashville, Tennessee 37215
Monthly newsletter

Maine Antique Digest
71 Main Street
P.O. Box 645
Waldoboro, Maine 04572
Monthly, regularly covers toy
    antique auctions and shows

Miniature Tractor and Imple-
    ment
R.D. 1, Box 90
East Springfield, Pennsylvania
    16411

Model Auto Review
P.O. Box MT1, Leeds LS17
    6TA
United Kingdom
Quarterly, for model vehicle
    collectors

Old Toy Soldier Newsletter
209 North Lombard
Oak Park, Illinois 60302
Bi-monthly

Polichinelle
14 Rue Andre-del-Sarte
75018 Paris, France
Quarterly, covers toys, dolls,
    games, in French

Sound Investment Toy Trader
P.O. Box 263304
Escondito, California 92026
Monthly, new publication

Toymania Magazine
60190 Avrigny, France
(4) 450–27–88
Quarterly, Paris Toy Show
    coverage

Public Toy, Train, Doll, and Game Collections

✳ ✳ ✳

Many museums, historical societies, and restoration villages will, on occasion, hold special exhibitions of toys on loan from the hobby's foremost collections.

Regrettably, one of the finest specialty museums in the country, the Toy Museum of Atlanta in Atlanta, Georgia, closed its doors in 1986. A new toy museum, however, in Pittsfield, Massachusetts, is scheduled to open soon.

The following sources mount impressive permanent collections.

NEW ENGLAND

Massachusetts—Andover: American Museum of Automotive Miniatures. Salem: Salem Children's Museum, Essex Institute. Sandwich: Sandwich Glass Museum, Yesteryear's Museum. Sturbridge: Old Sturbridge Village. Wenham: Wenham Historical Association and Museum.

Vermont—Shelburne: Shelburne Museum.

MID-ATLANTIC REGION

Delaware—Winterthur: Henry Francis du Pont Winterthur Museum.

New Jersey—Flemington: Raggedy Ann Antique Doll and Toy Museum. Newark: Newark Museum.

New York—New York City: Forbes Museum, Brooklyn Children's Museum, Cooper-Hewitt Museum, the Smithsonian Institution's National Museum of Design, the Metropolitan Museum of Art, Museum of American Folk Art, Museum of the City of New York, The New York Historical Society. Rochester: The Margaret Woodbury Strong Museum.

Pennsylvania—Douglassville: Mary Merritt Doll and Toy Museum. Philadelphia: Perelman Antique Toy Museum. Strasburg: Toy Train Museum.

Washington, D.C.—National Museum of American History, Smithsonian Institution, Washington Dolls' House and Toy Museum.

SOUTH

Kentucky—Bardstown: The Sterling Collection.

Virginia—Williamsburg: Abby Aldrich Rockefeller Folk Art Center; Colonial Williamsburg.

MIDWEST

Illinois—Chicago: Art Institute of Chicago, The Field Museum of Natural History, Museum of Science and Industry.

Indiana—Auburn: Auburn-Cord-Duesenberg Museum.

Indianapolis—Children's Museum of Indianapolis.

Iowa—Dyersville: Scale Model Farm Toy Museum.

Collecting Organizations

A number of the collecting organizations listed on these pages may lack a permanent headquarters address. The mailing address, therefore, could vary from time to time. Check your toy periodicals to stay posted on such changes; listed in italics are titles of various organizational newsletters or bulletins.

> *Note:* Membership in some of these organizations may be contingent on recommendations by at least two members in good standing of that club or society. There also may be restrictions due to size limitations.

American Flyer Collectors Club
P.O. 13269
Pittsburgh, Pennsylvania 15243

American Game Collectors Association
Game Box 1179
Great Neck, New York 11023

American Model Soldier Society
American Military Historical Society
1528 El Camino Real
San Carlos, California 94070

Antique Toy Collectors of America
Rte. 2, Box 5A
Baltimore, Maryland 21120

LCB Model Railroad Club
3329 White Castle Way
Decatur, Georgia
(404) 987-2773

Lionel Collectors Club of America
P.O. Box 479 (Business Office)
La Salle, Illinois 61301

Lionel Collectors Club of America
P.O. Box 11851
Lexington, Kentucky 40511

Lionel Operating Train Society
7408 138 Place N.E.
Redmond, Washington 98052-4008
(206) 885-6636 (evenings and weekends)
Contact: Geoffrey Swan

*Maerklin Enthusiasts of
   America*
P.O. Box 189
Beverly, New Jersey 08010

*Marble Collectors Society of
   America*
P.O. Box 222
Trumbull, Connecticut 06611
Marble Mania

Matchbox Collectors Club
P.O. Box 119
Wood Ridge, New Jersey 07075

*Mechanical Bank Collectors of
   America*
H. E. Mihlheim, Secretary
P.O. Box 128
Allegan, Michigan 49010

*Miniature Figure Collectors of
   America*
813 Elliston Drive
Wynmoor, Pennsylvania
   19118

Miniature Truck Association
3449 N. Randolph Street
Arlington, Virginia 22207
Miniature Truck News

*National Association of Mini-
   ature Enthusiasts*
P.O. Box 2621
Brookhurst Center
Anaheim, California 92804

*National Association of
   S Gaugers*
280 Gordon Road
Matawan, New Jersey 07747
Contact: Mike Ferraro

*National Capital Military Col-
   lectors*
P.O. Box 166
Rockville, Maryland 20850

*National Model Railroad As-
   sociation*
4121 Cromwell Road
Chattanooga, Tennessee
(615) 892-2846

Puppeteers of America, Inc.
2311 Connecticut Avenue,
   N.W. #501
Washington, D.C. 20008

Schoenhut Toy Collectors
Attention: Norman Bowers
1916 Cleveland Street
Evanston, Illinois 60202

Still Bank Collectors Club
62 South Hazelwood
Newark, Ohio 43055

Teddy Bear Club
P.O. Box 8361
Prairie Village, Kansas 66208

Toy Train Collectors Society
109 Howedale Drive
Rochester, New York 14616
Contact: Louis A. Bohn

*Toy Train Operators Society
   (TTOS)*
25 West Walnut Street
Suite 305
Pasadena, California 91103

*Train Collectors Association
   (TCA)*
P.O. Box 248
Stroudsburg, Pennsylvania
   17579

Virginia Train Collectors, Inc.
P.O. Box 7114
Richmond, Virginia 23221

Repair and Restoration Services

✳ ✳ ✳

The following listing of Restorers of Antique Toys does not constitute an endorsement of any kind. These people, however, have an established reputation for doing quality work in the hobby.

Marc Olimpio's Antique Toy Restoration Center
Marc Olimpio
Sanbornville, NH 03872
Specialty: Early handpainted German, French-American tin toys, iron and pressed steel, also cast iron

The Paper Conservatory
Nan and Bill Bopp
Box 33
Walpole, NH 03608
(603) 756–9096
Specialty: Paper and wood toys, boxes, games, puzzles

Phantom Antique Toy Restoration
Buddy George
1038 North Utica
Tulsa, OK
Specialty: Pressed-steel toys and pedal cars

Russ Harrington's Repair and Restoration Service
Russ Harrington
1805 Wilson Point Road
Baltimore, MD 21220
Specialty: Mechanical and still banks, iron toys

Tin Toy Works
Joe Freeman
1313 N. 15th Street
Allentown, PA 18102
Specialty: Tin toy autos, boats, go-rounds

Toy Glossary

Animated toys: Any plaything that simulates lifelike movements, whether powered or activated by spring, string, flywheel, rubberband, gravity, controlled movement of sand, gyroscopic mechanism, steam, electricity or batteries.

Artificial antiquing: Using burnt umber or a similar compound to disguise the fact that a toy has been repainted.

Automata: Plural of automat; refers to figures that are relatively self-operating and capable of performing multiple complex movements. Early examples featured doll-like bodies with composition or bisque heads. Modern day robot toys are the latest rage in automata.

Balance toys: Earliest European example was 16th-century French, although most widely known in the Orient. Swinging weight is usually above or below toy. Many popular papier-mâché roly-poly toys, circa 1900, were counterweighted with pebbles or buckshot.

Balance wheel: Most often seen on horse-drawn vehicles, it is a small rotating or stationary wheel that is normally attached to a front hoof or a shaft suspended between two horses, which eases passage across the floor.

Bisque: Unglazed porcelain, minus final firing and glazing.

Carpet runners: Transport or other moving toys used out of their proper medium (i.e., tin or cast-iron trains with smooth rims, rather than grooved wheels, that did not run on tracks but were usually hand-propelled).

Cast-iron toys: Made of molten gray high-carbon iron, hand-poured into sandcasting molds; usually cast in halves, then mated and bolted or riveted as one. More elaborate versions incorporated interlocking, nickel-plated grills, chassis, bumpers, people, and other accessories.

Chasing: process of engraving or embossing to decorate a toy or bank.

Clockwork mechanism: Made of machined brass and steel; used to animate toys for as long as 30 minutes as interlocking gears move as spring uncoils. Produced as drive system for toys by clockmakers beginning in 1862 and ending about 30 years later in the Northeastern United States, Connecticut in particular.

Composition toys: Material may be wood or paper pulp, sawdust and glue, molded into various shapes and painted.

Crazing: Aging lines that run through the paint on vintage toys and banks that distinguish them from new examples.

Die-casting: Method of mass-producing, under great pressure, molten zinc and white-metal alloys into permanent molds. Sharp clean detail can be achieved. Die-cast toys were very inexpensive and generally found in the five-and-dime emporiums.

D.R.G.M.: Often mistaken for a manufacturer's mark, the initials stand for Deutsches Reichs Gebrauchmuster (translation: in-use model).

Dribbler: Nickname for British, solid brass, steam-powered toy locomotives made from the 1840s to the turn of the century; so called because they were known to leave trail of water deposited from steam cylinder.

DRPOSR: An acronym indicating French patent registry.

Drive wheel: Attached to piston rod that transmits energy from power source, as on toy locomotives.

Elastolin: A type of composition material from Germany, molded around wire supports, which has questionable survival rate.

Flats: Two-dimensional lead soldiers with engraved decorations.

Floor runner: See Carpet runners.

Friction wheel: A central inertia wheel, also known as a flywheel, that is activated by spring in rear wheels to set toy in motion. American toys utilized a cast-iron friction wheel; Europeans used cast lead. Friction toys were popular from 1900 to the early 1930s

Gilded (or gilt): Covered with a thin layer of gold (or appearing so); paint usually contains powdered metal.

Hauberk ('ho-bark): A tunic of chain mail worn as defensive armor in the 12th to the 14th centuries. Term used with militariana.

Hollow cast: Also known as a slush cast, whereby molten lead alloy is poured into mold, which is then inverted, leaving a thin layer of cooling metal adhering to its surface. Pot metal toys, as they are commonly called, tend to have less definition and are more fragile than die-cast toys.

Horse-drawn vehicle terminology: These descriptions apply to toy replications of rigs from the 1880s and 1890s in Europe and the United States.

Barouche: Open four-wheeled rig with driver's seat higher in front and two seats facing each other.

Brake: Two- and three-seated sporting rigs, four-wheeled and open; two-seated brake toys are especially prized and are known in only a few advanced collections.

Brougham: Elegant closed carriage with exterior driver's seat; named after Lord Henry Peter Brougham, Scottish leader of House of Commons, 1830–1840.

English trap (as in "trappings," signifying elegance): Four-wheel rig is rarely replicated by U.S. toy makers.

Gig: A sporting two-wheeled vehicle, deemed too high off the ground for safe pleasure driving; often used to exercise a trotting horse.

Hansom cab: Popular covered, fast-moving two-wheeler for one or two passengers; driver controlled reins from platform at rear of cab.

Landau (Bavaria, Germany): Enclosed carriage with divided top that can be thrown back or let down; raised seat for driver.

Phaeton: Any of the various light, four-wheeled, graceful open carriages; also a type of touring car. The more fragile appearing spider phaeton often featured a rumble seat for coachman.

Tally-Ho: Posh "jolly country outing" or "to the hunt and races" rigs carrying as many as 12 passengers inside and atop the vehicle.

Japanning: A decorative technique that includes several layers of paint finished with a coat of lacquer; commonly applied on early American and European tin. In France, a cheaper "dyeing" method was used; a varnish paint mix was burned on in alcohol, then baked, achieving a thin hard translucence.

Jobber: A purveyor of goods manufactured by others; Ives, for example, manufactured toys as well as marketing those of other firms. George Borgfeldt of New York City, obtained manufacturer's rights for certain toys and then subcontracted their production. Butler Brothers and Selchow & Righter were major jobbers.

Lithographed tin: The process was introduced to toys in the 1880s whereby various colors and detail were printed on flat sheets of metal by a lithographic press; the toys were subsequently formed by tools and dies.

Living pictures: Lithographed paper or cardboard jointed figures against colorful backdrop and enclosed in glass-covered, framed wooden box. Clockwork activated. Popular toy in Europe in second half of 19th century. A. Schoenhut produced over 20 variations in this country.

Married parts: Mating of two parts of a toy that did not originally belong together, down-scaling it in desirability.

Nickel plating: Technique for coating cast-iron or steel toys with molten nickel to prevent rusting and enhance appearance.

Patent date: If the patent number appears on the toy or on the box it came in, one can get a good approximation of the year any U.S. toy from 1860 to date was manufactured. German toys produced after 1890 usually bear patent dates.

Pattern: prototype of the piece ultimately to be manufactured; usually of bronze or brass, sometimes lead; when pressed in the sand it creates the mold. Pattern mechanical banks are highly prized.

Plastron (plas tron): Metal breastplate worn under the haubach; also quilted pad worn in fencing. Term used with militariana.

Registering banks: Mechanical banks that visually indicate the cumulative total of coins received.

Sand toys: Graphically appealing and ingenious toys of lithographed paper and wood, whereby a complex mechanism powered by shifting sand provides animation. Popularized by the French, Italians, and Germans as early as the 17th century, they were usually in a glass-encased frame. One of the earliest United States toy makers, the Tower Guild of South Hingham, Massachusetts, produced wood and tinplate that used chutes and paddle wheels to cause jointed figures to perform, ca. 1850s.

Semi-mechanical bank: A bank which performs a mechanical function, but it is independent of coin activation, as with a mechanical.

Sheet metal: A toy material that is rolled into a thin plate made of brass, copper, and, in the case of most toys, steel; first toy usage in the United States dates back to 1895.

Short stride: Term applied to Barclay toy soldiers because its marching figures' feet were cast close together.

Solids: Three-dimensional figures, usually refers to lead soldiers.

Spring-driven: Stamped tinplate gears activate by a spring uncoiling on what are popularly known as toy wind-ups. Actually, they wind down after two to three minutes. Usually a key does the rewinding; in the case of Kingsbury, a flanged cover on a patented, sealed round housing must be turned; a lever activates certain spring-driven toy banks. Tin wind-ups date back to the 1890s.

Still bank: Not a bank that's quiet; the term merely differentiates between mechanical banks and banks with no moving parts.

Tab-and-slot: Applied to tin toys wherein two parts are mated, and small flaps on one half are inserted into corresponding narrow slots of the other half, then bent to secure the connection.

Wind-ups: A term often used interchangeably for both clockwork and spring-driven toys; the former offers superior quality and length of activation—30 minutes versus two to three minutes with the coil or barrel spring mechanism.

Bibliography

✳ ✳ ✳

GENERAL

Ayres, William S.: *The Warner Collector's Guide to American Toys.* Warner Books, NYC, 1981, 255 pp. (Features toys from the Perelman Toy Museum in Philadelphia.)

Baker, Linda: *Modern Toys/American Toys 1930–1980.* Collector Books, Division of Schroeder Books, Paducah, KY, Hardbound, 1985, 270 pp.

Barenholtz, Bernard, and McClintock, Inez: *American Antique Toys, 1830–1900.* Harry Abrams Pub., NY, 1980. (From one of our premier toy collections; captures the essence of what toy collecting is all about.)

Botto, Ken: *Past Joys.* Prism Editions, Chronicle Books, San Francisco, CA, 1978. (A visual treat using toys as part of a mixed-media celebration.)

Cadbury, Betty: *Playthings Past.* Praeger Pub., NY, 1976.

Culff, Robert: *The World of Toys!* Hamelyn, NY, 1969.

Daiken, Leslie: *Children's Toys Through the Ages.* Prager Pub., NY, 1953.

Dictionary of Toys Sold in America, Vols. I & II. Long's Americana Pub., Mokelumne Hill, CA, 1971 and 1978. (Rates toys on scale of 1–20; reproduces cuts from old catalogs.)

Foley, Daniel J.: *Toys Through The Ages.* Chilton Co., Philadelphia, PA, 1962.

Fondin, Jean and Remise, Jac: *The Golden Age of Toys.* New York Graphic Society, Greenwich, CT, 1967.

Fraser, Antonia: *A History of Toys*. Delacorte Press, NY, 1966.

Freeman, Ruth and Larry: *Cavalcade of Toys*. Century House, NY, 1942.

Fritzsch, Karl Ewald, and Bachman, Manfred: *An Illustrated History of Toys*. Translated by Ruth Michaelis-Jena. Abbey Library, London, 1966; reprinted Hastings House, NY, 1978.

Grober, Karl: *Children's Toys of Bygone Days*. Frederick Stokes, NY, 1928.

Hertz, Louis: *Handbook of Old American Toys*. Mark Haber Pub., Wethersfield, CT, 1947.

———: *The Toy Collector*. Funk & Wagnells, Inc., NY, 1969.

Hillier, Mary: *Pageant of Toys*. Tapplinger Pub. Co., NY, 1966.

Ketchum, William: *Toys and Games*. The Smithsonian Institution, Washington, D.C., 1981.

King, Constance: *The Encyclopedia of Toys*. Crown Pub., NY, 1978.

McClintock, Inez and Marshall: *Toys in America*. Public Affairs Associates Press, Washington, D.C., 1961.

McClinton, Katherine Morrison: *Antiques of American Childhood*. Clarkson N. Potter, Inc., NY, 1970.

Murray, Patrick: *Toys*. Vista/Dutton, London, 1968. (Murray was Curator, Museum of Childhood, Edinburgh, Scotland.)

Perelman, Leon J.: *Perelman Antique Toy Museum*. Wallace-Homestead, Des Moines, IA, 1972.

———: *Toys/Beloved Survivors of the Playroom*. Encyclopedia of Collectibles, Vol. 15, Time-Life Books, Alexandria, VA, 1980, pp. 85–109.

Schwarz, Marvin: *F.A.O. Schwarz/Toys Through the Years*. Doubleday & Co., Garden City, NY, 1975, hardbound, 144 pp. (Reprinted catalog pages of F.A.O. Schwarz through the years.)

White, Gwen: *Antique Toys and Their Background*. Arco, NY, 1971.

Whitton, Blair: *Toys*. The Knopf Collector's Guide to American Antiques Series. Alfred A. Knopf, NY, Chanticleer Press Edition, 1984.

The Wonderful World of Toys, Games, Dolls, 1860–1913. Follett, Chicago, IL, 1971.

MECHANICAL AND STILL BANKS

Bellows, Ina Heywood: *Old Mechanical Banks.* Lightner Pub., Chicago, IL, 1940.

Davidson, Al: *Penny Lane/A History of Antique Mechanical Banks.* Al Davidson, Oyster Bay, NY, 1988.

Ellinghaus, Bernard: *Other Old Mechanical Banks.* Vol. I. (Booklet) Mechanical Bank Collectors of America, Allegen, MI, 1977.

————: *Other Old Mechanical Banks.* Vol. II. (Booklet) Mechanical Bank Collectors of America, Allegen, MI, 1982.

Griffith, F. H.: *Mechanical Banks.* F. H. Griffith, 1972.

Hertz, Louis: *Mechanical Toy Banks.* Mark Haber Pub., Wethersfield, CT, 1947.

Long, Earnest: *Dictionary of Still Banks.* Long's Americana Pub., Mokelumne Hill, CA, 1981.

McCumber, Robert L.: *Toy Bank Reproductions and Fakes.* Self-published, Glastonbury, CT, 1970. (Contains base tracings of original mechanical banks.)

Meyer, John D.: *Handbook of Old Mechanical Banks.* Rudusill & Co. Pub.,* Lancaster, PA, 1952. (Meyer reference numbers are used in the Mechanical Bank section of this book.)

Moore, Andy and Susan: *The Penny Bank Book: Collecting Still Banks.* Self-published, Chicago, IL, 1984.

Norman, Bill: *The Bank Book: The Encyclopedia of Mechanical Bank Collecting.* Accent Studios, San Diego, CA, 1984. (An annual or biannual supplement containing updated prices, trends, etc. is planned for the near future.)

Rogers, Carole: *Penny Banks: A History and a Handbook.* E.P. Dutton, NY, 1977.

Whiting, Hubert B.: *Old Iron Still Banks.* Self-published. Out-of-print. (Whiting reference numbers are used in the Still Bank section of this book.)

*Reissued as *Old Penny Banks*, with Larry Freeman, Century House, Watkins Glen, NY, 1960, 1979 (updated with section on Still Banks by Freeman).

COMIC AND CHARACTER TOYS

Harman, Ken: *Comic Strip Toys.* Wallace-Homestead, Des Moines, IA, 1975.

Heide, Robert, and Gilman, John: *Cartoon Collectibles: 50 Years of Dime-Store Memorabilia.* Dolphin Book, Doubleday & Co., Garden City, NY, 1983. (Main focus is on Mickey Mouse and other Disneyana.)

Hillier, Bevis: *Walt Disney's Mickey Mouse Memorabilia.* Harry Abrams, Inc., NY, 1986. (Our nomination for the best coverage of Mickey Mouse and his friends lionized in toys, games, and novelties.)

Lesser, Robert: *A Celebration of Comic Art and Memorabilia.* Hawthorn Books, NY, 1975.

Longest, David: *Character Toys and Collectibles, Second Series.* Collector Books, Paducah, KY, 1987, hardboard, 256 pp. (First series published in 1984.)

Munsey, Cecil: *Disneyana.* Hawthorn Books, NY, 1980.

Stern, Michael: *Stern's Guide to Disney Collectibles.* Collector Books, Paducah, KY, 1989.

Tumbusch, Tom: *Tomart's Illustrated Disneyana Catalog and Price Guide.* Three Vols. Tomart Publications, Dayton, OH, 1985.

LEADING MANUFACTURERS

Brown, George W.: *The George Brown Toy Sketchbook.* Edited by Edith Barenholtz. Pyne Press, Princeton, NJ, 1971.

Buser, Elaine and Dan: *Guide to Schoenhut Dolls, Toys and Circus.* Collector Books, Paducah, KY, 1976.

Cieslik, Jurgen and Marianne: *Lehmann Toys, The History of E.P. Lehmann: 1881–1981.* New Cavendish Books, London. (Now available through Schiffer Pub., West Chester, PA)

Fuller, Roland and Levy, Allen: *The Bassett-Locke Story.* New Cavendish Books, London, 1984. (History of one of England's eminent model and miniature railway model makers; also a producer of exhibition standard ship models.)

Hagerty, L.C.: *Ives Blakeslee & Williams Toy Catalog.* Circa 1893, reprint 1965, 142 pp.

Hertz, Louis: *Messrs. Ives of Bridgeport.* Mark Haber Pub., Wethersfield, CT, 1947.

Manos, Susan: *Schoenhut Dolls and Toys, A Loving Legacy.* Collector Books, Paducah, KY, 1976.

McCullough, Albert: *The Complete Book of Buddy "L" Toys.* Greenberg Pub., Sykesville, MD, 1984.

Murray, John J., and Fox, Bruce R.: *Fisher-Price/1931–1963.* Books Americana Inc., Florence, AL, 1987, softcover, 204 pp.

Parry-Crooke, Charlotte, ed.: *Toys, Dolls, Games: Paris 1903–1914.* Hastings House Pub., Inc., NY, 1981. (Catalog cuts from leading French toy makers reproduced.)

The Great Toys of George Carette. New Cavendish Books, London, 1975.

Whitton, Blair: *Bliss Toys and Dollhouses.* Dover Publications, Inc., in association with The Margaret Woodbury Strong Museum, NY, 1979.

MINIATURES

Force, Dr. Edward: *Miniature Emergency Vehicles.* Schiffer Pub., Ltd., Exton, PA, 1984.

——: *Corgi Toys.* Schiffer Pub., Ltd., Exton, PA, 1984.

——: *Dinky Toys.* Schiffer Publishing, West Chester, PA, 1989, softcover, 224 pp.

Gibson, Cecil: *History of British Dinky Toys, 1934–1964.* Mikansue and Modeller's World, London, 1966.

Ramsey, John: *The Swapmeet and Toy Fair Catalog of British Die-cast Model Toys.* Swapmeet Toys & Models Ltd., Suffolk, England, 1984. (Well-researched book, but seven pages are required to explain the value rating system!)

Richardson, Mike and Susan: *Dinky Toys and Model Miniatures.* Schiffer Pub., Ltd., Exton, PA, 1981.

Schiffer, Nancy, ed.: *Matchbox Toys.* Schiffer Pub., Ltd., Exton, PA, 1983.

Viemeister, Peter: *Micro Cars.* Hamilton's, Bedford, VA, 1982.

Wieland, James, and Force, Dr. Edward: *Tootsietoys.* Motorbooks International, Osceola, WI, 1980.

———: *Detroit in Miniature.* Miniature Auto Sales, Litchfield, CT, 1983.

MILITARIANA

Bard, Bob: *Making and Collecting Military Miniatures.* Robert M. McBride, NY, 1957.

Ferguson, Michael: *Model Soldiers/Historic Armies in Miniature:* Encyclopedia of Collectibles, Vol. 10, Time-Life Books, Alexandria, VA, 1979, pp. 40–53.

Garrett, John: *The World Encyclopedia of Model Soldiers.* Overlook Press, NY, 1981.

Harris, Henry: *Model Soldiers.* Octopus Books, Ltd., London, England, 1962, hardbound, 96 pp.

Johnson, Peter: *Toy Armies.* Forbes Museum, NY, 1984. (The Malcolm Forbes Collection, probably the premier collection of militariana in the world, is beautifully presented in this book.)

Kurtz, Henry I, and Erlich, Burtt: *The Art of the Toy Soldier.* Abbeville Press, NYC, 1987, hardbound, 324 pp.

Nicollier, Jean: *Collecting Toy Soldiers.* Charles E. Tuttle Co., Rutland, VT, Tokyo, Japan, 1967, hardbound, 284 pp.

Opie, James: *Britain's Toy Soldiers, 1893–1932.* Harper & Row, NY, 1986.

———: *Toy Soldiers.* Shire Publ., England, 1985.

MOTOR TOYS (SEE ALSO MINIATURES)

Bartok, Peter: *The Minic Book.* 1988, hardbound, 112 pp.

Crilley, Raymond, and Burkholder, Charles: *International Directory of Model Farm Tractors.* Schiffer, West Chester, PA, 1985.

Gottschalk, Lillian: *Toy Cars and Trucks.* Abbeville Press, NY, 1985. (The most beautifully photographed and designed book on American motor toys published to date; unlike most "picture books," this one is painstakingly researched.)

Marwick, Al: *Automobile Toys of Yesterday and Today.* Princeton Pub. Co., 1981, hardcover.

Massucci, Eduardo: *Cars for Kids.* Rizzoli International Pubs., NY, 1982. (Children's sidewalk pedal cars featured.)

Remise, Jac and Frederic: *The World of Antique Toys: Carriages, Cars and Cycles.* Edita S.A. Lausanne, Switzerland, 1984. Distributed by Schiffer Pub. Ltd., Exton, PA. (Beautiful pictorial coverage of European motor toys.)

TOY RAILROADING

Alexander, E.: *The Collector's Book of the Locomotive.* Clarkson N. Potter Pub., NY, 1966.

Carlson, Pierce: *Toy Trains: A History.* Harper & Row, NY, 1986.

Carstens, Harry A.: *The Trains of Lionel Standard Gauge Era.* Railroad Model Craftsmen, 1964.

Fernandez, Don: *Trains/Railroading for Grown-up Boys.* Encyclopedia of Collectibles, Vol. 15, Time-Life Books, Alexandria, VA, 1980, pp. 124–139.

Fraley, Donald: *Lionel Trains, Standard of the World: 1900–1943.* Train Collectors Association, 1976.

Godel, Howard: *Antique Toy Trains.* Exposition Press, Inc., Smithtown, NY, 1976.

Godin, Serge: *The Trains on Avenue de Rumine.* Giansanti Coluzzi Collection. New Cavendish Books/Editions, London, 1982.

Hertz, Louis: *Collecting Model Trains.* Mark Haber Pub., Wethersfield, CT, 1956.

——: *Riding the Tinplate Rails.* Model Craftsman Pub. Co., 1944.

Hollander, Ron: *All Aboard; The Story of Joshua Lionel Cowen and His Lionel Train Company.* Workman Pub. Co., NY, softcover, First printing 1981, reprinted 1989.

Jeanmaire, Claude: *Bing, Grandad's Model Railway.* Verlag Eisenbahn, Germany, 1982.

Joyce, J.: *Collector's Guide to Model Railways.* Model & Allied Pub. Co., Argus Books, 1977.

Levy, Allen: *A Century of Modern Trains.* Crescent Books, NY, 1986. Reprint of 1974 edition by New Cavendish.

Reder, Gustav: *Clockwork, Steam and Electric: A History of Model Railways.* Translated by C. Hamilton Ellis. Ian Allan, Shepperton, England, 1972.

Spong, Neldred and Raymond: *Flywheel-Powered Toys.* Antique Toy Collectors of America, Baltimore, MD, 1979.

Williams, Guy R.: *The World of Model Trains.* Andre Deutch Publishing, London, 1970.

TIN MECHANICAL TOYS

Bartholomew, Charles: *Mechanical Toys.* Chartwell Books, Secaucus, NJ, 1979.

Chapius, Droz: *Automata.* Central Book Co., NY, 1958.

Gardiner, Gordon, and Morris, Alistair: *Illustrated Encyclopedia of Metal Toys.* Crown Pub., Harmony Books, Avenel, NJ, 1984.

Hillier, Mary: *Automata and Mechanical Toys.* Jupiter Pub., London, 1976.

Pressland, David: *The Art of the Tin Toy.* Crown Pub., NY, 1976.

Weltens, Arno: *Mechanical Tin Toys in Color.* Sterling Pub., NY, 1979.

Whitten, Blair: *American Clockwork Toys, 1860–1900.* Schiffer Pub., Ltd., Exton, PA, 1979. (The definitive book on pre-1900 clockwork toys.)

Von Boehn, Max: *Puppets and Automata.* Dover Pub., NY, 1972.

Wind-Ups: Tin Toy Dreams. T. Kitahara Collection. Chronicle Books, San Francisco, CA, 1985. (Chronicles Japanese tin toys from 1900s to present.)

Wonderland of Toys. Tin Toys Vol. I. T. Kitahara Collection. Chronicle Books, San Francisco, CA, 1984.

Wonderland of Toys. Tin Robots Vol. II. T. Kitahara Collection. Chronicle Books, San Francisco, CA, 1984. (Covers post-war Japanese tin toys, robots.)

OTHER SPECIALTIES

Avedon, Elliot, and Sutton-Smith, Brian: *The Study of Games.* John Wiley & Sons, NY, 1971.

Baird, Bill: *The Art of the Puppet.* Ridge Press Book, Bonanza Books, NYC, 1973, 252 pp.

Bauman, Paul: *Collecting Antique Marbles.* Prarie Winds Press, Wallace-Homestead, Leon, IA, 1970.

Bell, R.C.: *The Board Games Book.* Marshall Cavendish, London, 1979.

Best, Charles W.: *Cast-Iron Toy Pistols-1870–1940.* Rocky Mountain Arms & Antiques Pub., Englewood, CO, 1973.

Coleman, Dorothy S., Elizabeth A., and Evelyn J.: *Collector's Encyclopedia of Dolls.* Crown Pub., NY, 1976.

Conway, Shirley, and Wilson, Jean: *Steiff Teddy Bears, Dolls, and Toys with Prices.* Wallace-Homestead, Des Moines, IA.

Eikelberner, George, and Agadjanian, Serge: *American Glass Candy Containers.* Two volumes. Belle Meade, NJ, 1967.

Gibbs, P.J.: *Black Americana Sold in America.* Collector Books, Paducah, KY, 1987.

Hannas, Linda: *The English Jigsaw Puzzle.* Wayland, London.

Heide, Robert and Gilman, John: *Cowboy Collectibles.* Harper & Row, NY, 1982.

Hewitt, Karen, and Roomet, Louise: *Educational Toys in America: 1800 to the Present.* The Robert Hull Fleming Museum, University of Vermont, Burlington, VT, 1979.

Kaiser, Von Wolf, and Baecker, Carlernst: *Toy Steam Engines and Accessories* (Blechpielzeug Dampfspielzeug). Berlin, Germany, 1984. (Printed in German only. Well illustrated, definitive work on a vastly underrated area of toy specialization.)

Lavitt, Wendy: *Dolls.* The Knopf Collector's Guides to American Antiques. Chanticleer Press Edition, NY, 1983.

Mandel, Margaret: *Teddy Bears and Steiff Animals.* Collector Books, Paducah, KY, 1984.

Milet, Jacques, and Forbes, Robert: *Toy Boats: 1870–1955.* Charles Scribner's Sons, NY, 1979.

Moran, Brian: *Battery Toys.* Schiffer Pub., Ltd., West Chester, PA, 1984. (Featuring over 150 color plates of battery-operated toys from the 1950s to date.)

Mullins, Linda: *Teddy Bears Past & Present.* Hobby House Press, Inc., Cumberland, MD, 1986, hardbound, 304 pp.

Murray, H.J.R.: *A History of Board Games Other Than Chess.* Clarendon Press, Oxford, England, 1952.

Orbanes, Philip: *The Monopoly Companion.* Bob Adams, Inc., Pub., Boston, MA, 1988, softcover, 208 pp.

Schiffer, Margaret: *Holiday Toys and Decorations.* Schiffer Pub., Ltd., West Chester, PA 1985.

Slocum, Jerry, and Botermans, Jack: *Puzzles Old and New.* Distributed by University of Washington Press, Seattle, WA, 1986.

VIDEO

Pressland, David: *The Magic of the Tin Toy.* Video version of Pressland's 1976 book. In VHS or Beta. Running time: 55 minutes. Available through *Antique Toy World*, Chicago, IL

Index

✳ ✳ ✳

526